N... 1945

e you
s. So much.
. to Heaven

d in your bed.

more green spread
et very cold tonight
the window.

you

·Mrs A.·

Dear Mother
Hope you received my ...
present and that you and
Barbara had a good time
together.
God Bless you dear
Affectionately
[signature]

Goodbye darling -
I shan't be long -
be good - eat well -
and sleep — alone"
Mrs A

Christmas
May. 1945

Tommy.
hopping with a
n now on.
on this one for 16
rest are smaller.
us birthday and I
her with some
apartment

Beloved Husband.
I adore the wheelbarrow
picture!! hope you don't
think you can push me
around anywhere you
please though!!! (or can you?)

GERTRUDE LAWRENCE AS MRS. A

Vandamm

This photograph of herself Gertrude gave to her stepson, Richard S. Aldrich, Jr., when he left for Korea.

GERTRUDE LAWRENCE

AS

Mrs A

AN INTIMATE BIOGRAPHY OF THE GREAT STAR

BY

Richard Stoddard Aldrich

A Pickering Press Book

GREYSTONE PRESS

NEW YORK

The Greystone Press
100 Sixth Avenue
New York 13, N. Y.

1551-25M

Designed by Sidney Feinberg

Library of Congress Catalog Card Number 54-11970

Manufactured in the United States of America
American Book–Stratford Press, Inc., New York

For Gertrude

"Thou art not gone, being gone,
where'er thou art
Thou leav'st in him thy watchful
eyes, in him thy loving heart."

John Donne

Chapter One

TO HER FRIENDS she was "Gertrude" or "Gee." Never to me after our marriage. Her wifely messages bore various signatures. On tour in a play that was doing big business, she might dash off a brief, jubilant note from "Mrs. Gotrocks." In what she felt was a subtle, literary mood, she became "Emily Brontë." And if she was acutely conscious of the distances dividing us, as during the war, she became "Your Bunkie." But at all other times in letters and wires, beginning with the first penciled note she left on the pile of handkerchiefs in my bureau drawer the day after we were married, to me she was "Adoringly, Mrs. A."

The name was her own invention. She never used it in writing to anyone but me, and she never referred to herself as "Mrs. A" except when we were alone. It had a significance for us both which made it peculiarly our own.

Of Gertrude Lawrence as a theatrical personality there is little I can add to what already has been told. In her autobiography, *A Star Danced,* she has recounted the story of her childhood, her early struggles toward a career and her ultimate triumph. The book ends with our marriage.

Gertrude Lawrence the actress is a beloved figure to millions.

But Mrs. A is a woman who was known slightly to not more than a dozen persons. And fully, intimately, to only one—myself.

Some have wondered how much of Mrs. A was real, and how much a portrayal by a highly accomplished actress. Years ago Pirandello devoted a whole play to this complex theme, without reaching a conclusive answer. Nor can I.

If Mrs. A was a role, it was one that Gertrude played spontaneously, without direction, and with ever-increasing delight. Performed for an audience of one, not for fame or wealth, it was the greatest role of her long and varied repertory. Even if it was nothing more than a role—which I do not believe—as Mr. A I have been privileged above the lot of most men.

* * *

"Poor Richard Aldrich. He thinks he has married Miss Gertrude Lawrence. He'll soon find out it's *Myth* Lawrence."

Constance Collier's quip, delivered at a party held for Gertrude and me shortly after our wedding on the Cape, spread quickly among our friends.

When it was repeated to me, I laughed. It was true that many myths had grown up around Gertrude. Her outrageous comic pranks; her many extravagances, which had forced her into bankruptcy; her celebrated admirers and friends, including young members of the British royal family; her fabulous clothes, furs and jewels; above all, her glamour—a word which she had brought back into parlance, and the only term our language affords which even haltingly describes her radiant charm—these are the stuff of which legends are made.

Bewitching and elusive as a moonbeam, she flitted from the terrace of the Carleton at Cannes to a millionaire's yacht off Palm Beach, enchanting her audiences, rekindling in their hearts something which in too many of us dims and flickers out after first youth—faith in an imperishable loveliness and romance.

"Myth Lawrence," I called her teasingly when we were taking our favorite late-night stroll arm in arm across the lawn toward the dunes. We stood at the edge of the grass with the sea breeze in our faces, breathing in the pungent smell of sea weed, wet sand, bayberry and cranberry bog which is the aroma of the Cape, and listening to the soft slur of surf on the beach.

I was unprepared for the seriousness with which she took the witticism. She drew closer and her hands—strong, capable and as eloquently mobile as her face—tightened on my arm. "Darling," she said, "those things get laughs, but only from people who can't find love. We have each other. But oh, do let's be careful."

Here, as I was to discover, was the keynote of all her thinking and feeling about our marriage: "We have each other, but do let's be careful." Her full meaning was not brought home to me until we had been married some time, and I had found my way through the surface contradictions that created her prismatic radiance, to the basic truth of Gertrude Lawrence.

I might never have learned this truth, as many men never reach a clear understanding of the women they love and marry, if it had not been for the separations that circumstances imposed on us. Gertrude and I were frequently forced apart, sometimes for long periods: by her career, by the war, by my four years' service in the Navy. We both chafed at these absences. Undoubtedly they put a strain on our relationship, especially in our first years together.

And yet, once we survived that strain, I believe that in the long haul our marriage was actually strengthened. The constant adjustments that had to be made, the challenges that had to be met, gave us an insight into one another which might have been dulled by the rub and wear of uninterrupted companionship. The provocative spices of surprise and change were always present, seasoning our marriage, giving it savor and zest.

Also, occasional distance gave us the perspective to appraise and appreciate each other; it was a built-in safeguard against taking our love for granted.

While apart, we kept in frequent and usually daily touch—by telephone, by telegraph, and, most often, by mail. Gertrude was one of those rare human beings who write without self-consciousness tugging at the pen. She had a freedom of expression, as well as a freedom of affection, that I envied from the bottom of my heart.

Her letters were never formal; often they were not more than a few lines penciled in her strong, square script on whatever paper came easiest to hand in hotel suites, theatre dressing rooms, on ships, trains and planes. If she couldn't write, she sent a telegram. These messages, however sent, were the intimate, spontaneous expression of whatever she was thinking or feeling at the moment. Reading them is like feeling her hand steal into mine.

Gertrude was the most outgiving person I have ever known. Her own need for affection, urgent as it was, was always surpassed by the need she felt for bestowing affection. This generosity of love was not to me only, or to her daughter Pamela and my two sons by my previous marriage; it extended to everyone within her orbit. It increased as Gertrude matured during our twelve years together, and developed new facets of character in response to the needs of other human beings close to her.

Her warmth—quickening as the spring sun shining on the rocky slopes of my native Massachusetts—inevitably had a softening effect on the Puritan sternness that was my own heritage.

This influence extended to other members of my family circle. None of us—Aldriches, Joys, Hobarts—are what we were, or what we would have been if she had not been a vital element in our lives. This is especially true of my mother.

Mother was in her eightieth year when I telephoned her on the morning of the Fourth of July, 1940, to announce our marriage. The wedding had taken place at a quarter past midnight—a concession to Gertrude's wish to start her life as Mrs. A coincident with her birthday, which was the Fourth. I put through the call to Groton from my cottage at Dennis, where we were married. I chose an hour when I knew Mother would have finished her breakfast, and before any of the Boston papers would have the news and their reporters might descend on her for comments. Anything Gertrude did, and especially whatever concerned her private life, was front-page copy.

My sister Barbara answered the telephone. While I heard her calling, "Mother, Richard wants to speak to you," I thought I could hear, far off, the Groton Town Band striking up for the Independence Day parade. I pictured Main Street with its arching elms and opposing lines of sedate white-painted houses, each with its prim white fence and neat apron of green lawn, prudently keeping the larger, pleasanter garden out of public view at the rear of the house. The flags would be out over the eighteenth-century front doors with their leaded fan-lights. It was a boast of my mother's that no new house had been built on Main Street for more than one hundred years. When, after my father's death and while I was still at Harvard, she went to live permanently in Groton, she made no attempt to conceal her pleasure in exchanging Brookline, which is "not what it used to be," for a village which so far had succeeded in ignoring the advent of the twentieth century.

Yes, I knew that Groton would be keeping the Fourth in tune with its neighbors, Concord and Lexington. The Boy Scouts would be forming in troops in front of the Unitarian Church, just as the minutemen did on April 19, 1775.

As I amused myself with these fancies I heard approaching footsteps, then a little preliminary cough as Mother prepared herself for the ordeal of a long-distance call.

She still regarded the telegraph and telephone as being primarily for the conveyance of bad news. Under the tutelage of my father, no Aldrich ever made a long-distance call or sent a telegram except in matters of life or death.

Her voice, slightly flattened by reason of a poor connection, inquired anxiously: "Yes, Richard. What is it?"

Speaking slowly and distinctly, I said I wanted her to know that I had been married that morning (no need to mention the hour, which would have shocked her) to Gertrude Lawrence.

I knew my mother had seen Gertrude on the stage once, at a matinee performance of *Skylark* on the Cape. But that had been a full year before, and I was not at all sure Mother would remember it.

I waited for her reply. There was none.

"Do you hear me, Mother?" I repeated, raising my voice. "I have just been married to Gertrude Lawrence."

"Certainly I hear you, Richard," Mother's voice came sharply. "But *who* is Gertrude Lawrence?"

Not only who, but what, Gertrude Lawrence was, Mother eventually was to learn and I believe to appreciate more fully than anyone but myself.

* * *

Two things Gertrude could never quite forgive me for: my glass of cold milk at breakfast, and the fact that I had not seen her in all the roles she had played in America.

It was never any use trying to make her understand that when she first came to this country to star in *Charlot's Revue* I was still an undergraduate at Harvard. At that time I served as part-time drama critic for the *Dramatic Mirror*—a position chiefly valuable for its free tickets to shows that opened in Boston. *Charlot's Revue* did not.

Although I was in New York a few years later when Gertrude did *Oh, Kay,* I was then concentrating earnestly on becoming a banker, to regain the caste I had lost with my relatives by coming to New York to earn a living.

No Aldrich of our branch of the prolific family had ever before turned his back on New England. The Joys, however—although Mother was reluctant to admit it—had done their share of wandering. Not only had two of her paternal uncles headed West after the Embargo Act of 1807 destroyed New England's commerce (the son of one of them, Mother's first cousin Henry B. Joy, became founder of the Packard Motor Company); but her adored younger brother, James Joy (my uncle Jim), had settled in Plainfield, New Jersey, after being graduated from Yale in the manner of Joys for many generations (the Aldriches traditionally went to Harvard). Uncle Jim became active in the publication of Methodist literature and ultimately editor of *The Christian Advocate.* In Mother's eyes, his career constituted a double defection—of Massachusetts and of Congregationalism.

I had put aside my undergraduate interest in the theatre (a "dangerous virus" which Mother attributed to Professor Baker's celebrated 47 Workshop), and had become a fledgling banker. As such, my choice of shows was limited largely to what was available at the cut-rate ticket agency in the basement of Gray's Drug Store. The hits in which Gertrude starred were never listed there.

Thus Gertrude Lawrence remained a name in lights on a theatre marquee until some years later, during the period of my marriage to Helen Beals, a New York girl. One afternoon we went with friends to see Gertrude Lawrence and Noel Coward in *Private Lives*. I remember I enjoyed the play.

Later that evening, my sister Barbara dropped in during her ten-thirty walk with her dog. As we discussed *Private Lives*, and Gertrude's portrayal of the volatile Amanda, Barbara observed, "I wonder what Gertrude Lawrence is like. Really, I mean. Off the stage."

"Human," I said, "like the rest of us. And probably dull when she hasn't clever lines to speak."

My sister exclaimed indignantly: "I can't believe it."

"There's no reason to assume that she herself is anything like Amanda," I argued.

"There's one thing I'll say for you," Barbara remarked. "You may have a weakness for the theatre, but not for actresses."

"No," I said. "I'm safe on that score."

The weakness, for which my mother blamed Professor Baker ("President Lowell never really approved of him, and I don't wonder") did not improve as the Depression cast a gloom over banking. Compared to the stagnation downtown, Broadway appeared more and more enticing. Like a timid but persevering bather, I began to dabble in the waters I had always wished to swim in. I began in 1930 to produce plays with Kenneth Macgowan and Joseph Verner Reed.

One of many pleasant things connected with being a producer is the necessity of going abroad to look for plays which might profitably be brought to New York. I was in London on this mission in May, 1933. One evening I dropped in at Wyndham's Theatre to see Nigel Bruce backstage after the performance. The play was Roland Pertwee's *This Inconstancy*. Gertrude Lawrence was starring in it with Nigel and Leslie Banks.

Wyndham's, on Shaftesbury Avenue, is separated from its neighbor, the New Theatre, by a narrow paved alley with the noble name of St. Martin's Court. The court runs through to where St. Martin's Theatre backs up against Wyndham's. Between the two is a small, square yard lighted by two lampposts. The stage doors of the three theatres are there, close together.

To anyone in the theatre I suppose that there is no equal space in the whole of London to compare with St. Martin's Court for thrilling traditions and memories. Practically every great actor of the English stage of the past seventy-five years has hurried up the narrow, sooty alley to one of these doors. They have come in trepidation before first nights, and a few hours later they have moved down St. Martin's Court as down a triumphal way, past stage-struck admirers waiting to touch their cloaks, to beg their autographs, to cry: "God bless you!" No people love the theatre and its people more devotedly than the English.

On the evening in 1933 when I visited Nigel, Sir Gerald du Maurier was playing at the New Theatre. I admired him greatly and expressed a wish to meet him. Nigel took me across to Sir Gerald's dressing room.

Our meeting, though pleasant, was brief. As Nigel and I left the New Theatre's stage door, the stage door of Wyndham's, directly opposite, opened and a young woman stepped out. She wore a white dress. The light from the two lampposts shimmered on the silver threads in the fabric, played over her fair hair and warm white shoulders and jeweled arms. She stood poised on the step against the background of grimy brick wall, her head tilted as she spoke to a tall man close behind her. Then she turned, caught sight of us and smiled radiantly.

"Why, Nigel darling," exclaimed the voice I remembered as Amanda's.

Nigel introduced me. She bowed, said something quick and gay, flashed us another smile and was swept away by her escort, a gentleman whose title, whispered in my ear by Nigel, took me back to my boyhood reading of *Kenilworth.*

She was gone. But I heard the quick light tap of her heels on the stones of the court. From out of the warm darkness came her throaty laugh.

Thirteen years later, when London was under siege by the venomous V-2 rockets, I was a lieutenant commander, quartered as a paying guest in the home of the Marchioness of Queensberry in

South Audley Street, Mayfair. In the midst of a party given by my titled landlady, a gentleman wandered through my bedroom, which had to double as a corridor. His attention was attracted to the photographs on my bureau, night table and walls. Belligerently, almost possessively, he asked why there were so many pictures of Gertrude Lawrence around the room.

"I put them there," I said quietly. "She's my wife."

"So you're the American who married Gertrude!" he said. I felt his eyes searching out the insignia of rank on the sleeve of my naval uniform. Then he looked at me and an expression of wistful camaraderie replaced the belligerence. "I was going to marry her once," he said.

Despite the passage of years, he became at this moment recognizable to me as the young Earl who impatiently had swept Gertrude away from me in St. Martin's Court and who—according to Nigel and prevalent London gossip—had laid his coronet at her feet.

After our meeting in London I did not miss Gertrude in any of her plays in New York, although I never met her again either backstage or at a party. The season she starred in Rachel Crothers' *Susan and God* was the year my marriage ended in divorce. Helen married a man who made her happier than I had been able to do, and I devoted all my attention to the theatre: producing in New York, directing the Summer Festival at Central City, Colorado, and managing the Cape Playhouse at Dennis, Massachusetts. During my summers at Dennis, Mother would spend a few weeks on the Cape, provided she would not be required to enter into or lend countenance to what went on at the Playhouse. A devoted supporter of Symphony, she drew a line at the theatre, as she drew it to exclude from her world drinking, card-playing, scandal and divorce.

The ending of my marriage by court decree had deeply distressed her. Less, however, for what divorce might mean of hurt to me than for what it revealed of the breakdown of family tradition and standards. I was the third of her three children to go through the divorce court. She repeated several times, almost fearfully: "I don't know what your father would say."

I thought I knew. Or close enough. As a pillar of the Congregational Church and an ardent supporter of the Northfield Movement led by the evangelist Dwight L. Moody, my father had confidently expected his children to follow undeviatingly in their parents' footsteps. When one of us stumbled a little, or took a path of his own choice, Father became like an Old Testament prophet foreseeing nothing but disaster. As a small boy I heard him rival the gloomy eloquence of Jeremiah on the subject of my older sister Joy. Joy had eloped with a musician and returned from Europe with two children and a crate of canvases she had painted; later on she received the first divorce among my father's descendants.

Father died long before Barbara, who is four years younger than Joy and ten years my senior, took the road to Reno. Returning from Nevada to Groton, Barbara had been met at the front door by my mother. A small but really imposing woman, she effectively blocked the way.

"You may come in, Barbara, because this is your home," she said. "But I cannot permit you to bring your suitcases with those baggage labels on them into my house. I must ask you to unpack them on the back porch, and then hide them in the woodshed."

It was tacitly agreed that my divorce, like my connection with the theatre, was not a topic for conversation even within the family circle. My mother succeeded for a number of years in keeping Groton in ignorance of the fact that I had severed my banking connection—which had kept me, by Groton standards, respectable—and had become a producer, a man beyond the pale.

When I taxed her with distortion of the truth she defended herself indignantly in these terms: "No one ever asked me pointblank if you were in the theatre; therefore I told no lies. I never mentioned your occupation unless I was compelled to do so. Then I invariably spoke of your 'business.' If people chose to think this was something to do with banks there was no need for me to inform them otherwise."

* * *

It was our policy at the Playhouse on Cape Cod to bring there the greatest stars available for one week's engagement, on the theory that the summer people would willingly pay Broadway prices for the best that Broadway had to offer. I was making plans for the 1939 season, congratulating myself on having secured Jane Cowl, Ethel Barrymore, Ina Claire, Walter Hampden and Edward Everett Horton among others, when playwright Samson Raphaelson called upon me at my office in New York.

Rafe asked how we were fixed for a supporting resident company that summer. His wife, Dorshka, wanted to try a season of summer stock. She was a friend of Murial Williams, whose husband, Francis Hart, was our press agent and my oldest friend.

Before committing myself on Dorshka, I asked Rafe how his new play, *Skylark,* was coming along. John Golden, the successful producer of *Susan and God,* had acquired it as a vehicle for Gertrude Lawrence. Rafe said that *Skylark* was then in rehearsal on the road; but, he conceded, it needed more work done on it to be ready for Broadway in the fall. My New England instincts toward a good trade prompted me to put forth the suggestion that Rafe persuade Miss Lawrence to star in *Skylark* at the Cape Playhouse the third week in August.

At that time—April—it seemed like a perfect arrangement by which everyone would benefit. Rafe worked his magic on Mr. Golden and Miss Lawrence. The deal was made. I saw our season, which was already very promising, mounting to a brilliant and successful climax.

This mood of exaltation lasted until July. Then deflation set in, under a barrage of commands and demands issued by John Golden's office as "from Miss Lawrence."

What the Golden office requested for Miss Lawrence's three weeks' stay at the Cape was a cottage by the lake, sufficiently near the Playhouse for convenience but distant enough for complete privacy. Besides generous accommodations for herself and for guests she might wish to invite, the star would need rooms for a personal maid and a secretary, garage space for her town car and grounds for Mac, her West Highland terrier. I was instructed to place an order with a florist to keep the vases in Miss Lawrence's cottage filled with fresh flowers, preferably lilies, her favorites. The Playhouse commissary should be at pains to see that Miss Lawrence's refrigerator was well-stocked with a list of delicacies that ranged from avocados and caviar and sweetbreads through melons, quail, pâté de foie gras, and rainbow trout.

Nothing in my previous experience with stars had prepared me for anything like this. Jane Cowl had exhibited no such delusions of grandeur. The previous season Miss Ethel Barrymore had arrived by bus—and in the middle of the night, unexpectedly, before we could prepare an appropriately gala welcome for the First Lady of the American theatre. If a couple of stay-ups had not noticed her strolling unconcernedly about the grounds, Miss Barrymore might have had to pitch her own tent on the grass for that night. Something which, she said offhandedly, she would not have minded at all.

What, I thought darkly, did Gertrude Lawrence think a summer theatre was? And who did she think she was? I could tell her in less than ten words: a spoiled, pampered actress with a prima donna complex. I had heard tales of Miss Lawrence's taste for the settings and properties of a royal existence; much of my rage was directed against myself, for allowing these tales to be outweighed by the memory of a slim, white-clad figure bringing a moment of magic to a grimy stage alley.

I recounted these demands indignantly to Radie Harris, a newspaper woman and friend of Gertrude's.

"Oh, that's not Gee's doing," Radie informed me. "She adores caviar, it's true. But most of that chi-chi is Golden's idea of building up her star value. Since *Susan and God,* John thinks nothing's too good for his Golden Girl."

I said that if Miss Lawrence expected a lot of kow-towing and adulation she was in for a considerable jolt. The Cape was neither Mayfair, nor Park Avenue, nor Beverly Hills, and she needn't expect to turn it into a star's paradise.

"You're the one due for a jolt if you think she's like that," said Radie. "Wait till you see her at the station."

"What station? I'm not going to meet her."

"You must meet her at the train," Radie counseled. "She'll expect it."

"She'll expect a strip of red carpet from Yarmouth to her cottage,

I suppose. No, indeed! If Miss Lawrence stages any tantrums, as I hear she's quite capable of doing if she doesn't get everything she wants *when* she wants it—she can take the next train back to the Plaza. Contract or no contract!"

Radie cooled me off. "Look, you started the summer theatre star system. You want stars, you'll have to treat them as stars."

"On the stage; not off."

I muttered that I doubted I would recognize Miss Lawrence without footlights between us.

"No danger of that," Radie assured me. "If Gertrude Lawrence were parachuted into darkest Africa, the first pygmy would ask for her autograph."

Finally I allowed myself to be persuaded to head the welcoming committee, which included Fran Hart, Radie Harris and the Raphaelsons. Actually I put up only mild resistance. As a producer, I resented the outrageous requests; as a man, however, I was not immune to the waves of excitement and anticipation set in motion by the mere announcement of Gertrude Lawrence's arrival.

* Chapter Two * * * *

IT RAINED the night she came.

Slanting curtains of rain and salty-tasting mist were blown across the bogs. The foghorn at Truro Lighthouse kept up its periodic wail. It was one of the nights when you have to like the Cape very much not to add your despairing howl to the foghorn's and depart at top speed.

Our little group of five huddled on the rain-swept platform and watched the Neptune's headlight blur a path through the foggy dark. The train drew to a stop and people began tumbling out of it, hurrying for shelter from the storm. A white-coated porter swung off the step of one of the cars and stood at attention. I watched a trim young colored woman descend, carrying a jewel case in one hand and what was patently a make-up case in the other, followed by another woman holding a supercilious white terrier. Porters began handing down piece after piece of handsome Vuitton luggage until they grew into a sizable hillock on the platform. We advanced to the car steps regardless of the pelting rain. Then, with a timing I mentally applauded, a slim, golden-haired figure appeared at the top of the car steps.

She stood poised, a little above me, darkness surrounding her, the lamplight on her eager face. She caught sight of Radie Harris and the Raphaelsons.

"Darlings!" she cried, and tripped down the steps to their embraces.

At Radie's call I emerged from behind the baggage to be presented for the second time to Miss Lawrence.

On the drive to the cottage she sat beside me, composed and deliciously fragrant. We two were alone, following the car's headlights through the dripping countryside. "That first dark rainy night," was how she spoke of it afterward. The night we were married there was also a driving rain. "I love rain," Gertrude said then. "It's a lucky omen. Rain brought us together. Remember?"

That night, fumbling for conversation as she was so quiet, I apologized for the weather. "But the glass is rising," I added. "It will clear by morning."

"Glorious! I shall lie for hours on the beach in the sun, alone. I'll pack a lunch. I adore picnics, don't you?"

"No," I said, flatly, "I don't."

It occurred to me afterward when I reviewed this conversation that if she had been graciously opening a gate through which I might slip to join her on her beach in the sun alone, I had slammed it rudely in her face.

This thought drove home the increasingly disturbing realization that I lacked by nature and training a certain facility in human relations which more and more seemed to me indispensable in the art of living. It was easy to blame this stiffness on my upbringing. Though it never occurred to me to doubt that affection existed between my parents, and between them and their children, I never witnessed any exhibition of it. I was inoculated early with the idea that demonstrative language, gift-giving—except books and a five-dollar gold piece at Christmas and on birthdays—or kisses, save at solemn moments, and then always on the forehead or cheek, were distinctly in bad taste. They were the sort of thing the foreigners employed in Father's factory at Watertown might indulge in. We were expected to have more restraint in the matter of physical manifestations of affection. I have no recollection of Mother and me exchanging kisses until the very last years of her life—after we had both succumbed to Gertrude's warming influence. Father's few and laconic communications to me were invariably signed bluntly: "Yours truly, Father."

As I drove through the rain that night, chafing under the bonds of my own repressions, I deplored my New England heritage. There had been a time, before the advent of Freud, when repression was called self-control, and inhibition labeled self-restraint; these were qualities to be highly regarded and closely treasured. Now I was beginning to wonder. The greater my urge to be charming and gallant, the heavier my silence lay as a pall on conversation.

Gertrude seemed unaffected by my moodiness. Presently I heard her humming a little tune to herself. A happy tune, I was pleased to observe. She broke it off to ask: "Do you mind if I let down the window?"

This was a harbinger of the future; for the next thirteen years, Gertrude was always to be opening windows, both literally and figuratively.

Before I could reach across her knees to turn the handle, she had done it quite competently herself. She held her face to the opening thirstily.

"How divine it feels!" she exclaimed, not so much to me as to the night. "So cool and clean. And good! Do you know what I would like? To get out and walk in it for miles and miles."

I thought of what was waiting for her at the end of the ride—a surprise party staged by Jules Glaenzer at the cottage Gertrude was to occupy during her engagement. Jules, who was vice president of Cartier's, was full of plans for giving "Gertie" a royal reception and had come over with a hamper full of champagne as a starter. He had been a good friend of Gertrude's and Bea Lillie's since their first season in New York with *Charlot's Revue*. From all accounts, Gertrude had been one of the firm's lucrative customers. But that was not the reason why Jules was giving her this party. He was providing her with a welcome which he, and many more friends of his and hers, thought suited her better than what the Cape Playhouse had to offer.

The party, which burst into startling noisy merriment the minute

Gertrude stepped across the threshold of the deceptively dim cottage, lasted most of the night. I stayed until almost the end, though I felt myself an awkward anachronism on the edge of the swirl of which Gertrude was the center. Once or twice I felt her glance on me. It was puzzled, and a trifle pitying.

* * *

Even though the Playhouse constitutes a small and closely knit community, I had very little to do with Gertrude until one morning during the second week of her engagement, when her secretary appeared at my office with a penciled note:

Dear R.A.

Tonight I have two young friends coming over to play piano for us after the show. They were here last night and they and Amos and Andy all 4 played together. It was *so* exciting.

Could we have 2 pianos in the private room at the Restaurant after the play tonight? And would you come and be my "Beau" for the party?

Please let Charlotte know so that I can go ahead and invite the gang and get the vittles.

Love,
Gee

It was a gay, youthful party, with Gertrude in sky-blue pajamas singing all the songs the guests asked for. She was a far cry from the imperious leading lady I had been led to expect. Before it was over I had asked her to have supper with me at the Playhouse commissary the following night.

Driving her back to the cottage after that supper I asked if she had been to Scargo Hill.

Some time afterwards she told me: "The name sounded Scandinavian. I thought you were starting on a travelogue. When you said you would like to show it to me by moonlight I thought: 'How ducky! By the time he gets around to it, I'll be too old to see!' Then, to my amazement, you drove off with me."

After the expedition to Scargo Tower, which overlooks the lake adjoining the Playhouse grounds, we explored the Cape by moonlight almost every night of Gertrude's stay. She was quickly responsive to natural beauty: to the pure lines that the elms lifted to the sky; the eerie emptiness of the cranberry bogs; the wind-wrought dunes; and the staunch, prim little villages. These things appealed strongly to something in her which may have been an inheritance from her Danish father. She told me about how she had gone to Denmark to try to find her father's people.

"His name was Arthur Klasen. That's my name, too, really. Gertrude Alexandra Dagmar Lawrence Klasen—if you care to remember."

I asked if she had found her Danish relations.

"Oh, yes. They turned out to be solid working people who still couldn't understand how they had produced a vagabond concert singer like my father. He wasn't a real *concert* singer, of course. But he managed very nicely at pub smokers and in small music halls. Especially in black face."

Despite her close identification with England—the land of her birth and of her mother's family—Gertrude was proud of her Danish blood. "I'm like the Klasens—a worker." She spread her hands out in the moonlight, and I was as surprised as others have been. Gertrude's hands were not the slim, tapering sort one might have assumed she possessed. They were handsome and capable.

"They're working hands," she said proudly. "There's very little I can't do with them. Or that I haven't done. If something were to stop my acting tomorrow—it would be horrible, I'd much rather die —I wouldn't starve. Not as long as I had the use of my hands."

She asked me about the early settlers on the Cape. It pleased her to learn that they were English. She said: "It makes me feel as if I belonged here."

It may have been after one of these drives that she wrote to a friend in New York:

> This is a haven if ever there was one. I have a bungalow on the rim of a beautiful lake with the sea and the sand less than five minutes away. Here the Happy People enjoy their life's work in the theatre in a healthy, sweet, eager and sane way and the whole site of the theatre center is like a large model farm.

Here I could live. Sorting, choosing, being, studying, doing a job of living in the winters and acting the plays of one's choice, new or old, in these wonderful surroundings during the summers.

Such a plan in such a place would make a life really worth while, with sometimes a winter season in New York or England.

You must come and see me. It's so simple after all the grandeur we have known, and there are some houses for sale over one hundred years old which could be divine.

I have a room in my cottage for you so just let me know . . . Pam would adore it of course. Do come. Wood fires. *V* quiet. Gee.

On the last Sunday of her stay she gave a luncheon for the Harts, Radie Harris and myself at Latham's Inn. When I arrived I found Gertrude much exercised because she had just heard that my mother and sister Barbara were guests there. Why hadn't I told her? Why hadn't she met them? Was it too late to ask them to join the luncheon party?

I told her Barbara was there to recover from an operation. She and my mother had been to see a matinee of *Skylark* the day before, a momentous occasion for Mother, whose previous experience of the theatre had been confined to a few moralistic dramas approved by Father. Today Barbara was resting and Mother felt she should stay with her.

Gertrude said she understood perfectly; but it seemed too bad for the rest of us to be having fun while my mother and sister were out of it. She would like to do something for them. How would it be if she sent them a bottle of champagne?

I didn't like to say that champagne at Sunday lunch was something my mother would not have understood. I doubt if she had ever seen a bottle. I am sure she had never tasted it. The Joys were rigidly "dry." Mother had never forgiven Shattuck's, the leading grocer in Groton for three or four generations, because after Repeal they had opened a package store. Regretfully, she took away her trade and gave it to a newcomer whose tenure in Groton was not more than seventy years.

Although Gertrude had shown a flattering appreciation of New England, I felt that she would not understand this aspect of our regional character. "No champagne," I said firmly. "Mother doesn't like it."

"What does she like?"

I told her: "Ice cream."

This, I reasoned, was entirely safe. In accordance with New England custom, the inn celebrated Sunday by serving vanilla ice cream with your choice of sauce—chocolate, or butterscotch.

"I'll see that some goes up to her," Gertrude said, and disappeared kitchenwards.

Once behind the swinging doors, Gertrude called for "Lots of ice cream, please. And a large spoon. And maraschino cherries. And somebody please chop some nuts."

Gertrude happily stirred the cherries and nuts into the vanilla ice cream, added a liberal amount of whipped cream and then poured on brandy with a generous hand.

The *coupe* was divided in two portions, heaped on fancy plates, given a top dressing of cherries, nuts and cream and then delivered to Mrs. Latham to be taken upstairs "with Miss Lawrence's compliments."

Mrs. Latham carried up the tray herself. Its elegance seemed to demand this degree of respect. My mother opened the door. The message from Miss Lawrence was overlooked in her excited admiration of the confection. She simply took it for granted that the inn had provided her and Barbara with this pleasant Sunday treat and she thanked Mrs. Latham graciously.

My sister had heard the message, and her nose had told her that the flavor which Mother declared delicious and unusual was nothing less than cognac. While Mother praised the thoughtfulness and culinary skill of the inn's new management, they finished their *coupe*.

Only then did Barbara enlighten Mother first as to the source of the gift—the actress who was starring at her son's theatre that week; and then, as to that delicious, refreshing flavor: "It's brandy, the finest brandy. Don't you feel it in your elbows?"

Barbara's use of that old phrase of my father's was calculated to make Mother feel the enormity of the crime committed against her. For my father, though he did not drink and would not allow liquor to be served in his home, was partial to wine sauces and brandied pressed duck in restaurants such as Foyot's or Fouquet's in Paris when he traveled abroad. After such indulgences, he would make the improbable claim that he "felt it in his elbows." Mother had never been persuaded to join him in these indulgences, of which she thoroughly disapproved.

"I don't know which made her maddest," Barbara told me later. "Having accepted a gift from an actress, or having been duped into tasting liquor, or having enjoyed both sins as much as she did. Of course, she was furious at me for letting her eat the ice cream when I knew what was in it. But most of all, she blames you for bringing 'that actress' to the Cape and to the inn where she is staying. I explained that actresses were part of your business now. 'He *has* to take her out to lunch, Mother,' I said. 'She works for him.' Mother wasn't convinced. 'Your father did not take the workers in his factory out to lunch!' she pointed out."

* * *

In New York City, during the next few months, I saw Gertrude again and again. Our friendship, which had put forth such tremulous shoots in August, was in full bloom by winter. I could not dispute Gertrude's accusation that I had been standoffish, at least during the first ten days of her stay in Dennis. Actually my reserve was compounded of longing, acute shyness, total ignorance of how to establish contact with a creature of Gertude's will-o'-the-wisp qualities, and the normal masculine fear of making a fool of oneself.

"You weren't very friendly," was the way she rebuked me on one occasion.

"I was terrified."

"All six feet four of you? Was that why you watched me when you thought I wouldn't know it? All through that first week when we were rehearsing, at odd times I would catch a glimpse of you somewhere—in the Playhouse or in the commissary. You never once came near my cottage. And you would be looking at me with that appraising look. Wary, suspicious. And yet rather wistful, too. Like a rabbit peering through a hedge."

"You fascinated me."

"You didn't show it. You made me feel that you didn't like me. Finally I asked Radie Harris: 'What's the matter with Richard Aldrich? He has never once asked me to have supper with him, or dropped around for a drink.' Radie said it was because you were born on Plymouth Rock. 'Born there?' I said. 'He *is* Plymouth Rock.' "

Our friendship had progressed to a point where I found myself waiting impatiently each morning until the hour arrived at which I might properly telephone Gertrude. Later I learned that I did not have to wait; she usually woke early no matter how late she had gone to bed. She always woke very alert and full of ideas, and wanted to share them with someone. She used to say plaintively that she could not understand why so many people objected to being roused for a chat on the phone before they swallowed their first cup of coffee.

Sometimes, during those morning calls, she would discuss with me the news from Europe which she had just heard from her bedside radio. It was the first winter of the war, the winter of what the quick-talking commentators were beginning to call the "phony war." Intensely loyal to her native England, Gertrude was acutely concerned over every turn of events.

The stalemate at the Maginot Line caused her qualms of uneasiness: "Richard, what *is* Gamelin about? Is France to be trusted? As England's ally, I mean?" She would repeat what some broadcaster had said and demand: "What does it mean? For us?" At other times she would read me opinions expressed in letters she had received from her friends in London—rather jaunty, most of them were, and in the light of what was to happen in a few months in Norway and on the beaches of Dunkirk, not very realistic.

But Gertrude would be immensely cheered.

Always pressing upon her was a keen sense of responsibility and anxiety for her daughter. Pamela was then leaving her teens. She had been whisked to New York from her Swiss boarding school in the autumn some weeks after the declaration of war. She was finding the adjustment to life in New York difficult. Gertrude was insistent that she keep on with her studies. "I don't care what she studies, but she must work at something until she decides what she wants to do with her life, and what she is best fitted for."

She talked to me frequently about Pam, who showed the usual teen-ager's reluctance to find herself with any definiteness. This was something Gertrude could not understand. From the very beginning of her own rough-and-tumble childhood, she had known exactly where she was going. And she had kept consistently "on target," despite the lack of a normal home life and the pressure of economic difficulties. The only advantage ever accorded her was free lessons at Miss Italia Conti's dancing school. In contrast, Pam had been sent to Brearley School in New York, to Roedean in England and to finishing schools on the Continent. In all these schools the fact that she was Gertrude Lawrence's daughter gave her immediate prestige.

"Pam was born on the night of London's worst air raid in the first world war," Gertrude told me early in our friendship. "I was in the chorus of *Charlot's Revue*. My husband and I needed the money desperately, so I worked much longer than I should have. Then, just as I was about to quit, my big chance came. Bea Lillie met with an accident and was laid up for some time. I was her understudy and got her part. Every night I laced myself into Bea's costume and prayed that the baby wouldn't come until I had proved that I was *good*.

"I just made it to the nursing home in time, one night after a performance. Later, as I lay there listening to the drone of the Zeppelins and the crash of the bombs, I said that I'd work to give my daughter everything I had never had. I so wanted her to be happy. I still do."

I told her that I didn't see how she could have done more for Pamela than she had.

"I wanted to spend more time with her," Gertrude said wistfully. "I couldn't. Not while I was working to support us. No matter where I was working, we've tried to spend our holidays together. I've treasured every day she could be with me, and every one of her letters to me, and her school essays. It hasn't been enough; there are so many things I would have loved to do with her and for her. Perhaps, if I hadn't pursued a career, I could have given her my entire attention."

"Nonsense," I said, "the psychoanalysts' couches are filled with girls trying to break away from doting, over-protective mothers. Stop worrying about Pam. She'll find herself and what she wants to do, one of these days. When that happens, she'll bless you for letting her take her time about it. Or she should."

* * *

Sometimes I wondered exactly how it came about that in a few short months I had become so intimate a friend and confidant. I could only surmise it was because that was what Gertrude wanted most at the time. Early in our friendship, in one of her rare moments of self-revelation, she wrote to me, "You have added to my life a joy that was strangely lacking."

Many men had been in love with her. They had given her amusing, sometimes exciting companionship. They had brought romance and gaiety into her life, and from her own abundant fount of these qualities, they had drawn in even larger amounts. But no man, as far as I could learn, had ever given her the one thing she had lacked all her life. Call it stability. Call it security. Gertrude at that moment called it friendship. I had my own name for it: love. But the time had not yet come when she wanted to call it that.

* * *

During those winter months in New York, it became a habit for me to drop in at Gertrude's apartment at about five-thirty in the afternoon. I would have a drink while she ate her simple but substantial dinner—chops or steak, green vegetables, potatoes, a salad, fruit—"You can't do good work on an empty stomach," she would say. "I've had to do it, and I know."

At six, her chauffeur would be at the door with the Rolls to drive her to the theatre. Like all good, sincere actresses, she liked to get there early, never later than half-past six. This gave her time for a rest on the couch in her dressing room, after which she would make up and relax in leisure. How different from those stars who dash into the theatre just before curtain time, exhausted after a whirl of engagements!

Sometimes I would drive down to the theatre with her and take her to the stage door, where the doorman—one of those battered, sardonic, elderly men in dusty hats who seem to have been minted for the purpose of watching suspiciously at stage doors—would be on the lookout for her. The doorman of every theatre she ever played was a friend of hers. She never forgot their names, their taste in cigars, the ball team they favored and the exact location of their rheumatism. She never came or went without a gay greeting. When she came back to a theatre and found a new face at the wicket she made it her immediate concern to find out what had become of his predecessor. If he were sick, she made it her business to see that he had proper care and a few luxuries. She believed in luxuries; not merely for herself, but for others.

When she arrived at the theatre, her maid would be waiting for her. Her dressing room would be immaculate, aired and filled with flowers, as she liked it to be. No one was ever permitted in her dressing room before or during the play. "The theatre is a place for work," she would say. "After the show is the time to have fun."

Surrounding Gertrude was a staff of experienced and devoted aides whom I came to know well: Dorothy, the English maid and companion who had been through innumerable ups and downs with Gertrude on both sides of the Atlantic; Corinne Turner, the nurse who often accompanied her on tour to look after her diet and health; and Carrie, her dressing-room maid for many years, whom Gertrude considered without peer until Hazel was engaged as Carrie's assistant during the long run of *Lady in the Dark,* with its many changes of costume. When faithful old Carrie, whose service in the theatre dated back to years with Marilyn Miller, retired, Hazel took over, to stay for the rest of Gertrude's life.

Heading the backstage team was Jack Potter, Gertrude's manager whenever she went on tour. A Princeton graduate and member of an old Philadelphia family, Jack had been introduced to

Gertrude in London by the Prince of Wales. Jack was not only expert in the ways of the theatre, which he loved; he was also familiar with Gertrude's personal enthusiasms, and was always obligingly on hand, whether it was for a few rounds of bezique (a rather rare card game) or to organize one of the backstage parties that Gertrude delighted in holding for the cast and crew on Hallowe'en, Christmas and similar occasions.

* * *

Gertrude had an extraordinary power for getting people to do what she wanted them to. My first encounter with this came early in 1940, when I had known her about six months. She and Pam, to whom I had recently been introduced, were lunching with me. Dick Myers and I had just produced *Margin for Error* following directly upon *My Dear Children,* with all the strain attendant on dealing with John Barrymore in his latter days. I announced casually that I was going to run down to Mexico for a ten-day vacation in the sun.

"Mexico? How wonderful!" Gertrude exclaimed. "Wouldn't you like to take Pam with you?"

The truthful answer would have been "No," but with Pam seated on one side of me, and Gertrude on the other, I was somewhat handicapped. I managed to mutter: "Pam wouldn't enjoy traveling with me."

"Of course she would!" said Gertrude enthusiastically. "Darling, wouldn't you enjoy Mexico with Richard?"

What could Pam say?

I tried to make my proposed trip sound as unattractive as possible. I intended to be a tourist. I was going to climb up and down pyramids, make myself conversant with Mayan and Aztec remains. There wouldn't be a bullfight, a night club or a party in the entire tour.

"Wonderful!" Gertrude exclaimed again. "That's just what Pam should have. You know so much about everything, Richard. It will be quite educational. And now that she thinks of studying art, this trip will be a real inspiration."

"But, Gertrude," I objected, "surely you realize that I can't travel around the country with a young girl. Especially with one who doesn't belong to me."

"Oh, she won't be a bit of bother," she assured me. "Pam's used to looking out for herself. She won't be in your way and you can forget all about her whenever you like. Oh, darling," she beamed on Pamela. "You'll have *such* fun."

Of course there was only one reason I didn't refuse firmly and unequivocally—I was in love. Of all the deeds that men have performed for the women they loved, few have been more quixotic than my taking my not yet prospective stepdaughter to Mexico.

For, as I knew I would all along, I took her. Not very graciously, I admit. But I took her.

I cannot honestly claim that my future stepdaughter and I became closer friends as we followed our Mexican guide through cathedrals, over Aztec ruins and floating gardens; nor yet in the market places where Pam bought baskets, pottery and silver with an abandon worthy of her mother. I know that I probably grinned most annoyingly at an incident that occurred on our return trip when the train stopped to take on water at some lonely little town in a waste of Texas desert. We had gotten out to stretch our legs on the platform. Pam looked about her with marked distaste.

In her high-pitched, well-bred English voice, she observed: "Why would anyone want to live in a place like this?"

From somewhere in the surrounding sagebrush a voice drawled: "If you don't like it here, Limey, go on back where you came from!"

The morning after I had deposited Pamela and her souvenirs at her mother's apartment, Gertrude telephoned me. She told me—what I could not believe—that Pam was delighted with her trip. She had loved every minute of it, she had reported, but she was afraid I had not.

"What makes her think that?" I asked.

"From the way you acted. She says you barely spoke to her. And never once looked at her or at anyone else."

I said I had merely tried to treat her "as any father treated his daughters." Wasn't that the way she had expected to be treated? What did Pam, or her mother, think I was?

"I'll tell you what Pam thinks," Gertrude said, laughter welling between her words. "She says you're hopeless."

"Do you agree with that?"

The laughter overcame her for a moment. Then, "Not having had Pam's opportunity," she said, "I'm not in a position to say."

Chapter Three

One member of Gertrude's household viewed our increasing intimacy with unconcealed distrust. This was her terrier, Mackie. Was he somehow forewarned of my intentions toward his mistress, and flatly jealous? Or were his dour resistance to all my overtures and his sinister interest in my trouser cuffs indicative of some deficiency he had discovered in my character?

Gertrude often said thoughtfully that dogs were notable judges of people. For herself, she would back a dog's judgment every time. Remarks like these increased my sensitiveness to Mackie's obviously low opinion of me.

The white rough-coated terrier, like every pet Gertrude ever had, was absorbedly and possessively in love with her. He was fond of her maid Dorothy and he tolerated Pam. The other members of Gertrude's inner circle he ignored. Me, he unqualifiedly despised.

"I don't believe you like dogs," Gertrude accused me one day when I accompanied her and Mackie on a brisk, healthful walk through the more remote regions of Central Park. Mackie's veterinary had prescribed more exercise in the fresh air and Gertrude had accepted the prescription as equally good for her. And for me.

"American men spend too much time in their stuffy overheated offices," she said. "Then they stuff themselves, and get potbellied. It will do you good to get the sun and lots of fresh air with poor old Mackie and me."

On this particular afternoon the sun was absent. A bleak wind blew off the Hudson in sudden tormenting gusts that compelled me to hold fast to my hat with one freezing hand. The icy air found its way inside my coat collar and up my trouser legs. My eyes watered and my nose grew blue at the tip. Gertrude, a scarf over her head, swathed to the ears in mink and in a British superiority to damp and chilliness, appeared to be enjoying the outing.

She had made straight for an unfrequented part of the park, where she encouraged the unlawfully unleashed Mackie to burrow in the shrubbery. I was posted to watch for and give the warning of the possible approach of a policeman. "You're so tall, Richard, you can see over the bushes in case one is lurking somewhere getting ready to pounce," she said. "And, too, you look so respectable. The copper's bound to be impressed."

Was this, I wondered, the only reason she had invited me on the walk? My position appeared in need of consolidation.

I replied hastily to her comment that I did like dogs, though my experience of them was not extensive. "I don't believe Mackie likes me," I countered.

"Well, you aren't very gracious," she said. "You haven't thrown a single stick for him all afternoon. Don't you think Mackie has feelings, too?"

I made an abortive effort to ingratiate myself with Mackie by finding a stick and hurling it into a thicket. But he was not deceived. Instinct, not gratitude, compelled him to retrieve the stick which, pointedly disregarding me, he laid at Gertrude's feet.

"No, he doesn't seem to," she said as though the fact impressed her.

"I really know more about cats," I said quickly. Whereupon I produced several anecdotes connected with Archimedes, the huge tiger cat of alley antecedents which was the only pet tolerated by my parents during my boyhood. Needless to say, Father gave him his name.

Two days later a pet shop delivered to me a pair of Siamese cats. The card attached to their velvet-lined basket read: "To Richard—from Gertrude." On the reverse were written the names she had given them—David and Wally, in honor of the Duke and Duchess of Windsor.

Beautiful, disdainful creatures, they promptly assumed possession of my hearth rug and of the apartment I shared with my sister and her husband.

Barbara, who has always been devoted to animals of any sort, and her husband, Harrison Hobart, looked at David and Wally with lifted eyebrows. My sister said: "You must be in love with Gertrude Lawrence."

Harrison came to my defense by saying that it was rather far-fetched to interpret my tolerant acceptance of two cats as a declaration of love.

"It would do you good, Richie, to be in love with someone like her," Barbara went on imperturbably. "In fact, the improvement has already begun. There's not so much of the dried salt cod about you."

I became uncomfortable; love was not usually a subject of conversation in our family. I told Barbara that merely because she wrote stories for women's magazines, she needn't attempt an analysis of my character.

"Do you *really* think Gertrude is in love with you?" she persisted.

"Is that so impossible?" I asked a little touchily.

"Of course not, Richie," Barbara assured me. "I was just thinking—wondering what she sees in you. Here is a woman with the world at her feet. She's at the top of her profession, an established success. She certainly doesn't need you as a producer. You haven't a million dollars to offer her—or a title. What have you, or any man for that matter, to offer—except—"

I waited hopefully.

"You know what Mother says," my sister mused. " 'You can depend on Richard.' And, like Mother, you have principles. You're—well—you're what our generation unfortunately feels embarrassed to call . . . good."

"That's ridiculous," I replied. "I'm no better than the next man."

Barbara continued: "It's only in late years I've realized that integrity of character—goodness—is better to live with than cleverness or shrewdness or a genius for making money. There aren't too many nice people in the world, either. When you find one of them you feel like holding him close."

I intercepted the look that passed between her and Harrison and I realized that Barbara's life, for all its earlier tragedies, had also its deep compensations.

"Maybe that's what Gertrude Lawrence sees in you," she said. "I hope so."

"Why?" I asked.

"Because if she does, and if that is what she wants, you will make each other terribly happy. I'd like you to be happy."

A little later, when my sister and her husband went out, she did something extraordinary. She put her arms around me and kissed me.

"Good luck, Richie," she whispered.

* * *

That winter—1940—was a busy one for me. As I have already mentioned, my partner, Dick Myers, and I produced Clare Boothe Luce's *Margin for Error,* which promised—and gave—us a long run. Early in the year Raymond Moore, under whose ownership I had managed the Cape Playhouse, died. Convinced as I was that summer theatres were not only an excellent training ground for young people and a boon to theatre-hungry communities, but could be made financially profitable as well, I arranged to take over the Playhouse on my own.

I was surprised and delighted when Gertrude endorsed this move wholeheartedly. Her experience of summer theatres had been limited to that one engagement at the Cape the previous summer—concerning which, when it was originally suggested to her, she had reportedly demanded, "What is a summer theatre?"

But she was, I discovered then and realized more fully as time went on, extraordinarily theatre-wise. She knew what pleases the public; partly by instinct, more by reason of her extensive hard-working experience in the years she was making her way entirely on her own talents from the chorus of third-rate musicals to stardom on two continents. She was proudly professional to her finger-tips; she had no patience with amateur, arty "little theatre" standards. The idea of running a theatre for any reason other than to make it a successful and paying business venture shocked her.

Like all professionals, she respected her public. She never made light of their reactions to a play or to players. She trusted the basic rightness of the public's judgment, which the cleverest and costliest promotion schemes cannot for long deflect. Above all else, she wished to stand well with that public. They were the people she worked for; not the critics.

Her instant interest in the Cape Playhouse when I took it over was shown by her agreement to play an engagement of *Private Lives* to open our 1940 season. This would cut into her all-too-short holiday between the closing of *Skylark* on Broadway and the start of the company on a four-month tour of thirteen states. She made one stipulation about *Private Lives*—the proceeds of the play were to be donated to Allied War Relief. Naturally, I concurred.

* * *

Our first talks together were gay, inconsequential, innocently childlike; or concerned factually with the war, the state of the world, or the larger aspects of the theatre. But gradually our conversation veered more to the personal, as our friendship grew deeper.

Gertrude began from time to time to mention incidents from her own childhood—always lightly and with a total want of self-pity. In a few striking phrases she made me see Kennington Oval in Clapham, with its dreary, shabby-genteel houses, the wandering organ-grinder, and little Gertie Lawrence leading all the other children of the neighborhood in a dance after him. Vividly she sketched in "Dad," her stepfather, with his ginger-colored mustache, his jaunty bowler, and his self-depreciating manner when there was no money to pay the rent and the only way to escape the irate landlord was by a "moonlight flit"; and her mother, who had been named Alice after a royal princess and had come down in the world from her original status as the daughter of a masterbuilder. When money was scarce (Dad was always being betrayed by unpredictable horses), Mother would make the rounds of the managers' offices during casting for the Christmas pantomime. She could sing a bit and dance a bit, and she was pretty. Only her lower limbs were too thin to find favor. Dressing for performances, she would stand on a chair and tell Gertrude how to stuff the calves and thighs of her flesh-colored tights to give her the alluring curves the patrons wanted.

Years later, Gertrude would more than once remark, "Thank goodness, plump legs have gone out"—meanwhile looking with warranted complacency at her own long, slim, beautiful limbs—"or I'd be nowhere."

Gertrude's first recollection of personal success as a performer went back to the age of six, when she was taken to Bognor Regis, the English seaside resort, for Bank Holiday. A concert troupe was entertaining on the sands. At the manager's invitation for anyone in the audience to "come up and have a twirl," Gertrude had stepped forward, held out her skirt, spun around lightly on her toes and sung her number:

"Oh, it ain't all honey, and it ain't all jam,
Walking round the 'ouses with a three-wheel pram,
All on me lonesome, not a bit to eat,
Walking about on me poor old feet,
My old man, if I could find 'im,
A lesson I would give.
Poor old me, I 'aven't got a key,
And I don't know where I live . . .
Boom! Boom!"

The vociferous applause and the gold sovereign presented to her by the manager had only confirmed her belief that she was an actress.

That song, by the way, was one that came first to her lips whenever she felt the need of strengthening her spirit. I have been told that she hummed it while flying in a bomber over the Pacific with a USO company, after they had been warned that Jap fighter planes might wing out of the clouds to attack them at any moment. And before that, in Normandy, jolting over roads from which all the mines had not been removed, just four days behind the enemy, on her mission to entertain the troops in the advance lines.

Though not a "happy tune," like the one she whistled in *The King and I,* it was a link with her childhood which helped her over many a rough spot.

Another favorite quotation of Gertrude's from her cockney days was the cheery credo of the carnival operator: "Wot yer loses on the swings, yer makes on the roundabouts." This carried her through what must frequently have been a trying adolescence. At the age of thirteen, Gertrude had run away from home and joined her minstrel-singing real father, Arthur Lawrence Klasen, who, "too fond of his glass," had separated from her mother long before. Klasen appeared professionally under the name Arthur Lawrence. For several years Gertrude toured and lived with him and with Rose, the warm-hearted show-girl who shielded Arthur when he was drinking and supported him when the managers fired him.

It was Rose who urged Gertrude to strike out on her own for the bright lights of the West End. "You've got something that goes down with a certain kind of audience, Gertie. But you've got to be seen by the toffs."

From then on, Gertrude was entirely on her own. When she was lucky, she found a job in the chorus of some musical show touring the provinces; when she wasn't, she lived on short rations in the Theatrical Girls' Boarding House (known in the profession as the "Cats' Home"). So it had gone until she found her first chance to be seen by the right people in one of André Charlot's revues.

Whenever Gertrude engaged in these reminiscences of her early life, I found myself thinking how very different my own background had been. Literally from birth, I had been surrounded by well-ordered stability.

My parents were both middle-aged when I was born. The staid pattern of our family life is recorded vividly in Mother's photograph albums.

We are all there: Mother in a well-boned basque and a stiff

sailor hat, with a croquet mallet on the lawn of Great-grandfather Joy's house in Groton; Father in a frock coat, a Bible under his arm, about to depart for his Sunday afternoon Bible study class; my sister Joy seated on a bicycle, in a stiffly starched Gibson-girl shirtwaist; and Barbara as captain of the Wellesley hockey team.

It is somewhat embarrassing to recognize myself in the scrawny boy in tweed knickerbockers and stiff-brimmed straw hat; again in floppy, striped bathing drawers and shirt, looking apprehensively at the sea; and on the steps of our Brookline house, proudly wearing my Noble and Greenough school cap.

Our homes are there, too—the old Joy and Hartwell houses on Groton's Main Street—and Great-grandfather's ultimate resting place in Groton's cemetery surrounded by forebears and descendants, and protected from lesser breeds by a handsome white-painted wrought-iron fence of which Mother was exceedingly proud. No other family in the cemetery had such an ornament. She always spoke condescendingly of my father's family, who were buried in Upton—"a town with no historical associations, and in an unfenced, open plot."

The first home I remember was a bow-windowed mansard-roofed house on Gardner Street in Boston. My father had three brothers, all married and living in Back Bay and Brookline; Uncle Samuel Nelson Aldrich, as head of the family, exercised patriarchal authority from his large Back Bay house.

Every Sunday afternoon, except in summer when the various Aldriches scattered to their country houses, Uncle Sam's brothers, their wives and progeny paid a ceremonial call on the head of the tribe.

While our elders conversed, we children sat as quietly as we could on the somewhat scratchy horsehair-covered furniture, and looked at each other disparagingly. As the youngest of the younger generation, younger even than many of Uncle Sam's grandchildren, I came in for the largest amount of disparagement.

After Uncle Sam died, the chieftainship passed to my father. The relations began coming to our house on Sunday afternoons. This was a little easier on me because I could make a pretext of getting a drink of water and duck up the back stairs to my own room and to the book I had previously concealed beneath my pillow.

The topics considered suitable for Sunday conversation were rigorously limited. Nothing worldly, except investments—in bonds, naturally; not in common stocks—was mentionable. As no Sunday papers were permitted in our home, there was no up-to-the-minute discussion of current events, except the sermons at the various churches attended by the family.

We were all Congregationalists; and, as such, militantly opposed to Unitarians. Father was anti-Unitarian not only on doctrinal grounds but because entire congregations, switching to the newer faith, had taken with them the title deeds of their meeting houses and other church property. The sight of Groton's beautiful historic church, originally a Congregational meeting house, now turned to Unitarian use, while the diminished Congregationalists worshipped in a smaller, plainer building, never failed to infuriate him.

In spite of his prejudice, my Father's religion was sincere and deep. As fervently as he believed in the Commonwealth of Massachusetts and the sanctity of private enterprise, he believed in the efficacy of prayer and the working of Divine Grace. He gave conscientiously and generously to the Lord's cause, tithing his wealth and spending time and energy in personal service. He was until his death a strong supporter of the missions established by Dwight Moody in the slums of the great cities. Whenever he went to New York on business, he would visit the Bowery missions and take part in the religious services there.

For many years he and my mother used to attend the Bible conferences which were held every summer at East Northfield, Massachusetts. These had been organized by Mr. Moody when he conceived the idea of making a religious and educational center out of the little village where he had been born. So fond did my parents become of these gatherings, and of Northfield itself, that they rented the Swiss chalet which belonged to Father's Boston friend, the Reverend Henry Mabie, as a summer home. My earliest memories of Northfield are of this steep-roofed, timbered house with the text carved on the central gable: "God's Providence Is My Inheritance."

I was still a schoolboy when Father bought land on Rustic Ridge and built on it a house which he named, not inappropriately, "Sunny Shadow." This became our home through summer vacations which increased in length as Father gradually cut down his business activities at the Hood Rubber Company, tire and rainwear manufacturers, of which he was one of the founders.

Sunny Shadow offered a simple outdoor existence in which a boy had time to think his own thoughts and dream his own dreams without interruption. Permeating this existence was the life of Northfield itself. All summer long, successive Bible conferences filled the village with earnest young men from the colleges, then with equally earnest and frequently pretty young women, some of them preparing for service in the foreign mission field. Later would come the Bible students, and finally the missionaries on furlough from posts in distant lands, speaking as familiarly of Bangkok and Dakar as I would of Boston Common. "Native Christian" missionaries would appear at the conferences in the dress of their countrymen, mingling colorful saris and long, straight Chinese robes with the clerical black when the faithful gathered for prayer meetings or sedate afternoon receptions.

My parents had a special fondness for the foreign missionaries. In planning Sunny Shadow, Father included a large dining room and front porch adequate for entertaining twenty guests. I recall his arriving from Boston one morning with a crate from which twelve heads of cauliflower tumbled out onto our lawn. To my mother's remonstrances, Father retorted: "I just thought anyone who'd been doing the Lord's work on a diet of rice and bitter herbs would find some nice Maine cauliflowers with cream sauce a welcome change."

My mother's interest in the missionaries was more educational than evangelistic. She liked hearing about the distant countries, the customs of the people, the lives lived by the missionaries themselves. Through these stories she traveled vicariously to African jungles and Chinese rice paddies. She read all the literature the Mission Boards published and the books which retired workers wrote of their service in foreign lands.

Sundays at Northfield presented a joyous contrast to Sundays in Boston. The welcome churning of the ice-cream freezer sounded through the house by mid-morning. There were no family gatherings to endure. And although there was the same taboo against newspapers and light reading, Barbara and I, after attending services twice with our parents, were encouraged to enjoy the outdoors.

Our greatest pleasure at Northfield came from the daily sunset services on Round Top. From Round Top you had an unobstructed view up and down the rich Connecticut Valley. Whenever Mother sang one of the favorite Northfield hymns on Sunday evenings at home:

> *"Shall we gather at the river*
> *The beautiful, beautiful river . . ."*

to me the river was the Connecticut; the saints assembled on its brink were the conference students and missionaries; and the Throne of God was Round Top, bathed in golden light while dusk settled on the valley.

The services on Round Top were preponderantly musical, led by George C. Stebbins to the accompaniment of a portable organ. None of my musical memories surpasses that of hearing and joining in the great hymn by Ira D. Sankey, *The Ninety and Nine:*

> *"There were ninety and nine that safely lay*
> *In the shelter of the fold,*
> *But one was out on the hills away,*
> *Far off from the gates of gold . . ."*

More and more, I found myself telling Gertrude of my boyhood experiences. Many of them I had not thought of for a long, long time, and I supposed they had vanished forever from my mind. But now they surged back with wonderful vividness and life, as she sat by my side, listening. I had not felt so relaxed, nor talked so freely and gaily to anyone in years.

Chapter Four

SPRING HAD COME early in 1940, with a burst of balmy weather in mid-March. Suddenly New York looked frowsy and down-at-heel; I longed for country sights and country smells. When some family business came up that could conceivably best be settled by discussion with my mother, I jumped at the opportunity to drive up to Groton.

I phoned Gertrude, whom I was seeing quite frequently by then, to explain that I'd be away for a few days.

She was frankly and rather pathetically envious. She would give anything, she said, to get out into the real country for even a single day.

"When you get back we'll go off for a long day in the car," she planned. "Some day when I haven't a matinee or an appointment I can't break. We'll take the picnic basket, and we'll find some lovely place where we can walk in the real woods the way you used to do at Northfield."

"Northfield?" I said, surprised.

"I don't believe you realize how often you talk about it," she said. "Your house, Sunny Shadow, and the chalet with the text carved on it, and the hill you used to climb so you could see all the colored mountains."

"The Green Mountains and the White Mountains aren't all the ranges you see from Northfield," I informed her. "South are the Berkshires. And on very clear days, off in the northwest there's a line of blue that people say is the Adirondacks."

"You see," she pointed out. "You remember every little thing. The part about Northfield is the part of your boyhood that you like best."

There was a great deal of truth in what Gertrude said, though I had not suspected her of discovering it. I realized that she knew me better, had fathomed the reserves of my nature more deeply than I thought possible of one as volatile and buoyant as she.

Saturday afternoon found me in Boston conferring with Fran Hart, publicity director of the Cape Playhouse and my closest friend since boyhood days. We were discussing scripts and stars. But the premature spring seemed to engage our attention as much as the imminent summer, stirring the primeval urge to get out into the country and feel the quickening earth under our feet. Unexpectedly, Fran asked what the family had done with Sunny Shadow.

I said we had sold it.

"Too bad," was his comment. "It would be great to see it again. You know, I've tried to explain Northfield to Murial. But one has to see the place to understand it. I really ought to take her there someday."

"Like tomorrow?" I suggested. Though I spoke laconically, his words had aroused within me feelings which were both strong and deep.

Fran agreed readily. We arranged to drive to Northfield the next day, stay overnight at the Northfield Hotel and return to Boston on Monday. We drank a toast to our trip.

When Fran left, I saw that it was five-thirty—a good time to call Gertrude. She would be in her dressing room resting between the matinee and evening shows.

"When will you be back in New York?" was her immediate question.

"Not before Tuesday," I replied. I told her of my plans for Sunday with the Harts.

"How wonderful!" she exclaimed, her voice singing through two hundred miles of wire. "Oh, how I envy you—getting out into the real country. That's what I ought to do; even for a day. I never seem to be able to. Oh, Richard, I do believe I can manage it. I *could* catch the midnight sleeper, couldn't I? That would give me two days."

"Sleeper? To where?"

"Darling, to Boston! And we could all motor to Northfield in the morning. That is," her voice dropped, becoming suddenly wistful, "if you want me."

There was only one answer to that, and I tried not to give it grudgingly. If it had been a question of San Francisco, London, Paris or Rangoon, I could have thought of nothing more delightful than to have Gertrude's unexpected company. But Northfield and Gertrude (as I knew her then)—they simply did not seem to fit together!

I said quickly that we were not going to a gay or smart resort, and that the hotel might not be up to her standards of luxury.

"But I don't want a fashionable hotel. I long for fresh, clean air! And sun! And the four of us together! I can hardly wait. Ten o'clock tomorrow at the Ritz in Boston, Richard. I'll be rested and ready to go," she said gaily.

For a full minute, after she hung up, I sat with the receiver in my hand and a premonition of disaster in my mind.

By morning I had reconciled myself to the possibility of having a successful and satisfying trip, when Fran called to tell me that Murial had developed flu overnight. He would have to stay in town to take care of her. "Let's go later in the spring," he proposed.

"Later may be fine for you," I said, "but what am I going to do about Gertrude Lawrence? She's at the Ritz right now, waiting for us to call for her."

Fran's answer was no comfort. "Why don't you keep her amused in Boston?" he suggested. I reminded him tartly that amusement in Boston on a Sunday is not the easiest thing to come by. "Besides, Gertrude is all charged up with visions of spring in the woods."

As usual, Fran stood staunchly by me. He agreed to go with me to the Ritz to help explain the change of plans to Gertrude. His final words were disturbing. He reminded me that the Northfield Hotel, out of deference to the continued observance of a Puritan Sunday in Northfield, did not encourage arrivals or departures of guests on that day.

I had forgotten about this tradition. This lapse of memory only revived my uneasiness about the trip. There were so many things that I had grown away from.

Fran met me at the Ritz promptly at ten. He suggested that if we failed to dissuade Gertrude from going to Northfield, I should defer the start of the drive and then dawdle along the way. "That way you will arrive in Northfield after dark, and you won't be so conspicuous."

"With Gertrude on my arm, just in time to spend the night at the hotel? You've forgotten too much, Fran. You and Murial would have made it all right. But Richard Aldrich and Gertrude Lawrence traveling alone—"

Fran suggested as an alternative that I take Gertrude somewhere else. I had the whole of New England at my disposal, he pointed out.

"And run the risk of exposing her to gossip? That would be worse. Think what the columnists would make of it if someone reported seeing us. And someone would. It would be my luck."

Fran ruefully agreed that this was a contingency to be avoided at any cost. "We'd better go up and see what we can do to persuade her to abandon the whole idea," he said. "Anyway, what's wrong with the Ritz? Why can't she be happy staying here? I can think of a lot of people who would!"

I said I could, too. But unfortunately Gertrude had come primed for country air and a complete, refreshing change from luxury.

The moment Gertrude opened the door of her sitting room, I knew that I could not disappoint her. Though she had arrived early that morning after a night on a train, her suite looked as if it was her permanent home, with bowls of flowers, a scattering of books and magazines. And a few framed photographs without which she never went anywhere, even for a night. She herself was dressed in a sea-green gown whose train swept the floor. I caught a glimpse of gold slippers and the tinkle of bells on her toes.

Her first words came as a jolt:

"Mackie and I are so thrilled about going to Northfield!"

I hadn't counted on Mackie. The Northfield Hotel did not welcome pets. Suddenly this seemed to offer the way out. I interrupted Fran's account of Murial's illness and the reasons why they could not leave Boston, to announce that Mackie's presence put the trip out of the question for everyone. "I'm sorry, Gertrude. I ought to have told you that the hotel has a rule against dogs."

For a moment I thought it was going to work. Then Gertrude shook her head. "Poor old Mackie, he's going to lose his country holiday. We'll leave him with you, Fran. I've set my heart on seeing Northfield. Richard has talked about it so much and I want to get out on the ground and walk in the woods. Maybe there will be wild violets."

I threw Fran an agonized glance. Loyally he came to my rescue.

"We'd love to have Mac," he told Gertrude. "That is, if you think he'll get along with our dog. He'll be good company for Murial while she's in bed."

"Oh, he can't stay with Murial," Gertrude objected. "Not if she has flu. Dogs are terribly susceptible to infections, Mackie particularly."

For a split second my hopes rose again, only to fall when she said decisively.

"No, he'll have to go along with Richard and me. You can explain to the hotel people, Richard. Wasn't your father one of the pillars of Northfield? And didn't you always spend your summers there? Surely, they will make an exception for an Aldrich!"

* * *

A few hours later, Gertrude, Mackie and their six pieces of assorted-sized luggage were fitted into my car. Fran waved us off. His grin threatened the moorings of a lifelong friendship. I had succeeded in delaying our departure for a little while, at any rate, by persuading Gertrude that I was expecting an important long-

Culver Service

Gertrude as she appeared in *Skylark*.

Gertrude's favorite photograph of Pamela and herself. It traveled with her wherever she went.

John Bennewitz

Gertrude in the role of Susan, in Rachel Crothers' *Susan and God.*

George Maillard Kesslere, B.P

Gertrude, my sister Barbara, and I at our favorite "bistro."

distance call. Even with the delay, I knew I would have to find the longest route to Northfield in order to avoid arriving at the hotel before dusk.

As we drove through the Commonwealth that afternoon, gray clouds blotted out the feeble sun; the promise of spring faded into a threat of returning winter.

My mood turned equally sombre, and I sat at the wheel deep in thought. Gertrude had the rare gift of sensing moods. Dressed in a tweed suit, and looking very much the country gentlewoman, she sat close to me and fell in with my humor. Occasionally she would comment briefly on the bleak landscape. When the hills began to rise, she would say, "Surrey—just like Surrey." A close-nestled white clapboard farmhouse might provoke her to remark, "How beautiful! It seems to grow right out of the earth."

For my part, I was assailed with contradictory emotions. Despite earlier misgivings, I was happy to be alone with Gertrude. A speeding car has a way of seeming like a private world. With Gertrude, it seemed like the best of all possible private worlds.

However, we were not spinning through some remote and timeless galaxy, but along Route No. 2 in the Commonwealth of Massachusetts. Each mile brought me closer to a place which I realized, with increasing clarity, represented to me something different from every other place I had ever known.

I was afraid that something inside of me would instantly shrivel if Gertrude should condescendingly characterize Northfield as "quaint."

The chill March dusk was settling in the Connecticut Valley when we drove along Main Street under the bare arching elms and on up to the hotel, a long, rambling structure which—except for a coat of stucco over its red clapboards—had scarcely changed since I had roamed freely around it, cadging cookies in the kitchen. On both sides of the entrance, the empty porches stretched away, with green-painted rocking chairs up-ended inhospitably against the wall.

Gertrude surveyed them and laughed, "Bottoms up!" She jumped out and stretched herself. "Couldn't we take the chill out of our bones?"

Quickly and in warning accents, I said, "The hotel is dry."

"What I really meant is tea," she said cheerfully. "Can you think of anything better than a big steaming pot of tea in front of a huge log fire?"

The lobby was quiet except for a sizzling of the radiators. We walked across to the reception desk, where Ralph Forsaith, the room clerk, looked up at me. Though it was a good many years since my last visit, Ralph, who had been a fixture there for as far back as I could remember, showed no awareness of the passing of time.

"Evening, Richard," he said. "Looks like another storm coming up."

I was home.

I signed the register and said that the lady—indicating Gertrude at my side, who was smiling and filling the air with a most unevangelical perfume—would like the best room he had available. As for me, I would like a room in the annex.

Ralph frowned. He said: "You won't be comfortable in the annex in this weather, Richard. There's plenty of room here. It isn't as if the conferences were on."

"I like the view from the annex," I answered firmly.

"Suit yourself, Richard," said Ralph as he turned to the key rack.

I surprised a dangerous twinkle in Gertrude's eye and I felt myself reddening. Before I could speak, the door of the large parlor opened and a tide of clerical black flowed into the lobby. It was led by a portly, balding man whom I knew—my father's old friend and fellow-pilgrim to the Holy Land, Dr. Webster.

The sight of him brought back vividly a terror which had stimulated many a nightmare during my early years.

One Sunday in Boston he had visited us for dinner, bringing Billy Sunday with him. The evangelist, in his florid and persuasive manner, placed a hand of benediction upon my head while saying to my father: "Mr. Aldrich, I trust that you are going to give this fine young lad to the Lord."

"If the call is given," Father replied solemnly, "he will be dedicated."

Instantly a picture I had seen flashed to my mind. I saw myself a small, naked and shivering Isaac, bound to a pile of blazing fagots. My father, in Abraham's flowing garments, took a long knife out of his Boston bag and brandished it, while Dr. Webster, Jehovah-like, supervised the sacrifice from a nearby cloud bank.

From that moment on I had felt uneasy in Dr. Webster's presence.

It was at least twenty years since he had seen me but he recognized me at the first glance and bore down on me with both hands outstretched cordially.

"Richard, my boy! How good to see you here in Northfield!"

His richly sonorous voice embraced me and Gertrude, on whom his eyes rested with interest.

"This is Miss Lawrence," I murmured. And to Gertrude: "Dr. Webster was a friend of my father's."

Dr. Webster moved to take her hand. Suddenly his expression turned to one of alarm. He stepped back swiftly.

"Mackie!" Gertrude cried sharply. She bent and picked up her pet. "Behave, angel." Then she turned, beaming reassurance on Dr. Webster. "Don't mind Mackie. He never bites anyone. At least, only those with evil in their souls."

Gordon Moody, the hotel manager, who had come out of his office to inspect the new arrivals, now announced: "We don't allow dogs in the hotel. You should know that, Richard."

Gertrude lifted wide, beseeching eyes but they were wasted on Gordon. He turned back and went into his office. Gertrude looked at me, indicating that this was my cue.

Before I could enter a plea for Mackie, Ralph beckoned to the bellboy carrying our bags. "All right, Bob. Take care of this animal."

Before Bob could advance upon the growling terrier, Gertrude spoke in a voice vibrant with emotion. "Oh, please don't take Mackie away. His feelings get hurt so easily. If he stays in Richard's room he can't bother anyone. You said no one was in the annex in this weather."

Ralph wavered noticeably. Gertrude smiled, and he was lost.

"Well, I guess that'll be all right," he muttered, though with a dubious glance toward the manager's office. "So long as he stays there, Miss —er, Miss. . ."

"Gertrude Lawrence," Gertrude supplied. The name, however, meant nothing to Ralph. Gertrude turned happily to me. "Darling, Mackie can sleep with you. It will be a wonderful chance for you and him to become really good friends. And that way he won't be lonely."

As I have said, I am not a man to quarrel with the inevitable. The inevitable had arrived.

"And now, darling, won't you please order some tea?" she asked.

Dr. Webster and his colleagues had entered the dining room on the left of the lobby. A silence, made reverent by the low murmur of grace, was followed by the scrape of chairs and the rattle of dishes. I looked at the clock. It was almost six.

"No tea," I told Gertrude firmly. "There isn't time. The dining room closes for supper at the dot of seven."

"Supper?" She stared at me incredulously. "Supper, *now?* It's nearer teatime than supper."

"It's never teatime in Northfield, Massachusetts," I informed her.

To my surprise and relief she accepted this meekly. "Very well, dear. In that case I'll just go up to change, and meet you here in twenty minutes."

Before I could add that in Northfield no one changed for Sunday night supper, she had thrust the unwilling Mackie into my arms, and entered the waiting elevator. The doors shut irrevocably behind her.

The bellboy, relieved of the problem of the dog, set about making a lazy-man's load of the six pieces of luggage and tottered away with it. Ralph's eye went from the bags to me. "Staying with us quite a while, I see," he said, apparently feeling interrogation was superfluous. I muttered noncommittally. The thought occurred to me that it might seem quite a while by morning.

I took Mackie and my own small suitcase over to our room in the annex. On my way back to the lobby to check on the fire I had ordered, I became uneasy. Gertrude was changing, but to what?

In New York, I had been proud to see her in the lovely—and often dazzling—creations which were appropriate to supper at the Colony or the Pavillon. Suppose she dressed like that for supper here? I remembered the sea-green tea gown in which she welcomed Fran and me that very morning and which must be in one of those bags. In it she had appeared Spring incarnate. But now the warmth had changed to a Lenten chilliness. I shivered, and sent up a fervent prayer that she would not come down in her gold, tinkle-toed slippers.

I should have known her better. When Gertrude appeared—prompt to the minute, as she always was—she was wearing a starkly simple black frock, relieved only by a string of pearls at her throat.

I breathed more freely. I was to learn that Gertrude's instinctive fine taste and her respect for the sensitivities of others always kept her in harmony with her environment. As it turned out, such uneasiness as I was to experience that evening was to be caused by her desire and her ability to get into her environment only too well.

We sat down in the dignified, rather austere dining room, to an excellent but plain Sunday-night supper of cold cuts, fried potatoes country style, cole slaw and custard pudding. After supper the reverend gentlemen, shepherded by Dr. Webster, rose and went to an adjoining parlor. From the low murmur of voices we heard, it was evident that a prayer service had started.

"Didn't you say that the conferences were held only in the summer?" Gertrude asked.

I explained that we seemed to have run into a meeting to plan the summer season. "Twice a day, this coming summer, there will be conferences and prayer meetings, with reports, hymn singing and sermons. It all takes planning, scheduling, budgeting."

"Like your summer theatre."

"Exactly, even down to the special attractions and stars. Moody imported hymn singers and revivalists from England—men with great personalities, who commanded huge audiences and brought drama and excitement to the prayer meetings. One of the great ironies of my life is that Father brought us to Northfield so that we would live a religious life in the summer, far removed from such sinful pastimes as the theatre; yet, it was here at the prayer meetings that I first developed my love and instinct for the dramatic."

Gertrude was fascinated, as she always was, when the technical details of any new field were explained to her. And as was her habit of mind, she had to relate herself to it.

"I never had any religious training," she said. "Except what I got from Granny. She was my mother's mother and I loved her more than anyone else in the world. Strict Church of England, she was. She used to take me along with her at evensong. But, poor dear, she was so deaf she couldn't hear the sermon. We'd come home and she'd have me repeat it, word for word. I'd do it, too—with all the proper clerical intonations and gestures. She loved it, and so did I."

I said I could well believe it.

"I've often wondered, Richard," she went on more thoughtfully, "what it is that I have always seemed to miss in life. Sometimes I think I have a longing to believe in something. Or someone. I'm not an atheist, of course; but though I believe in God, I'm so terribly independent I'm afraid I don't leave Him much to do for me."

I regarded her wonderingly. Gertrude had never spoken to me before about religion. Was this a true and intimate revelation of how deeply she felt and thought about it? If so, I was flattered.

But a nagging doubt persisted. Was her speech merely fashioned to match her dress and her environment? At that moment, I admit, I did not have the breadth of understanding to judge.

* * *

When we finished supper, we went to the parlor, where a fire had been lighted. The blaze gave forth a heart-warming, cheerful glow. I was hoping for an evening of relaxed privacy, especially as the other guests, released from prayer meeting, seemed to be congregated in an adjacent parlor, where a trio of elderly females was entertaining with a concert of chamber music.

But no sooner were Gertrude and I installed, than Dr. Webster's head appeared at the door.

"Ah, a fire!" His bulky, black-clad body followed the head into the room. "And you are here, Richard. And Miss Dorrance."

"Lawrence."

"Ah, yes. Lawrence."

"Won't you join us?" Gertrude said. "Richard and I are having such an interesting talk. About religion."

The doctor came in and settled himself. As an eminent religious leader, he considered himself an ex-officio participant in any conversation on this topic. He began to talk about religion and the world crisis.

Soon the music next door came to a halt and one by one the other guests drifted in to sit by our fire and listen respectfully to Dr. Webster's views.

He had just delivered a bitter denouncement of war—even in a righteous cause—on the grounds that war destroyed men's faith in God, when Gertrude's clear voice cut in decisively. "I cannot agree with you, Doctor. As I said in a sermon I gave recently, 'The people are turning to God as their Saviour, as men have always turned to God when beset by trouble, war or violence.' "

The words, and her delivery of them, instantly focused everyone's attention on her. I felt a premonitory pricking under my collar. My throat went dry.

Halted in midstream, as it were, Dr. Webster gasped. Gertrude went on serenely:

"Yes," she observed, and her glance around the circle of listeners drew us all irresistibly together, "it's a poor, sick, unhappy world, as you say. Civilization's a failure. What's the good of all our inventions, if we haven't made the human race happy and better?"

The question did not seem to me to follow logically what had gone before, but the good people in the room appeared to be impressed by it. They nodded to each other. Dr. Webster cleared his throat, preparatory to taking off into his accustomed realm, but Gertrude canceled his flight of oratory.

"The world," she announced, "is full of bitterly unhappy people. They run around trying to fill up the awful emptiness with parties and sports and love affairs." I winced. "They don't know, poor things, that what they want is God."

"True, true," Dr. Webster concurred. His experienced eye quickly took the spiritual temperature of the group. He appealed to Gertrude: "Let us pray to our Heavenly Father that we may be permitted to find Him."

Gertrude turned to look him squarely in the eye. She lifted her hand in a gesture which was disturbingly reminiscent. "I don't think God is out *there* to pray to," she said thrillingly. "I think He's *here.* In us. And I don't believe He helps us till we dig, and DIG, and *DIG* to get the rottenness out of ourselves."

Again she made a gesture and then I remembered—too vividly for comfort. Her voice was that of Susan, the heroine of Rachel Crothers' play *Susan and God.* The lines were from the play's memorable last scene. The entire performance, down to the last nuance, was one which she had played to packed houses all across the country a thousand times.

I did not know then, nor do I know now, whether Gertrude was consciously putting on an act, or whether she was instinctively swept away in a familiar characterization. Undoubtedly these oft-repeated lines had found a permanent lodging in her subconscious, just as surely as the prayers and hymns which I had said hundreds of times as a boy had found their way into mine. But whatever the cause, nothing was more certain than that she would soon get into deeper and more dangerous theological waters. If the ministers should discover the truth, they would certainly believe they and their most cherished beliefs were being ridiculed by an actress. Their humiliation would inevitably be mine.

Clearly, the moment for drastic, decisive action had arrived.

I stood up quickly and announced with a loud brusqueness which caused Dr. Webster to blink, "If you will all excuse me, I'll say goodnight. I'm going to my room. In the annex." The last words were almost a shout.

Bewilderment clouded Gertrude's face. "So soon, Richard? But why, darling?"

"Perhaps you had better go up to your room too, Miss Lawrence," I prompted. "We must make an early start tomorrow."

She showed no sign of complying. I took her by the elbow and propelled her, with no dignity, toward the door.

As we crossed the lobby to the elevator the manager called out: "Snow's falling. Looks as if it's getting colder."

"It definitely is," Gertrude snapped. Her eyes were the blue of arctic ice. "Good night, Richard. Give my love to Mackie."

* * *

As soon as I was settled in bed, Mackie began trying to get out of the room. His efforts were accompanied by a pitiful whining squeal. In order to muffle the noise I pulled the covers over my head, only to have my feet exposed to the shivery night air. I realized that there were not enough blankets for the chilly night, which was becoming frostier by the moment.

Mackie's squeals had now prolonged themselves into a doleful howl. I was thankful that he and I had the annex to ourselves. Still, the outlook for a peaceful night was dim. Then I remembered a photograph which Gertrude had shown me, of herself in bed in her luxurious apartment in Portland Place, with Mackie snuggled in her arms. I whistled and patted the bed beside me invitingly. Mackie stopped howling and regarded me dubiously, but made no move to accept the invitation. I thrust an arm out of the bedclothes, seized his collar and lifted him in beside me.

"*Faute de mieux,* old man," I muttered. "Suppose we try keeping each other warm."

That night, *Mackie* slept exceedingly well.

* * *

At dawn I arose with a cold coming on. Aside from the longing to be warm again and the fear that I never would be, my thoughts were dominated by one overwhelming desire—to make sure that Gertrude and the ministers did not meet. Soon I was in the kitchen, where I persuaded the cook to send breakfast up to Miss Lawrence's room—a luxury which, in Northfield, usually is reserved only for guests who are ill. In the welcome and familiar warmth of the kitchen, I chatted with the cook over a bowl of hot cereal. Later, as I passed through the dining room, I noticed Dr. Webster and his friends, deeply involved in a hearty Northfield breakfast. I tried to slip by unobtrusively, but before I could do so Dr. Webster looked up.

"Good morning, Richard," he intoned. "I'd like to talk to you—"

Reluctantly I went over to his table; he rose and, taking my arm, led me out to the lobby.

"Richard," he began hesitantly, "we've just been talking about Miss Lawrence. She has a most devout and convincing manner. I would imagine that when she is in the pulpit she holds her audience."

"Yes," I readily agreed. "She does hold an audience well."

"Ah, you've heard her, Richard?"

"Many times." (What else could I say?)

"Good! Good!"

I tried to get away, but Dr. Webster held my arm.

"She's British, Richard?"

I nodded.

"All the better. It's a long time since we've had a British evangelist here. Remember the throngs who came to listen to Campbell Morgan! Now, we have two dates open—one in early July and the other in August. Which would the young lady prefer?"

The walls were closing in on me. "I really can't speak for her, Dr. Webster. Why don't you write her?" I said in desperation. "That would be best."

Dr. Webster pulled out a memorandum pad and carefully spelled out the name. "And the address is?" he queried. I was about to supply this when, to my horror, Mackie suddenly and illegally appeared, coming out of one of the parlors. He caught sight of me, then of Dr. Webster. Growling menacingly, he made for that gentleman's trouser cuffs.

I stretched out an arm and collared him as he passed. With no more ado, I rushed him out of the front door into the whirling snowstorm. There, at least, I was safe from Dr. Webster's questions. For the first time in our somewhat uneasy acquaintance, I gave Mackie a friendly pat.

* * *

"And now," I said reprovingly as we drove away from the hotel an hour or so later, "you have led that good man to believe that you're some sort of Aimee Semple McPherson."

Gertrude lifted her head haughtily. "I said nothing that wasn't true."

"Really?" I said with heavy sarcasm. "What about that alleged sermon?"

"*Alleged* sermon? I *did* preach that sermon at Dr. Christian F. Reisner's Broadway Temple in New York. And to a full house too, I might add."

"When was that?" I asked skeptically.

"Not long ago. Just before *Susan and God* closed."

I said nastily that I supposed it was a publicity stunt.

The suggestion infuriated Gertrude.

"Just because you spent your summers here, you needn't think you have a monopoly on religion," she retorted. "Yes, Reverend Aldrich, I preached that sermon from the pulpit of the largest church in New York to a capacity audience. Not for publicity, but because Dr. Reisner asked me to do so, one night after he saw the play. Of course, the news services picked up the story. It appeared everywhere. Even in London. I had a cable from Cocky [Charles B. Cochran, the British producer] that he'd book Queens or Albert Hall if I'd come home and be the English Aimee McPherson."

As Gertrude talked I suddenly recalled the New York *Times* story I had read, followed by a satirical report on "Preacher Gertrude Lawrence" in the *New Yorker* magazine.

"Nevertheless," I said grudgingly, "you had no right to make Dr. Webster and his committee think you were so spiritual and holy."

"Did you wish me to appear *unholy?*" she demanded with increased hauteur.

"There was no need for you to launch out into what is their province."

"I was just trying to talk about a subject of interest to *them.* I wanted to be warm and friendly. Some people like to be warm and friendly. Or didn't you know?"

Her remark snapped like a whip across my face, which was already tingling from the frosty weather.

As I searched for a fitting reply, we reached the foot of a steep hill. I stopped the car and pointed up the icy grade. "There's our old house up on the mountainside. The car can't make it in this snow. So we'll drive on now and see the Swiss chalet."

As I started the engine, Gertrude, sizing me up from head to foot, said quietly, but with a determination I could not ignore, "The car may not be able to make it, but *we* will." She swung wide the door and sprang out into the snow. "Come along, Richard."

Short of arguing with her—which, instinctively, I knew would be useless and only lead to more serious quarreling; or seizing her bodily, placing her in the car and driving off with her, which, I was equally sure, would please her inordinately and give her a feeling of triumph, I had no choice but to follow. I called to Mackie.

"No," Gertrude objected instantly. "It's too cold for him. Let him stay in the car. Are you coming, Richard?" She plunged ahead through the unbroken snow.

I looked at her striding purposefully up the slope. As always, she was dressed for the occasion. She might have been going skiing or bobsledding at St. Moritz. As for me, I was equipped to cross Madison Avenue with the traffic lights in my favor. True, my feet were somewhat protected by rubbers but, under my Homburg, my ears were at the mercy of each gust that whistled through the pines. As for my coat, my tailor had never recommended it to me for mountain climbing.

Gertrude did not deign to look back to see how I was faring. It was just as well. As I climbed, stumbled, slipped, and fell my way up the hill, I was very far from presenting the kind of appearance a man wishes to make before any woman, even one with whom he is quarreling. The head cold which had been hovering since I awoke, now gripped me. I sneezed violently. As I pulled out my handkerchief, some half-forgotten lines of poetry fluttered through my mind: *"A banner with the strange device—Excelsior."* All the props were at hand and the last stanza might be a prophecy of my imminent fate:

"A traveler, by the faithful hound,
Half-buried in the snow was found . . ."

Finally we reached Rustic Ridge, where Sunny Shadow stood blanketed by snow. But I was far from feeling any nostalgic exaltation at my return to this treasured spot. It was the one moment in my life that I can recall wishing I was a West Highland terrier.

Gertrude had not completed her impish persecution. "And this is the place you carved your initials on a tree when you were eleven?" she inquired coolly.

I admitted it was.

"Do show it to me!"

I said that I was not at all sure I could find the tree. After so many years, and in the snow.

"Of course you can," she challenged.

Circling around a wooded mountaintop in a snowstorm, trying to locate some initials carved on a tree almost three decades earlier, is something I cannot recommend as a pastime. I was strongly tempted to push the persevering Miss Lawrence face downward into a snowdrift. That, however, would have given her too much pleasure. It was plain she was all-out to make me surrender, but this I stubbornly refused to allow her to do. Not if we two spent the rest of the winter on Rustic Ridge squinting up at bare trunks trying to find the letters R.S.A. carved on one of them. Shivering, sneezing, miserably aware of the snow water in my shoes and of a chill that was coming on, I went from tree to tree under Gertrude's mocking gaze.

"There it is," I pointed suddenly.

"Where?"

I waggled a finger at some vague notches in the wood about ten feet above the ground. I saw at once that she did not believe these were my initials, and I realized she was quite capable of demanding that I climb the tree and verify my find.

"My!" she observed, measuring the distance from the ground to the markings on the tree. "For an eleven-year-old, weren't you the tall little man."

Now it was my turn for hauteur. I said acidly (and mistakenly, as I later learned), "If you knew anything about nature, you would know that as a tree grows higher it carries its scars along with it."

We trudged down the hill in grim, angry silence. When we had rejoined Mackie in his snug warmth I said stiffly, "We've seen Sunny Shadow. Now where would you like to go? To the Swiss chalet? The auditorium? The seminary?"

"Really, Richard, we mustn't overdo this sentimental journey!"

If I had known her better I would have been warned by her tone and the manner in which she clipped her words. Gertrude was now very angry. At such moments, I later observed, her back would stiffen, and her head would come up—inches, it seemed—giving her a deceptive appearance of greater height.

Blind to these storm signals, I persisted along my own way. "I don't know about you," I said sarcastically, "but that's what I came to Northfield for—to view the landmarks."

"Very well, then," Gertrude snapped. "There's one more landmark I would like to see. At once."

"And that is—?"

"The railroad station. Fully equipped with a fast train to New York."

I put her on a through train at Greenfield. Such goodbyes as we said were mechanical. Without waiting for the train to pull out, I headed back to Groton and the warmth of my mother's house, which was comfortably undisturbed by the theatrical temperament. I felt that I had had as much of that as I could stand for a very long time. Perhaps forever.

Tuesday found me again in New York, at the Harvard Club; my sister, with whom I lived, was in the throes of moving. My cold still hung on, making me morose and irritable. It was difficult to settle back into the routine of my working day. On Wednesday, my cold was nearly gone, but my restlessness was worse. I was conscious of a loneliness I had never felt before. By Thursday the loneliness was much increased and I experienced a dread of the dull days and weeks ahead. I discovered in myself a tendency to stare at the telephone. But the Aldriches are stubborn; we give in slowly.

On Friday I suffered a serious relapse—reason rose above anger. It informed me that in no single act in our little Northfield comedy had Gertrude been at fault. She had been entirely and genuinely herself, whereas I had been wrong from the start when weakly, under the guise of politeness, I had encouraged her to make the long trip in hope of a pleasant country week-end. When the plans for this miscarried, she had adjusted herself to the change with good humor. It was I who had succumbed to apprehensions and to a miserable self-consciousness which (I had to admit) the presence of Dr. Webster had aggravated.

To crown my stupidities, I had sunk to scolding her, like a schoolmaster. And when she had served me back—as anyone of spirit would have—instead of turning the whole misadventure into a joke which both of us might have enjoyed to the full, I had pulled my bad temper around me like a cloak and sulked within its folds.

I spent the greater part of Friday night with these reflections, and I found myself very poor company indeed. The previous week-end had become an incredible and fantastic nightmare from which I longed intensely to escape. There was only one way out of it—to admit that I had been at fault and to ask Gertrude's forgiveness. Though I had no basis for believing that she could, or would forgive me, I realized that I would have no peace within myself until I had taken that step.

On Saturday I went out very early and headed for the flower shop. It was closed. I waited till the florist opened up his store and then had him select a large bunch of his best long-stemmed roses.

I wrote a note to go with them: "Will you be free after this evening's performance? I should like to apologize and explain."

When I stopped at the desk for my key at the end of the day, there was a telegram in my mail box. It read:

RICHARD S. ALDRICH
HARVARD CLUB
27 WEST 44TH STREET
NEW YORK, NEW YORK

YES

GERTRUDE LAWRENCE

Chapter Five

I COULD NO LONGER sidestep the realization that I was in love. Until now, I had been pleasantly content to have in Gertrude a compatible, entertaining companion who valued her own freedom and who allowed me to enjoy mine. But what had begun as an amusing, lighthearted friendship between two adults who moved in the same world of interests, had broadened and deepened into something which compelled recognition.

The recent Northfield experience had shown me that between Gertrude and myself the former agreeably indefinite *status quo* was no longer possible. Either we must drift apart, or we must go forward. And together.

This was not what I had expected or planned. At that time I had no wish to marry again, nor to be in love with anyone. Certainly not with someone in the theatre. Still less with a star of Gertrude's disturbing magnitude.

The man who marries a star, who takes her into the intimate confines of his life, invites one of two major disasters. Either he destroys the elusive loveliness which has enchanted him, and dims its radiance under the pall of domesticity; or he must sacrifice much of his own individuality. He must reduce himself to consort status and find fulfillment in providing a useful neutral background for his wife.

I could not see myself in either role.

Everything Gertrude had accomplished in her career was by her own efforts, by her own indomitable fortitude and intuitive genius. Others possibly became stars in the theatre because some men had put them there. Not Gertrude. No one had smoothed the way for her or helped her climb to the top. Being of the theatre myself, I admired her achievement so profoundly that I never once entertained the thought of asking her to give up her profession to become my wife.

But was it possible to combine marriage with a career such as hers?

Also not to be ignored was the matter of money. Gertrude's yearly earnings amounted to a sum which any banker would treat with respect. I was doing quite well, but I was not in her bracket. I was appalled at the prospect of being married to a wealthy woman, especially one whose wealth was of her own making, in circumstances where I would not have (nor would I wish to have) any authority over her finances.

If anything could have put me out of love with Gertrude Lawrence it would have been her salary and her attitude toward it.

Gertrude's extravagance—of which I have spoken previously—was the sort of thing to strike terror into the heart of a man like myself, who had been reared in the tradition that only criminals and madmen ever live up to their incomes. Father had instilled in me at an early age the idea that to let February's bills remain unpaid beyond the third of March was to give oneself a good head start toward ruin. And for some years I had been a banker, an occupation which leaves indelible marks.

Largely because of the penury she had known as a child, Gertrude's zest for luxury was insatiable. It had been fostered by her success in a profession which tends toward display.

Gertrude had never been able to retrench, even in lean periods. She was on a toboggan on an icy slope and she could not stop. An entry in one of her diaries made when she was playing in

London during the thirties records: "Haven't a bob or an ounce of strength after six days in bed with a temperature. Blood count very low and weight 105 lbs. Have a nurse, but God knows who will pay her. Picture doesn't start for a week. But shall find some cash *somewhere* and go off to St. Moritz for a week's sun and rest. Just Pam and me. Funny how everyone thinks I'm so happy and so well. And *well off* . . ."

That runaway holiday in the Alps was as gay as she could make it. No one who welcomed her at St. Moritz, no one with whom she went skiing, would have guessed that she was literally down to her last shilling. The diary entry ends rather grimly: "Went to ski-jumps in afternoon with Doris Duke (Millionairess!). Twenty francs Swiss for her and her boy-friend's tickets. I meant it to be Dutch treat but got stung again. Paid hotel bill (one week 1654 francs) with cheque. Fortunately Pam and I have our tickets home . . ."

Knowing how her luxurious possessions and free spending figured in the Gertrude Lawrence legend, she was not above making publicity of these when an opportunity invited. Another entry in the same diary records:

Eric Barker of the Evening News came to lunch and to spend the afternoon. He wanted an insight into the private life of a popular star. I took him to look at a new Rolls. I shan't (can't) buy it but the story will do me and his column good. Though I suppose all my creditors will increase their demands. From there we went to Schiaparelli's where he was much impressed by a mink coat I tried on. I saw him squinting at the price tag. And by an evening cape of silver fox I told them to send home. More good news for his readers. But what he and they don't know is that the foxes were my four-year-old skins being remodeled.

At Schiaparelli's we found Adele Astaire and husband, or should I say Lord and Lady Cavendish? More plums for the Evening News readers. Then I took Eric along to hear me sing at Gwynne Davies'. That, I must say, was the most genuine thing in the whole afternoon, but I could see he got more out of the mink and the Rolls . . .

Shortly after this, Gertrude's creditors took matters into their own hands; she was declared bankrupt, and evicted from her West

End apartment. Her affairs had become so scrambled that a thorough overhauling was necessary.

Then Noel Coward prevailed upon her to turn over all her economic problems to the law firm of Fanny and David Holtzmann, who had helped to solve her financial difficulties in America in the early years of the depression.

Their chief problem, the Holtzmann office discovered, was to cope with Gertrude's erratic flights of spending. After a few attempts at conveying basic arithmetic to her, they came to the conclusion that the only way to keep Gertrude out of financial trouble was to exercise an almost complete control over her expenditures. They therefore set up a budget, and arranged for all bills to be checked and paid through their office. The system required a few adjustments, to deal with Gertrude's sometimes ingenious evasions; but ultimately it worked out. Since Gertrude's legal, professional and personal affairs were inextricably intertwined, her relationship with Fanny and David inevitably grew close.

After the Holtzmanns came into the picture, Gertrude professed to be relieved; now, she said, her money was in responsible hands. But she continued to be overwhelmed by occasional impulses to splurge—to become what Noel Coward characterized as "insanely generous." At such times she would go on wild buying sprees, charging all manner of things at the stores and cautioning whoever was near, "Don't tell Miss Fanny or Mr. David." Gertrude did not relish being confronted by the Holtzmann queries, which made her feel like a naughty child who has been caught with her fingers in the cookie jar.

In her *Skylark* days, Gertrude was still given to luxurious display. Her duplex penthouse apartment on West Fifty-fourth Street was decorated in a style that suggested the Arabian Nights, with satin curtains and chairs that looked like colored bonbons. She was driven to the theatre in an eye-catching Rolls—"not a patch," she assured me, on the Bentley she had lately owned in England.

When I took Gertrude out after the theatre I asked her to dismiss her chauffeur, and we used my convertible or a taxi. Once I commented casually that an ostentatious limousine maintained by a certain Hollywood star was not in the best of taste. Gertrude, perceptive as always, was quick to sense the purport of my remark.

When spring came, she turned her Rolls in. "For a Ford," she told me proudly, pausing for my approval. I commended her sincerely, and could hardly retract when an elegant Ford town car rolled up, its expensive Brewster body covered with a lacquered basketwork design. In its way, it was at least as dazzling as the Rolls.

But Gertrude was delighted by this act of "economy." She informed me, and others, that showy, very costly models appealed only to people who felt insecure.

Her chauffeur was dismissed a good many nights in that spring of 1940, following our trip to Northfield. Three or four times a week Gertrude went out to supper with me. Afterward I would often urge her to go directly home and get some rest.

"I can't sleep if I go to bed too early," she told me. "Like poor Nijinsky, I have to run down after a performance. Going home and to bed doesn't help. Going out after the play may not be much fun for my companion, but it's relaxing for me. And it helps me sleep."

So we went out. To the well-known supper clubs where there were always parties of Gertrude's friends who would beg us to join them. Immediately Gertrude became the life of the party. She seemed to feel that it was her responsibility to be entertaining, to keep the merriment at its height. And this after her performance—sometimes after two performances that day.

As a change from the Stork, "21" and the rest, I introduced her to a small French restaurant in the East Fifties that I liked. The food and wines were excellent. There were no crowds. My—later, our—corner table was always ready for us. The music was unobtrusive—soft, familiar songs that did not demand our attention and never interfered with conversation.

Gertrude fell in love with the place. "Our bistro," she called it. We went there often in those months and we continued to go there when we wanted to dine quietly alone in surroundings which had romantic associations for us. For years we celebrated there the anniversary of our making up after our first quarrel over the Northfield incident, until our friend, the proprietor, closed the place and retired.

On other nights that spring I would drive Gertrude out into the country. It always rested and refreshed her. Sometimes, on those drives through Westchester or Long Island, she would say suddenly, "Let's stop at that diner." Perched on a stool at the counter, she would eat ham and eggs or a Western sandwich with as great enjoyment as when lunching at the Colony. Frequently she got into conversation with a neighboring truck driver.

On many predawns I would be sneaking up the three flights to my rooms in my sister's top-floor apartment and would meet my brother-in-law, Harrison, in his work clothes, starting for his job as supervisor of the early deliveries of one of the big baking companies. He would grin at my tails and wilted boutonniere.

But it was a kind grin. Neither he nor Barbara asked any questions. Only, more than once, I surprised in my sister's eyes a look compounded of amusement, pity and exasperation. It said, more clearly than words, "Why don't you get on with it?"

* * *

Barbara adored Gertrude from the moment of their first meeting. She loved her bubbling, infectious gaiety, her childlike absorption in whatever was at the moment uppermost in her thoughts, her quick generosity, which included the gifts of sympathy and tolerance no less than material wealth. Gertrude had a way of taking the best from everyone and every situation, and letting the dross go by. She wasted no time or energy on censure, regret or self-pity. As she expressed it: "All my life I have leaned on myself in trouble or disaster or in any crisis—financial or physical. I know I have just got to look in a mental mirror and say, 'Come on, Gee, we are in a hole. We must stand together and find a way out. Being sorry for yourself won't pay bills. Blaming someone else won't fill stalls. People don't want your woes. And it doesn't do to be too proud of one's wells either.' "

How good her entertaining best could be, only her intimate friends knew. Barbara and Harrison found unceasing enjoyment in her extraordinary combination of extreme fastidiousness with an earthy Shakespearian humor.

Gertrude not only loved but understood Barbara, who, until that time, had met with meager understanding in the family. Until Gertrude enlarged my comprehension, I had vaguely shared the family's disapproval of the way Barbara managed her life; in particular, of her second marriage.

Harrison Hobart came of old Massachusetts stock, which, of course, pleased the family. He was a person of charm—ambitious, attractive and gay. However, his business ventures, which always started so promisingly, never quite worked out. It utterly baffled my mother and Aunt Alice that Barbara, after the failure of an early marriage and the tragedy of her seven-year-old son's death, should have fallen in love with Harrison instead of with some solidly established business man.

They were equally mystified by Barbara's improvidence in circumstances which seemed to demand the utmost in prudence and thrift. Barbara, as I have said, is a writer; whenever she sold a story, she and Harrison celebrated the event by promptly dining at the Ritz, where, in ordering, they made it a point of honor never to glance at the right-hand column of the menu.

This defiance of the Puritan principle of grimly expecting seven lean years to follow one fat one, and preparing for them even at the cost of not enjoying the temporary fatness, shocked the good ladies in Groton. They felt it their duty to take the matter up with Barbara on every occasion. Not unnaturally, Barbara had become extremely sensitive to the family's disapproval of what they termed her "Bohemian ways."

Perhaps to atone for this, Gertrude's gifts to Barbara were always beautiful, costly and impractical. I remember one Christmas when the Hobart finances were exceptionally low and the elder generation had notified me as titular head of the family, that *"something has to be done about Barbara."* That year Gertrude's gift to Barbara, delivered on Christmas Eve, was a six-foot orange tree in a tub. Two men and unlimited oaths were required to get it up the stairs and into the Hobart living room. There it stood: beautiful, exotic and incredible.

Barbara was gazing at it with misty, devotional eyes when Uncle Jim, the Methodist editor in our family, arrived with a hamper of groceries and a check.

"Just think, Uncle Jim," she exclaimed, "you can't even eat the oranges. They are merely good to look at. Only Gertrude would have thought of sending me such a gift."

"Humph! I should hope so," Uncle Jim commented, adding that "the thing" must have cost "an awful lot of dollars" and it would have been more sensible of Gertrude to have sent the money instead.

"Thank God she didn't," Barbara shocked him by retorting. "You don't know what that tree does for me. What hunger it feeds. But Gertrude knows. She understands because she has really hungered—not only for food, but for a touch of brightness and beauty, without which life can be so drab and empty."

Then, sorry for his evident dismay, she hugged him.

"Uncle Jim, you're an angel. Harrison and I just love the Christmas dinner you've brought us. We'll eat it under Gertrude's tree and bless you both for being what you are."

Mischievously she added, "Cheer up. Maybe that tree will be useful anyhow. Perhaps we'll find one orange on it soft enough to slice and we'll make some Old Fashioneds." Uncle Jim looked relieved, though I doubt if he knew what an Old Fashioned was.

Gertrude's understanding embraced Barbara's marriage and disclosed certain aspects of it to me.

"What if Barbara does make more with her writing than Harrison makes at his job?" she demanded. "That might be terribly important to some people; it isn't to them. Fortunately they are alike. They see it the same way. If they didn't, their marriage would be impossible. But they have an equal partnership in loving; and to them, that is what counts. Harrison understands Barbara. He supplements her. He is patient when she is tired or irritable because she is worried about her work. He knows that she will never get over little Peter's tragic death. He doesn't expect her to. He makes allowances for her grief and he brings her a gaiety that she can't create. Above all, he lets her be herself."

She went on to expound her theory: "Women like Barbara and

me, who could be financially independent, don't judge a man's worth by the money he offers us. I think we are infuriated when men assume that we can be bought. Why don't they realize that we can get most of the things money buys for ourselves? What we would like from them is something else. Harrison gives Barbara that, and so they are happy and right for each other."

Some years before this, Gertrude told me, she had fancied herself in love with a popular motion-picture star. He had followed her to England and begged her to marry him. He pointed out that their marriage would benefit her career and his. They could act together—a romantic and appealing husband-and-wife team. Dancing with her one night at the Café de Paris in London he had slipped on her finger a ring set with a spectacular diamond. It was hers, if she would only confirm the announcement of their engagement, which the papers already proclaimed imminent.

"That diamond fascinated me," Gertrude said. "It was simply fabulous. I didn't know a woman, except royalty, who had a stone to match it. When I looked at it blazing on my hand I felt I simply could not give it up. And I believed I was in love with the man. He was great fun to be with. Pam adored him. And naturally I was flattered by his devotion to me. Any woman would have been. Many of my friends kept urging me to marry him.

"But something made me hold off. I asked myself why so many of our good times together ended in quarrels. Always about trivial things. I began to dread our rows. I got so I expected one every time we went out together. One week-end he drove me down to stay with some friends who had a house by the sea. I took the dogs along. They needed the sea air as much as I did. And I like to walk with dogs; you walk further and it is more fun. Driving down, I was dreadfully uneasy for fear the dogs might be sick, as they were sometimes when motoring. I knew if they were, he would fly into a temper. The bad mood would last and the week-end would be spoiled.

"Wonder of wonders, the dogs were models of propriety all the time. But I did not get over my uneasiness. There was always the dread of something else happening that would send him into one of his black moods. I came back to town more tired than when I left, and that night I gave him back his beautiful sparkling diamond and said: 'No, thank you kindly, sir. I won't marry you.' Nearly everyone thought I was foolish to let a chance like that go. Except Mother. She was pleased because she had an idea if I would only play my cards right I might have a coronet. Perhaps I might, but somehow or other I couldn't do that either."

To my inquiry whether she had subsequently regretted the diamond she said: "Once or twice. When I've been feeling Mondayish. But not for long. Surely, it's better to be happy and what people may call 'crazy,' than prudent and always blue."

"What about the coronet?"

She looked slightly rueful. "I have to admit," she said, "if you've been brought up in Clapham Common to revere royalty and the peerage and all that, you can't help feeling there's nothing like a good title. No matter what doesn't go with it."

"But you would marry?" I asked. "If the man was someone you felt was right for you? If he loved you enough to leave you free to be yourself."

She said slowly: "I think I would. Someone who would give me what I have never had and what I can't get for myself."

I asked what that was.

She glanced at me quickly out of the corner of her eye. It was the startled, wary look of a forest creature that feels you getting dangerously close and that keeps very still until you apprize it of your next move. Did some depth of emotion betray me? Suddenly her quietness was swept away by a roguish impudence which, I was learning, often served as a mask to protect her sensitivity. She began to sing under her breath, but not too low for me to catch the words:

"I want someone to watch over me . . ."

* * *

That spring the Germans invaded Norway. From then on, the phrase oftenest on Gertrude's lips was "I want to go home."

All over the world Englishmen were quietly resigning from jobs and going home to get into uniform to fight the Battle of Britain, which loomed closer every week. No one felt this summons more keenly than Gertrude.

"I want to go home and be of use," she said one Sunday when she came to tea at Barbara's. There were just the four of us gathered around the fire in the Hobarts' big, untidy but very comfortable living room. As usual Gertrude had arrived bearing gifts—daffodils and Easter lilies. Her flowers filled the room with beauty and fragrance.

I understood and sympathized fully with Gertrude's desire to serve her country, but reason told me that her emotions were rapidly running away with her common sense. Actually she was in a better position to give practical aid to her country if she stayed here. It was high time someone brought her to face reality. Otherwise, under the impetus of patriotism, she might conceivably set off on a quixotic trip to London.

"I shall cancel my tour," she went on. "As soon as my play closes, I'm going. I know I can be of use. I can cook, scrub, sew, nurse, sing songs and be generally useful."

As she enumerated her qualifications it was apparent that she saw herself in uniform performing every one of these services.

"Mr. Chamberlain's girl Friday," I said.

She swung round at me, all indignation.

Before she could give vent to it, I continued: "What about the show you are going to do at the Cape for the benefit of British War Relief? Are you going to cancel that to go home and roll ten shillings' worth of bandages a day? What can you possibly do in England that is worth half as much as this practical financial support?"

"Whatever my King and my country wish me to do," she retorted grandly. "Do you think all I'm good for is to act? I can be a nurse. I know the Red Cross would take me. Perhaps I shall join the WRENS."

"And what will you do with Pam in the meanwhile?" I asked. "Do you plan to walk out on her, too? How will she live? In any of the services you mention you wouldn't earn the price of your uniforms. Which, if I know you, would have to be made by Hattie Carnegie or Molyneux. Where would you live? I doubt if you'd rate a suite at the Savoy."

Gertrude's eyes shot blue sparks.

"Stop being an actress and start behaving like a human being," I told her. "Think with your head, not with your emotions. Of course you want to do something for England. Well, do it! Do what any intelligent man does under these circumstances; go and see your consul. Or better still, your ambassador. Ask him, as your King's representative, what he wants you to do."

"I hadn't thought of that," Gertrude said slowly. "I could get in touch with the embassy."

"Why don't you?" I said, adding that I had met Lord Lothian, the ambassador. "He's charming. And, in case it interests you, a bachelor."

She disdained replying to this thrust, changing the subject with the air of offended royalty. When she left, she haughtily declined my offer to see her home.

"You've hurt her feelings," Barbara said. "You have about as much tact as a bulldozer. She'll never forgive you."

Gertrude's temper was quick and hot. And her pride was intense. But underneath was a firm core of common sense which had brought her through many difficult situations. I was banking on that.

Two days passed without my hearing from her. Then she rang to tell me excitedly that she had just talked with Lord Lothian. She was bursting with pride because her call to the British Embassy had been put through at once to His Excellency. "He treated me as if I were Somebody," she said pointedly.

"Why not? You are."

"You seem to have changed your mind since Sunday. But, oh, darling, don't let's quarrel."

She said that Lord Lothian was coming to New York in a few days and had said he would call on her. She asked me if I would be present at the interview. "After all, it was your idea I communicate with my ambassador."

Lord Lothian, when he came, was so unaffectedly pleased to be calling on Gertrude Lawrence and so genuinely interested in her eagerness to be of service to their country that he put her instantly at ease. He spoke feelingly of the usefulness of persons like Gertrude in the important field of public relations and in building good-will between the two great English-speaking countries. He said: "I was with Northcliffe in the first war. I know how valuable people like you can be. There are jobs to be done in the United States which Gertrude Lawrence can do more effectively than the embassy staff."

At that time the America First group, favoring America's isolation from the war in Europe, was exceedingly active. A number of influential congressmen and senators supported the cause, as did many prominent men and women in all parts of the country. Lord Lothian suggested that Gertrude's services might be enlisted in winning friends for England from that group.

No cause could have made a stronger personal appeal to her. Her loyalty to England was fervent, but she also felt a kinship with America which I think sometimes surprised her by its intensity. In contrast to many English actors who spend much time in the United States but who remain aloof from and alien to American life and thought, Gertrude, from her first season in New York, had identified herself with our national life. She sought and made friends of Americans. She steadfastly refused to live within any of the tiny English colonies which exist in Hollywood and in New York. She was always quick to adapt to American ways which seemed to her worth while. There were many of these, she would boast to her British friends.

She was an enthusiastic reader of the women's magazines, and was always the first to discover one of Barbara's stories, which she would then advertise to all. She accumulated files of clippings on every subject connected with running a home—including hundreds of recipes which, she affirmed, she intended to try someday. I was astounded by her knowledge of how American women thought, kept house, brought up their children and managed their husbands. She knew these things because she was sincerely interested in human beings and she wanted to know as much about them as possible.

Though she might have been as aware of the life of any other country in which she spent much time, I doubt if her interest would have brought about so intimate an identification. The truth is, Gertrude possessed many of the qualities which are generally thought of as American.

After her meeting with Lord Lothian, she was increasingly occupied with British War Relief. She personally sold thousands of dollars' worth of emblems. Her brief vacation at the Cape that June was used to start a chapter there. Through an old friend at the British Embassy in Washington, she kept informed on British-American relations and occasionally surprised supper companions by her accurate information on matters about which they were vague. I know that she astounded Hamilton Fish.

When the measure for the arming of American merchant ships, many of them carrying sorely needed war material to England, came before Congress, Ham, a member of the Committee on Foreign Relations, was a leader of the opposition. Gertrude was incensed by the newspaper reports of the fight in the House. If only someone—if only she—could explain the case and Britain's need of help to Congressman Fish!

"I'll bring Ham back to your dressing room some night," I said, "and you can have a go at him."

I knew Ham slightly. He had been at Harvard before me, but his fame on the football field was still very much alive in my day. I saw him occasionally around the Harvard Club. He and I stood on opposite sides in the matter of American aid to the Allies. I had no patience with isolationism; but, basically opposed as our ideas were, I did not doubt his love for his country.

Not long after my promise to Gertrude I ran into Ham at the club. He joined me willingly and we went to see her in her play. After the curtain, we went back to Gertrude's dressing room, where I had alerted her to be ready.

There and at supper she turned her attention and all her arguments on Ham. He listened and was visibly impressed. When the measure was approved with Ham voting for it, Gertrude's satisfaction made her so cocky I had to remind her of my part in what she called gleefully, "hooking our big Fish."

* * *

Plans for the 1940 summer season at the Playhouse were promising. Fran Hart reported that we were sold out in advance for every performance, matinee and evening, of opening week.

This was not surprising, since Gertrude was to open our season with a busman's-holiday appearance in *Private Lives.*

Noel Coward's witty comedy occupied a special place among Gertrude's theatrical successes. For one thing, it was frequently held that the part of Amanda had been written not only *for* Gertrude, but *about* her. While I have always felt that Amanda represented only one facet of Gertrude's complex character, there were undeniably strong resemblances between her and Noel's hot-tempered, fascinating heroine. It was extraordinary on how many occasions Amanda's lines would come spontaneously from Gertrude's lips. When tempers flared, she momentarily seemed to become Amanda before my eyes.

Alexander Woollcott, the critic and litterateur, whose habit it was to address Gertrude by the names of her successive roles, gave up after she appeared in *Private Lives.* From then on, aptness triumphed over whimsy, and to "Uncle Alec" she became forever "Amanda."

Noel's play was also the source of an arrangement between Gertrude and me which, after we were married, averted many a domestic crisis. In *Private Lives,* a code word is used between the two lovers which instantly silences their quarrels. Noel's word was "Sollocks." In borrowing the device, and recalling our serio-comic week-end in Massachusetts, we substituted the word "Northfield."

* * *

As soon as *Skylark* closed its New York run late in May of 1940, Gertrude left town at once for the Cape, where she had taken a spacious old house at East Dennis. She wanted to rest as much as possible before going on tour in *Skylark* in mid-July. Pam chose not to accompany her mother that summer, as she was absorbed in serving an apprenticeship at Hattie Carnegie's in hat designing. Another, possibly more compelling, reason for her wishing to stay in town was a young medical student.

Gertrude left a week ahead of me. She telephoned from the Cape that the rose garden of the Playhouse was "as lovely as a dream of England." A small guest cottage near the rose garden had been reserved for my use that summer. Its surroundings were romantically lovely, but actually the cottage was rather dark and uninviting. At least I remembered it so. When I came, I found the place transformed; it had a fresh coat of light paint, crisp curtains and other gay accessories.

"All from Woolworth's," Gertrude informed me.

As one perfect June day succeeded another, as the roses spent themselves in a riot of fragrance and color, the horror of Dunkirk broke on the world.

The news and its implications struck Gertrude to the heart. She hovered close to the radio. "How *dare* they?" she cried, when the announcers recounted the toll of destruction. She would go out across the lawn to stand where she could look at the sea, as though by looking she could send encouragement and hope to the men fighting on the Belgian beaches, struggling into all the unseaworthy little boats that had gone gallantly to rescue them.

In those grim days I realized what work meant to her. Tense and anguished as she was, she went steadily on with the rehearsals for *Private Lives*. Her zeal for perfection increased. "Let's try it again," she would say to the company. "Let's get it right. It must be right." It was her way of keeping up her morale. And the play, when it opened, was as brilliant and polished in its performance as Broadway would have demanded. Never was Amanda so enchanting, so provocative, so deliciously, outrageously amusing.

Before that week was up I knew that I could not let her go off on the four-month *Skylark* tour without asking her to marry me.

"If only you were not Gertrude Lawrence," I said when we were alone after the final performance. I had taken her for a drive so she could "run down," as she expressed it. Her house, when we came back to it, was very still. "If only you were not Gertrude Lawrence, it would be easy."

"What would be?" she asked.

"To ask you to marry me."

Her reply was steady and in a voice suddenly low and grave.

"Please ask me, Richard," she said. "Only please don't—unless you are very sure you want me to say yes."

* * *

Caution dies hard in a New Englander. Unwilling to trust the good fortune which smiled on me, I insisted on going into particulars. "You know, Gertrude," I explained, "my income as a producer is uncertain. I've had hits before and I'll have them again, I hope. I'll have flops, too. But, whatever the future, we'll live as I can afford without regard to your income. I won't be a kept man."

"I wouldn't want you, if you were willing to be one."

"And are *you* willing to be Mrs. Aldrich?" I asked incredulously.

"Try me!" she challenged, with a smile.

We commenced to make plans at once.

"Darling," Gertrude said, "Fran mentioned there would be a full moon on the Fourth. I've always longed for a moonlight-and-roses wedding, so do let's be married on my birthday, the Fourth of July, a few minutes after midnight. And, oh, do let's keep it very, very quiet until it's all over."

Nothing could have pleased me more than to be spared the glare of publicity.

Early the next morning I stopped by to see the town clerk in Dennis about our marriage license. I knew I could depend on him to keep its issuance a secret.

"Just bring along your birth certificates," he stated, "and divorce decrees, if any. Nobody will learn about it from me," he added dryly.

Greatly relieved, I arranged for my papers to be rushed to me by messenger from New York. Then I called Gertrude to see about hers.

"They are in the vault, darling."

"Can David or Fanny Holtzmann get at them?"

"No, darling, the vault is in *London!*"

"*London,* did you say?" I exclaimed.

"Yes, darling, I am trying to think who could get at them there."

I took a deep breath. The Battle of Britain had just started; London was under fierce bombing. Airmail had been halted by the war; even if there were access to the vault it would take many weeks for the documents to reach the United States. I hurried to see what I could do with my friend the town clerk. He was sympathetic but helpless as he read me the law of the Commonwealth pertaining to remarriage.

Gertrude took the news sportingly although her disappointment was keen. She tried to cheer me.

"Don't worry, Richard dearest, we'll just put off our wedding until I return from the tour," she said.

"No, we will NOT!" I stated definitely, as I paced the floor. "Too many things can happen if we postpone the marriage. There must be *some* solution to this legal snarl."

Gertrude laughed. "Oh, if it's only a legal snarl we're all right. Let's telephone Fanny Holtzmann—she promised to come for the week-end anyway."

I listened dubiously as Gertrude urged Fanny to get to Dennis as soon as possible to disentangle a legal problem which had arisen. Up to that time I had known Fanny Holtzmann only socially, through Gertrude. Her reputation as an international lawyer was difficult for me to grasp. My idea of a lawyer was personified by my uncle Samuel Nelson Aldrich, who, in dignified cutaway and striped trousers, could meet the majesty of the Law on equal terms. Fanny, by contrast, was described by Moss Hart in an article in the New York *Times,* as "a small, delicate, mouselike creature given to wearing flopping hats in the spring and creating a first impression of wistful helplessness." She did not fit my mental picture of a legal adviser; nor was I reassured after her arrival that evening, when she nodded approvingly as I told her of the town clerk's adamant refusal to make an exception for us.

"Who's the county or probate judge here?" she asked.

"Judge Colin Campbell, in Hyannis."

I watched with trepidation as Fanny telephoned Judge Campbell and arranged to see him immediately.

Fanny was gone an inordinately long time, it seemed to us, and we became worried. I regretted not having stopped her from invading the privacy of a Massachusetts jurist's home late at night. I was speculating on the consequences when we heard her car.

"Oh, Fan," Gertrude called breathlessly. "What kept you so long?"

"I'm terribly sorry, I didn't realize it was so late, Gee," said Fanny, looking at her watch. "I've had the most wonderful time at the Campbells'. They're such a delightful family. They were celebrating the graduation of their son, Peter, who received the highest honors. He enters Yale in September. We talked about the war and everything. Here's a piece of the delicious cake Mrs. Campbell baked. She gave me the recipe, too. She . . ."

"But, Fanny," I interrupted. "What about the *marriage license?* Remember? That's why you went there."

"Oh, yes, I forgot to tell you. You can go ahead with your July Fourth wedding plans."

"You mean you have obtained Judge Campbell's permission to by-pass the law?" I asked.

"Certainly not! We must start a court proceeding to ask for an order that the license be issued to you."

"Oh," I said, completely let down. "That would only mean more delay."

"Not if you get me a typewriter so I can get started," she said. "Judge Campbell's all right," she added.

"What argument did you use with the judge?" I asked, more hopeful.

"That the Commonwealth of Massachusetts should not interfere with your *constitutional* right to the pursuit of happiness," she replied.

I understood what Moss Hart meant when he observed: ". . . actually Fanny is about as helpless as Bethlehem Steel."

After we settled Fanny at a typewriter, she went to work drawing up the petition stating that she had seen Gertrude's documents and could swear to the facts.

As Fanny waved us out of the room, Gertrude turned and called back, "Good luck, my Counselor-at-Law—and at-Love!"

* * *

After completing the necessary technicalities and obtaining our marriage license, Fanny gave us her blessing and returned to New York to cope with any inquiries that might arise there. But I did not let her leave before legal arrangements had been made by which the Holtzmanns would continue to control Gertrude's personal finances. I refused to have anything to do with her money. This arrangement remained in force from then onward. No arguments about money were ever to come into our life together.

On the morning of the third of July, I told Fran that I wanted him and his wife to witness my marriage to Gertrude. And Gertrude told Dorothy, her devoted maid, whom she had brought over from England. No others were to be present at the ceremony, which the Reverend Paul Wilkinson, the local Presbyterian minister, had promised to perform immediately after midnight.

Buying the wedding ring in Hyannis without arousing speculation and conjecture was not an easy task, particularly since the ring that Gertrude fancied was displayed in the window of a store that was closed. However we located the owner, persuaded him to open the shop and explained to him that the ring—a two-dollar circlet of silver engraved with the Navajo good-luck symbol—was needed for a prop in one of our plays.

Dorothy had secretly ordered a cake from a baker as a birthday surprise. At the last moment the cake was given another layer decorated with sugar roses and the figures of a bride and groom. The bottom layer had the words in icing: HAPPY BIRTHDAY. The top one said: CONGRATULATIONS. Red and white roses wreathed the cake, and two miniature flags, the Stars and Stripes and Union Jack, were stuck on either side of the bridal pair. No sentiment connected with the day and the occasion was forgotten.

Gertrude had set her heart on a moonlight-and-roses wedding. But, just before midnight, a sudden storm came tearing across the Cape. The rain sent us all scurrying into my cottage. There Gertrude and I were married.

After the ceremony and before the news reached the press, Gertrude sent off several dozen telegrams to the friends here and abroad she wanted to tell first. The message was the same to all. It read:

LOVE FROM MRS. RICHARD STODDARD ALDRICH. THEATRICALLY KNOWN AS

GERTRUDE LAWRENCE

Chapter Six

My own announcements of our marriage were quickly disposed of. They were limited to a message to my sons, and the telephone call to my mother which I described earlier.

The boys sent a punctilious congratulatory reply, presumably dictated by their mother. She added a cordial message of her own, wishing Gertrude and me every happiness. From Barbara came another telegram of loving greetings, "in which Mother joins."

I passed this over to Gertrude, whose hands were filled with the yellow sheets, which relays of boys on bicycles kept bringing to our cottage.

Gertrude read Barbara's message with evident disappointment. She said quickly: "I suppose your mother is writing us. She will want to say more intimate things than she would feel like putting into a telegram."

"Probably," I agreed noncommittally. I could not tell Gertrude about the chill silence which had met my telephoned announcement that morning. Or the question: "WHO is Gertrude Lawrence?" I congratulated myself that Barbara was in Groton and could be counted on to try to break down the family reserve. I said to myself that Mother would come around in a day or two.

But even as I tried to make myself accept this comfortable assurance, all that I knew of my mother's character—her obstinacy when it was a matter of adhering to her principles, even to breaking with members of her family, as she had almost done with her sister over her marriage—warned me that if Barbara did succeed in getting her to welcome an actress into the family it would be by some extraordinary persuasive powers. Mother was not only a Joy, a Boynton and a Pickering; she had been for forty years the wife of Edward Irving Aldrich. Superimposed upon her own heritage of prejudices was the stern Puritanism of the Aldriches and Stoddards. What Father and Uncle Sam would have said, had they not both been safely laid away in Upton, would be sure to color her thinking about her new daughter-in-law.

Though I loved my mother deeply, I was able to think objectively about her. I could smile at many of her old-fashioned ideas, so at variance with those of the world in which I lived in New York. But I respected the integrity of her character and the tenacity with which she held to her ideals. Remembering her oft-expressed axiom that "Tolerance is merely an excuse for the lowering of accepted standards," I hoped that her principles would not prove too formidable a barrier against her acceptance of my actress wife.

From Barbara, I later learned what happened in Groton. Any hopes that Mother might have entertained of concealing this latest dereliction of mine from the neighbors, as she had formerly hidden my connection with the theatre, were promptly dashed. As soon as the papers got news of my marriage to Gertrude, reporters appeared like a plague of locusts, eager to gobble up anything that savored of story. One intrepid cameraman sprang up in the backyard and snapped away at the house until Mother jerked down all the shades as if for a death. A "sob sister" from a Boston paper banged so imperiously on the front-door knocker that Aunt Alice, mother's widowed sister, chose to disobey orders and open the door rather than let its seventeenth-century panels be cracked. The interviewer pinned my little aunt into a corner of the entry under a barrage of questions until Uncle Jim stamped downstairs and routed the intruder.

In a back-parlor conclave the three Joys decided on a course of action before the world. They would treat my breach of tradition with dignified aloofness. Loyalty forbade condemning my marriage publicly. The early American tradition of burying the dead in the road and tramping over the grave to keep the enemy from knowing their losses, still held. Uncle Jim pointed out that every New England family of prominence had swallowed and lived down at least one distasteful marriage. To which Barbara impudently added: "Think of our Salem cousins. Didn't one of them bring home a Chinese bride?"

Mother gave as her opinion: "We will not mention it to anyone. Naturally none of the people we know will mention it to us."

* * *

Leaving Groton to seethe, and the Cape to lay bets on how long the marriage would last, Gertrude and I drove to New York, to the comparative seclusion of her apartment. Pam, having warmly expressed entire approval of our marriage, declared a total lack of interest in any honeymoon but one of her own. She packed her bags and moved into my former quarters at the Hobarts'.

Gertrude was scheduled to leave for the West Coast opening of *Skylark* on the fourteenth of the month. Meanwhile daily rehearsals were called to break in several new members of the cast. Our time together was short and broken by our many obligations. Lord Lothian had sent his congratulations, adding that *lèse-majesté* had been committed in not asking him to give the bride away; as His Majesty's representative he stood *in loco parentis* to Gertrude. He asked us both to lunch at the embassy in Washington.

I told Gertrude we could not go. There were no planes available for civilians without top priorities. She looked at me aghast. "Darling, we have to go. It's the same as a royal command."

We went by crowded train on one of the hottest days of that July, returning at night as uncomfortably. Gertrude made no complaints. For a person who reveled in luxury she could adapt herself to a total lack of it, when circumstances demanded, with better grace than any woman I ever knew.

Three other visits of ceremony which she insisted we make together were at no distance. The first was to the family of Dr. Downes, the renowned pediatrician who had saved Pam's life when Gertrude brought the frail little girl to New York in her second season in *Charlot's Revue*. From that time they had been adopted by the Downeses. "I used to have three daughters, now I have five," Dr. Downes was fond of saying. His eldest daughter, Helen, was about Gertrude's age and the two had become fast friends. The youngest daughter was a playmate and school companion for Pam.

I realized from what Gertrude had told me of these old and close friends that she was very anxious I make a good impression on them. She wanted them to approve of her choice. But I was highly embarrassed when, having introduced me, she suddenly exclaimed: "Wasn't I right? Doesn't he look *exactly* like Abraham Lincoln?"

Our second visit was to Fanny Holtzmann's parents, Henry and Theresa Holtzmann. There, a clover-shaped glass curio cabinet in the living room, its shelves crowded with an assortment of objects, caught Gertrude's fancy.

"This is the family museum; we started it when we were married," Mrs. Holtzmann explained. Opening the cabinet, she picked up a small box. "Decorations from our wedding cake," she murmured softly—"a long, long time ago." There were a yellowed bit of lace from her wedding veil, baby shoes of many vintages, and dozens of other mementos of a long, happy marriage.

Mr. Holtzmann turned to Gertrude. "The children tease Mamma for treasuring these. They say sentiment went out with the horse and buggy. But what would life be without memories?"

Gertrude caught my arm. "Oh, Richard, how wonderful! We must start a museum of our own. I'll look around for a cabinet."

She never had a chance to, for the next day the curio cabinet was delivered to us as a wedding present, with a note from Mrs. Holtzmann: "May God send you happy things to remember."

Our "family museum" was installed in a conspicuous corner of the living room, where it remains to this day. In it went the bride and groom from our wedding cake, which Gertrude had preserved with sentimental care. Not even Noel Coward's cynical smile in their direction, when he visited us, could dislodge them from their place among Gertrude's treasured possessions or from her heart.

Her preparations for our third visit, which was to the playwright Edward Sheldon, showed Gertrude in a new light.

I had never met Sheldon, who had been a Name when I was at Harvard—the most brilliant graduate of Professor Baker's 47 Workshop. His *Salvation Nell* had been played on Broadway by Mrs. Fiske; his later successes included *Lulu Belle* in collaboration with Charles MacArthur. For years Sheldon had been crippled by arthritis and blind, confined to a sofa in his New York apartment. But he was still in many respects the most important man in the theatre, because to his book-lined, sunny room, in which no evidences of illness and no talk of it were permitted, thronged the town's leading playwrights, producers and stars. Gertrude had been welcomed there. For years she made it a practice to visit Ned Sheldon once a week when she was in New York. That he enjoyed and looked forward to her visits was clear from the affectionate tone of his congratulatory telegram, which closed with the plea not to go off on tour without coming to see him, and bringing me along.

On the afternoon we were to go, Gertrude spent an unusually long time dressing. Her reappearance in the living room was accompanied by an unusual rustle of silk.

"Ned's petticoat," she explained, and twirled to show taffeta ruffles beneath her summer print frock. "I bought it on purpose to wear when I go to see him. Poor darling, he remembers that ladies used to rustle. He knows they don't nowadays, but deep inside him he thinks they *should*. The frou-frou is such a little thing to give him pleasure."

With the same loving wish to satisfy the blind invalid's nostalgia for romance, Gertrude catered to his unimpaired faculties of touch and smell. For her visits to him, she carefully chose clothes with recognizable textures—a brocaded silk scarf, a pair of velvet gauntlets, or perhaps a chiffon handkerchief. She avoided the modern heavy perfumes, using only simple, old-fashioned scents such as lilac, lavender or sweet pea.

The first time we went to Sheldon's big shaded penthouse, we could hear, as we entered, the cooing of pedigreed pigeons that were fluttering around on the adjoining terrace; they were carriers, trained to fly messages to the little group of Sheldon's friends who summered at Alec Woollcott's place on Lake Bomoseen. Our host remained inert on the sofa, but his greeting was fervent. "Darling Gertrude!" he exclaimed. "You come like a breeze from an English garden."

In introducing me to these friends Gertrude was sharing with me her closest and dearest associations in the United States. They were in a way her family. In the same spirit she asked me to go with her to Sulka's to choose some silk shirts to be sent to Clay Smith, from us both.

The American vaudeville team of Lee White and Clay Smith, big-time headliners before World War I, had started Gertrude on her road to fame. Vacationing in a seaside resort in England, they had happened to see the musical show in which she was touring the provinces. They went backstage and invited her to supper. They told her that she had talent. She should be in West End. Moreover, they promised to look out for an opening for her when they returned to London for an engagement in *Charlot's Revue*.

Each week, for many weeks, Gertrude sent them a postcard giving the name of the town and the theatre she was playing. She was in Yarmouth when their wire came saying that if she would come to London immediately there was a place for her in the chorus.

It was not in her nature ever to forget a kindness; least of all the one which had opened the gate to stardom. Years later she learned that Lee White was dead and that Clay Smith, blind and his savings gone, was a charity case in an institution. She immediately arranged with the Holtzmanns to give the old vaudevillian a monthly allowance which allowed him to board with a private family in the midwestern town where he grew up. She would write him or send him gifts, like the silk shirts.

I suggested that broadcloth or woolen shirts would be more useful, and added I had several suits that I could include in the package.

Gertrude shook her head. "Not *used* clothes. And not useful ones. He will feel the silk shirts and they will remind him of old times. They are what he used to wear. Besides, think how he'll adore showing them off. Probably nobody else in Prairie du Rocher, Illinois, has Sulka shirts."

She was right, of course. As she was in dressing specially for Sheldon. And in sending Barbara the fabulous orange tree. Under her influence I felt my understanding of human beings and their needs begin to stretch.

* * *

Meanwhile, letters, wires and gifts continued to pour in on us. I noticed that Gertrude scanned each batch of mail eagerly and would put the letters down with some disappointment. I surmised that she was looking for the expected letter from my mother welcoming her into the family. But day followed day, and there was no letter with the Groton postmark.

One morning, Gertrude picked up the newspaper. As she was scanning one of the Broadway columns, she encountered an item to the effect that, since I had married an actress, my name would be dropped from the Social Register.

She put the paper in front of me indignantly.

"They can't do a thing like that to you," she said. "Who do they think they are? Richard darling, do you mind very much?"

"Do I look unhappy?"

I added that to be married to her was worth being dropped from twenty Social Registers.

"It seems so silly," she commented. "If I were poor at my job, a miserable flop, or if I were drunk and disorderly, I can see there might be some excuse for thinking you had come a cropper. But I'm not. Debrett isn't fussy minded. Think of all the Gaiety girls who are in it. And in *Burke's Peerage*. I would have been in if I had married Eric Dudley or one of the others. Americans are very funny in some ways. I find them hard to understand."

And then she said, with a wistfulness that struck my heart: "Do you suppose your mother feels like that? You know she hasn't sent me one word."

"She will," I promised.

While Gertrude was rehearsing I put in a call to Groton. To Barbara, who answered the telephone, I said: "I've got to speak to Mother. This is important."

Presently I heard Mother's preliminary cough and her voice saying stiffly: "Well, Richard?"

At this distance in time it is impossible to recall all that I said or the pressures I brought to bear. Realizing that it was futile to attempt to argue with Mother's prejudice against the theatre, I did what I had never yet done with her or with anyone: I begged her, if she loved me and valued my love for her, to set aside those prejudices and to write my wife, expressing her love for us both and her hope for our happiness.

"You will love Gertrude when you know her," I said.

"That remains to be seen," was her reply.

"But you will write?"

"I will think about it, Richard."

With that I had to be content.

Now I, too, began to watch the mails. I was counting on something in Mother which I believed was stronger than what she considered her "principles"—perhaps because it is the first principle of all. This was her love for her only son. Inarticulate as she was in expressing it, unaccustomed to any form of affectionate demonstration, even rigidly trained against what might be called effusiveness—just as she had trained me—I had no reason to doubt the deep well of love that lay beneath her reserve. If I had tapped that as I had meant to, as I hoped I had. . . .

Two days later I handed Gertrude an envelope addressed in Mother's old-fashioned spidery hand. It contained this letter:

Groton, Massachusetts
Thursday, July 11th, 1940

My dear Miss Lawrence,

When I saw you at Dennis in *Skylark* last summer how little I dreamed that I should be closely related to you some day.

I can't realize it at all, but I hope to know you better and be charmed as everyone seems to be. Richard thinks you "very remarkable" and I hope when you return to New York I may really come to know you.

I am sure you and Richard, having the same interests, will enjoy a very happy and worthwhile future.

Yours, with my best love—
Mary P. Aldrich

"It isn't very warm, is it?" Gertrude said slowly. ". . . 'Dear Miss Lawrence' . . . And the signature. Why couldn't she have said 'Mother'?"

"Because she's a New Englander," I said. "And she is nearly eighty years old. When she attended Lawrence Academy in Groton, letters were supposed to be formal, dignified. The people she knew in Boston and Concord didn't call each other 'darling' and 'dearest.' They would have thought that the height of bad taste. My father's letters to her were signed, 'Your loving husband, Edward Irving Aldrich.' She would have been shocked by any other signature. You say you find Americans hard to understand sometimes. Well, we New Englanders are like that. You've married one and you'll have to try to understand the way we are."

She looked at me as if she was finding it hard to reconcile herself to the idea of a husband who was in so many respects the direct antithesis of most of the men she had known.

"Read it again," I advised. "She says: 'With my best love.' Take it from me, if Mother wrote that, she meant it. Up to the hilt. She isn't like the people we know who toss endearments around like confetti. And don't get the idea that because New Englanders seem stiff and standoffish and reserved, we don't feel deeply and love deeply, too."

An impish grin suddenly lighted my wife's features. "Like those old Congregational deacons buried in the Cape Cod cemeteries," she said. "I explored one of them. Most of the old boys had three wives and at least fifteen children."

"That should have warned you," I retorted. "Dear Miss Lawrence, I am surprised you married me."

* * *

Up to this time Gertrude had never met my sons. Dick, Jr., was now eleven; David, nine. At my request they came to lunch with us at the apartment. They came dressed in blue shorts; so scrubbed, so painfully polite, so agonizingly shy that I knew their mother and stepfather must have drilled them in the behavior considered proper to such an occasion. Even Gertrude, whose way with children usually broke through all barriers, made little headway at first.

The boys were quite different in appearance and temperament. David, still chubby and rosy, made friends readily, was interested in many things outside himself and found life constantly entertaining. Gently encouraged by Gertrude, he was soon chatting easily about a new pet he had acquired, a canary which he had named Henry.

To the not unnatural inquiry as to why he had chosen this name, he replied gravely: "Because he is my friend."

"Of course," Gertrude breathed. "Henry is a *very* friendly name."

But though David responded to her advances, Dick remained miserably aloof. He was too tall, too thin, too grave and too inexpressive. He was an embarrassing replica of myself at his age.

His shyness, silence and unhappy withdrawal from the luncheon conversation irritated me unreasonably. I found myself booming at him as Father used to boom at me when he felt I had failed to do him proud at those Sunday gatherings at Uncle Sam Aldrich's. When Dick's shaking hand dribbled chocolate sauce from around the sundae, which Gertrude had ordered as a special treat, onto the table and himself, my annoyance was loud and harsh.

I felt Gertrude step, not too lightly, on my foot.

A few minutes later, Gertrude reminded me pointedly that I had to read a certain play script at the office. Her hint was not too delicate for me to understand; I left her alone to make friends with the boys.

While David occupied himself with a pile of illustrated magazines, Dick wandered into the library. He was standing by the desk, looking at a letter with foreign stamps, when Gertrude came in. Startled, as if caught in something wrong, he dropped the letter and hung his head.

"Do you like stamps?" she inquired gently. "I can give you those and lots more. I get letters from all over the world. I'll save the stamps and send them to you if you wish." (She did do this, and much more.)

He tried to thank her, but the words would not come. In their place came tears.

Suddenly he felt Gertrude's arms around him. She was holding him close. She was crying, too.

Presently she whisked him into the bathroom, and washed his face and hers. In a few minutes he was telling her how much he hated loud noises, and how deeply my shouting had upset him, making him only shyer and more awkward.

"We won't tell Dad," she said. "It will be a secret just between you and me."

When I returned two hours later, a furious game of cassino was in progress. After the children went home, I asked Gertrude how they had all got along.

"Oh, famously. Your boys are darlings, Richard. David has a twinkle in his eye that tells me we are going to have fun together."

"But what about Dick? Could you break through his shyness at all?"

"Dick and I are going to understand each other very well," she replied. "Bless his stout little heart. If you will keep Edward Irving Aldrich out of the picture, everything will be all right."

She said nothing more. I left it at that. It was not until quite a while later that I discovered what had happened between Gertrude and Dick that afternoon. And then it was not from Gertrude that I learned it, but from the grateful Dick himself.

* * *

Our honeymoon—if one can properly call those frantically busy ten days a honeymoon—ended on July 14 when Gertrude left for Los Angeles and her *Skylark* tour.

Gertrude's departures for a tour always followed an established ritual, in which each member of the court had an assigned role. With Jack Potter as chief dragoman, the party assembled at her house. Hazel, her dresser, was custodian of the make-up box. Dorothy had the overnight bag and picnic basket. Nurse Catherine

The bride and groom in reality, and as they appeared on our wedding cake.

My mother, Mary Pickering Joy Aldrich. A daughter of old New England, she was shocked to learn I had married an actress.

My sons, Dick and David, with their little half-brother, Teddy Corballis.

Turner attended to Mackie and his luggage. The other fifty-odd pieces, including a case filled with the blue silk sheets and special blankets for Gertrude's berth aboard the train, were the chauffeur's affair.

The caravan got away to an early start. Gertrude insisted that no one who knew anything about traveling would arrive at the station less than forty minutes before train time. She was always early herself.

I saw her off and then returned to the Cape and the problems connected with the imminent arrival of our star of the moment, Miss Tallulah Bankhead, squired by a pet monkey. In those familiar surroundings, and with the numerous duties of my job, my marriage began to seem as improbable as a dream.

Gertrude's letters, sandwiched into a schedule that included performances, war benefits, reunions with old friends in Beverly Hills and selling British War Relief emblems in a department store, were warm and witty. Their very intimacy, however, emphasized the distance between us.

"Hullo, my darling," she wrote on arrival. "Arrived here this A.M. at 8 o'clock to find your beautiful roses. My first bouquet from the groom. Do you realize that? . . . How are you, my beloved husband? I am so glad we did it when we did and that we belong to each other. It helps during this horrid separation. . . .

"By changing in Chicago, Jack and I got in a day earlier than the company, which gives me a chance to see the Press, write my speech for my opening campaign for B.W.R. and rest before the Garden Party at the Lubitsches."

This was a supper given for the Red Cross. "Everyone was there," Gertrude reported. "Lotte Lehmann sang and the guests drank $25,000 worth of wine, whisky and bewilderment."

Her comments on life in the motion-picture colony were far from admiring: "This place always was awful and now it's even worse. Everybody is being hard-working for charity while cutting each other's throats in order to show up the best at it. My telephone has not stopped ringing since we came in, and even though none of my activities will clash with theirs, they are all fighting for my time. I know that those I refuse will never have a good word for me after I am gone. Still, it's all for one cause, so it doesn't really matter who does the work as long as it's done. . . . The emblems are going splendidly. I could have sold over one hundred on the train coming out . . ."

In spite of these reservations about Hollywood, she was enjoying reunions with people she had known in London and elsewhere:

"Today I am going to see Mary at Pickfair," she reported. "Then on to see Mary Lee and Douglas's baby. Then to dinner with Jessie Barthelmess and Dick. Then to the Warners to see the private showing of a picture. Some Sunday! Saw Bette Davis last night. She was thrilled about us, as is everyone. Nigel and Bunny came last night, bless them. Bill Powell and Garbo and that nice Billie Burke are coming tomorrow . . ."

I might have thought myself forgotten in this whirligig, but for an occasional penciled note, "I AM MISSING YOU MORE EVERY MINUTE WHAT ARE WE TO DO? MRS. A." Or a telegram like this: "SUCH A GLORIOUS DAY AND I HAVE A MATINEE BUT I WANT YOU TO GO TO THE BEACH AND GET PLENTY OF SUN."

Even more flattering in its implications was the photograph of herself which arrived one day with the note: "This is for your office so that all those producer-struck ootzie-wootzies will know you have the most beautiful and dangerous woman for a wife, so HANDS OFF."

Her concern with the fateful march of events in Europe continued.

"Today I am tired and could so easily be depressed," she wrote. "The news is bad. Still, things aren't going as well as Mr. Hitler thought. England isn't France. There is something in good old Shakespeare's *Henry the Fifth,* I think, about small showers lasting a long time and sudden storms of short duration. Look it up. It's Act II . . . Bless you for being you. Please always be just the same, and love me."

The affectionate postscripts were comforting, but they hardly made up for Gertrude's absence. We had been married two weeks and our relationship was still new. Now I had no expectation of seeing Gertrude for another five months. It was most disturbing.

Many a husband has to leave his bride after the briefest of honeymoons, especially in time of war. But then it is the man who goes into a life of exciting variety and action, while the woman waits for him to return. In our case the usual procedure was reversed. I remained at home, tied to an accustomed—even humdrum—job. Meanwhile Gertrude entered upon a life of constant and stimulating change; she would renew her old ties of friendship and camaraderie with people I did not know; she would live in a world which I could not share.

It was not the ideal way to start a marriage.

Subtly and against my own better judgment, I found myself affected by the amused comments on my anomalous status, the raised eyebrows, the questions: "When is Gertrude coming back? Or isn't she?"; and the "friendly" reminders of my wife's tendency to change her mind without notice. I grew irritable and morose.

This condition was not relieved, a while later, by the knowledge that Gertrude had reached San Francisco, a city which had long ago taken her to its warm, impulsive heart. I knew she had many friends there, one or two of whom had wanted to marry her. It was clear from her letters that she was enjoying herself, being feted and made much of.

San Francisco was in the throes of the Fair. It was inevitable that Gertrude should be swept into the publicity and the promotion of the enterprise. A Gertrude Lawrence Day was held, at which she, escorted by the mayor, did the honors.

Gertrude always enjoyed the company of newspapermen, and was immensely popular with them. On one of her previous tours she had been elected a member of San Francisco's century-old Press Club, and her favorite dressing-room mascot was an enamel-and-gold cat given her by Joe Cauthorn, president of the San Francisco *News*. She was a frequent dropper-in at the luncheon Round Table at Jack's presided over by Louis Lurie, owner of the Curran Theatre. It was there that she met Lurie's friend, Damon Runyon, and became the model for the "lady" in Runyon's series of short stories about that glamorous figure.

Reporters would frequently drift into her dressing-room after the play and pass along stories which they knew she was too astute to repeat indiscreetly. I was continually amazed by the bits of information she had about politics, sports events and, occasionally, the stock market. "One of the boys told me . . ." she would explain.

Not all her fun with the boys was confined to backstage or to the club. There was a wild streak in Gertrude which made it impossible for her to resist a dare or, occasionally to do something which was highly dangerous—particularly if she had been warned against it. In this spirit she had once joined a party of newspapermen on an all-night crabbing trip in the waters off the California coast.

I had heard the story from Jack Potter, who was managing Gertrude's company.

Three of the boys had dropped into Gertrude's dressing room on a Saturday night already dressed in rough clothes and sou'westers. They were going out at 2 A.M. with one of the boats of the fishing fleet—a crabber, with an Italian skipper. One of the boys was a cameraman who hoped to get a story out of the expedition.

"Could I go along?" Gertrude asked.

The boys demurred. They were divided between their eagerness for a story and their knowledge that the trip was not only unconventional but dangerous.

"You couldn't take it," they said.

To tell Gertrude she couldn't take something was sufficient to turn her will into iron. She announced that she was going; and let anyone just dare to try to stop her. Her determination was increased by Jack Potter's firm reaction to the plan. "You can't go, Gertrude," he ordained. "It's absolutely out of the question." He reminded her that he and she had been invited to a supper dance that night and it was time they set out.

"I might have known by the docile way she took this that she was planning to bolt," Jack said when telling me the story. "She said, 'All right, I'll go back to the hotel and dress.' I was to go on to the party with one of the girls from the cast. She would join us.

"I had just arrived at the party when I was given a telephone message: Please accept Miss Lawrence's apologies. She was so tired that she had decided to go to bed.

"After the party I went up to the country with some friends. About midday, I rang Gertrude at her hotel, and her maid said she was asleep. With that assurance I had a relaxed week-end. Not until I saw the Monday papers did I know what Gertrude had been up to."

She had gone back to the hotel after arranging for Carolyn Anspacher of the San Francisco *Chronicle* to join the party. At 1:30 A.M., per schedule, the boys and Carolyn came by to pick her up. Gertrude was dressed in slacks, sweater and heavy coat. Two more sou'westers had been obtained from the Fire Department for Gertrude and Carolyn, and the hoods were drawn well over their heads.

The skipper of the crabbing boat might not have known that two of the five passengers coming aboard were women if a sudden gust had not whipped the hood from Gertrude's head. Then he flatly refused to take her, claiming that women were bad luck aboard ship at any time; they got sick and demanded to be waited on. Besides, he was a respectable married man and he wanted no wild parties on his boat.

One of the newspapermen promptly headed for a telephone booth and rang up the waterfront boss, telling him the predicament, and that the women were Gertrude Lawrence and a newspaperwoman friend.

"I'll fix it," the boss promised. He did, through a call to the head of the pier. The alarmed skipper was told to take the party, "ladies, too," and take good care of them or find another dock.

From all accounts, this was but the beginning of an adventure-packed night. The sea was rough. There was a drizzle of rain. When the crabber pulled up to the mother boat of the fleet for bait, Carolyn accidentally let her hood fall back. This promptly drew catcalls from the crew of the mother boat. The skipper's conviction that he was in for trouble was strengthened by the increasing roughness, the cameraman's falling on the slippery deck and spraining an arm, and the seasickness of all the "boys."

Gertrude alone, to the shame and fury of her fellow-passengers, remained impervious to the pitching and tossing, even played Florence Nightingale to them.

Topping it all, the skipper cut his hand while opening a can of beer. Gertrude found the ship's first-aid kit and dressed the cut competently.

"As you can imagine," Jack growled, "she was having the time of her life."

Through all this the skipper's fear of women aboard ship was lightened by his mounting liking for Gertrude. "She was the best of the whole bunch," according to him. When she joined him at breakfast and did full justice to the muddy coffee and meat stew with no criticisms for its service, he was completely won over.

Only one thing caused him worry: they had caught no crabs. It might have been the weather, or it might have been having women aboard; they were coming back to port in the morning with nothing to show for their night's work.

"How much would you have made if you'd had a good haul?" Gertrude asked.

He told her.

"I'll see that you get it," she promised.

The money and two passes to her play went to him before he sailed that night. When he and his wife came to her play, and went backstage, he told her that she could go out on his boat any time she wanted. "But next time leave those reporters ashore."

In the light of such past performances I was constantly worried by what Gertrude might be up to. I wired Jack Potter to keep an eye on her. His reply:

DOING MY BEST BUT YOU KNOW GEE

did not allay my anxiety.

Consequently, when I was wakened one night shortly after 3 A.M. by the ringing of my telephone, my immediate thought was: Something has happened to Gertrude.

But it was her voice that came over the wire. "Are you all right?" I demanded.

"Of course! It isn't me . . . It's the children. Richard, you've got to do something."

I asked what children.

"Noel's," she told me. "Of course they're mine too . . ."

I sat down on the edge of the bed and took a firmer grip of the receiver. My wife's voice was going on in a rush of quick phrases: "We're so distressed . . . Noel has been here with me this evening

. . . We don't know what to do . . . Those babies can't stay in England, with the blitz . . . We had planned to evacuate them . . . our arrangements were made, or we thought they were till YOUR government stopped it and now everything's tangled in yards of red tape and . . ."

"GERTRUDE!"

I had to shout to stem the flow. And I continued to bellow: "What is all this? Your children and Noel Coward's? How many children?"

"Fifty-eight . . . No, wait, only fifty-seven. But, Richard, those helpless babies . . . and the bombs . . . We've got to save them. I told Noel that you would surely think of a way . . ."

The thought flashed through my half-wakened mind that Mr. Coward's children, however numerous, could hardly be considered my problem. I had never met the gifted Mr. Coward but his name figured so often and so intimately in Gertrude's conversation that I had developed toward him the instinctive jealousy that every husband feels for a man his wife knew before she met him.

I repeated my query: "What do you mean—your children and Noel's? I want a straight answer."

Ultimately I got it. Though it took a long time, punctuated at regular intervals by a bored voice reminding us that our time was up. To each of these interruptions Gertrude and I chorused from opposite sides of the continent, "No, no, don't cut us off, operator. We want more time, please . . ."

The children—by final count fifty-seven—were inmates of the Actors' Orphanage in Britain at Chertsey in Surrey. For a number of years, Noel Coward had been president of the British Actors' Orphanage, which maintained the Home. Gertrude was a director and a vice-president. She had never mentioned this to me. Nor had she told me that a committee of British actors in Hollywood, headed by Dame May Whitty, was trying to arrange for the evacuation of the children, as a group, to this country. No doubt this lapse was due to the hasty circumstances of our marriage and Gertrude's subsequent departure on tour. This therefore was the first knowledge I had that my wife was plumping into my lap fifty-seven orphans, for whom the United States Department of State, through our

London consul, had refused entry permits. Gertrude felt that she—and inferentially I, as her husband—would be personally responsible if the children were not evacuated before a bomb was dropped on the orphanage.

"Richard dearest, promise me you will unwind all that red tape in Washington. Didn't you tell me you were a Son of the American Revolution? That ought to help."

"It will help more if you will stop getting hysterical and let me think," I replied. A glance at my watch told me it was nearly 3:30 A.M. I dismissed the hope of any more sleep, and, having enjoined Gertrude to leave the orphans to me, and to get some rest herself, I hung up and faced the problem.

Through the ensuing weeks Gertrude's "babies," as she insisted on calling them, though the youngest was a child of five and many of the others were entering on a lanky adolescence, figured prominently in my life. I set to work trying to live up to the reputation my wife had given me as someone who gets things done. I was determined on one thing: this was a British Actors' enterprise; I, as an American and without professional standing, did not wish to figure in it publicly. I would act in an advisory capacity, but "Keep me out of it" I told both Gertrude and Fanny Holtzmann, who was acting as Noel's lawyer as well as Gertrude's.

The children were to be sponsored by various persons, many of them British subjects. The State Department's ruling against granting them individual entry permits was based on the fact that they were institutional children. This eliminated the plan of the English colony in Hollywood, which had been to place the children in private homes, at least until an estate could be secured large enough to house them all under one roof. It had been suggested that the entire orphanage be enrolled in a California private school, but this promised to be so costly, what with the prospect of the war continuing for years, that it had to be abandoned.

Meanwhile, though we had as yet no roof to cover the children, the necessity of their removal from England grew daily more imperative. The hourly radio reports of the blitz kept Gertrude in a state of acute anxiety. Every night she telephoned. What was I doing? When could the children be put on a convoy? When? When? When?

It was useless to remind her that every port in England was jammed with would-be émigrés waiting for places on the ships. Or that the convoys put out into a sea infested with U-boats.

Finally I was able to report that her "babies," shepherded by a representative of the British Actors' Orphanage, were all at an unspecified British port of embarkation. There the American consul had promised to see the orphans board the S.S. *American Legion* sailing in the next convoy.

Meanwhile the West Coast newspapers had learned of the enterprise and of the celebrated stars who were sponsoring the children. The story of the orphans was played up in all its tear-jerker aspects. It appeared inevitable that the children would be publicized, photographed and exploited—something which I knew Gertrude and Noel Coward would dislike and which I, as a parent, knew was bad for them and for their education in America.

We had been notified that the convoy was expected to dock at Montreal. The cost of transporting the orphans and their guardians from that city to Los Angeles was not negligible; not to speak of the difficulty of procuring transportation on already overcrowded trains.

I mentioned this to Gertrude.

"Oh, I've arranged for that," she told me. She had remembered that an old friend of hers in Chicago was the owner of a celebrated motor transport company. She had written him and had secured from him the offer of private buses to convey the orphanage across the continent.

It was now September and I had moved from the Cape to New York, occupying Gertrude's apartment. I felt like a trespasser in that satin setting. She may have sensed this, because she sent daily wires from the stops on her tour with instructions for my comfort: "Order blue coal for apartment . . ." "See that Claire does the flowers . . . She knows how. One low bowl in the living room and one on the desk in the library, because unless the apartment looks and feels homey you might as well be at your club. I want your friends to think you are being taken care of and not neglected."

One day I dropped in on Uncle Jim, at his office at *The Christian*

Advocate, and took him to lunch. He looked me over as if seeking signs of deterioration since my marriage outside the family pale. "What do you do with yourself while your wife is away?" he asked.

The orphans' plight could not fail to stir him. I told him about them. He asked what would become of them after they arrived in the United States. I explained that the plan was to move them on to Hollywood, where there was a large colony of British actors.

"You can't let those children go to Hollywood," Uncle Jim protested. "That's no place for them among motion-picture people and motion-picture standards and morals. We must find a home for them where they can have proper Christian training. I shall start making inquiries."

My uncle's inquiries resulted in the discovery that the Gould Foundation owned a large estate on Pelham Parkway, in New York, dedicated to the use of needy children, but at that time had no children to house in it. Fanny Holtzmann immediately took the matter up with the State Child Welfare Committee, and also with Noel Coward and his committee. The fact that the foundation offered to house, feed, clothe, educate, supply medical and dental care to the refugees for eight dollars a week per child, and would do this for as long as needed, was an advantage which the British Actors hailed with relief. The expense was well within their means.

Just as I was thinking that the evacuation of the orphans was successfully under way, came the shocking news that the convoy in which they were traveling had been attacked. Two ships had been sunk. Whether one was the *American Legion* was still unknown.

Gertrude was then playing in the Northwest. Her tour of many one-night stands had exhausted even her apparently inexhaustible strength. All her letters spoke of being tired: "Some tour, nine states in nine days . . . I must be running for office or something . . . A million thanks for the beautiful roses. Please order the casket to match for the end of this tour . . ."

I realized at once that she must be spared additional anxiety. The news must be kept from her at least until we had definite information of the children's fate.

I wired that I would join her in Denver, where she was scheduled to arrive in a few days. I would bring the architect's plans of the house we proposed building on the Cape and about which she was now writing in every letter.

I flew out to Colorado and we spent a happy week-end studying the plans the architect had drawn, and on which Gertrude immediately drew additions, until I reminded her that she had said she wanted a simple country house, a cross between a Danish farmhouse and a Cape Cod cottage.

On Sunday we drove up to Central City, whose theatrical festival I had managed for several seasons and which I wanted her to see. I said nothing of the reported attack on the convoy. Gertrude was delighted with the plan for placing the children at the Gould Foundation in New York.

That evening, as we came into the Brown Palace after our trip to Central City, I was handed a telegram. Gertrude stood at my elbow.

When I attempted to stuff it into my pocket, she demanded: "Why don't you open it?"

With a sinking heart I tore open the yellow envelope and read:

CHILDREN SAFE THANK GOD FANNY

When I returned to New York I met Noel Coward for the first time. He was busily engaged in preparations for the children's reception. Gertrude appeared exceedingly eager that Noel and I should become friends. And even more eager that he should be impressed that ours was a love match.

I had expected that Noel would meet the *American Legion* in Montreal. But this he refused to do. His reason revealed a side of his complex character which only his closest friends know; he was resolute against doing anything which might throw the spotlight of publicity on him in connection with his work for the orphanage.

Fanny, armed with the required papers and funds, had gone to Canada to bring the orphans to their new shelter in New York. Back in town, she telephoned me "mission accomplished."

Later, talking to Noel, I observed that I did not know how I could have faced Gertrude if things had been different.

He regarded me a moment, a quizzical smile playing across his lean and elegant face. "You're a brave man—marrying Gertie."

I said: "I happen to love her."

"I love her, too, but she terrifies me. She's so devilishly clever at getting whatever she wants."

I said that I wondered sometimes why she had married me.

"So did I," Noel said with unabashed frankness. "When I saw her in San Francisco I asked her. She said: 'Because he's the only man who never yessed me.'"

He smiled again. "Keep it up, old boy. If you can."

Chapter Seven

As I look back over the first year of our marriage, I am conscious of a strong animal flavor. For in marrying Gertrude I had married her pets as well as her devotions, her enthusiasms and her extraordinary capacity for interesting herself in a hundred different things. Hazel, her invaluable theatre maid—"my wonderful Hazel," Gertrude called her—expressed it, almost with awe: "I'll tell you about Miss Lawrence—she's always into something."

There were the canaries: a saga that began over a luncheon table in Cincinnati during Gertrude's *Skylark* tour. Her host was the rotund and voluble Alec Woollcott. An unexpected additional guest was a plump canary who made a nonchalant entrance on Woollcott's shoulder, then lunched serenely on hearts of lettuce shredded by an unhappy waiter.

It developed that the canary was a gift from Uncle Alec's friend, Dr. Gustav Eckstein, the Cincinnati physiologist, whose book *Canary* had been highly publicized by Woollcott on his radio program. The Man Who Came to Dinner was in Cincinnati in honor of Dr. Eckstein's fiftieth birthday.

"Now that you have arrived so opportunely," he informed Gerture grandly, "you may join me in a private tour of Dr. Eckstein's laboratory."

Uncle Alec would have been surprised to learn that Gertrude's immediate acceptance of this invitation had nothing to do with his eloquent talk on the rare qualities of his pet. Her wanting to go along was linked to a small boy with a canary "friend" named Henry.

Gertrude had a wonderful time at the laboratory. Eckstein beamed at her intelligent interest in his birds and answered her questions with such volubility that the visit prolonged itself until Gertrude had to rush off to the theatre. Woollcott preened himself on her capitulation to the canaries, characteristically taking full credit for it.

Before leaving Cincinnati, Gertrude ordered a copy of *Canary* which she immediately wrapped as a Christmas gift for my son David. On the flyleaf she wrote:

> Dear David,
>
> If you are impressionable—and I am sure you are—your poor mother will in all probability never forgive me for giving you this book. But please tell her that "actresses will happen in the best of regulated families," and that there is no real harm in us.
>
> My love to Henry, dear David.

My young son's reply, printed in pencil in awkward capitals, was put away among Gertrude's treasured possessions. David wrote:

> Thank you very much for the book about canaries. I like it very much. I am going to raise a family of canaries. I wish you would come to see my canary named Henry. He doesn't sing much. I think the book about canaries is very amusing. My canary takes to bathes a day. I hope you feel well,
>
> Love,
>
> David

Gertrude returned from her *Skylark* tour in November of 1940. She was home only a few days when she—or rather we—acquired a canary all our own. It came in the form of a belated wedding present from Woollcott.

The canary's name, Woollcott advised his "Darling Amanda," was Franklin. Woollcott's admiration of our recently re-elected President was intense.

Mackie surveyed the new arrival with his customary dour disdain. However, Wally and David, our Siamese cats, displayed a horrible interest in Franklin. Slinking in despite the concerted efforts of the household to keep the door shut between them and the canary, they would sit for hours beneath the cage, staring up greedily, their tails moving slowly back and forth.

I had to hand it to Franklin; he sang on, unruffled. The rest of us, however, lacked his assurance. After five days of strain, Gertrude relieved our nerves by beseeching Barbara to take the cats home with her, which she did; a happy turn of events for which I was grateful to Franklin.

The canary's name caused Gertrude some misgivings. If she was going to have a pet named for an important personage, she preferred that the namesake be British. And she was aware that I was anti-New Deal and did not share Uncle Alec's and Barbara's unqualified enthusiasm for F.D.R.'s policies and personality.

"All right, let's call him something else," I said. "I don't suppose he knows his name."

She studied the canary thoughtfully.

"I don't think we can change his name," she said. "Look, Richard. Who does he make you think of? Those very bright eyes. And that stiff, backward tilt of his head . . . Doesn't he appear to be looking through pince-nez down an elongated chin?"

She was right. The bird bore an extraordinary resemblance to F.D.R. as an ornithologically-minded cartoonist might have pictured him.

"You'll just have to put up with the name, darling," she decided. "After all, he's *your* President."

"And a good friend of *your* country," I reminded her. That was one Roosevelt policy I wholeheartedly endorsed.

Until Gertrude called me to acknowledge the resemblance, it had never occurred to me that one canary was not an identical replica of every other. On my way to the office that morning, I found myself stopping instinctively before a Sixth Avenue pet shop. A number of canaries fluttered appealingly in individual wicker cages in the window. One, high up on the wall, caught and held my eye. He was a large, puffy bird. "Corpulent" was the word that came to mind. His round, small-beaked head was sunk between his shoulders. There was something dogged and aggressive about him which was heightened by a bald patch on top of his head. If his beak had held a thick cigar. . . .

I told the shop to deliver the bird to Gertrude. On the card I wrote: "Call me Winnie."

From the moment of their introduction, Winnie and Franklin took to each other. They shared a large cage. Winnie moved along the perch to one end (did my imagination deceive my eyes, or was there a nautical roll suggestive of a certain famous Former Naval Person?). With an unmistakable wink, he invited Franklin to hop up on the other end. This Franklin did immediately, with his accustomed self-assurance. There the two chirped and chuckled to each other, sang duets and occasionally solo serenades, one pouring out his song, to which the other listened attentively and courteously, with head cocked.

Some time afterward, to Gertrude's great delight and pride, she was invited to Sunday lunch with President and Mrs. Roosevelt at the White House.

I asked her what she had talked about.

"Oh, nothing very serious," she replied. "Mrs. Roosevelt once told me that she welcomed any diversion for the President in these grim days—especially amusing stories. So I told him how Alec gave us Franklin, and how you had completed the pair of canary statesmen with Winnie. The President threw back his head and roared with laughter. Then I said to him, 'Why, when you do that, you are the very image of *our* Franklin.' "

* * *

During our hectic ten-day honeymoon the previous July, Gertrude had signed a contract to star in Moss Hart's musical play *Lady in the Dark* beginning late in December. This allowed only one month between the closing of her *Skylark* tour and the opening of her new show: one week for costume fittings, and three for intensive rehearsals of her new lines and songs. It was a tight schedule. Despite the mounting frenzy of preparing a musical show of grand-scale dimensions, Gertrude did not become tense or temperamental. As Moss Hart wrote about her, no one he ever knew had her ability to make fun out of the hard grind of rehearsing and putting a show together.

The last week of preparation took place in Boston, where the show was to get its pre-Broadway unveiling. Although I had not seen nearly enough of Gertrude during the *Skylark* tour—only brief flying visits to spend a few days with her in California, Colorado and Tennessee—I did not accompany her to Boston. I felt she should be completely free in those hectic final days to concentrate on her role.

Lady in the Dark was undergoing the usual last-minute cuts, substitutions and revisions. Between performances and rehearsals Gertrude sent me hurried notes. "I don't wear the white dress you did not like, and the Rah-Rah stuff is out," she wrote after elimination of a scene which had given her two rapid costume changes. "Thank Heaven! We are better without it."

Two days before the scheduled opening, I flew to Boston. Gertrude greeted me affectionately, her amazing vitality clearly undiminished by the grueling round of rehearsals. At her request, I dropped in at one of the final run-throughs of the show.

What I saw left me considerably dismayed. *Lady in the Dark* had a fresh concept and many amusing scenes—no question about that—but Gertrude's role was eclipsed by the material furnished to a young, and at that time unknown, featured player—Danny Kaye. Danny had what to my mind was the only show-stopping song in the score, a specialty number called "Tschaikowsky." Since his role in *Lady in the Dark* was distinctly a minor one, this struck me as a serious imbalance.

When Gertrude asked how I liked the run-through, I expressed my misgivings forcibly.

"It's all right, darling," she assured me brightly. "Moss Hart has been worried about the same thing. He's persuaded Kurt Weill and

Ira Gershwin to do a new number for me. We're trying it out tonight."

The new number was "Jenny." I stood in the back of the house that night for dress rehearsal, as Gertrude did it for the first time. I was frankly unimpressed. "Jenny" was not at all the kind of song that Gertrude was accustomed to sing, or that her audience expected of her. I felt it would be an anticlimax after Danny Kaye's tongue-twisting "Tschaikowsky."

As Gertrude's husband, and a man not without experience in the theatre, I was considerably upset. I had seen more than one play, carefully constructed around a star, go all awry because its focus shifted to a lesser player. The performance I had just seen could be disastrous both for the production and for its star—my wife.

On the other hand, Gertrude and I had agreed at the time of our marriage that we would never interfere with each other's careers . . .

I phoned Fanny Holtzmann in New York. What exactly did Gertrude's contract as star stipulate?

Fanny assured me that, under her contract, Gertrude could, if she wished, have the Danny Kaye song cut from the show.

That evening, as Gertrude and I were having dinner, I casually mentioned this to her.

Gertrude's reaction was immediate and emphatic. "Danny is a talented performer and he's entitled to his chance. As for my not being able to top his song—don't worry about me, Richard. I can take care of myself."

She insisted that "Jenny" would not be an anticlimax on opening night. "Just wait till I get out in front of a paying audience. You're due for a surprise, darling—I promise you!"

At the opening, I watched the first act tensely. Act Two, in which the two key song numbers appeared, was what I was waiting for. I knew from the faces of the producers and authors that they shared my apprehensiveness. "Tschaikowsky" was a known quantity. But what, if anything, was Gertrude going to do with "Jenny"?

The curtain went up on the second act. As anticipated, Danny's Russian number was a howling success; the audience kept up its applause for two minutes. I watched Gertrude, lolling idly in a swing on stage, and held my breath.

Then I witnessed one of those instantaneous and complete metamorphoses on Gertrude's part which never ceased to amaze me through the years. Evidently the thunderous applause the audience gave Danny was the challenge that she needed, and knew she needed, to stimulate her into an all-out performance. As the clapping of hands died down, she slid off the swing. The song she had to do did not fit her; but this did not prevent her from fitting herself to the song.

Taking the stage, she went into "Jenny." But not as she had sung it at rehearsal, and not with the smart, sophisticated elegance for which she had been celebrated since André Charlot introduced her to American audiences. Suddenly, startlingly, the exquisite, dreamy, glamorous Gertrude Lawrence was transformed into a tough, bawdy dive singer. As a piece of impromptu impersonation it was superb and with few parallels. It left everyone—backstage as well as in the audience—aghast for a moment; and then madly, vociferously enthusiastic.

A miracle in showmanship was accomplished that night; two tremendous hits followed each other immediately and with equal effect. The success of Danny Kaye's number did not cut down Gertrude's prestige. Instead, it made possible, by its challenge, her triumph with "Jenny."

Not only that night, but at every performance through the six or seven months Danny Kaye remained with *Lady in the Dark,* this miracle was repeated—with other singers after Danny Kaye left to accept his first starring role. Meanwhile Gertrude continued to deliver "Jenny" with undiminished verve and with bumps that "outminskied Minsky." Her performance added another unsuspected facet to her professional career; one which was on a par with her playing of the slatternly British housewife in *Fumed Oak,* and the down-at-heels singer in *Red Peppers.*

Danny was deeply appreciative of Gertrude's warm encouragement, which had begun the first time she saw him perform at rehearsal. The friendship between the two remained firm. After Danny had achieved his enormous success, he was playing in London at the same time Gertrude was starring in Daphne du Maurier's *September Tide.* She, Danny, the Garson Kanins and the Oliviers frequently made a lively party at the Café de Paris. Gertrude wrote me:

"I went to Danny's opening night, rushed over after my play and joined a party in the stage box. He was a sensation. Afterwards we all went on to the Café de Paris but he asked me to go in his car with him and his manager and Mrs. Parnell. We had an escort of 12 stout London bobbies and 2 inspectors to get us safely from the stage door into the car. It was great fun. . . ."

Separately, they were both asked to appear on the Bebe Daniels-Ben Lyons broadcast, "Hi, Gang," and they conceived the stunt of singing each other's songs from *Lady in the Dark*. Gertrude sang "Tschaikowsky," which everyone associated with Danny. He, when his turn came, did "Jenny."

Gertrude even looked forward to doing a play with Danny for her next season in New York. She became enthusiastic about one titled *A Dame for Don Juan,* and sent me a copy, urging me to read with her in mind.

> I have a mad idea that with a few vital songs by Cole Porter it could be the greatest musical ever with Danny Kaye as Don Juan. It's time he did a play, and this is a great story but should only be played as a comedy drama, and by two stars who are adored and considered the tops in chic and glamour by the public.
>
> It would make a fortune. We could do it in New York first until June, then here [London], and then the road in America for a limited period. It couldn't miss.
>
> I urge you to discuss this with Gilbert Miller, no matter where he is. Danny has a picture to do when he leaves here, which would make him free by the autumn. But it should be arranged soon, and I am sure Cole would see the great wisdom and the money angle. . . .

The idea came to nothing because Gertrude went to Hollywood to make *The Glass Menagerie* immediately after her return to the United States. Before the picture was released plans were afoot for *The King and I.*

* * *

What with Gertrude's long tour in *Skylark,* followed almost at once by bringing *Lady in the Dark* to Broadway late in January, it was February and a full seven months after our marriage before Gertrude and I could be said to have accomplished that process the British call "settling in."

We were still occupying her penthouse in West Fifty-fourth Street, but we had arranged to give this up and move into another apartment in the same building which was less spectacular, and more suited to our needs and my budget. However, this would not be available until September. Knowing how much Gertrude loved space and country walks, and how important these were to her well-being when she was working very hard, I proposed leasing a house on Long Island and moving into it until Gertrude's play closed and we could go up to Dennis for the summer.

Gertrude fell in with the plan. The winter at Ballybrook Farm was to be our belated honeymoon. I made efforts to arrange my work so as to be able to do part of it at home.

The house belonged to Mr. and Mrs. Henry Alexander. Gertrude had been entertained there with the Duke of Windsor and his party when, as Prince of Wales, he made an American tour. It was exactly the sort of country house Gertrude loved: white, spacious, homelike, built in colonial days. The grounds were extensive and wooded; handsome even in winter. Mackie, in the gold-trimmed collar which his mistress had lovingly wrapped and tied on the Christmas tree for him, inspected the shrubberies and expressed approval.

Gertrude and Mackie went for daily brisk walks and runs through the gardens, while I pleaded business letters to dictate or scripts to read. Gertrude said regretfully that I was not the hearty, sports-loving type she had hoped for; my size had deceived her. But though she pretended to have accepted these deficiencies of mine with graceful resignation, actually she never stopped trying to turn me into a tennis-golf-squash-playing champion swimmer, skier and surf-boat rider.

Another ideal of hers which I obdurately refused to live up to, and which died hard, was that of the leisurely pipe-smoking country gentleman. It did no good to point out to Gertrude that I was not a smoker. In several trips to Dunhill's, she laid in all the equipment calculated to lure me into becoming a pipe addict. Pipes and handsome jars filled with the most expensive tobaccos were placed within reach of all the chairs I showed any tendency to sit in. From time to time the collection was augmented. For years she periodically emptied and replenished the tobacco jars, with pathetic hopefulness. "If only you would become a smoker, it would be so much easier to know what to give you," she would sigh when Christmas or my birthday drew near.

It was years before her patience became exhausted. Then, one day, I found her dumping all the tobacco from the jars into a large biscuit tin. She had bundled up the pipes as well.

"One of the stage hands at the St. James Theatre smokes a stumpy little pipe as he works," she said. "It has a frightful smell. I'm going to give him all this good tobacco and the pipes you spurn. Somebody might as well enjoy them."

All the time we were at Ballybrook Farm, she longed to see me in perfectly fitted tweeds, pipe in mouth, gun under arm, strolling about the place. Not that she ever wanted any living creature shot; but the gun was an indispensable part of the picture. The stroll over, she would have liked me to lounge in front of the open fire, wearing the needlepoint slippers which she was busily making for me, and a brocaded silk smoking jacket. I found one hanging in my closet one day as a hint.

Another of her domestic concerns was my diet. She was always trying, openly or by subterfuge, to get me to "Eat up." My predilection for ice cream and homemade chocolate cake in preference to French soufflés, Hollandaise sauce and lobster mousse she condoned as a hangover from childhood. But my steadfast refusal to become a morning tea-drinker she took as a personal affront. If I discouraged some impractical scheme of hers or failed to share one of her sudden high enthusiasms, she would fling at me: "What can you expect of a man who fills himself up with *cold milk?*"

One part of the farm we both avoided. This was the road leading to a large, empty carriage house. There was a forbidding gloominess about the building which was sufficient to make me shun it even if I had not known its tragic associations.

Several years before our tenancy the carriage house had been the scene of the suicide of a beautiful society actress, who reportedly killed herself out of hopeless love for a man well known in the theatre. Although Gertrude was acquainted with both principals in the tragedy, she was in England when it occurred and there was no reason to believe she knew where it had happened. I warned several of our guests against mentioning it. Apparently none did, because her delight in the estate continued through the five months of our lease.

Ours was not a selfish honeymoon. Pam would come to see us, sometimes bringing her young Doctor Bill. They planned to be married after his graduation that summer. Gertrude had decreed that the wedding should take place at Dennis, and already was deep in plans.

Old friends of ours sometimes came down for the night and part of the next day. Only matinee days were strictly guarded, since on these days Gertrude followed a special schedule. Once in her dressing room, Gertrude stayed there until her evening performance was over; her lunch and dinner, both light, were served her there.

After the day-and-night of work she would be weary and ravenous. At such times there was nothing she enjoyed more than steak tartare—the chopped raw beefsteak mixed with chopped green onion and a whole raw egg favored by stars of grand opera after an exhausting performance. With this she would drink a tankard of Canadian ale.

I would watch her put away this hearty—and to me repulsive—bloody provender with an awe bordering on horror. Being one of those brought up to regard any meat that shows a tinge of red as unfit for human consumption ("Take it back to the kitchen," Father would roar at the terrified waitress if a single drop of ruddy juice oozed from under the stroke of his carving knife. And to my mother: "Why do we keep that woman in the kitchen, Mollie, except to *cook?*"), it came as somewhat of a shock to discover that the exquisite, ethereal creature, which was the public's idea of Gertrude Lawrence, could put away a meal I had hitherto associated only with ponderous Brunhildes and the drivers of transcontinental trucks.

Blessed by nature with a healthy appetite and a digestion to match, her figure remained the same, no matter what she ate. She was able to wear the riding habit which had been made for her in 1932 over the next two decades.

* * *

Sundays were set apart for the family. When we first talked of renting the Long Island place, Gertrude had said: "We can have your boys with us. They'll adore it. And it will be so good for them to be in the country."

By the terms of my divorce I was allowed to see my children whenever I wished and have them with me six months of the year. As they were very young when their mother and I separated, it had seemed best for them to make their permanent home with her and her second husband, Wing Commander Edward Corballis. A well-traveled Englishman, educated at Sandhurst, Teddy Corballis was the type of man I would wish my sons to be with when they could not be with me. He and Helen were always amenable to my seeing the boys at their apartment. Before I married Gertrude I had been in the habit of dropping in at the Corballises' several times a week late in the afternoon to spend an hour with Dick and David before their early supper. On Sundays I sometimes took them to the zoo or to the American Museum of Natural History.

In all this Helen and I were following the behavior pattern established by other divorced couples of our generation. We were inclined to pride ourselves on our courteous tolerance of each other, once the marriage tie against which one or both had chafed was dissolved. When we happened to meet on the street, we would walk a block or two together. Only one thing betrayed us: our conversation was always in the present tense. We had no future.

It was an article of our code that the children should not suffer. To this end, each parent was honor-bound not to mention the other. Questions about the past were discouraged. I now realize that on those afternoon visits it must have struck Dick and David that I put in my appearances with the jerky, unrelated suddenness of a puppet, let down in the entr'acte to speak his lines, do his tricks, and exit on cue. That I had an environment, a life and people to whom I belonged, all of which, being mine, were also theirs, was something I am sure never entered my sons' minds.

When did Gertrude begin to plan to share our life with Dick and David? I do not know; but plan it she did, quietly, unobtrusively and as creatively as she planned any step in her career.

In that plan there was no intention of wooing the boys from their mother; or from their stepfather, of whom they were extremely fond, as he was of them. In fact, Gertrude was always at particular pains not to compete with Helen for the boys' affection. She never presented herself to them in a maternal role, but as an understanding, amusing companion. I am sure that no tribute in her entire career meant more to her than the love they gave her.

Soon after we took the Long Island house she suggested to me that we ask the boys to spend their Sundays with us. When I said I would like this, she proposed to meet Helen in town and talk it over with her. "I don't want her to think I am trying to wean the children away from her." She was unfailingly punctilious about not interfering in Helen's plans for the boys or with any schedule or discipline that Helen and their stepfather had instituted.

So it came about quite gradually and naturally that Helen and Gertrude should discuss amicably matters relating to my sons' welfare and happiness. Largely because of Gertrude's wholesome and realistic approach to the problems involved, I am sure neither she nor Helen was ever jealous of one another. All of us were determined on one thing—the boys should never feel pulled by one set of parents away from the other.

Gertrude could not help anticipating Christmas and making the boys the center of her plans for the season. This immediately evoked the question: what about Helen and Teddy? And their son, little Edward Corballis, whom my boys loved? All these were Dick and David's true family as much as Gertrude and I were.

Gertrude—and I, when she brought the problem to my attention—felt that one of the best things we could do for my sons was to give them the experience and the memory of happy, harmonious family Christmases. There should be no struggling of one set of parents against the other, no invidious comparisons, no criticisms and resentments. So it came about, at Gertrude's instigation but wholeheartedly accepted and encouraged by Helen and her husband, that starting with Christmas, 1941, the three Corballises and Dick and David, whenever possible, shared our Christmas Eve party and our Christmas tree.

There were a few people who appeared startled and somewhat shocked by the apparently congenial gathering in which former marital relations and differences were forgotten or ignored for the sake of the children and the spirit of the feast we were celebrating. But this innovation came to be accepted by our relations and intimate friends as something which we adults did for the sake of the children. And, too, because doing it was good for all of us.

The festivities began Christmas Eve in our living room, which was dominated by the tree, on which Gertrude had hung a gift for every one, with a humorous, often rhymed message written in her own hand. Next day we dined at the Corballises'.

The tradition of Christmas as a time for family and close friends, for quiet singing of carols at intimate gatherings, was always deeply important to Gertrude. To ensure that no one of her scores of friends throughout the world should be overlooked, her Christmas shopping was a year-round affair that began in January and mounted into a vast pile by December. Each gift was wrapped by Gertrude and accompanied by a personal note.

She enjoyed Christmas parties with the fresh enthusiasm of a child wherever they were held—at home, on tour, in Europe. Always she insisted on putting the last-minute touches to the tree and supper herself; always her voice led us in "The First Noel." And when the party was over, she would go about the room tidying up, still singing.

"I can't bear leaving things in a mess," she would reply to my call to come to bed. "A Christmas party is so lovely it shouldn't be allowed to peter out in a lot of debris."

In setting aside our Sundays at Ballybrook for the boys' visits, Gertrude planned menus of their favorite dishes and provided gadgets to entertain them. Although we did not invite friends for the week-end, Pam was always welcome, as were Barbara and Harrison; sometimes the three turned up together.

More than once I caught my sister looking at me quizzically to see if I enjoyed these stay-at-home Sundays which were so different from the life I had lived since coming to New York, and were curiously—though pleasantly—reminiscent of our Sundays at Northfield as children.

These were only one of a number of changes which marriage to Gertrude had introduced into my life. Not all the changes were as easy to adjust to. Take dinner, for instance. Being married to an actress means that you no longer dine in leisure at seven or seven-thirty. You do not dine at all—at least, not with your wife. On most days Gertrude ate lunch, exercised out-of-doors, slept from four to six, had tea and left for the theatre at the time I had been accustomed to start my evening.

Dining out with friends was now a thing of the past. Cocktail parties came at the wrong hour. Through the first year of our marriage I was constantly, and not always successfully, trying to find a happy medium between the kind of day I had been accustomed to, and which business would not let me drop completely, and the schedule which Gertrude had to keep.

Though I sorely disappointed her in refusing to play the role of country gentleman, she persisted for a long time in playing the devoted little English wife, despite my efforts at discouragement. I would find she had spent a morning rearranging the contents of my bureau drawers and my closet. According to her ideas of arrangement, not mine. I would look for a suit or an overcoat and not find it. Gertrude had decided it should go to the cleaners, or to the tailor for repairs. Any man knows this sort of thing can provoke a quarrel out of all proportion to its importance. After a few such experiences I laid down a law: no one was to touch my clothes and personal possessions but myself. I had never had a valet and I had never wished for one. Still less did I want my wife to wait on me.

The order held until I had to go out of town one day on sudden notice. I rang up to tell Gertrude I would be home to pick up my bag and drive to the airport. When I arrived, with fifteen minutes to spare, I found her in a swirl of tissue paper, packing two large suitcases with enough of my clothes to see me around the world.

I hate unnecessary luggage, and tissue paper stuffed into my clothes infuriates me. Besides, this tissue paper was perfumed.

Before I could stop, I found myself shouting at Gertrude.

She started as if I had shot her.

"Why can't you leave my things alone?" I stormed.

She burst into tears.

At the risk of missing my plane connections I sat down and drew her into my arms. I had the embarrassing feeling that I was playing in a comedy written by Noel Coward. It was all too silly for any but the cleverest lines. And I did not know them.

Presently Gertrude sat up, sniffed, wiped her eyes on my handkerchief and said resolutely, "All right. I've learned my lesson. I'll never do it again."

She never did.

I knew I was forgiven when, in the midst of a business conference the next day, I was handed this telegram:

DEAR MR. A WHEN YOU'RE AWAY MY LIFE IS JUST A MUDDLE SO FOR YOUR PLAY HERE'S A HIP HOORAY SINCERELY MRS. PUDDLE

Not quite so quickly healed was our quarrel over the gun.

Among the chief delights of Sunday for Gertrude were the advertisement-filled newspapers. She went through them page by page, scissors and pencil in hand. Whatever caught her fancy—and how easily it was caught—was clipped, and a note made for one of the girls at the Holtzmann law office who did various errands for her.

At first I was appalled by the number of things she was ordering —gadgets for the kitchen, the garden, the house, a cocktail tray that played "Drink to Me Only" when you took a glass from it, boxes and bags for closets, china, glass and linen. Then I discovered that a conspiracy existed involving Gertrude's personal maid, Dorothy; her dresser, Hazel; and the Holtzmann office. None of the orders for expensive items was sent to the shops. This was found to be practical because Gertrude seldom remembered after Monday what she had thought indispensable on Sunday. If she did wonder aloud why some object had not been delivered, Dorothy or Hazel would offer to call up the Holtzmann office and inquire about it. This was always effective in ending Gertrude's interest in the matter.

It was part of her agreement with the Holtzmanns that she

would make no purchases without their O.K., except those she paid for out of her weekly allowance. But sometimes she would evade this and order things to be sent C.O.D. to Mrs. Richard Aldrich. To forestall the maneuver, I gave orders that no C.O.D.'s were to be accepted.

One day Gertrude confronted me in a high rage. "Who gave orders that my purchases were to be returned?"

She had seen an advertisement of a rifle which struck her at once as exactly what was needed to lure me into sportsman's tweeds. She wrote Abercrombie and Fitch to send the gun C.O.D., planning to give it to me as a present for St. Valentine's Day. When it failed to arrive, she rang up the shop and made inquiries, only to be told that two attempts had been made to deliver the rifle, and in each case it had been refused.

It took me some time to make her see—longer to get her to admit—that she was quibbling with a financial agreement which was in existence before our marriage and which she had promised me to observe.

"Well, you've done yourself out one present and a lot more," she said finally. "Always Right Aldrich."

The name, coined in that moment, became her retort whenever she resented what she felt was my interference with her pet projects.

These frequently involved giving presents—a favorite delight of Gertrude's. Every holiday became an excuse for sending messages and presents to those she loved. Until our marriage I had been unaware of Valentine's Day, St. Patrick's Day, Hallowe'en, etc., except as these brought out a rash of appropriate favors in the candy and flower shops. Now they and the greater feasts were marked on my calendar. That this sort of thing is infectious I found when I turned up at the Hobarts' one February fourteenth with a heart-shaped box of candy. My sister looked at me with such astonishment that I said quickly, thrusting the box at her, "It's Valentine's Day."

"It's the millennium!" Barbara exclaimed. "I knew Gertrude Lawrence was wonderful but I never knew how wonderful till this minute. If only Father and Uncle Sam could see you now!"

When Gertrude was on tour her zest for giving and sending presents mounted. Every mail brought packages from the cities she played in. Seeds, plants for the garden, gadgets for the house flowed in until I would send an admonitory wire to her company manager, Jack Potter, to try to keep Gertrude in bounds. Whenever she opened in a new play she would say to him and to Hazel: "Don't tell Richard or the Holtzmanns, but make a list of all the stage hands and their families, particularly the children. And any grandparents." She kept a list of the birthdays of the stage crew and she never failed in their observance. When members of their families were sick or their children graduated from school, Hazel was supposed to tell her in order that she might send appropriate gifts.

No matter how much affection Gertrude lavished on the human beings within her orbit, there was always an abundant surplus left over for other living things. It was a never-ending temptation to her to increase her circle of animal friends.

Thus, shortly before Easter, I returned home to Ballybrook late from an out-of-town trip. When I switched on the light in my bathroom I was greeted by excited quacks and splashings. Two ducks were very much at home in my tub. Someone had thoughtfully arranged for them a beach of bath towels and provided a mass of revolting mushy vegetable matter.

My objections showed a lamentable want of scientific curiosity, Gertrude complained. Didn't I want to study ducks as Eckstein studied canaries, pigeons, and cockroaches?

"No," I retorted, adding that there was a comfortable suite at the other end of the corridor which either the ducks or I would occupy that night and thereafter. Gertrude could decide which of us was to make the move.

As Easter drew nearer and her plans for entertaining the boys progressed, I adjured her, "No rabbits. And if I come home and find a baby lamb in my bed, I'll send it to the butcher. This business of pets has to stop somewhere."

She may have remembered my threat about the lamb. When, some time later, Constance Bennett gave her a lamb at the Cape as a birthday-anniversary present, she secreted it for one night in her bedroom. It bleated so piteously no one slept. Next morning, she had her chauffeur drive it back to the farm it came from.

At breakfast on Sunday mornings, Winnie and Franklin would join us. Gertrude would open the cage and the birds would come out to perch on her finger, eager for the toast crumbs she offered them.

"There's a good deal of the show-off in Franklin," she would comment, watching him preen before a mirror. When Franklin felt our attention wandering, he would burst into brilliant song.

Winnie's blandishments were less spectacular. He would snuggle against Gertrude's neck, chuckling fondly as though confiding his heart's secrets—a tactic that earned him thickly buttered crumbs, which he pecked from Gertrude's lips. He grew fatter, more pompous and more spoiled with every week.

On one of David's visits, at Gertrude's invitation, he brought his canary. The object was to introduce Henry to Winnie and Franklin. Gertrude and David, standing by, pencil in hand, were prepared to take down all the reactions and to report these to Dr. Eckstein.

The reactions were immediate. They left no doubt in my mind that Henry should be rechristened Henriette. Franklin's interest in Henriette, however, was short-lived. He withdrew in favor of Winnie, an arrangement which seemed to suit Henriette. Winnie and Henriette settled down to domesticity, with Franklin, a rather bored and condescending bachelor uncle, sharing the roost with them. David proved amenable to the suggestion that he leave his friend with us in confident hope of raising a "family of canaries." The fact that we had arranged for him and Dick to spend the summer on the Cape at a camp near Dennis may have had something to do with it. So had a growing interest in airplanes which Gertrude abetted by giving him *Jane's Flying Ships* with this inscription:

Dear David:

Flying without feathers is not easy, but someone once said (I think it was a certain Bishop Wilkins) that the time would come when gentlemen, when they were to go on a journey, would call for their wings as simply as they would call for their boots. (Somewhere around 1800.)

Here's the record up to date for your digestion.

Bless you, David, and may peace come soon to our world!

Gertrude

Only the canaries saved us from one or several kittens. When Barbara telephoned that the Hobart family now included seven pure-bred Siamese, I saw an acquisitive gleam in my wife's eye. I reminded her quickly of her duty to our feathered ménage. Besides, hadn't she said, in persuading Barbara to take the cats, that there was a market for pedigreed kittens? She wouldn't want to do Barbara out of a good thing.

She contented herself by going to call on the new arrivals, bearing offerings in the shape of flowers and a bottle of fine cognac.

"The stage doorman says you should put a few drops in the milk for nursing mother cats," she informed Barbara.

"Without being a stage doorman I can think of a lot better uses for aged Courvoisier," my sister replied. "Wally will do very well on a half pint of California brandy."

* * *

"Darling, it was a lovely honeymoon," Gertrude said, when we drove away from the house on our last day. Her play had closed the night before and we were starting for the Cape for a holiday.

"Was there anything you would have had different?" I asked.

"Not a thing." She breathed deeply. "But, darling, now that we're leaving Ballybrook, I can tell you. All the time we were there I was terribly worried you would find out and hate the place. You know that deserted carriage house. . . ."

"I know," I retorted, "that I have married the most wonderful woman in the world: one who can know something and not tell it."

Fonssagrives

My wife, with several of her animal friends—Mackie, two ducklings, and the Siamese cats, Wally and David.

Town and Country
Fonssagrives

Gertrude as the "Lady in the D
—with Danny Kaye in the b
ground.

Bob Golby

Her singing of "Jenny" won the song nation-wide popularity.

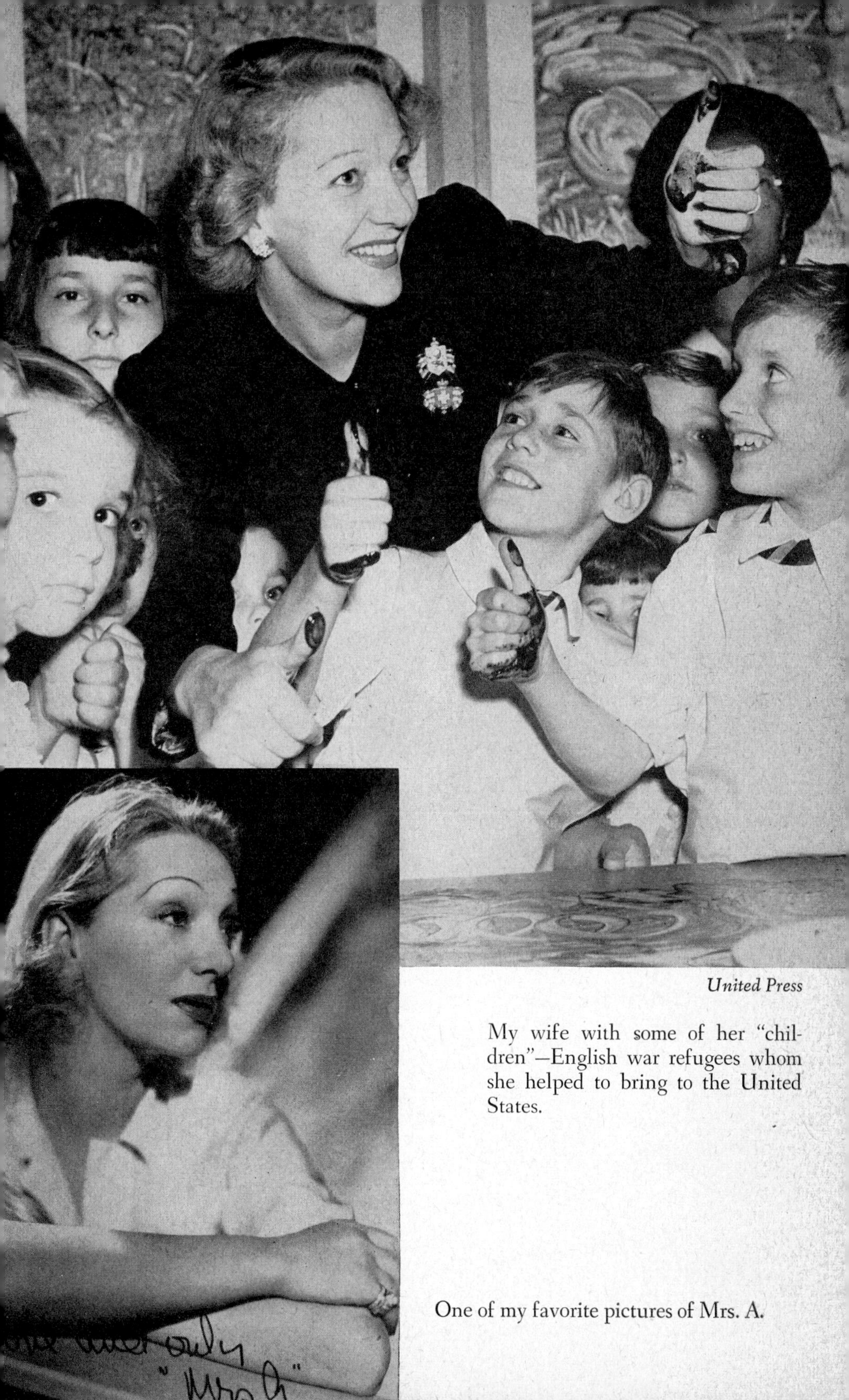

United Press

My wife with some of her "children"—English war refugees whom she helped to bring to the United States.

One of my favorite pictures of Mrs. A.

Fonssagrives

Gertrude loved the country, and was always trying to lure me into playing the part of a country squire.

"I *adore* the wheelbarrow picture!" she wrote. "Hope you don't think you can push me around anywhere you please, though! Or can you?"

Chapter Eight

GERTRUDE AND MY MOTHER had met at last. Twice.

Neither meeting was propitious. The net result was a stiff silence on the part of each whenever the other was mentioned.

My mother was accustomed to making a short visit every winter to her brother and sister, Uncle Jim and Aunt Alice, at their New York home on Perry Street. Though Mother preferred Boston as a city, she felt that New York offered certain advantages in the way of concerts, lectures and missionary meetings. When she came, she would also enjoy talking about the state of religion with Bishop Welch of the Methodist Church, who was Uncle Jim's brother-in-law.

In addition, I think she felt that it devolved upon her, as head of the family, to keep an eye on Aunt Alice's increasing devotion to spiritualism. The three Joys had grown up during the eighties, when a craze for Ouija boards, table rapping and clairvoyance swept New England. But while Uncle Jim and my mother had dismissed these parlor games, Aunt Alice, in later years and especially since the death of her husband, had taken them up again; seriously. Her cheery remark one morning at the breakfast table: "Mollie, Ed Aldrich just came in. He looks extremely well and he thinks we should sell the Fitchburg property," drew from my mother the retort that her husband, alive or dead, would have the good taste to stay where he belonged and leave the living to manage their own affairs without interference.

I had planned to have Mother spend the first Sunday of her visit at Ballybrook, where the two Mrs. Aldriches would meet in favorable circumstances and—I dared hope—discover qualities in each other to respect and ultimately to love. However, this plan did not work out, because Mother chose on this particular visit to stay with Barbara.

Barbara suggested that Mother should see the Saturday matinee of *Lady in the Dark* and be taken backstage to meet Gertrude after the show. I had grave misgivings about the choice of the meeting place. Mother's disapproval of the theatre was so strong that she had once confiscated an article about me as a producer which she found displayed on the Groton Public Library table. Still, I thought that she might be impressed by the regard in which Gertrude was held by her audience. With difficulty, I was able to secure a pair of seats in the second row, which she was to use with Uncle Jim.

Unfortunately, since these were "house seats" reserved for Gertrude, she learned of the arrangements a day or so before the performance. I do not think that until that moment even she was fully aware of how much she wanted my mother to like her. From then on, she became increasingly concerned about the impression her performance would make on her mother-in-law. In particular, she wondered and worried about her big number in the second act—"Jenny"—in which the repressed Lady in the Dark loses all her inhibitions and sings with the abandon of a burlesque queen. For Gertrude's theatre following, who associated her with the brittle sophisticated comedy of Noel Coward, low-down "Jenny" was the high spot of the show. But what would it be for Mother, who had never before been exposed to the dazzle and glitter of a Broadway musical?

Mother arrived early with Uncle Jim. She had not come to disapprove. With the best of good-will she had worn her favorite dress and had her hair fixed for the occasion.

As the audience came into the theatre, however, she and Uncle

Jim felt more and more out of their element—quite lonesome and apart. Sitting so close to the stage, the two elderly Joys were bewildered by the glare of the lights and the blare of the orchestra in the pit a few feet away. When the curtain went up on a scene which portrayed the fast-talking, wisecracking staff of a smart New York magazine, Mother was completely baffled. She reacted as she would have to an unorthodox sermon: by fixing her gaze straight ahead with impassive dignity. Uncle Jim, equally mystified by these unfamiliar theatrical goings-on, followed suit.

It was this dismaying picture that met Gertrude's gaze as, a moment after her entrance, she looked across the footlights. More than a little upset, she made a point of playing directly to Mother and Uncle Jim on her next comedy line. There was no reaction.

As the play went on, and Gertrude kept searching Mother's face for a sign of approval that never appeared, Gertrude became increasingly nervous. Her usually spontaneous performance became subdued and self-conscious.

A desultory clapping of hands at the end of her second song made Gertrude realize what was happening. Her audience had, as she put it later, almost "gone dead" on her. In her futile attempt to get a response from Mother, she was disappointing the hundreds of others who crowded the theatre.

This realization acted on her like a bracer. What was one woman —even her husband's mother—compared to all those who had come to be entertained? She could not let them down.

Nor did she. From that instant her mood changed. As her self-control returned, her pride in her ability to enchant audiences mounted. Once again, she became the star instead of the daughter-in-law. When the moment came for "Jenny" she slid off her swing and went into the number with a verve that made her audience tingle. The performance, which had gotten off to such a bad start, ended in triumph.

I had hoped to meet Mother at the end of the performance, but I was delayed in traffic. In my place, Jack Potter brought the two visitors backstage. They were escorted through the group of friends and fans who always clustered around Gertrude's door after a show, and the two Mrs. Aldriches, each in her own way equally frightened, met face to face.

Gertrude greeted her two visitors and asked, "And how did you like the show?"

Uncle Jim was the first to speak. His comment was, "I didn't hear a word of it."

Gertrude, who prided herself on her diction, hid her disappointment. She turned to look inquiringly at Mother. "And did you enjoy the play?"

Mother hesitated briefly before she answered, "The music was very nice but I didn't quite get the play's message."

The conversation was at this impasse—which Hazel was attempting to surmount by offering the guests some champagne—when, fortunately, I arrived. I headed Hazel off and hustled Mother and Uncle Jim into a taxi and to tea at the Plaza, explaining that Gertrude had to nap before her evening show.

Away from the strangeness of the theatre, Mother confided to me that she found Gertrude "quite vivacious." As for Uncle Jim, it was some months before he told me he would like to see the show again. "I didn't hear a word, that first time, because the battery in my hearing aid went dead!"

On the following afternoon—Sunday—Barbara had invited all the family to tea. When Gertrude came downstairs, ready to drive into town with me to the Hobarts', she was dressed with ostentatious demureness in a tailored navy blue suit and a small, plain hat. She was wearing no jewelry. Her only ornament was the British War Relief emblem, which she wore constantly and proudly in those days. A similar emblem was pinned to my lapel.

I saw Mother's eyes go to my emblem in the first moment of our meeting. And from it to the gold wrist watch and seal ring which had been Gertrude's Christmas gifts to me.

"What has come over you, Richard?" Mother asked. "I never saw you blazing with jewelry before."

I started to draw off the ring to show her the Joy crest engraved on it. Gertrude had conspired with Barbara to get the design for Cartier's. Mother stopped me.

"You are entitled to wear that. But that badge on your coat. It would be better to remove it."

To placate her, I unfastened the emblem and was about to drop it into my pocket.

"Richard!" Gertrude's voice rang out. "If you take that off I'll never forgive you." She turned to Mother with the mien of an affronted Britannia. In her deepest, most resonant tone she said: "You and Richard may be entitled to wear your family crest. The coat of arms of England is MY crest. I wear it with pride. And I expect my husband to do so, too."

Mother was effectively silenced. I refastened the emblem. Barbara asked hastily who would take milk and who preferred lemon.

Characteristically, Gertrude instantly regretted the explosion. To atone, she began explaining to Mother that the "badge" was that of the British War Relief organization, of which she was an officer. To prove that wearing it in no way contaminated my standing as a Mayflower descendant, she informed Mother that B.W.R.S. was headed in the United States by Mr. Winthrop Aldrich, "one of your distant cousins."

This remark brought back to my mind a quip reputedly made at the time of our marriage by one of the cleverest of Gertrude's circle of friends: "Gertie got the wrong Aldrich. She thought she was marrying Winthrop."

If Gertrude had not known of the distinction between the Aldriches then, Mother lost no time in setting her straight. Though an Aldrich only by marriage, and strongly convinced of the superiority of her own line of Joys and Pickerings, Mother was too loyal a daughter of the Commonwealth not to share the sentiment of her husband's family. She declared crisply that the Aldrich who deserted the Massachusetts Bay Colony and the strict tenets of Puritanism back in 1650 or thereabouts, to become a dangerous liberal with Roger Williams and the Rhode Island Baptists and Quakers, was a renegade. His descendants, no matter how prosperous and illustrious, could not be considered the equals of our pure Massachusetts stock.

Gertrude's bewildered expression revealed that she had become hopelessly lost in the tangle of New England tradition and prejudice which Mother spread before her.

"But, darling, I thought she'd be pleased," Gertrude said to me later, when we were on our way home. "I don't understand."

"Don't try to," I advised. "Nobody can understand who wasn't born in Massachusetts." I explained that foreigners were always expecting Americans to be as free from bigotry and pride of family or place as the noblest statements of our noblest minds would indicate. Our failure to live up to these high standards too frequently puzzled and disappointed visitors from other lands. It was better, I advised, to take us as you found us. And not too seriously.

The rapport which I had hoped would be established between my mother and my wife stubbornly refused to sprout. Each of their meetings had resulted in a draw. I was relieved when I saw Mother off on the twelve o'clock, bound for Groton.

Curiously enough, it was through Uncle Jim, and quite by accident, that the first breach in Mother's wall of hostility was made. Since our collaboration on the problem of the orphans, Uncle Jim had formed the habit of dropping into my office on his way to the Yale Club. His prestige there, he told me, had gone up appreciably since he had become known as Gertrude Lawrence's uncle by marriage. Members who formerly had only nodded, now made sure to stop and say they had just seen and enjoyed *Lady in the Dark*.

Uncle Jim was amused but not deeply affected by his new popularity. Then, one day, he told me that, the evening before, he had dined with his old college roommate, Dr. George Vincent, President of the Rockefeller Institute. Dr. Vincent warmly congratulated him on my marriage; he said that he had once spent a week-end at a celebrated English country house where Gertrude had also been a guest. He had been quite impressed by the regard shown her by their distinguished hosts.

"I never quite realized," Uncle Jim concluded, "how honored we should feel to have Gertrude in the family. Nor has your mother. I really must tell her what Dr. Vincent said when I go to Groton next week."

Later that spring, when we visited Groton, it was evident that Uncle Jim had performed his mission—perhaps too well. As we entered the house, Mother greeted Gertrude graciously, but with ceremony—I might almost say with a respect which widened rather than bridged the gulf between them.

In anticipation of our visit, the house had more than been put in order; the old furniture was polished till it glowed, silver candlesticks and vases I hadn't seen for years had been brought out to shine with a new lustre. Flowers from the garden filled the room with festive color. Gertrude was charmed.

"Oh," she exclaimed, "what a lovely home this is!"

"Thank you," Mother replied, "but I'm sure it doesn't compare to the stately old castles you're accustomed to."

"Oh, but this is so much warmer! Everything here looks so intimate, so *contented*—each piece *belongs* in its place. And oh, what a beautiful old clock," she declared enthusiastically as we went into the hall.

"That is my Grandfather Joy's clock."

"Each piece looks as though it has had loving care throughout the years," Gertrude continued.

"Yes," Mother answered, "they do take a lot of care. This clock has brass trimmings which must be polished regularly. It has to be oiled and checked—the mahogany waxed and rubbed just so . . ."

She turned to Gertrude. "But of course you wouldn't be interested in such details, Miss Lawrence—"

"Of course I am interested in such things," Gertrude broke in—rather sharply, I felt. "I am afraid you are laboring under a misapprehension concerning my luxurious background. I have been working since I was a child actress. The fifteen shillings a week that I brought home to Mother and Dad kept us in bread and tea and sausage. I've done my share of housework—and still do. Mother was not one to let me 'get above myself,' as she put it. She made me clean and scrub when I was home, and polish the grate and do the brights and learn to appreciate a tidy home. Oh, I have never regretted that; when I see a home such as this I know what it means."

Inadvertently, Gertrude had said the very thing that could not fail to win Mother's approval. That someone accepted by great and important people should also glory in lowly honest labor, and not be ashamed of her humble origins, satisfied Mother's notion of aristocracy, which was founded on the ideals of Concord's sage.

From that moment, the thaw set in.

* * *

"Let's make it a family summer," Gertrude had said.

In that summer of 1941, by virtue of a clause that Fanny had insisted on inserting in her contract, Gertrude could look forward to a ten-week vacation from her role in *Lady in the Dark.*

Her hunger for a family, for the feeling of belonging to a secure group in which the personal relationships were firmly established, was strong. It revealed how unsatisfied she was with her former butterfly existence.

I had agreed. We rented the same large house at Dennis which Gertrude had leased the previous summer, and moved up—pets, servants and children, including two British boys from the Actors' Orphanage.

"It will do all the children good to get to know one another," Gertrude said when she proposed it. "I chose the brothers, Ernest and Christopher Gifford, because they are the same age as our boys. It will be fine for them to play together and learn to understand each other. It will be an experiment in Anglo-American friendship—like our marriage."

Her personal concern for the orphans had not lessened since their establishment at the Gould Foundation. Besides her weekly visits, she had made a point of finding out each child's birthday. She arranged to have a Western Union messenger deliver a singing telegram to the child at a festive birthday tea.

Our first week on the Cape was dedicated to Pamela's wedding. The house was filled with a mist of bridal white, flowers, presents, sentimental music and young love. I gave my stepdaughter away, and Gertrude played Mother of the Bride in silver gray by Hattie Carnegie and a medley of tears and smiles which only April could rival.

Gertrude's love for Pam was never entirely freed from the anguish she had suffered during the child's infancy. As I pieced the story together later from what was told me by several of Gertrude's old friends—Bea Lillie, André Charlot, and others—Pamela had come into the world prematurely, just when her parents were finding it impossible to continue their life together. Their relationship was not helped by the fact that Gertrude was attracting flattering notices in a successful West End revue while her husband, who had been a stage manager for twenty years, was out of work.

In order to meet the heavy expenses of Pamela's special care in the nursing home where she was born, Gertrude had to rush back to work in Charlot's *From A to Z*. When Gertrude refused to continue to support her husband in addition to supporting the baby, he took advantage of the English law which gives the guardianship of the child to its father. He took Pamela from the nursing home, and removed her to some place unknown to Gertrude.

For weeks Gertrude went on singing and dancing every night. Her days were spent in an agonizing search for her child, making inquiries at police stations and hospitals—anywhere she might find some trace or clue of her daughter.

One night at the theatre she received a terse telegram:

CHILD DESPERATELY ILL NEEDS YOU MEET ME
AT USUAL PLACE FRANK

When they met after her performance, he told Gertrude that the baby was back in the nursing home but he could not pay for its support. If Gertrude would advance him some money he promised to leave her and Pam forever. She emptied her purse—six pounds and a few odd shillings. In anticipation of a demand for money, she had paid a visit to a friendly pawnbroker on her way to the rendezvous. The money-lender had refused to accept the security she offered when he learned she needed the money for a sick child.

Her husband swept the cash into his pocket, shrugged his shoulders and went out of her life.

From that moment Pamela became the center about which Gertrude's plans and ambitions revolved. The little girl's frailty was a constant source of anxiety. Neither the climate of London nor that of New York suited her. As soon as she could afford it, Gertrude engaged a French nursery governess to supervise the child's daily life. Mademoiselle continued to look after Pam until she went to boarding school.

The progress of Gertrude's career prevented her from being her daughter's companion except during holidays. She always regretted this. On some pages of yellow pad paper she had jotted down in pencil some observations on the subject of motherhood and careers. These began with a quotation from Wilde's *A Woman of No Importance*: "Children begin by loving their parents. After a time they judge them. Rarely, if ever, do they forgive them."

"What happens," Gertrude wrote, "if the failure of a too hasty marriage leaves a woman with the responsibility of a young child to support?

"If she decides to fight her battle alone and give her child all the advantages and good times in life, including a top-drawer education which she hopes will enable the child to grow up and face the world with confidence and poise, how is she to execute these good intentions?

"There is only one way; she must sacrifice the natural longings of her heart and substitute for motherhood a career.

"As the years pass, this career mother sees less and less of her child, who, in turn, receives a high education at the expense of close affection.

"Children are honest and critical and inclined to compare their own lives with those of their schoolmates. Thus this child feels lonely and thrust aside, and judges her mother without justification. What the mother deems necessary travail and toil, the child regards as indifference, neglect, and in some cases even a light-hearted means of thrusting her into the dim background of her mother's life. From this point she begins to condemn and not to forgive. She cannot realize that her career mother may regret the years which have been lost and which she can never explain to the child without it sounding like an appeal for gratitude.

"One wonders whether the years apart can ever be bridged by these two people. One can only hope that they will grow into intelligent and close companions later on. . . ."

And in one of her early diaries, when she was taking stock at the beginning of a new year, she wrote: "When the shouting is all over, my child is all I have."

From the moment of Pam's birth, Gertrude began putting money aside for the child's future security. She continued doing this even after Pam was married, investing in war bonds for her daughter out of her personal spending money.

A gold-framed photograph of Pamela as a four-year-old with enormous dark eyes, clinging to her mother, always stood on the table beside Gertrude's bed. It went with her wherever she traveled. A duplicate stood on her dressing table in the theatre. After Pam was married, a photograph of her as a bride took its place next to each of the others.

* * *

Our neighbors in Dennis were the Hydes—Dr. Fritz and Dr. Harriet. We had been friends since I had first come to the Cape. Dr. Harriet, a sister of Mrs. Ruth Baker Pratt, New York's first congresswoman, was a native Cape Codder whose grandfather had married a Hartwell. This, she announced with characteristic authoritativeness, made us distant cousins. She promptly removed the distance by giving me the freedom of their big house and private beach, both overflowing all summer long with children and grandchildren.

Theirs was the first home I took Gertrude to after our marriage. The warmth of their reception to Gertrude—not because she was a celebrity, but for herself—did much to atone for the chill which emanated from Groton in those days.

Dr. Fritz Hyde, shy, sensitive, loving the arts as much as his chosen field of surgery, presented a striking contrast to the vigorous, extrovert wife he had adored since their meeting at medical school more than forty years before.

"She's like an English duchess," Gertrude said. "Nothing happens in Dennis among the all-the-year-round residents that Dr. Harriet doesn't know within an hour. This is her domain. She feels responsible for everyone living on it, physically and spiritually.

Fortunately for darling Dr. Fritz, he has his studio and can escape to it when Dr. Harriet's vitality becomes overpowering."

Gertrude's immediate comprehension of Dr. Fritz and Dr. Harriet became the basis of a strong tie with each of them. In later summers Gertrude accepted Dr. Fritz's invitation to visit his studio while he painted. "My Fritz," she called him, always in her tenderest, deepest tone. This, and her way of putting her arms around his neck and kissing him, sometimes caused strangers to start and glance apprehensively at Dr. Harriet to see how that forthright New England wife was taking these theatrical blandishments.

But Dr. Harriet's understanding of Gertrude outmatched Gertrude's understanding of her. From the start she saw the makings of a woman to whom ultimately she might pass on some of her cherished local responsibilities and interests. Only she would have thought of taking Mrs. Richard Aldrich to meetings of the Ladies Aid Society over which she presided. And of putting into Gertrude's hands aprons and pot-holders to sew for the annual bazaar. She was not even surprised when Gertrude did the work quickly and neatly. She also enlisted Gertrude's interest in the Cape Cod Hospital and in the Red Cross classes in first aid. During the war Gertrude, who had taken a first aid course in New York, assisted Dr. Harriet in instructing recruits.

On our first visit to the Hydes, as soon as congratulations were over, Dr. Harriet demanded: "Now where will you live?"

I said that Gertrude had fallen in love with the Cape. We planned to build a small summer home near Dennis. The problem was to find a site.

"We will give you a piece of our land," Dr. Harriet said at once. "It will be our wedding present. Come on, we'll walk around the place and choose a location."

On a low hill overlooking a richly colored expanse of cranberry bog Dr. Fritz said gently: "I've often thought a house here would be perfect."

"Build here," Dr. Harriet told us. "It's yours."

The Hydes generously let us have two and a half acres, which we insisted on paying for. Later we were able to add to our holdings, until we had twenty-five acres. As the house took shape through 1941 Gertrude bestowed on it a number of names, trying them out as it were before we actually took possession. Ultimately, the name that stuck and remained most appropriate was "The Berries." The house was not to be ready for occupancy until the summer of 1942.

The Hydes hospitably gave us the freedom of their beach. There Gertrude swam, sunbathed, ran races with the boys and the Hyde grandchildren. There, every day, she carried her little portable radio and would lie for hours lulled half asleep by the sea wind, the sun, the sound of the waves and the ebb and flow of a succession of soap operas. Her tolerance for this sort of entertainment was extraordinary. She followed them all—*Stella Dallas, Backstage Wife,* and the rest of the sisterhood whose difficulties with their husbands, children and employers supply drama to the lives of millions of women. It was one of the things about Gertrude which I never thoroughly understood. Finally, I put it down to her insatiable desire to help people who were unfortunate.

She was thus occupied one day and sunbathing on the deserted beach with no more than a towel over her midriff when one of the Hyde grandsons arrived at their house for his vacation. He had heard that Gertrude Lawrence was at Dennis and he immediately announced his desire to meet her. It would be something to boast about when he went back to school.

"She's probably on her beach right now," Dr. Harriet told him. "Go down and you'll find her."

The lad departed. He was back remarkably soon, and his face was very red. "Well?" his grandmother inquired. "Did you see Gertrude Lawrence?"

"I sure did," he stammered. "All of her."

* * *

Gertrude's adoption of Cape Cod began in earnest in 1941, during our Family Summer.

Dick and David came over from Camp Monomoy to play with Ernest and Christopher, the English evacués. If the first ten minutes after the four got together were quiet, that was the only time between daylight and dark that was not full of shouts, shrieks, laughter, the banging of doors, the barking of dogs and the wails of the two Siamese cats, which arrived with Barbara and Harrison to round out the family group.

As I look back to it, my keenest memory is of noise.

Every morning I escaped gladly to my office at the Playhouse. The throes of managing a summer theatre with stars coming and going weekly, with a lot of eager and occasionally irrepressible young apprentices to keep in order, even with Tallulah Bankhead and her lion cub, were peaceful compared to life with the family.

But Gertrude loved it. The fatigue of the winter dropped from her. Every morning she was the first one up, singing gaily, planning the day's events—a picnic on the beach, a ball game, surprises and practical jokes which the boys enjoyed only slightly less than she did. Only one thing caused her to frown—my steady refusal to play baseball with her and the boys.

"Get Harrison Hobart to play," I told her. "He's really good at that kind of game and I'm not."

"But it's so good for *you,*" she insisted. "You need the exercise."

Partly to shame me, and partly because she never could resist attempting any sort of game, Gertrude started playing baseball—rounders, she insisted on calling it—on the team which Harrison organized with the assistance of several Hyde grandchildren and friends. Dr. Harriet volunteered to act as umpire. My sister Barbara was given a place in the outfield. But it was unanimously declared that the Queen of Swat was Gertrude. A quarter of a mile away from the diamond, I could always tell by the shrieks of joy, the groans, hoots and cheers, when my wife went to bat.

"She really hits 'em, Dad," David confided to me.

To preserve the careful balance of our Anglo-American ménage, Gertrude rang up Fanny Holtzmann and asked her to send all the proper equipment for playing cricket. But, after baseball, this game proved too tame. Even Gertrude admitted it, though she loyally continued bowling to the English boys every day, apparently afraid that their Americanization would proceed too fast.

Our pets now included Bounder, a large, shaggy English sheep dog contributed by Moss Hart from a litter raised at his Bucks

County farm. Bounder was so determinedly amiable as to be practically impervious to punishment. Spanked, he would roll over on his back, wave his feathered paws pleadingly and, the instant the spanking ceased, leap upon you with delighted barks and lick your face.

This overflow of affection was visibly disgusting to Gertrude's terrier, Mackie. But my young cousin, Bunny Lee, found it enchanting. Bunny, a granddaughter of Mrs. Henry B. Joy of Grosse Pointe, had been taken on as an apprentice when she found life with her grandmother at Watch Hill lacking in artistic atmosphere. Bunny lived and worked with the other apprentices but managed to spend a lot of time at our house, where she followed Gertrude around and fell hopelessly in love with Bounder.

The dog situation got out of hand when Corinne Turner, a nurse who had occasionally looked after Gertrude, arrived with a squeaky-voiced, unattractive Pekinese named Evie. As the dog had been given to Turner by Gertrude in an attempt to console her for the loss of a former pet, I was constrained from indicating my low opinion of it. Not so Mackie. He made a pointed exit whenever Evie appeared.

Unfortunately the Peke was not content to let Mackie sulk in peace. She harassed him constantly, leaping out at him from behind trees and shrubbery. If Mackie, exasperated, finally turned and snapped at her, Evie's shrieks echoed across the bog. This would generally bring up Bounder on the run, eager to get into the game. He would hurl himself upon the hysterical Evie, rolling her over and over until her cries brought Turner to the rescue.

This sort of thing was nerve-shattering enough as a constant refrain out-of-doors. But when it moved inside the house and took place under the dining room table while we were supposedly enjoying a pleasant lunch *en famille,* I asserted myself. There would be no dogs in the dining room.

"You can't shut Mackie out," Gertrude protested. "If he goes, I go."

"Well, Mackie if you insist," I conceded. "But no Bounder. And definitely no Evie."

The two outcasts were removed, leaving Mackie looking insufferably smug.

Somehow, nevertheless, Evie sneaked back to torment Mackie. There was small comfort in the drily detached comment of Matthews, the English butler who had served us at Ballybrook Farm and had asked to go on with us to the Cape: "When I was in service in England, His Lordship never sat down at table without three wolfhounds beside his chair."

Under the circumstances, the fact that Barbara and Harrison had brought their Siamese cats along was hardly calculated to help matters. The cats, far from being intimidated by the presence of so many dogs, threw themselves wholeheartedly into the fray. They baited Evie mercilessly; between sorties, they made life miserable for the canaries.

I found it increasingly difficult to suppress my irritation, especially when I began to suspect that the boys were egging the animals on.

There came a night of full moon when Bounder set up a wail which continued long after everyone was snugly in bed. The banshee quaver stirred a responsive Gaelic chord in Mackie and he joined in. Upstairs Evie resisted her mistress's efforts to restrain her and started to scream maniacally.

I leaped out of bed shouting: "This finishes it. Either this wild animal show moves out of here, or I take the next plane to Reno. I thought I married an actress, not the keeper of a zoo!"

I threw on my clothes, got out my car and drove over to the inn at Falmouth, where I finished out the night.

Next day, though I worked at the Playhouse, I kept away from the house. Late in the afternoon Bunny wandered into my office. She was beaming.

"Oh, Cousin Richard, what do you think?" she exclaimed. "Cousin Gee has given me Bounder. She said his devotion to me was so great she couldn't bear to separate us. I'm to take him home at the end of the summer."

"What happens till then?"

"Cousin Gee has that all figured out. There's a man near here who trains dogs. She's giving me Bounder's training for a present. I do think she's wonderful."

I agreed: "Wonderful."

Encouraged by these straws, I drove over to the house. Gertrude lay on a long garden chair, industriously knitting. A beautiful and rare silence spread over the place like the wings of a gigantic dove.

Gertrude did not seem surprised to see me. She said: "You know, your mother is coming the end of this week. Everything must be perfect and peaceful. I've told the boys they are not to play close to the house, and they are to have a picnic lunch on the beach every day. Harrison and Barbara have promised to look after them."

She knitted half a row before continuing, still in a light conversational tone, "Corinne Turner is sending her Evie down to board with the vet in New York. And in case your mother has a phobia about cats, the vet here is going to keep them until Barbara goes back to town."

"So the zoo is reduced to Mackie and the three canaries?"

"Poor Mackie," Gertrude sighed. "He scratches himself and his nerves are very much upset. *Your* Helen Mahoney has probably been feeding him scraps in the kitchen."

My Helen Mahoney was the cook-housekeeper whom I had engaged the summer before, while Gertrude was on tour. She was the one member of the household who was not of Gertrude's selection.

"If you would stop feeding rich food to Mackie at the table . . ." I began.

"Exactly, darling," Gertrude cut in. "Well, I've sent him down to New York, too. He and Evie left an hour ago in the station wagon."

From the terrace, where the birds' cage hung, came Winnie's contented chuckle. Matthews came out of the house and approached us across the grass, bringing drinks. I said: "With no dogs around, I'm afraid Matthews is going to be lonely for His Lordship's wolfhounds."

Gertrude was silent while the butler served us and went back toward the house again. She eyed me across the rim of her glass.

"I had a talk with Matthews," she said. "I told him that while your mother is here everything is to be done in the *New* England way. Matthews can forget His Lordship for the rest of the summer."

"Bunny is right," I affirmed. "You *are* wonderful."

The gamin grin vanished as swiftly as it had come. My wife lifted her face. Her eyes were starry bright.

"Darling Mr. A. Promise you'll go on thinking so, forever."

* * *

"Everything in the New England style," Gertrude repeated a dozen times that week as she made ready for Mother's coming.

Mother was to arrive late on Saturday afternoon. Gertrude's preparations for her visit centered on the Sunday morning breakfast. She issued minute instructions about the menu and its service.

As she had not taken me into her confidence, I was as amazed as Mother and Barbara on Sunday morning when Matthews brought in a platter of smoking hot fish balls and another of hot fried cranberry pies.

To those who are unacquainted with this specialty of the Cape, let me say that the pies are triangle-shaped and about the size of a doughnut. Two rich crusts hold the cranberries and sugar. The pies are fried like doughnuts in deep fat and served very hot, sprinkled with powdered sugar.

If you have been out in a dory for three or four hours fishing, a plate of cranberry pies is a welcome adjunct to a cup of coffee. But on a warm Sunday morning, when you have just risen from a good night's sleep, and have already had fish balls, the addition of cranberry pies is definitely gilding the lily.

"Where did you get this idea?" I demanded of my wife.

Gertrude smiled sweetly from her end of the table. "Darling, you told me about them yourself. You said you used to love them when you were Dick's age. And your father always had them on Sunday mornings."

It was true that we occasionally had the pies as a special breakfast treat on Sundays or holidays.

"You don't have to eat them," I warned Mother.

"I would like one," she replied firmly. "And a fish ball, please."

"Aren't you afraid you'll have indigestion?" Barbara interposed.

"Cranberry pies never bother me," Mother replied tartly.

It struck me that the senior Mrs. Aldrich was doing her best to meet her daughter-in-law more than half way. This was the only time I ever knew my mother to eat a cranberry pie.

After breakfast, seeing no papers about, I asked Matthews whether the chauffeur had driven down to the village for them. I was informed that, by my wife's orders, no papers were to be brought into the house on Sunday. I sought out Gertrude in her room, where she was dressing to accompany Mother and the boys to church.

"What's the idea—no newspapers?" I demanded.

She reminded me that I had told her this was a rule at my home when I was growing up. "Darling, we want your mother to be happy with us, don't we? And she won't be if things aren't what she is used to."

"Well, it's time she got used to some other ways," I grumbled.

Gertrude regarded me with disapproval. I saw that she was playing the role of a proper New England wife and daughter and she did not wish me to disturb her interpretation.

"Are you coming to church, Richard?" she inquired.

I told her that I would drive her and Mother and the boys to church and leave them there. Then I was going down to the village for the papers. I would spend the morning very pleasantly reading them in the garden. But, as a concession to her, I would gather up the incriminating evidence and hide it before Mother came back from church. I did not add that I intended having a conference with the cook to discover what, if any, bits of local color Gertrude had added to Sunday dinner.

My plan worked out very well. The garden was peaceful and quiet. Dr. Harriet had offered to drive the churchgoers home, so I had time to enjoy my papers and to gather them up and carry them off to my own room before the family assembled for midday dinner.

Just before dinner was announced, Matthews appeared with cocktails. I enjoyed Gertrude's surprise. She glanced fearfully at my mother, who stiffened suddenly.

"This is just another Cape Cod fashion," I said pleasantly. "Like the fish balls and the cranberry pies, no one has to take one unless he wants to. But I enjoy a drink before my dinner and, as I usually have one, I see no reason for pretending otherwise."

"Congratulations," Harrison said approvingly.

From that point dinner progressed happily. Afterwards Mother sought me out. She appeared slightly shamefaced as she asked me if I thought I could find her a Sunday paper. She was in the habit, she confessed, of taking the New York *Times* upstairs with her on Sunday afternoon when she lay down for a rest.

"I know your father did not approve of reading newspapers on Sunday," she said. "But I have grown a little lax in late years. However, I always read the church notices first."

I got her the paper and tucked her up on her bed with it.

"Richard," she said, "don't tell Gertrude, will you?"

I asked why not.

"I wouldn't want to hurt her feelings. She has tried so hard to make everything homelike for me. Too few young people respect the principles of others these days."

I bent down and kissed her. She seemed surprised. "Why, Richard!" she said.

"Just some of Gertrude's influence," I told her. "Have a good time with your Sunday reading. And if you'd like a tabloid, maybe I can find one."

* * *

Gradually the household reverted to its normal ways. Mackie completed his cure in New York in record time and returned to us. Without Evie to incite him, he was his usual dour self, paying no attention to anyone but Gertrude.

The boys took up baseball practice again and Mother was invited to umpire in place of Dr. Harriet, who was busy elsewhere. Mother told me that she was having the happiest summer she had known since our summers at Northfield.

Nothing revealed Mother's fixed intention to get along with her daughter-in-law so clearly as the way she accepted Gertrude's name for her—Mother Mary. To Puritan ears it was somewhat disturbing at first. But Mother was determined not to hurt Gertrude's feelings. She grew to cherish the name. In later years, when Gertrude spoke and wrote to her simply as "Mother," she would sign her letters "Mother Mary."

One Sunday the Cape was swept by a chill northeaster, just as it had been the night Gertrude stepped from the lighted train into my life. I had put in a good part of the day going over some papers upstairs in my room. The afternoon was well advanced toward dusk when I finished. The house seemed unusually quiet; so quiet that I would have thought everyone out of doors but for the rain and the assaults of the wind. Yawning, I went downstairs to see what was what.

Halfway down the flight I stopped. A log fire was blazing in the living room. Before the fire Gertrude sat cross-legged on the floor, Dick and David sprawled beside her. In a chair at one side of the hearth, under the reading lamp, was Mother, book in hand. Her voice floated up to me in words that took me back about thirty years:

"This is the story of a bad boy. Well, not such a very bad, but a pretty bad boy; and I ought to know, for I am, or rather I was, that boy myself. . . ."

Did a stair tread squeak? Or was it Gertrude's acute sensitivity that caused her head to turn? She smiled and beckoned silently. I tiptoed in. Surprised, but—I was happy to see—not displeased, the boys made room for me to drop down beside the three in front of the fire.

Mother alone paid no heed to my appearance there except—or did I fancy it?—that a smile played with unusual tenderness about her moving lips. With a fluency born of long practice, she continued the timeless tale of *Peck's Bad Boy*. Page after page, she led us through familiar Rivermouth with young Tom Bailey, Pepper Whitcomb and Sailor Ben, with Captain Nutter and Miss Abigail.

I was well aware that Mother had not opened the volume without delivering a little introductory talk to let the boys know that the Bad Boy and their own Great-grandfather Aldrich had been cousins. And that she had crowned this triumphantly with the announcement that on his mother's side *the Bad Boy was a Pickering!*

Watching my sons being made aware of this part of their heritage, I thought how strange it was that they owed their enlightenment, not to me, but to the Englishwoman I had brought into the family. It was she, first regarded with a reserve bordering on distrust as coming from an alien world, who had welded that quiet, close group before the fire, and had brought me to sit with her and my sons at my mother's feet.

* * *

The boys had left the Cape to join their mother, and the English children had returned to their school in New York. Mother was back in Groton. Gertrude and I, for the first time, were alone.

"Isn't it heavenly!" she sighed. "I do love your boys, Richard, but I must say the peace and quiet, after what we have been through, are wonderful. Isn't it?"

I said that I felt that I could do without the sight of a boy for a long, long time.

We sat quietly, waiting for the moon to rise.

Presently Gertrude sighed again.

"What is it?" I asked.

"The stillness, darling. Of course, it is heavenly. But isn't it a little *too* still?"

Chapter Nine

IN THE FALL OF 1941, Gertrude had written to the New York *Times:*

"Kind Friends and Gentle People."

These were the last touching and most beautiful words ever written by your own beloved Stephen Foster.

It has always seemed to me that they were meant to be used to some great purpose by that truly great man, and so in his beloved memory I address these words to the readers of this letter.

"Kind Friends and Gentle People of America":

I want to tell you, as an Englishwoman, of my heartfelt gratitude for all your generous, spontaneous aid to Great Britain in her hour of struggle and strife.

A cable from England last week told us "it is most urgent to equip some homes for shell-shocked and blitzed-out babies of 5 years of age and under!"

Isn't that an agonizing cry?

Children are citizens of God's Kingdom all the world over and innocent of all the evils of war . . .

In the meantime comes once again the day of the Heavenly Birthday—Christmas. How saddening to realize that this Christmas there will be no toys manufactured in England for home consumption for the first time in history. No dolls, no roller skates—no sugar-cane umbrella sticks or any of the simplest things which delight the heart of the poorest or sickest child!

So Americans are sending "The Happiness Ship"—to take the place of Santa Claus. Only, where he had his reindeer, our ship will have America's watchful convoys to escort her on her perilous journey.

We want to send a ship such as only children dream of—packed full of happy surprises—like the one I sing about in my play:

"My ship has sails that are made of silk—
The decks are trimmed with gold
And of jam and spice
There's a paradise
In the hold!"

Please, once again, America, and your more fortunate children, who are now beginning to write their notes to Santa Claus—please sent us a gift for our Happiness Ship! Each gift should bear a label with the sender's name and address on it so that the lucky little mite at the other end can send you back words of a dream come true on Christmas, 1941.

God bless you all and grant you yet more safe Christmases in this vast and bounteous Land of the Free.

Gertrude Lawrence

Gertrude's prayer for a peaceful Christmas for America was not to be granted.

In company with several million other American husbands and wives, Gertrude and I were spending a quiet Sunday afternoon at home when the broadcast report of the attack on Pearl Harbor ended one phase of our life together and rang up the curtain on another.

By the beginning of the New Year I had been commissioned a lieutenant in the United States Naval Reserve and was getting used to the uniform, the service idiom and to giving and acknowledging salutes. I had turned my share of the firm's responsibilities over to my partner, Dick Myers, while I reported daily to the headquarters of the Third Naval District at Ninety Church Street, in

New York City. There I quickly discovered that the production of a play isn't a patch on the production of a global war.

I was fortunate that my duties permitted me to remain at home for the time being. However, my schedule and Gertrude's allowed us very little time together.

In order to keep Navy hours, I had to be up shortly after six. In accordance with her British ideas of a wife's duties, particularly those of the wife of a man in uniform, Gertrude insisted on being up at the same time to get my breakfast. This, despite the fact that *Lady in the Dark* had reopened early in the autumn, which meant that she was seldom unwound and in bed before 1 or 2 A.M.

Under these circumstances, Gertrude's care of me was thoroughly heartwarming, but equally unnecessary and a threat to her health. When I suggested that she could not carry on her arduous role and her many activities on so little sleep, she took offense. As a last resort, I reported that my superiors had instituted breakfast conferences downtown at which attendance was compulsory. After that, Gertrude slept while I slipped out of the house to the corner drugstore. I was seldom home again until just before she left for the theatre.

Whenever my duties permitted, I would join her briefly backstage at the Alvin Theatre before curtain time. Once the play began, even I was barred from her dressing room. The rapidly changing scenes, each necessitating a change of costume and make-up, kept the two maids—Carrie and Hazel—constantly on the double-quick, and left no room for an unessential husband.

In order to be awake and alert when it was time to take Gertrude to after-theatre supper, or to sit with her while she supped at home, I fell into the habit she had sought to inculcate in me ever since we married—that of taking one or two hours' nap at the end of the day. She always did this when she was working. It was difficult for me at first, but, once I had acquired the habit, I realized its value.

It was during those months of our topsy-turvy existence that Gertrude took to writing me notes and leaving them about the apartment where I would be sure to discover them. Though they were far removed from the romantic messages Orlando pinned to

Arden's oaks for Rosalind, they were like Gertrude—merry, tender, solicitous.

The solicitous side of her character was very much to the fore now. The instant that I appeared before her in uniform I lost my status as someone who took care of her, and became someone for whose welfare she felt responsible. I came home one bitter cold evening to find a sheet of writing paper filled with her distinctive handwriting propped against a vase of holly in the hall. It read:

> Darling—
>
> Hot water bottle in your bed.
>
> Please don't remove green spread as room will get very cold to-night when you open the window.
>
> Hot milk on stove. Remove glass top from kettle and you will find milk in silver flask inside.
>
> I have to go out early to photographer. Come in and see if I am awake before you leave. Bless you,
>
> Mrs. A

On another occasion, when Gertrude had to be away from home overnight to attend a week-end war rally, the greeting was:

> Goodbye, darling,
> I shan't be long. Be Good.
> Eat well—and sleep—alone.
> Mrs. A

One morning I found a pocket-size photograph of her in a leather case, accompanied by the message:

> This is in case you have an accident so they will know whose old man you are. Bye, bye, Angel. Thanks for the 'earts, they ain't 'arf a bit of orlright.

In all these notes, as in many of her letters, her own mark of special affection, a heart pierced with an arrow, followed the signature. Gertrude was never one to underplay.

She was one of the few persons I have known in whom the necessity for writing a telegram aroused no inhibitions. Her wires to friends and to me were only slightly less demonstrative in tone than her letters. Mother, to whom the sight of a telegram was nearly as ominous as a crape on a door, never became accustomed to communications via Western Union beginning "DARLING MOTHER MARY. . . ."

I do not think that it ever occurred to Gertrude that the messages she wrote rapidly on the telegraph blanks she always carried about with her were heard and read by a number of strangers before they reached the person to whom she addressed them. I am not likely ever to forget the face of the sailor who saluted—ironically, I suspected a moment later—and handed me a telegram one February morning when I was at my desk at Ninety Church Street. No Navy wife was more acutely aware of the war than Gertrude. But for all that, she was hardly the girl to let St. Valentine's Day get by without wig-wagging in my direction. What she did not know was that all wire and radio communication with Naval Headquarters, whether personal or official, is handled by a central communications office. Except for reasons of security, the message is delivered on an open-faced office form. Thus, on that morning, I received this message:

> AHOY THERE SAILOR ON THIS DAY MANY VOWS MAY COME YOUR WAY BUT SHOULD YOU TO OTHERS STOOP I STILL WOULD LOVE YOU CAUSE YOU'RE MY OLD POOP REMEMBER ME I'M THAT GAL YOU MARRIED.
>
> MRS. A

And, in the appropriate place along the margin, the telegram was littered with scribbled initials—and not a few exclamation points. My valentine had been cleared through all the proper channels.

For some time after that I was referred to as "Lieutenant Poop."

Ever since our visit to Lord Lothian in July of 1940, when the British Ambassador had encouraged Gertrude to consider herself as a kind of unofficial builder of closer Anglo-American relations, Gertrude had forwarded suggestions in this connection to highly placed friends in Britain. A typically appreciative cable received in response from Lord Beaverbrook, then in over-all charge of England's war production, said:

MY DEAR DEAR GERTRUDE I AM SO GLAD TO RECEIVE YOUR LETTER STOP WILL YOU PLEASE WRITE ME FREQUENTLY STOP GIVE ME THE WHOLE PICTURE

MAX BEAVERBROOK

With the United States' entry into the war, Gertrude increased her Red Cross activities. She even attended faithfully a comprehensive course in first aid. With typical thoroughness Gertrude not only took full notes in the classroom, but afterward transcribed them meticulously into a leather-bound notebook at home. An overelaborate three-page summation of the proper steps for treating a victim of poisoning, listing as the final instruction, "Keep the victim quiet until doctor arrives," winds up with Gertrude's capitalized comment: "YOU NEED HIM YOURSELF BY NOW!"

Gertrude also began to make regular appearances at the Stage Door Canteen, operated by the American Theatre Wing, of which she was one of the founders.

At the first call for volunteers for civil defense, she signed up as air raid warden and took the course, being tremendously proud of her official helmet and badge. Her duties in our block made her known to a great many of the residents of West Fifty-fourth Street, to whom she was forever after not just Gertrude Lawrence, the star, but a neighbor with whom they exchanged friendly greetings.

She kept up her work for, and generous gifts to, Allied War Relief. Parcels of necessities and little luxuries in the way of sweets, tea and clothing went regularly to old friends and former retainers in beleaguered England. One of these was Evie Williams, her long-time secretary, who had gone back to London after accompanying Gertrude on her tour in *Susan and God*. Evie was deeply devoted to "Lady Jane," her name for Gertrude, and Gertrude, who never undervalued affection and had a gift for bestowing it, reciprocated this devotion. She worried constantly about the Williams family in Teddington Road. Later, when I was sent to England on duty, she gave me a list of "People I Love" to look up "and see if they need anything." The list was an indication of Gertrude's wide friendships. It began with Evie and included two teashop waitresses who were among her staunchest fans, a marchioness, a celebrated theatrical producer, a stage-door man, two ultra-smart Mayfair hostesses and her stepfather—Dad, as she called him.

She never felt less than kindly toward Dad, who, whenever he had had one of his rare strokes of luck with the ponies, had taken her mother and her to Brighton or Bognor Regis for a day on the sands. For years she had supported him. Now he was old, frail, and lonely. She was tormented by thoughts of his being bombed out; perhaps maimed, pinned under fallen beams in some cellar in which he might have sought refuge.

But Dad survived the blitz and the buzz bombs. He died in his sleep from natural causes about one month before V-E Day.

Gertrude's English fans were a story in themselves. At that time I did not understand the place these groups have in the life of an English star. We have nothing like it in America. They are not to be compared to the autograph-hunting bobby-soxers who indiscriminately mob virtually all motion-picture celebrities, crooners and night club entertainers in this country. An English star's fans stand loyally behind her—or him—alone. They constitute an audience of repeaters, who deny themselves other luxuries in order to see their idol ten, even twenty times in a season. When they haven't the price of a ticket they queue up outside the theatre just to cheer or murmur, "God bless you!" when the star arrives or leaves. Not only are they fully conversant with the star's career; they manage to keep informed of all events connected with her private life. Whenever one fan picks up an item of interest connected with the star, this is promptly sent along the grapevine until in a matter of hours it is known to hundreds of persons in all parts of the United Kingdom. It can best be compared to a kind of underground.

Gertrude's fan following was always enormous. Most of the hundreds who made it up had followed her in every play since she made her debut in Charlot's *From A to Z.* They had watched her meteoric rise, collecting scrapbooks of clippings and photographs. They talked of her romances, the houses she lived in, her escorts, her jewels, her clothes. She was a compensation for much that was drab, hopeless and hard in their own lives. And for this they worshipped her.

At the time of her bankruptcy, when her story was front-page news in the British press, she had to restrain a group of these fans from organizing a benefit on her behalf.

Many of the English fans wrote to Gertrude in the United States. Before the war, hardly a mail came from England without some letter or touching little gift. To all these Gertrude replied with personal letters, written by hand. When I discovered the extent of her personal correspondence, how much attention she gave it and the warm personal relationships she had established with hundreds of people all over the world, I was dumbfounded. She never kept a correspondent waiting for a reply, no matter how busy she might be.

This was not to build box office. It was an indication of a genuine and heartfelt appreciation of the affection showered on her by her fans throughout her career.

* * *

In June, 1942, *Lady in the Dark* closed its New York run. Gertrude was free until autumn, when the company was to start on "that familiar three-thousand-mile trek." Leaving me in New York, she went up to the Cape to supervise the last touches to our new home, The Berries, which was now ready for occupancy. Whenever I could snatch forty-eight hours' leave I traveled to Dennis to be with her. Meanwhile she and our cook-housekeeper, Helen Mahoney, and a handy man had their hands full of exactly the sort of work Gertrude reveled in.

How she loved a house, and especially setting one in order! Her flair for this sort of thing was amazing, considering the other facets of her temperament. Give her a room to clean and she would roll up her sleeves, tie up her hair in a kerchief, and get to work with pails of water, scrubbing brush, rags, and polish, singing gaily as she scoured and shone everything in sight. She could clean a room more quickly and thoroughly than any three servants.

Watching Gertrude attack a job about the house—and in the

course of time she tackled nearly everything, from papering a room to shingling a roof—I was often reminded of the day, early in our acquaintance, when she spread out her strong hands and said they would earn a living for her, if her acting did not. It was part of her nature to loathe incompetence, ineffectuality, dilettantism in anything. She never undertook a task, however humble, that she did not give her undivided attention and try to do expertly. She was never less than a professional.

Early in the war she had joined a class in home repairs given by the Women's Volunteer Services. Thereafter, no portion of the house's anatomy was safe from her. She could, and did splice electric wires, take apart sockets, putty a window sash, and even straddle a gable of the roof to clean out a clogged gutter. I accused her of clogging up the kitchen sink in order to display her plumbing skill to Helen Mahoney and me. Her denial was not convincing.

The house repairs were not confined to The Berries. For years she insisted on getting Star Cottage ready each season for the visiting celebrities. Each year she would try out a different color scheme, usually painting the woodwork herself and once even attempting to hang the paper she had suddenly decided to try.

She was most dangerous when she got hold of a brush and a can of paint advertised as "Quick Dry" but seldom living up to this description. After one or two unfortunate experiences I learned never to step into any room in our various dwellings in the dark. I was likely to find that she had created a happy surprise for me by installing new draperies in the Harvard colors and repainting my long-suffering furniture to match. I never could tell when she would change all the furniture around, and forget to inform me until after I had scraped my shin on a low table placed where I had no expectation of finding one.

She was always thinking up improvements in the way of decoration and comfort. As when she had the black and white-tiled floor of my bathroom in our city apartment covered wall to wall with red velvet carpet. This brought about a scene, and for several days she was exceedingly haughty, remarking about the disadvantages of being married to a man without a taste for beauty and luxury.

Therefore, when I drove into our garage at Dennis one afternoon and found the floor spread with a coconut fiber rug I merely asked, in my most tactful tone, "What's it for, darling?"

She explained that the garage looked so bare with nothing on the floor. Weakly, I let the rug remain where it lay.

One windy night I went to get the car in a great hurry. The motor started but the car refused to move. Investigation with a flashlight showed that the wind had lifted the rug until it had become entangled with the car's vitals. It took a garage mechanic hours to extract all the coconut fibers.

Gertrude had a poor idea of my usefulness about the house and often shook her head over my clumsiness with tools and my refusal to improve myself in that direction. In consequence she always insisted that I did not, and could not, value the work she and our various helpers did around The Berries.

"Richard is simply not a home maker," she complained in a letter to David Holtzmann. "Like most men, he thinks the flowers grow because God planted them. He thinks the house is clean because it's in the country and not in the dirty city. He thinks things get done at The Berries because we have ladders and paints and tools, and the pixies do the jobs in the night."

Needless to say, she enjoyed herself immensely carrying all the responsibility for settling in the new house and laying out the garden. Perhaps she felt a little ashamed because she was having so much fun while I was serving my country in the stifling city, because she never failed to tell me in the course of our daily telephone calls: "Darling, I miss you yelling GERTRUDE all over the place."

* * *

That summer at Dennis, the Gertrude Lawrence Branch of the American Theatre Wing was organized, dedicated to the entertainment of men in the coast defenses and various training camps on the Cape.

Every village on the Cape was engrossed in work for the services and, in all this, Gertrude was Dr. Harriet's eager lieutenant. Every week there were bazaars, lawn parties, clambakes, community rallies, and auctions to raise funds.

Dorothy Wilding

Her devotion as a Navy wife was thoroughly heartwarming, but her wit earned me the nickname of Lieutenant Poop.

Herman E. Krawitz

The Queen of Swat

Thanks to Gertrude's planning, Mother felt very much at home when she visited us.

Cape Cod Portfolio

Auctioneering for a benefit at the Cape.

She bought as well as sold. "I must have the hobbyhorse," she declared. "Mother says it's exactly like the one Richard rode in his nursery."

No serviceman ever failed to get a lift from this Red Cross driver.

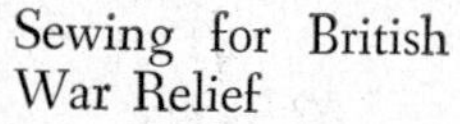

Sewing for British War Relief

Cape Cod Portfolio

Gertrude was a founder of the Stage Door Canteen and a regular worker there.

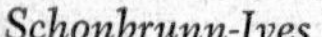

Schonbrunn-Ives

It was at the auctions that Gertrude outshone herself; not merely as a bidder-in, but as auctioneer. No one else could start the crowd bidding so eagerly for cakes, preserves, crocheted bedspreads, Cape Cod novelties and heirlooms dragged from attics. She always returned from these jaunts with a car full of purchases which no one else would pay money for. The Berries broke out in a rash of wooden windmills, sailor weather vanes, braided rugs, ships in bottles, hand-painted shells and clamshell pincushions. But all, she pointed out when I remonstrated, "for the cause."

In her Red Cross Motor Corps uniform Gertrude drove herself about, stopping to pick up anyone in uniform who thumbed a ride. She scoffed at our warnings that this might make her an easy prey of thugs and kidnappers; nothing could happen to *her,* no matter what happened to other people.

I was constantly worried about her, knowing that her fearlessness might lead her into paths that were hazardous, as on that famous all-night crabbing trip. It was as though, periodically, she rebelled against the ordered security of her life—against the very thing she had always longed for, and which, she once told me, she had never known until she married me. It seems probable that by these flirtations with danger she worked off some of the emotional tension which other more temperamental stars, male and female, release through bursts of bad temper backstage and in public. Or which they appease by chain-smoking or excessive drinking.

Gertrude's release—for a release of some sort was imperative for one of her intense, high-strung nature—came through ceaseless and constantly varied activity, both physical and mental. If at times the new interest into which she hurled herself was something actually dangerous, it was because her momentary need to escape was acute.

My understanding of all this did not come at once, nor did I attain it without repeated misunderstandings of her. I might never have gained it, and with it the power to help her at times when she needed my help (not that she ever admitted her need), but for that wise and forthright woman, Dr. Harriet Hyde. I grew to realize how often her eyes must have been on Gertrude and me, appraising the development of our contrary natures, seeking that center where we met in complete accord.

Gradually, I became prepared for Gertrude's "flings," though I was never sure when one of them might send her up in a space ship or over Niagara in a barrel. A speculative, longing look would come into her eyes when she watched someone do something daring and dangerous, that told me she was wondering how it would feel to have that experience herself.

Once, when Gertrude was appearing in Los Angeles, she spent the week-end at a nearby San Fernando Valley ranch. She was still there on Monday morning when I flew out from New York on a surprise visit.

I traced her to the ranch and drove directly there, only to learn that she was out riding in the hills.

I hurried over to the stable and, before long, perceived a figure on horseback coming in my direction. It was Gertrude, dressed in full Western regalia, even to the lariat looped over her hand.

When she saw me there, she edged her horse over.

"What a nice surprise, darling," she exclaimed excitedly. "You've come just in time to see me rope my first steer!"

On another occasion, Gertrude and I were at a party given for a group of newspaper publishers and editors at the country home of Arthur Hays Sulzberger, publisher of the New York *Times*. Gertrude was chatting with Mrs. Sulzberger and Mrs. Kent Cooper, wife of the manager of the Associated Press, when they heard a loud, whirring noise in the air above. They looked up to see a helicopter slowly coming down toward the lawn. On the side of its cabin, the aircraft bore in bold letters: "THE CHICAGO TRIBUNE, AMERICA'S GREATEST NEWSPAPER," a statement which did not go unchallenged by Colonel Robert R. McCormick's assembled competitors when he stepped down from the cabin of the plane.

Later, the colonel extolled the virtues of the helicopter as the air transport of the future, and invited us all to come up for a ride with him.

The publishers and editors felt they could well afford to wait for their first helicopter ride until it was a more tested and conventional method of transportation; they hastily declined, offering as their excuse that they did not want to endorse the *Tribune's* slogan by entering the ship.

Gertrude, however, had no such qualms. She accepted with pleasure, and had already started down the slope of the lawn toward the aircraft. I jumped up and strode after her.

"You're not going up in that helicopter," I warned her quietly but firmly.

"Richard, don't be a spoilsport. If it's safe enough for the colonel —"

I was not married to the colonel, I pointed out, but I was to her.

"I'm going up," said Gertrude, "no matter what you say."

I had to think fast. "Very well," I improvised, "I'll tell you what I just overheard one of the guests saying: 'Some people will do anything for publicity.' "

Gertrude turned quickly. I heard a sharp intake of breath.

"Oh, darling, you know that's not the reason," she exclaimed.

I said that I understood, but others might not. We rejoined the party.

Gertrude would never turn away from any challenge. Even in her work, there were dangerous territories she longed to explore. As she once told me, "Playing in a circus is one piece of show business I have yet to experience. It must be a thrill riding bareback. I'd like to train for that. And perhaps a wire-walking act. Then I could do a play or a film of real circus life . . ."

* * *

At the Playhouse, Bunny Lee was again Gertrude's adoring Girl Friday. My young cousin's passion for the stage showed no sign of abating. She was back among the apprentices, but minus Bounder. To her intense delight, she had been made prop girl, a job which necessitated driving around to the houses of generous friends and borrowing from them furniture, clothes, draperies—whatever might be needed to put on the next week's bill. Bunny took her job seriously. When she was asked to double with the sound effects during performances, she started talking gravely about her "career." Mother, who at the request of Bunny's grandmother had urged us to let Bunny be an apprentice again, became alarmed. But her fears were groundless; Bunny was no more immune to wartime romance than most of her generation.

She dashed into The Berries early one morning waving a telegram and shouting for "Cousin Gee." To Gertrude she revealed that she faced the dilemma of her life. A young man she had formed an attachment to—a lieutenant in a midwestern training camp—had wired her that he had obtained leave and did not know whether he would get another before being shipped overseas. As Bunny saw it, unless she could manage to meet him in Chicago, where he expected to spend a few days, the chances were that the Japs would get him before she could stake a claim.

"Oh, Cousin Gee," she wailed. "What'll I do?"

"Do?" Gertrude demanded. "Go, of course. First we'll see if we can get my friends in Chicago to look after you. Then we'll call your mother at Watch Hill and ask her permission."

"But my job!" Bunny's voice grew anguished. "What will happen at the Playhouse? There are all the props for next week to get. And there's that telephone bell that has to be rung three times in the second act tonight."

"I'll carry on for you," Gertrude said, as she placed a call to the railroad station.

"Oh, Cousin Gee! Would you? *Could* you?"

"I can try," Gertrude said solemnly. "It will be an effort, but anything for young love." Seeing that Bunny still looked dubious, she added, "You'll have to go through the script with me before you leave, and give me the cues."

Bunny's mother consented to her daughter's journey, once she was satisfied that Gertrude's friends would provide proper chaperonage. Having put her on the train, Gertrude drove the station wagon around on a series of calls on people who had been inviting her to their houses and whose invitations she had regretfully refused on the plea that she had to rest when she was not engaged in her war duties. She returned with the car brimming with collector's pieces that had been entrusted to her for use as props; what was more, she had started a rush for tickets for the show.

That night, Gertrude took her stand in the wings and rang bells on cue. When Bunny telephoned from Chicago to say that she had just seen her young man off to camp and that they were engaged, she finished: "We wanted you to be the first to know, Cousin Gee, because but for you it would never have come off."

Gertrude's congratulations were cut short by Bunny's anxious inquiry: "How's my job?"

"Waiting for you," Gertrude replied. "We have all decided, Bunny darling, that nobody can ring a bell as you do it."

"Oh, Cousin Gee, really?" came ecstatically over the wire. "Just wait till I tell Bill!"

* * *

Across the road from The Berries stretched acres of bog—wild, sweet-scented, and colorful as the Scotch moors. When Gertrude learned that this picturesque but apparently waste land produced an edible and salable crop of cranberries, she was interested and urged me to buy as many acres as possible. Early in the year our purchase of nine acres was completed. Gertrude immediately joined with the local Ocean Spray Cooperative and set about winning the war with cranberries. Bunny's pride in her bell-ringing was matched by Gertrude's when the Falmouth *Enterprise* spoke of her as "not one of your front-porch growers. When it comes to cranberry picking, the glamorous Miss Lawrence wields a mean scoop . . ."

A representative of the canning company, coming around to check on this report, was slightly apologetic about calling at 10 A.M., having heard that stars of the theatre seldom rise before noon. His first shock came when he was told that if he wanted to talk to Mrs. Aldrich he would have to seek her in the bog. This was nothing to what he subsequently learned—that Gertrude had already transplanted a lilac, painted a new window sash, driven to the village post office for the morning mail, and put in half an hour weeding the vegetables in her victory garden before joining the pickers.

People often have wondered how she came by her boundless supply of energy. Dr. Herman Rubin, her physician for many years, told me he was once asked by a patient for some of the vitamins he gave Gertrude Lawrence. "She must use a lot," the inquirer surmised.

"Vitamins could use Gertrude Lawrence," was the doctor's reply.

When I went up to the Cape for a brief leave I was welcomed by a sunburnt, scratched, and mosquito-bitten wife, who bore slight resemblance to the "Goddess" that Brooks Atkinson had called her in his review of her play.

"What price glamour?" I inquired. Which she parried with: "Glamour is as glamour does, my lad."

Only my uniform saved me from being inducted into her land army along with the household staff and all guests who unwarily accepted her hospitality. Mother alone was exempt.

Fanny Holtzmann's experience was typical. She had no sooner arrived and had not yet unpacked before Gertrude presented her with a scoop and orders to join the bog party. Fanny, a child of the city, demurred; "It's not in my legal retainer," she said.

"It's part of your duty as a citizen to help the war effort," Gertrude retorted. "Come on. The berries are ripening and must be picked."

Fanny obligingly got into the regulation costume and joined the gang, following faithfully behind Gertrude with her wooden scoop. Presently the sight of her distinguished client pausing to scratch various parts of her body, simultaneous with a pricking on her own ankles and calves, gave her an unpleasant idea. She said: "There's more than cranberries in this bog of yours, Gee. There's poison ivy."

"Of course there is," Gertrude replied.

"Well, doesn't it make you itch?"

Gertrude reached an arm around her bent back and dug viciously at her thighs. "Of course I itch. But is that any excuse for not doing a job that has to be done?"

Between shifts in the bog, Gertrude experimented in the kitchen with recipes in which cranberries—fresh or canned—were the main ingredient. You were apt to meet the tart crimson berries at every meal, and in every guise. Aware that Mother and Aunt Alice habitually refused orange juice at breakfast, preferring to take their vitamins in blueberries sprinkled over their cereal, she proposed: "Why not cranberries?"

Next morning a compote of cranberry sauce was placed temptingly before the two older ladies.

"Is it Thanksgiving?" Mother demanded with slight but understandable asperity.

In one venture along these lines Gertrude was highly successful. Whenever she had guests for lunch it was her custom to serve Dubonnet as an *apéritif*. A tray with filled glasses was passed, and the bottle was set out for refills. Mother had gradually accepted this practice and the serving of cocktails before dinner. When she was with us two glasses filled with tomato juice would be on the tray; one for her, the other for Gertrude, whose courtesy made her choose to drink what Mother took.

On one of my visits I noticed the absence of tomato juice. All the glasses on the tray were filled with liquid of the true Dubonnet hue. Mother had taken one and was sipping it with nonchalance.

To my interested: "How come?" Gertrude informed me: "It's my own invention. Blackberry and cranberry juices mixed. Isn't the color perfect? Mother Mary feels much less conspicuous—besides liking the flavor better than tomato."

It was not only that Mother felt less conspicuous, I discovered when she visited us in New York during the winter. At one Sunday luncheon at which Aunt Alice and Uncle Jim were guests, Mother took her glass from the tray without any show of self-consciousness.

"Why, Mollie!" her sister gasped. "What would Ed Aldrich say if he could see you?"

Mother sipped her *apéritif* before she replied calmly: "Ed was first and foremost a business man, Alice. He would have thoroughly approved of supporting a family industry. Didn't he always insist that all of us should wear Hood rubbers because they were turned out by his own firm? As long as Richard and Gertrude raise cranberries for sale, it is my duty to drink cranberry juice. And you and Jim and anyone else may think what you please."

Uncle Jim drew me aside to speak as man to man.

"Something has come over your mother," he said. "When I think how severe she was with me when I told her I had been at a dinner where cocktails were served and that I took one, not drinking it, of course, but just held it so as not to cause comment. She wanted to know what had happened to my principles. She actually preached me a sermon on the text 'Abstain from every appearance of evil. . . . !' What's become of *her* principles? It certainly has every appearance of evil. And what's more, it's meant to."

I told Gertrude later that Uncle Jim thought she was leading Mother astray.

"First it was that crimson silk shawl you gave her. Now it's drinking, or pretending to drink, cocktails. They probably expect to find she's dyed her hair the next time they come to take her out to Sunday church."

"They are just finding out things about your mother that have been true all the time," Gertrude said. "Who was it that told me she always loved a bit of bright color but had never dared wear it? She did. That's why I got her the bright shawl. She doesn't want to drink, but she does want to be a part of our lives. If cranberry juice will make her feel that she is, then I'll drink it to the end of my days. Do you know what else she told me? When Uncle Jim was at Yale, his roommate, George Vincent, invited her to the junior prom. The family made quite a to-do about it. No girl of the family had ever done such a thing. They were willing she should go, but she must not let a young man put his arm around her waist and tempt her into the polka. She sat out all the dances because she was afraid to break the family tradition."

"You aren't planning to teach her to jitterbug?" I inquired. "I wouldn't put it past you."

"Swing isn't her style," Gertrude said, and she was not laughing. "But I was thinking, after this war is over, and there are lots of young people around, and Dick and David bring their friends, we could have square dancing. She would adore watching it. It would help make up for that beastly Yale prom nearly seventy years ago."

* * *

As everyone who has served in the United States Navy knows, a lieutenant is very small potatoes. A lieutenant's wife, when admitted to the company of the wives of full commanders, captains, and an admiral, is expected by unwritten protocol to show herself unobtrusive, quietly respectful, and as shy of the limelight as an oyster of the sun.

Would Gertrude be able to do this, I wondered? Could she become merely Lieutenant Aldrich's wife, sinking into the background with the wives of my fellow officers whose coat sleeves displayed no more gold braid than my own?

The Navy is a very close world—even in wartime, when its ranks swell abnormally. And it is an exacting one. It views as unforgivable any attempt to carry prominence in other spheres over into Navy life.

However, my worry about how Gertrude would acquit herself as a Navy wife proved needless. She accompanied me to several cocktail parties without anyone but a few of my close friends being aware she was the star whose singing of "Jenny" was the delight of Broadway.

Eventually, of course, her identity became known, but this was not Gertrude's doing. She had set herself to play the role of the little wife and she played it consistently and, I think, with considerable enjoyment. We both realized that the era of incognito was up when we were invited to the admiral's party, an honor above my rank. The Old Man was exceedingly gallant to Gertrude, even to the point of adding a commendation of me as an officer.

"Oh, but, Admiral," I heard my wife exclaim in the voice that wooed and won thousands of fans, "Richard doesn't want to spend the war at a desk job at Ninety Church Street. I'm so proud to have a husband who longs for sea duty."

She conveyed the idea that I was an embryo Nelson champing to lose first a leg, then my life, on the bloody quarter-deck. Several times in the course of the party I caught the admiral eyeing me speculatively, as if considering a particularly hazardous spot to put me in.

"What are you trying to do?" I demanded humorously of Gertrude when I got her alone. "Become the world's most glamorous widow?"

It may have been purely coincidence, but shortly after her remark to the admiral I found myself detached from the work I had been doing at Ninety Church Street to enter upon sea duty aboard a new destroyer, the *Maddox.*

Gertrude promptly adopted the ship and her crew. When the *Maddox* was still in the Brooklyn Navy Yard, the skipper invited Gertrude to lunch aboard, after which she inspected every inch of the destroyer from gun turrets to engine room. As an active worker at the Stage Door Canteen, she saw to it that the men from the *Maddox* had tickets for the popular shows, even if this meant her telephoning the managements herself to get the passes.

The term of my service afloat was brief; after a few weeks I was back at Third Naval District Headquarters. But I still had a feeling of belonging to the destroyer. Consequently I took more than a casual interest in plans for the farewell party which, in those days, the crew of every ship gave before she sailed to one of the war zones. These entertainments were usually very simple beer-and-pretzels affairs enlivened by whatever entertainment could be rounded up at no cost.

Commander Eugene Sarsfield, U.S.N., captain of the *Maddox,* was a friend of my C.O. This, and Gertrude's well-known interest in the ship, led me to reply: "We'll see what we can do," when he asked if we could arrange for something unusual in the way of a party for his crew.

Someone knew someone in the management of the Waldorf and was able to get the Starlight Roof for the evening. Gertrude made herself, and me, responsible for the entertainment. At the time she was busy with a series of broadcasts known as *Broadway Calling,* a production of ENSA, the British organization which was the equivalent of our USO. Gertrude was the founder and president of its American branch. The foremost stars of Broadway and Hollywood appeared on her programs. She got several of them to agree to come to the Waldorf and entertain the boys from the *Maddox.* Not content to stop there, she also took a hand with all the arrangements —music, menu, decorations.

Word went around that this was to be a "really bang-up affair," and, when the night came, practically every member of the crew of the *Maddox* turned up at the Starlight Roof for what was becoming known as Gertrude Lawrence's party.

The name was not misapplied. She and Commander "Doug" Gessford took turns emceeing. Gertrude sang, danced and told stories; in between her turns at the mike she danced with every man from the ship. She posed for photographs and signed autograph books and pictures of herself which the men begged for.

During one of Gessford's turns as M.C., he noticed a slim, inconspicuous young man standing in line behind stage, apparently waiting to be called on to entertain.

"What do you do, sonny?" the commander asked.

"I'm supposed to sing a couple of songs," the young man said shyly.

"All right, you're next." Gessford beckoned him forward to the mike. "Don't be nervous. What's your name? Sennett, did you say? Oh, Sinnott." He led the boy out to the audience. They were met by tumultuous applause and a few unnautical feminine squeals.

The commander's face grew stern. "Give the boy a chance to sing," he pleaded. When the room was quiet, he announced, "Mr. Sinnott, here, will sing a little song."

The audience reacted to that with inexplicable laughter. Quickly Gertrude made her way to the platform. She took over the mike and announced, "Our next singer needs no introduction, except to the Master of Ceremonies. Commander Gessford, I'd like *you* to meet—Frank Sinatra!"

The singer, who just that year had created a peak of hysteria among the younger generation, shook hands with the commander and went into his song.

Next day, the *Maddox* put to sea, going into the silence which cloaked ships in those dangerous days. When the silence lasted too long, we began to entertain fears—which unfortunately proved to be justified. One July morning, at 5 A.M., when the *Maddox* was engaged in the invasion of Sicily, she was caught squarely amidships by a string of bombs. In sixty-five seconds the ship went under; and of the hundreds of men whom Gertrude had helped to entertain a few short weeks before, only four officers and thirty men survived. Captain Sarsfield went down with his ship.

Weeks later, Gertrude was still receiving delayed letters from boys who had gone down with the ship, thanking her for the wonderful party and telling her she was the pin-up girl of the *Maddox*, with her photograph on nearly every bulkhead and a "blow-up" of her in the wardroom.

The fate of "her" ship saddened her more than any other single event of the war. It had brought the war very close.

* * *

In the autumn of 1942 Gertrude commenced her tour in *Lady in the Dark*. But her war activities did not cease. She had made many coast-to-coast tours, and had friends in all the major cities en route. Everywhere she was in demand for benefits, bond-selling drives, special broadcasts, launchings, and official visits and presentation of awards to airplane plants, arsenals and shipyards. And, of course, at the servicemen's canteens.

"Were you up in time to hear the broadcast?" she wrote me from San Francisco. "It was for the Red Cross blood bank. I see a possible 10,000 pints or more, plus my own measly one. I gave on Saturday, and I feel wonderful, though at the time I was terrified that I would not be able to fill the bottle. But it came out beautifully, a deep, dark American Beauty rose. . . ."

San Francisco, she reported, was "like an ant hill . . . Millions of people in steel helmets going on and coming off shifts all the time . . ." The industry of the shipyards amazed her and commanded her respect. "Just think, they turn them out at Sausalito one every seven days. One launched at 6:30 last night, and the keel for the next one was in the slips at 6:30 this morning. I toured one today which goes out in five more days. Real tankers with the lines of a battleship . . ."

Perhaps to keep me from feeling neglected she added a postscript: "They could do with a man like you out here.

"I must fly, Angel, because I am lunching with Admiral and Mrs. Nimitz. I've been asked to christen a ship next Tuesday . . . the first time a British actress has had such a privilege. Aren't you thrilled? Now I'm becoming a real sailor's wife."

I *was* thrilled. But I wished I could have felt sure that she had not blithely advised Admiral Nimitz that he needed me to help him do his job.

* * *

On this tour she began the custom of sending my mother a gift from every city she played in—a bit of old Honiton lace, a book of memoirs "which I thought would make gentle reading for you," a piece of Sandwich glass, or a first edition of one of my mother's favorite poets.

"Always I thank you for something lovely," Mother wrote Gertrude in acknowledgment of one of these presents. "Do you realize that all my pretty gifts come from you?"

Their correspondence revealed the two Mrs. Aldriches to each other. Mother wrote:

My dear Gertrude:

I feel an urge to write to you this morning before I go to the post office. Do you think I shall get a letter from Richard? In the last one he said, "I have a wonderful wife, and she loves me." Isn't that a comfort? It means more than words, too, for we New Englanders are very undemonstrative and find it hard to express our devotion. I am so used to depending on Richard that I feel lost and can't decide things myself. You must feel the same.

Yours with much love,
Mary Aldrich

Chapter Ten

GERTRUDE'S TOUR in *Lady in the Dark* ended in July of 1943. She went at once to the Cape, where Helen Mahoney had the house ready for us. I had obtained leave for that week-end to spend it at Dennis. Both of us were glad that, in this first meeting in several months, we could be by ourselves at The Berries.

The house already had the look of being lived in by an active and thoroughly extroverted American family. The blasé Mackie, who was accustomed to making himself at home in Pullman drawing rooms, hotel suites and theatre dressing rooms, so far forgot his role and his thirteen years as to caper the minute he was let off his leash on the lawn of The Berries. The three canaries, Winnie, Franklin and Henriette, expressed their delight at getting out of the city by singing and chirping their heads off.

The trustees had decided to close the Playhouse "for the duration" after the 1942 season, which, quite apart from my own unavailability because of Navy duties, I had advised them not to undertake. I had felt—as it turned out, rightly—that gas rationing, blackouts and similar wartime conditions would make successful operation impossible.

Our week-end reunion on the Cape was the first time Gertrude and I had been there together when there was no Playhouse to engross me. Without the horde of eager young apprentices swarming over the grounds and the continuous coming and going of cars, trucks, station wagons and bicycles, with no production problems, no visiting stars to be entertained, placated, temporized with and finally seen off like comets trailing a wake of sparks, the Cape's real character emerged with startling clarity. In the village, cleared now of sightseers and vacationists by the war, the Yankee face—long, lean, unperturbed, slightly wry—was conspicuously in evidence. Several times during my stay I caught Gertrude looking at me as if she was seeing me for the first time.

She said: "I'm discovering something. These are your people; you belong to them and they to you. You're a piece of New England, like the characters in O'Neill's plays."

I told her that, like most New Englanders of my generation who had escaped through the universities to New York, I suffered a morbid self-consciousness whenever anyone identified me with my native habitat. The midwestern writers who had discovered New England and had set out to interpret it in Freudian-angled novels and plays had done that to us.

Though I spoke lightly, I was busy realizing that during my early years in New York, and while married to my first wife, I had made a deliberate attempt to divest myself of my New England traits in order to appear as a young man about Gotham. I had done this, as I realized, from the basest of human motives—fear of ridicule. In the circles I moved in, a New Englander was regarded as amusingly quaint or as definitely psychopathic: at best an Ethan Frome; at worst one of the less admirable characters of *Our Town* or *Desire Under the Elms*. Because the authors of these works had written strong dramas, it seemed to be taken for granted that they had also written sociological truth . . . whereas the whole truth had been barely glimpsed.

I did not burden Gertrude with these observations, which, after all, could mean little to her. But I told her she would find more of New England in my mother and in Dr. Harriet than in the heroine of *Mourning Becomes Electra*. She, better than most, should know how untrue to life good drama can frequently be.

My leave was short; headquarters was very busy at the time. I had to take the late Sunday night train in order to report at Ninety Church on Monday morning. I left Gertrude tucked up in bed with her little radio beside her, turned low, as she liked to have it all night. She always said she felt better for hearing soft music or a voice close by when she woke suddenly in the dark.

"Try to come soon again," she begged when we said goodbye.

I asked her if she would like to return to New York and stay at the apartment. She shook her head. "No. The Berries is more ours than anything we can ever have in New York. Here I'm not Miss Gertrude Lawrence; I'm Mrs. Richard Stoddard Aldrich. When you're away, that helps a lot."

New York was stifling under a blanket of humidity. I was glad Gertrude was in cool Dennis. She always wilted and lost weight in exceedingly hot weather.

The train was late, which meant no time for the shower and change I longed for. I bolted a glass of milk at Grand Central and darted, like thousands of other rabbits, into the burrow of the subway to ride downtown to my desk.

When I showed my identity card to the guard at the entry of Ninety Church Street I thought he looked at me strangely. Not suspiciously, but rather—if the notion had not seemed so ridiculous—almost as if with pity.

Entering my office, I found a group of my fellow-officers in earnest, low-voiced conversation before an open window. They broke off abruptly when I came in. On one or two faces I surprised that same look of commiseration—or was it anxiety?—that the guard had directed toward me.

Heading toward my desk, I found myself wondering if they had advance knowledge that I was going to be transferred. Or reprimanded. Demoted, perhaps?

I felt awkward and apprehensive.

I sat down at my desk, where the telephone already was making insistent demands. The pressure of the day's business took precedence over everything of a personal nature. I told myself that any disturbing orders from the C.O. which the others might know about would reach me in due course through the proper channels.

No orders came through, however. My telephone continued to ring and my work took me out of the office a number of times during the morning.

Hurrying back from one of these absences, I found the message that Dennis, Massachusetts, had been trying to get me. Also that David Holtzmann had called several times; he had asked that I ring him on a matter of personal importance. I planned to do this and to call Gertrude in Dennis as soon as I had free time.

At noon, John Lodge—later Governor Lodge of Connecticut—who had been in my class at Harvard and who was then one of my brother officers, stuck his head in the door and asked if I wasn't going out for a bite to eat. I told him I couldn't get away just then. "Later. Say, half an hour."

Instead of going on, he came in, his usually cheerful face rather grave.

"What are you doing for dinner tonight, Dick?" he asked.

I said I had no particular plans.

"I'd be glad to meet you at the club." Again that oddly solicitous look.

"Fine," I told John. "But I couldn't make it till around eight. I have to—"

"Any time that suits you," John assured me. Still he made no move to go.

I shot a glance at him. He looked troubled.

"Anything wrong, John?" I asked.

"Well, I don't suppose you want to talk about it," he blurted. "And I don't blame you. But I want you to know we're all with you. We think it's a shame."

"What is?"

John was too intently following the course of his own thought to stop to enlighten me. "It doesn't make sense. Francesca can't get over it. She rang me from Westport last night the minute she heard it. It's something neither one of us thought would ever happen. Not to you and Gertrude. We'd have bet on it."

"WHAT?" I demanded. "What's happened?"

John's jaw dropped. "Do you mean you don't *know*?"

"Know WHAT?" I shouted.

I was aware that several officers had stopped at the door and were crowding around my desk. Tom Dewart, of the New York *Sun* publishing family, laid a consoling hand on my shoulder.

"We think it's a rotten deal, Dick," he said. "Somehow, I never thought Gertrude would do a thing like that."

I pushed back my chair and stood up. I felt better on my feet. I looked at the ring of faces—kind, concerned, showing that instinctive, if frequently inarticulate, sympathy which unites males, even of quite different types, when confronted by the enigma of woman.

"Look," I said. "All this is a mystery to me. If it has anything to do with Gertrude, I'd like to hear it—straight. And quick."

Tom said: "We're talking about the divorce, Dick. About Gertrude divorcing you to marry some rich Californian."

I found myself looking from one face to the next, seeking confirmation of Tom's incredible statement. The others nodded. So I had heard aright.

"Where did you hear this?" I asked Tom.

John spoke up: "It's in one of the morning columns. But Jimmie Fidler broadcast it last night. That's how Francesca got it."

"And about half the country," growled Tom.

Before I could reply, my telephone rang again. It was David Holtzmann's secretary. David would be on the wire in a moment.

While I waited, I reflected rapidly on Gertrude's admirers. I could think of at least three wealthy Californians, any one of whom might, conceivably, be a man Gertrude might marry. None of them had ever been at pains to hide his devotion, and Gertrude had enjoyed accepting this. She had even encouraged it. I knew that each of these men (and several others in both America and England) had a large photograph of her, specially and lovingly inscribed, and decorated with a heart pierced by an arrow, which was her mark of deep affection. I had occasionally teased her on this score, calling her an outrageous hussy.

"But darling, it makes them happy," she had said. "So why not? And they are all perfect dears. Besides, they are all so wonderful to me whenever I play in their cities."

I had believed in the innocence of these flirtations chiefly because she was so open about them: not hiding them from me, but boasting about them, like a seventeen-year-old girl flaunting her dates. She had even asked me to stop in at Mark Cross and buy a leather frame to hold one of these inscribed photographs destined for a man's desk. With shameless practicality, she had said my taste would probably suit the man better than hers.

But suppose these relationships were not as innocent as I had thought them? I was under no illusion about my own powers to charm and hold a woman of Gertrude's volatile temperament. I had been through one divorce. My hopes of holding Gertrude lay in my determination not to attempt to hold her, any more than I would clench my fist around a hummingbird. Before our marriage I had promised her that she should never lose the sense of being free.

If she had turned from me to another man who offered her more than I could give, how could I blame her? During the two days we had just spent together she had been tender and loving—everything that a man could want of a wife. But might this not have been a final bestowal of affection—a parting gift of love?

David came on the wire. "Dick? I've been trying to get you for hours! So has Gertrude. She's fit to be tied!"

"Is she?" I snapped. "Tied to whom? Who is this fellow Gertrude is supposedly divorcing me for?"

John's voice prompted me: "A Pasadena business man."

"Divorcing you? NUTS," David shouted in my ear. "Snap out of it, will you? I've had enough with Gertrude ringing me every fifteen minutes to find out what I've done about Fidler, without your going off the beam, too. She's been wild since she heard the broadcast last night. There's no foundation whatsoever for the story. When she couldn't reach you at the apartment this morning, and you weren't in your office when she called, she was sure you had heard it and were 'keeping away from her.' "

I was beginning to feel exceedingly foolish. I put my hand over the mouthpiece and turned to my friends. "Everything is all right," I assured them. "Fidler is one hundred per cent wrong. There is no Pasadena business man. This talk about divorce is nonsense!"

A wave of smiles spread through the group—along with various remarks unflattering to the tribe of radio gossip-dealers. The crowd melted away, muttering down the corridor. I did some muttering of my own to David.

"That's what I called you about," he said. "The American Broadcasting Company are as upset about it as we are. At least they should be," he added grimly, "after what I've just said to them. Anyway, they've offered to put on a special broadcast tonight refuting what Fidler said and apologizing to Gertrude and you. They're not going to wait for the show's regular hour next Sunday."

I could not fail to accept this formal apology. But there was a further *amende honorable* to take care of—the one due to Gertrude from me for those thirty seconds in which I had doubted her. I rang a florist and ordered two dozen white roses to be delivered to Mrs. Richard Stoddard Aldrich in Dennis, Massachusetts. No message of any sort was needed; the flowers would speak for themselves.

After our first falling out at Northfield I had sent Gertrude red roses, and from that occasion red roses had come to have a special meaning for us. They marked the end of a quarrel. Later I had learned that Gertrude preferred white flowers to any others, and I would send her these when I wished to express my special appreciation of her. She used to say: "Your white flowers always tell me when I'm being a very good girl."

Would she understand their significance at this time? She was exceedingly astute in all the delicate phases of human relationships. Silently, I thanked God that her astuteness was more than equaled by her generous forbearance. She never expected human beings, even the human being who was her husband, to be perfect in all ways at all times. She could always allow for a human failing, believing, as part of her creed for living, that this was usually compensated for by an abundance of some other virtue.

As she expressed it in her favorite phrase: "Wot yer loses on the swings yer makes on the roundabouts."

* * *

The relationship between the two Mrs. Aldriches deepened during the summer of 1943. Mother spent August with Gertrude at the Berries. I went up to join them whenever I could get leave.

Gertrude had again enlisted under the banner stoutly upheld by Dr. Harriet. When she was at home and not working in garden or bog, she and Mother knitted steadily. Aware that Gertrude needed more rest than she seemed willing to take, Mother, at a hint from me, proposed to read aloud to her for several hours every afternoon. Gertrude accepted the offer with alacrity. She loved being read to, and I had found this was sometimes the only way to get her to relax. Although I did not myself particularly enjoy reading aloud, I had formed the habit of reading to her at times until she would drop asleep, to awake hours later refreshed.

Mother, like so many of her generation, was an experienced and adept reader. That summer at the Berries she read to Gertrude from the books which had meant much to her all her life—Browning, Wordsworth, and the New England writers whose sunset glory had illumined her own girlhood. One or two of them she had known. She spoke of meeting "Mr. Emerson" at a literary tea; and among her treasured books was a volume of Longfellow's poetry given her by Mrs. Dana, the "Edith with golden hair" of "The Children's Hour."

As a young matron in Boston, Mother had belonged to a Browning Circle whose members read, explored and discussed the meaning of Robert Browning's often difficult verse. It was inevitable, therefore, that she should read some of his shorter poems to Gertrude: "Oh to be in England, now that April's there," and "Prospice," and "My Star." Inevitable, too, that Gertrude's sensitive ear and quick, retentive memory should seize and hold fast many of the lines. Her interest in them and in their author was grounded in her enjoyment of *The Barretts of Wimpole Street,* which she had seen many times, first in London, later in New York.

Contrary to popular belief, Gertrude was not by nature a gay, frivolous butterfly reveling in the delights of Café Society. Her sorties into the smart set were all made, so to speak, in the line of duty; she felt it was part of her job to be seen in certain circles. As with her other roles, she played the carefree glamour girl so well that all but those closest to her were thoroughly deceived.

Actually, Gertrude was happiest in a small, intimate circle; or among young people. Otherwise, she needed a stage; a part to interpret; and, above all, a goal to achieve.

Knowing this, I occasionally lured her into a pleasant social evening by representing it as a matter of personal importance to me. Faced with an ostensible opportunity to be of service in furthering my plans, she would be willing and eager to attend a small dinner. Once there, in her effort to do me proud, she would be her most charming, warmhearted self.

As a result, everyone enjoyed her, fell in love with her, and she discovered that she liked them; thus close friendships were developed with John and Francesca Lodge, Cassie and John Mason Brown, Mary and Oswald Lord, and Ellie and Tom Dewart.

She would be especially shy among intellectuals, or people who spoke of world affairs. Yet, so great was her reverence for learning, it was just such people that she longed to meet. One of her unfulfilled wishes was to meet Professor Albert Einstein.

I am sure that the basis of Gertrude's shyness among people not of the theatre was her awareness of her own total lack of formal education. Yet, although she spent no more than a few months in any school, and grew up, so to speak, backstage in variety shows and musical comedies that toured the English provinces without ever coming into London, Gertrude had a fluent and beautiful command of the English language that would put the majority of American college graduates to shame. Her handwriting had great distinction. She could express herself in a note, even to a stranger, with a clarity, a feeling for words and an unaffected, warm sincerity that came close to genius. She made no mistakes in grammar, and her misspellings were limited to a very few words which she consistently spelled in her own chosen way.

Her spontaneous interest in and curiosity about whatever was new to her sent her to books on an extraordinarily wide range of subjects. Everything, from conchology to cooking, engaged her at one time or another. When she was teaching a class in the Drama School at Columbia University, at the same time that she was appearing in *The King and I,* she had a habit of going to the campus at least a full hour before her class was scheduled. Availing herself of her faculty privileges, she would drop in on some lecture or browse in the library.

One afternoon I found her at home in bed, reading a thick volume on archaeology. She looked up excitedly as I came in. "Did you know there are places where you can dig history right out of the ground? Cyprus. And Crete, and places like that."

I admitted to this knowledge.

"Darling! We must go and see those Greek isles, just as soon as we can!"

Chapter Eleven

On her return to New York from the Cape, Gertrude began making elaborate arrangements for the family to put up a united front at Thanksgiving. But the Navy Department had other plans. In October of 1943 I was ordered to overseas duty with the amphibious forces based in England.

At that time Gertrude was working regularly at the Red Cross and the Stage Door Canteen. She had accepted no play for that season, hoping that arrangements would be made for her to go to England to entertain Allied troops there. Meanwhile she had signed up for a weekly radio program sponsored by Revlon. She made no bones about her envy of my "luck" in getting into the European Theatre of Operations ahead of her.

"I hate being a civilian," she said bitterly. She was sitting in the sunny bow window of our apartment living room sewing name tapes on intimate articles of my clothing, a task she had stoutly refused to let her maid take over. "I know my duty as a Navy wife," she said proudly, and sent her needle through the cotton of a pair of shorts with a vicious jab. "But I think it's unfair for me to be left high and dry on the beach while you sail away to all the excitement. And it's my homeland you're going to."

She extorted from me a promise to see Basil Dean—the veteran English producer who was arranging shows for the British equivalent of our USO, and with whom her friendship dated back to her childhood appearances in pantomimes he directed. "Make him cut all the red tape and get me across as soon as possible," she instructed.

She was not impressed by my observation that the Navy was sending me to help stage a war, not to meddle in the entertainment of the troops, and that it was unlikely I would have any opportunity to contact Basil Dean.

"It's being left behind that always hurts most," she said.

Gertrude had a habit, probably dating from adolescence, of starting a diary whenever she felt depressed and a trifle afraid. Although her personal code prevented her from confiding her low feelings to anyone, her diary afforded a safe vent for the blues. Alone at night, before going to bed, she could pour onto its patient pages her anxieties, her hopes and ingenuous self-revelations. For a time she would make regular entries in it. Then it would end suddenly, when her life became too active, exciting and successful to require this kind of introspection.

One of Gertrude's diaries, a small, crimson leather-bound volume with gold tooling, is inscribed on the title page: *My Life Without Richard.* Pasted below is a small photograph of me at the age of six, wearing a blue sailor's hat atop a Buster Brown haircut, and an expression of such unhappiness that only a mother, or a wife capable of the sentimentality Gertrude sometimes displayed, would have saved it from the wastepaper basket.

"*Wednesday, October 20, 1943,*" she wrote. "At 11:30 A.M. this day, my dear one left the house and the homes we have made together and, like many other millions, he and I may not be husband and wife again for longer than either of us can, or dare to, imagine.

"It was a hard bitter parting, not being allowed to go with him, but I drove down later and stole a look at the ship and I think I feel better. She is large and very seaworthy and safe-looking. There seems evidence of a good escort. I came home, tried to eat, was violently sick and then went out for air.

"I shopped for this book, in which I intend to write day by day while Richard is overseas.

"I returned and asked my telephone operator if there had been any calls for me. She calmly said: 'No, but Lieutenant Aldrich is upstairs.'

"It seemed as if the world was swimming around me as I rang and waited for the lift and tried not to believe that my mind had gone wrong.

"At last I reached my door and, still not believing it could be true, I called his name. The door opened and there was Richard and we were holding each other closer than ever before, laughing and crying at the same time. At that moment I knew the goodness of God's mercy—Richard had snatched thirty minutes ashore to dash to me, and I could so easily have missed seeing him had not His hand led me back in time. We sat and just looked at each other, and this time I drove with him as far as I dared. Now he has gone, but some strength has been given me from that thirty-minute reprieve . . .

"*Same day, 7:15 P.M.* I cannot settle down in any room. No more word from R., just the low cry of the boats from the river, and each one sends a knife through my heart. I used to love to hear such sounds; now each one may be the signal which means Richard is underway. I long to dash to the pier, yet dare not leave the house lest he should call me . . . O stupid people, in such a splendid world to permit so much misery and heartache . . . Richard . . .

"*9:30 P.M.* I have sat here in my room, just sat doing nothing, and now the sky is full of planes and the sounds from the pier are unmistakable. Richard is putting out to sea. I wish I had gone down to try to see him go but the police would probably have turned me back . . . The pain is choking me . . . I'm cold and, oh, so lonely and unhappy, and yet I'm supposed to be one of the lucky ones . . ."

The daily entries continue faithfully for three days. Then there is a silence of seven months—a gap which the diarist bridges with characteristic nonchalance: "Well, it certainly is some time since I wrote in *My Life,* but the truth is, I have no life without Richard."

This entry is more literary than literal. Far from having no life, Gertrude had been up to her ears in so many things that winter that she had felt no need for the solace a diary offered. It was not that she did not miss me; every one of her almost daily letters breathed that. But, constitutionally, she was no moper. Her instinctive way of meeting any problem, even that of loneliness, was to do something.

Among her constant occupations that winter were her weekly radio show and her *Broadway Calling* broadcasts to the armed forces, for which she enlisted the talents of guest stars ranging from Lily Pons to Jimmy Durante.

In December, she undertook to open New York's new City Center of Music and Drama. Typically, that civic-spirited venture ended up with Gertrude revamping the acoustics of the theatre to save the entire project.

City Center was a pet idea of Mayor LaGuardia and Newbold Morris, then president of the City Council. The ornate Mecca Temple building on West Fifty-fifth Street had become city property for default of taxes. Morris, a devotee of the theatre and long one of Gertrude's fans, conceived the notion of turning the building into a playhouse where good music and good plays could be given for short runs at popular prices. When he approached Gertrude and asked her to open the Center with a two weeks' run of *Susan and God,* she enthusiastically agreed.

Rehearsals were held elsewhere while repairs to the building were being completed. On the opening night, ten days before Christmas, it became dishearteningly apparent why the original owners of the big auditorium had abandoned it: the actors could not be heard beyond the first few rows. The acoustics were so poor that many of the distinguished audience left at the end of the first act.

After the final curtain, a melancholy group gathered backstage to assess the failure. Their case seemed hopeless. Clearly a whole public address system was needed; and sound equipment, as well as the engineers to handle it, was simply not to be had in those days of wartime restrictions. LaGuardia hunched his massive shoulders and threw wide his hands in a gesture which implied silently his famous remark, "When I make a mistake, it's a beaut."

Gertrude alone was undismayed. As Jack Potter reported it to me by letter: "The next morning she phoned the Bell Laboratories and got on to the President of the company, Dr. Oliver Buckley. Dr. Buckley confirmed that, under regulations of the War Production Board, he was unable to sell electronics equipment for civilian use; he certainly couldn't sell the city a complex public address system. Still Gertrude persisted. . . Ten minutes later—somewhat to his own surprise, I suspect—Dr. Buckley found himself agreeing that while he couldn't *sell* a p.a. system without a priority rating from WPB, there was nothing to stop him from *lending* one to Gee—which she in turn could lend to the city."

Gertrude gratefully accepted the offer—and the services of the two technicians who were dispatched to install the system. However, her problem was not yet over. The technicians were agreed that, by getting to work at once and keeping at it through the night, they could have the amplifiers and other equipment in working condition in time for the next day's matinee.

What to do, however, about that evening's performance, for which thousands of tickets had been sold?

The engineers conferred, and came up with an interim suggestion: If the walls of the Center could be padded thickly, the acoustics would be improved enough, they thought, to make the actors reasonably intelligible in the evening performance.

The next question was: What sort of padding?

"Would blankets do?" Gertrude inquired. "And what about down-filled coverlets?"

Yes, the engineers said—if enough of them could be obtained to line a large area of the walls. But then there was the problem of concealing them from view.

Every eye in the group measured the height and breadth of the walls. "It would take a lot of bedding," Fanny Holtzmann observed.

LaGuardia shook his head. "The city can't go out and buy blankets—" he began.

Gertrude cut him short. "Who said anything about buying

them? We'll do just what they do at the Playhouse when props are needed. We'll borrow them. From our friends, of course. Everyone here must get together all he can. Off your own beds and off everyone's you can think of. Fortunately, it's only for one night and we'll hope the weather doesn't turn any colder."

Dubious glances went around the little circle. Fanny broke the ice. "We've *got* to make Gertrude's plan work," she announced. "We simply can't have a dark house tonight. The very idea makes me furious."

LaGuardia grinned at Fanny. "Now you girls are talking my language," he said. "Fury."

That was all the encouragement Gertrude needed. Sparked by her, the whole group took fire. They scattered to round up bedding from every quarter of the city. Fortified with five dollars in nickels, Gertrude's dresser Hazel took her post at the backstage telephone and rang her friends in Harlem to "help Miss Lawrence out." Helen Mahoney, our cook-housekeeper, canvassed her Greenwich Village neighbors in Perry Street.

In an hour's time taxis, trucks, and people on foot began arriving at City Center with bedding of every description. Judge Learned Hand, Newbold Morris's father-in-law, brought his family's quota and his daughter Connie Morris's regrets that her illness prevented her from joining the campaign. A police car with shrieking siren brought trophies from the Mayor's house.

Up they all went on the walls—a pied patchwork that was symbolic of the city itself. A red cotton featherbed which could only have come from somewhere in Central Europe hung beside the gray satin down quilt off Gertrude's own bed.

Meanwhile she had made a personal appeal to two old friends, the distinguished producers John Golden and Lee Shubert. For her, they had opened their huge storehouses and emptied them of all the dark velvet draperies. These were hung over the bedding, concealing it completely. The last fold was in place a quarter of an hour before the doors of the City Center opened.

Fearful that the report of the building's bad acoustics would have its effect on the night's audience, Gertrude had notified the

Stage Door Canteen that all empty seats would be available free to men in uniform.

The curtain rose on a good house. The acoustics were not absolutely perfect, but they were more than adequate.

In a few days all the bed coverings were returned to their owners with Gertrude's thanks. "You see," she said, "New York is like the Cape at heart—a friendly community."

Mayor LaGuardia was profuse in his gratitude to Gertrude for saving his project. A large box of flowers arrived with his card, on which was written: "To My Commissioner of Sound." A similar offering to Fanny was inscribed: "To My Commissioner of Fury."

* * *

In every letter in that winter of 1943-44, Gertrude expressed her longing to go to England: in part because I was stationed there (as she repeatedly said, "We could have some days together"), but also because she wanted to be with her countrymen at that critical time.

She had received from Basil Dean a cable asking her to come and tour the camps for ENSA, the British USO. The difficulty was to get a priority to make the crossing. In those weeks of waiting, hoping, being disappointed, and hoping again, she returned to her diary.

"*May 5, 1944.* Three suitcases have been bought and all proved too heavy to keep my air weight down to 55 lbs. I have packed and unpacked a dozen times . . . new songs have been written, orchestra parts made, dance routines rehearsed, taxes paid, visas and exit permits procured, also a re-entry permit—when suddenly, like going off the Gold Standard, England declared a law forbidding the entry into the U.K. of any civilian, British or Allied, for any short period. And no exit from the U.K. for the duration.

"I lost my space in one flight while I awaited word from Richard what to do . . . He cabled not to worry, that the ENSA people would arrange everything, and for me to leave immediately. So I reapplied for the next trip, which goes today. I have said goodbye to everybody, sent everything I possess ahead, shut up everything, dismissed the maids, cut my hair, and *now* I am told by ENSA that they cannot guarantee everything. I have been waiting for this trip since *Lady in the Dark* closed last July—almost a year. Richard, meantime, has been promoted, bless his heart, and moved into another base which he now commands. I haven't the faintest idea where they have sent him and he hasn't written, because he thought I was on my way.

"Maybe the ban will be lifted later, and then I can go home, but as things are it would be madness to go over for 12 weeks for ENSA and find myself shut in. But if that is what Richard says to do I shall go by the next plane.

"I wish I could keep my sense of humor about this, but I feel utterly frustrated.

"My Pamela and her husband came to have a farewell luncheon, as they are leaving for California. They seem so happy and complete, and once more I realize how lonely I am and have been and always will be until Richard is with me again. . . . Tomorrow I shall go up to our home in New England. I can keep busy there. . . ."

As always, activity overcame loneliness. There is no entry in *My Life Without Richard* for ten days. Then she wrote jubilantly:

"*May 16*. Sudden call . . . mind made up, shall take my chance and make the trip, no matter what consequences later.

"Leaving for Baltimore 4:30 and for Great Britain at the stroke of midnight.

"Give my regards to B'way. Piccadilly and the White Cliffs of Dover, here I come."

* * *

My first intimation that she had arrived was a trunk call from London to our base at Southampton. She promised to take an early train from Waterloo the following morning, a Saturday. We could have together as much of that day and the next as my duties as C.O. of the base would permit.

My quarters were at the Star Hotel, which had been requisitioned as H.Q. for the United States Navy. Naturally I could not take Gertrude there, since it was out of bounds for civilians. Finding an empty room anywhere in Southampton just then, when the top-secret preparations for the invasion of Normandy were engaging the Anglo-American forces to the exclusion of all else, was a formidable task. After much telephoning and resort to official pressure, I was able to get the promise of a room at the Dolphin Hotel. It had no private bath and was at the head of the stair landing, with the w.c. a long way down the passage, but under the existing circumstances I felt we were fortunate.

I went to the station to meet the nine-thirty from Waterloo, which was the train Gertrude had said she would take. I found a posted notice saying the nine-thirty had been canceled. There was nothing unusual about such changes in those days. The next train from London would be the eleven-thirty. I settled myself philosophically to wait.

In due time the eleven-thirty train arrived and disgorged a horde of servicemen—British, Canadian and American—and a small quota of civilians. But no Gertrude.

I tried not to think that a bomb might have dropped on the Savoy the night before. Much as I longed to see Gertrude, I could not help wishing her back in Dennis, with the wide Atlantic between her and constant danger from the air.

Inquiry at the stationmaster's wicket brought the cheerless information that the next train on the schedule had been taken off. The one-thirty from Waterloo was my next hope. Meanwhile, Saturday was slipping out of our grasp. At best it would be teatime before I could expect Gertrude.

I was back at the station in time for the London train. This was even more crowded than the preceding one. As sailors, soldiers and marines jammed through the gates I began to believe my luck had failed. I had been reflecting that I was perhaps the only American officer in Europe lucky enough to get a visit from his wife. Now, with anxiety overwhelming expectation, I would have exchanged what had seemed my extraordinary good fortune for the assurance of Gertrude's safety.

My unhappy reverie was shattered by a series of shrill whistles and unmistakable wolf calls. They came from the troops milling

"The glamorous Miss Lawrence wields a mean scoop," said a local paper when she made a going enterprise of our cranberry bog.

Arthur Griffin

A gift from Gertrude—photographs of the two Mrs. A's.

Our summer home, The Berries.

American Home

about the gate. A voice exclaimed: "Hey, fellers. Pipe the Red Cross dream girl."

"I'm for sale, baby."

"What do you say, sister—you busy tonight?"

Over the craning heads I saw my wife in her American Red Cross Motor Corps uniform, making her way through the mob with considerable difficulty.

At the same time she saw me.

"Richard!" she called, and started to run. I ran, too. As Gertrude flung herself into my arms and we embraced, I was conscious but proudly defiant of the stares, grins and long-drawn-out whistles from all parts of the station.

The Red Cross uniform, Gertrude explained later, had been an inspiration born of desperation. At the station in London she had found herself at the end of a long queue of civilians waiting for places on the earlier train. Realizing that she had practically no chance of getting on as a civilian, since people in uniform received preference, she had hurried back to the Savoy, pulled her Red Cross uniform from her luggage and donned it, and returned to Waterloo. There she inserted herself into the queue of uniforms lined up by that time for the one-thirty.

"It's a good thing I didn't wear it in the plane coming across," she said. She had brought with her a dozen eggs as a present for her old friend Evie Williams. In her excitement at her first glimpse of "home" she had bounced in her seat, breaking two of the eggs, which she had on her lap. Ernest Hemingway, in the adjoining seat, had helped her mop up the mess and grinned broadly to see her twist her skirt back to front, hiding the egg stain under her coat, in order to make an impeccable entrance at Croydon.

Her time in London had been too brief for her to see much of the damage done by the air raids. The devastation of Southampton, as we drove to the Dolphin, shocked her.

"And you've been through this," she said, several times, almost incredulously.

I told her she was liable to go through some of it herself that night or fairly soon. Southampton was getting a lot of hammering these days. Perhaps the Jerries suspected that we were almost ready for the Big Push. Punctiliously, Gertrude avoided asking any questions about my work or about my plans. At that time, with D-Day just two weeks off, the tension had mounted to such a pitch that it seemed as if no one could be in the United Kingdom twenty-four hours without feeling the imminence of something tremendous.

I took Gertrude to dinner at our mess. I wanted her to see and meet the men of my command, and I wanted them to see her. I don't think I'd ever been prouder of her than that night. It wasn't exactly her beauty, in the conventional sense of classically perfect features. She had something far more arresting and more unforgettable than beauty. The word that comes closest to it is radiance.

Our accommodations at the Dolphin amused and pleased her. It seemed the right setting for a reunion in the midst of war. She understood and was interested in the black-out which the chambermaid had "done" before we went upstairs. When I came back from a trip down the passage, I found Gertrude smothered in the voluminous heavy black-out drapes, trying to open the window behind them.

"Here," I exclaimed, "you can't do that."

"Why not?"

"Because if you do, you'll half choke to death."

I explained that an important part of Southampton's defense against enemy planes was the hundreds of smoke pots planted throughout the city containing a chemical compound which, when electrically ignited, sent up a dense, acrid smoke that helped hide the target.

"There's no smoke now," she persisted, sniffing out the window.

"No. But there will be if they come over."

"But, darling, we can't possibly sleep in this room without any fresh air."

"You'll have to."

"But I can't. You know I always have to have the window open."

I knew, as most husbands know. Gertrude had been opening windows, insisting on fresh air, since the night we met. I wasn't going to have our first time together spoiled by any farcical husband-and-wife bickering, so I gave in.

"Have it your own way," I told her. I told myself that maybe Jerry would give us a night off.

* * *

I was awakened by Gertrude clutching me as an air raid siren went off. She was sitting up in bed, coughing. Smoke fumes were pouring into the room.

"Oh, Richard, get up and shut the window," she gasped.

"You see," I told her, padding across the worn carpet on bare feet to struggle with the black-out. I banged down the window. "Now, perhaps you'll believe me."

She looked up at me with streaming eyes. "Always Right Aldrich," she wheezed.

I fetched her a glass of water and gradually the paroxysm subsided.

"I am a one for having my own way, aren't I?" she whispered contritely.

"You are."

But I spoke perfunctorily. I was listening, thinking. The smoke meant enemy planes. Of course they might pass over us bound for targets inland. Again, they might not. I told Gertrude what we could expect and asked her if she wanted to go down to the hotel cellar, where a good many, if not all, of the guests and staff would take refuge.

"Not the cellar," she said. "I'd rather take our chances above ground and just us together."

I said I would, too, so we waited.

The first one that landed—I estimated it fell between the docks and the gas works—shivered the Dolphin's stout old timbers but caused no immediate damage.

Gertrude came closer into my arms. She whispered against my shoulder: "That sound brings back so much I'd rather forget . . . the first war, and the night Pamela was born. Things looked awfully black just then. I was facing up to the fact that my marriage was all wrong. I hadn't the ghost of an idea what to do . . . Darling, this is a thousand times better. Whatever happens, we've had nearly four years of happiness. I've loved every minute of being Mrs. A—"

I told her that we had a lot of time ahead of us. I felt confident of it.

"Well, let's not waste a single minute," she said practically. "This is better than sleeping, and I've simply oceans to tell you. First, about the boys . . .

"I knew you'd want the latest news about David and young Dick. David's doing well at school, though he says he gets high marks only to earn more time off for play. And Dick is practically as tall as you are—but he's thin and pale and sort of quiet."

I said most growing boys passed through that stage.

"The best thing for them both," Gertrude went on, "would be to run wild on the Cape for a few months. I'm trying to sell our cranberry separator. We don't use it, now that we belong to Canners, Inc. If I can get some money for it I'll clear the cranberry house out and put bunks in it; then the boys can camp out there. They can work in the bog and run on the beach, and Helen Mahoney will see that they eat up."

She gave me details about The Berries. She had taken Mackie's ashes there and buried them under a pine tree in the garden. (The little dog had died only a few days after I had left, the previous October.) Of all our menagerie of pets, only Winnie remained.

"I shan't get another dog until the war is over and we are settled again," Gertrude said sadly. "And, of course, there'll never be another like Mackie. Darling, do you remember him at Northfield?"

I said that I could not forget.

"He very nearly bit your father's friend, Dr. Webster." She began to laugh.

I did, too. We clung together, laughing.

Jerry selected that moment to drop another. This one was closer. Gertrude began to talk very fast.

"I hate having The Berries empty," she said. "It seems such a waste when it's so lovely at the Cape. The garden has come on a lot. Barbara and Harrison will go up, they promised me. But your mother refuses to leave Groton."

I asked about Mother. Gertrude said she had talked with her on

Mother's Day a few weeks before, and then had gone up to see her before leaving. "She is well, but she seems just a tiny bit older. She worries about you, naturally. She's terribly proud of you. She has a photograph of you in uniform on her desk where she writes her letters. She's been looking up all your English ancestors and where they came from. She asked me to walk with her to the cemetery in Groton to see the Joy graves and the beautiful white iron fence around them. She doesn't like the idea that she will be buried beside your father in Upton, and not among her own people in Groton."

I said this had been one of Mother's worries for years.

"She went over to Upton one day this spring," Gertrude informed me, "and she had an awful shock. The tombstone of some strange woman has tilted over into the Aldrich plot. 'The intruder,' Mother Mary calls her. She's terribly indignant about it. She pointed out that such a thing couldn't happen to the Joys. Because of the white iron fence, I expect."

"No doubt you told her I would push the tombstone away," I ventured.

"Of course, darling," Gertrude said seriously. "I promised her you would attend to it the minute you came home."

I did not like all this talk about cemeteries. To divert her, I said I was sorry Mother had been so depressed. "The visit couldn't have been very much fun for you."

"On the contrary," Gertrude said quickly. "She told me those things and she took me to see the graves because she feels now that I *belong*. It was a tremendous compliment. You're the head of the family and I am your wife. She unlocked her desk and showed me the letter your great-grandfather James Joy wrote to his wife Sarah Pickering when he knew he was going to die. It is her most cherished possession.

"And oh, darling, I almost forgot to tell you. Mother said we could have Grandfather Joy's lovely old clock. You remember the one I mean, don't you?"

I most certainly did. Gertrude was right. Mother had taken her into the family's innermost sanctuary. I could see that the two Mrs. A's had had a wonderful time together.

"She was so sweet, trying to comfort me about your being away," Gertrude went on. "She offered me a helpful thought to repeat in the lonely moments: 'This, too, shall pass.' "

I remembered the quotation well. Mother summoned it up invariably in times of crisis.

"This conversation is rather like a chorus girl's tights," Gertrude said. "It touches everything and covers nothing."

She began to speak of her proposed tour for ENSA. Hers was to be called the Gertrude Lawrence Unit. She had no idea where they were to go—their destinations were to be kept secret from day to day—but they would tour Great Britain for eight weeks, giving two shows or more a day and motoring from place to place. Some of the shows would be given in war plants, others for the troops.

She was interrupted by sudden heavy firing. It sounded close.

"Richard, what's that?"

"The rocket guns." I did not add that these were not usually fired unless they could be aimed directly at the target. It meant the planes were flying low overhead.

"How about going down to the shelter?" I asked quietly. Inwardly I cursed my eagerness to see her, which had led to her coming down. I should have made her stay in London.

"I really think we ought to go," I said.

But she refused. There would be all the others. "I want us to be alone. Especially when we have so little time." Her hands held me tight, but her voice was determinedly gay.

I realized that she had allocated to herself the role of sustaining me, fortifying me against fear. While the guns kept up their firing, and now and then a bomb exploded, she chattered on about a multitude of things—future plans: "Darling, when this is all over, let's have a theatre of our own. We shall call it the Commander and make ourselves some steady rentals . . ."

She talked about people we knew—Dr. Fritz and Dr. Harriet, the people who own the grocery in Dennis, and the auction held for the local church, at which she had acted as auctioneer.

"Darling, I must tell you about the awful *faux pas* I made in Dennis. We had a tea to raise money for British War Relief at Helen Rich's house. The committee had asked me to award the prizes to the ladies who had knitted the most mittens or sold the most raffle tickets, or whatever. Well, Richard, as I was making the awards, I suddenly noticed that I was short one prize, so I picked up a loving cup from the mantel and presented it 'temporarily' to the winner, saying: 'We all know no one deserves this as much as you.' The lady, one of the most dignified and respected of the group, purred in appreciation. Then she put on her spectacles and looked at the cup she was holding. Do you know what was engraved on it, darling? 'To the best bitch!' "

She interspersed these anecdotes with jokes. It was a magnificent performance; I was sure that in the course of it Gertrude convinced herself that she was keeping up my morale.

It was a long time before we slept, and the housemaid's rap came all too soon. After a hurried breakfast I saw Gertrude off on the train back to London.

* * *

I was to see her again several times during her stay in England. We were within a few days of D-Day when I came out of my quarters one afternoon to find the town plastered with bills announcing the arrival of the Gertrude Lawrence Unit at Southampton's Guildhall next day.

No sooner was the news out than my office was besieged with requests for leave to see the show. Very few of those who asked knew that Gertrude was my wife: this was something I had thought best to keep secret. It was known only to my superior officers and to the few men of my command she had met at mess.

I managed to catch the show, and the party which the top British brass put on for her unit afterward at the Polygon, the V.I.P. hotel where Gertrude and her company were billeted. Gertrude and I were extremely circumspect throughout the party. Very dutifully, I let the admirals, captains, and generals dance with her, without cutting in. None of these suspected the presence of a husband. After the party was over I bribed a discreet hotel porter to let me up the back stairs to Gertrude's room. I left very early the next morning by the same route.

"Just the same, that porter wasn't so discreet. Or you didn't give him enough," Gertrude told me later that day, when we went for a walk down by the docks. "There was an unmistakable look in the faces of the hotel staff when I came down. The gossip is going around that Gertie and the tall Yankee commander are having an affair."

It was our private joke, which we enjoyed while she remained in the Southampton area. We kept it up when her unit did a show aboard *H.M.S. Collingwood* at Portsmouth. As she came forward to sing "A Lovely Way to Spend an Evening," she all but missed cue when she saw me seated among the ranking British brass in the front row.

"You nearly lost your false eyelashes," I teased her later, when we had a moment together.

"If they were to go, I'd jump overboard after them," she said. "They're the most important part of my make-up. I can tell you, trying to be glamorous in this ENSA uniform takes some doing."

Her tour through that spring of 1944 took Gertrude from Portsmouth to the Orkneys, from Cardiff to Canterbury. "If anyone ever again mentions this tiny little island, I shall scream," she wrote later. "Its vastness is one more of the wonders of the world, when one is routed by ENSA."

She traveled every day in an ENSA car. "I am never told where we are going until I open my orders in the car. I do two shows every day, one at 12:30, the other at night. Sometimes we work under canvas for as many as two thousand men. Once we played to eight thousand of all the services of all the allied nations . . . With all this motoring I now have a gait like a permanent drunk. And, oh, the beds! Sleeping in one is like trying to relax on a charging camel. But, boy, am I tough! When I get home I'm going to live a life of ease, smothered in perfume, soap, and decent lavatory paper. Darling, I have read the latest headlines in the oddest places . . ."

At the conclusion of the tour she spent several days in Salisbury. This was near enough to our base for me to run over one evening, and we had a few hours together. She was weary, but determined to go on to Normandy to entertain the troops who had made the landing there a month earlier and were now fighting their way toward the Belgian border. I did not approve of her going into an area which was still dangerous and where the living conditions were not only uncomfortable but unsanitary. But no resistance I put up could hold her back.

She went over with the first ENSA unit to go into France, making the crossing in an LST. Others in the party included Ivor Novello, Margaret Rutherford, Diana Wynyard and Bobbie Andrews. In her autobiography, *A Star Danced,* she has given a graphic account of their landing on the Normandy beach and of the progress of her unit through the wrecked towns, where there was still no water or electricity. Shows were given in shell-torn movie houses and hastily lighted casinos.

The physical discomforts—the sleeping in attics, the total lack of sanitation, the scanty and poor food—Gertrude could and did take as fortunes of war. What bothered her more was the breakdown in communications with me. Always dependent upon getting frequent letters from those she loved, she chafed and worried because no mail reached her.

"I know now how a soldier feels when he doesn't hear from home," she wrote pathetically. "No word from you. This really is not my idea of being married, not even in the vaguest, most wartime way. Don't you love me any more? Or what?"

Her letters to me were as slow in coming through as mine to her. I had no idea where she was. Twice I crossed the channel and was within thirty kilometers of her, but had no idea where her unit was or whither it was routed. No one seemed to know. I sympathized with her complaints about disorganization in ENSA, though I could realize better than she what they were up against.

"Without the good spirits and guts of the artists, they could never carry on," she wrote. "The gold-braided back-room boys in charge should be sent out on one of these tours for a few weeks and learn what's what. They would pass out.

"Thank God you can't see me. I haven't had a bath since we landed. (How often she blessed her luck, which allowed her and others in the party aboard the LST to have a swim while waiting for the low water to beach the tanks.) Nor have I washed my hair for three weeks. I'm a mess."

Many of the towns they stayed in were still mined, and warnings were placed everywhere not to pick up souvenirs or to go into the fields to gather flowers.

"All have now had or now got dysentery," she wrote. "I have now got. And most painful and inconvenient it is. The M.O. says it's the flies, as they are now here in millions and come straight from the dead lying around here and nearby. The shelling is very heavy but at least it is going in the opposite direction. What about Paris? I long to see you before I fall to pieces . . ."

Our meeting in Paris never came off. I was kept at Southampton, from which port men and material moved in steady streams across the channel. Gertrude went on, into Belgium to Brussels and eventually to Antwerp. She played in that city when it was still "the front" and when the firing nearly drowned her voice, despite the excellent amplifiers which the Germans had installed in the enormous Sportspalast and had left behind in their retreat.

"The men are marvelous," Gertrude wrote. "Many have been in all the major battles since Tunis. They are tough. But they are simple people with simple emotions, and being so close to them has been a great experience. They come to our shows in thousands. Some are wounded—they would rather see the show than go to the dressing station. All are terribly tired. There will never be any applause to equal what they give us. Ever. It's better than all the greatest First Night successes rolled into one . . ."

* * *

In October, 1944, just two months after Gertrude left for France and when I had not heard from her for ten days, one of my fellow-officers came into the office and, after fiddling around self-consciously for a minute or two, said: "I think I ought to tell you, Dick. There's a rumor going around that Gertrude Lawrence has been taken sick and is being brought back to England."

I telephoned ENSA headquarters in London. Yes, a voice said; the unit was expected back that day. Miss Lawrence had been taken ill in Antwerp. How ill she was, or what the illness was, he was unable to say.

I went straight to the admiral and asked for forty-eight hours' leave. It was the first leave I had requested, and it was granted. I was able to commandeer a staff car and drove at top speed to London.

Inquiry at ENSA brought the information that Gertrude was at the Savoy. I hurried to the hotel and phoned Gertrude from the lobby. There was no answer.

The desk clerk, to whom I was of course a stranger, was understandably reluctant to let me go up to the room. I appealed successfully to Charles Hofflin, manager of the Savoy, who got a boy with a pass key to accompany me to Gertrude's room.

It was fortunate that he did. We found Gertrude on the bed, just as she had flung herself down when she came in. She still had on her worn, faded ENSA uniform and she was in a semi-coma.

I telephoned downstairs for a doctor and a nurse. I was told no nurses were available.

While waiting for the doctor, I undressed Gertrude, bathed her, and got her into bed. She seemed to accept my presence as quite natural; true to her nature, she admonished me feebly not to worry. "I'm not ill, Richard. Only so terribly, terribly tired."

When the doctor arrived, he confirmed this. He said that Gertrude's condition was the result of a recent attack of dysentery in Normandy, plus the shock effect on a sensitive nervous system of battlefront conditions, and the wearing grind of the tour itself. He gave Gertrude a sedative; soon she was asleep.

For thirty-six hours I did not leave her. As the hours passed I was immensely relieved to see her condition improve, although she was still weak and was drowsy from the medication.

My immediate concern was to find someone to look after her when my leave was up. Gertrude seemed to catch some of my worry. In one of her short wakeful periods she whispered, "Get hold of Evie, Richard darling. She'll know what to do."

Evie Williams was Gertrude's former secretary, who had toured with her in *Susan and God.* After Evie returned to London, Gertrude had kept in constant touch with her, writing her regularly and sending her parcels.

Evie's address in suburban Teddington Road was listed in

Gertrude's small address book. I sent a hotel porter out there with a note. He brought the reply that Mrs. Williams would hurry to Gertrude as soon as she could make the necessary arrangements to have someone take over her civil defense duties; this could not, however, be before the next day.

I was sitting by Gertrude's bed, one eye on my watch—for it was getting close to the time when I would have to drive back to Southampton—and dreading the prospect of leaving Gertrude to the already overburdened hotel staff, when there was a knock at the door. I opened it to find myself staring down at a gentle-looking little woman of indeterminate age.

"I'm Lou Hollis," she said. "I've been one of Miss Lawrence's fans ever since she started on the West End. I heard, in a roundabout way, that she was ill. I came to see if I could be of use to her."

Gertrude moved restlessly in the bed. I stepped out into the corridor and closed the door behind me. I suggested to Mrs. Hollis that we move down the corridor in order that our voices should not disturb Gertrude. I realized I owed her visit to the working of the grapevine of Gertrude's fans, one of whom might have seen her arrive at the Savoy, or learned of her return through someone connected with ENSA.

Standing by a window looking out on the river, which flowed gently under a veil of October mist—a view so peaceful that it was difficult to realize nightfall would bring squadrons of death over the twisting river and the city sprawling along its reaches—I told Mrs. Hollis what I knew of Gertrude's condition, my plans for her, and my hope that Mrs. Williams would arrive to nurse her the following day.

"I'll stay until Mrs. Williams comes," Mrs. Hollis offered. "And afterward I can come every day for a few hours after my work, until Miss Lawrence is well. Don't worry, sir. She won't be neglected."

I said that Gertrude should go home to the United States as soon as she could make the flight. I would see to that.

When I looked in at the door she was sleeping. I did not rouse her. Lou Hollis had taken off her jacket and seated herself where I had been sitting, near the foot of the bed. When Gertrude awakened and opened her eyes she would see Mrs. Hollis at once and know that she was not alone.

As I drove to Southampton I began to comprehend, and to marvel humbly at, the almost mathematically precise workings of a law which operated consistently in Gertrude's life. All her life long, whenever she was in any sort of trouble, someone appeared unexpectedly and providentially who could, and was even eager to, give her whatever she needed most acutely at the moment. Life had tried her, had tossed her about, had brought her to the brink of disaster. But never had she been deserted.

If there is a psychological explanation for this, it may be found in the fact that she herself, as I have already related, was always a ready giver; not merely of material things, but of interest, appreciation, and affection.

In her giving, her criterion was never merit, but need. She was at once too proud and too simple to be a respecter of persons.

In addition to being one of life's givers, Gertrude had the rarest of all graces—gratitude. She could forgive a slight or an injury; but she could not forget a kindness. She never undervalued friendship, affection, courtesy, loyalty; but was touchingly grateful for what measure of these came her way. Perhaps in consequence, and by the working of the law I have mentioned, they were given to her by all sorts of people, at extraordinary as well as at ordinary times.

Once, when I had remarked on this, adding that it was almost uncanny how often this sort of thing happened, Gertrude said thoughtfully: "Perhaps that's what is meant by something my Granny used to say when I was a child—'God pays debts without money.' Granny believed one has only to do what is right and kind at the time, without wondering or worrying about being repaid or even thanked. Because you will get it back, with interest, from God—when you need it most."

Though Gertrude rarely spoke of this philosophy, she lived by it consistently. I could see that it spared her a great deal of agony in a profession which is full of ups and downs, petty and big jealousies, feuds and resentments. In a sense, her motto, on which her creed was built, was just another way of phrasing the sentiment proclaimed on the gable of the chalet at Northfield, "God's Providence Is My Inheritance."

Chapter Twelve

I BREATHED EASIER when I knew Gertrude was out of England; easier still when her cable came announcing: SAFE LANDING DEAREST. Things were bad in Britain that fall of 1944, and steadily getting worse. And Gertrude was never cautious.

On the heels of her cablegram came a letter full of news. She was at The Berries "resting." Later Helen Mahoney told me that Gertrude's rest was as energetic as I feared it would be—climbing up and down ladders, cleaning out roof gutters, painting shutters.

Gertrude wrote nostalgically of earlier and happier days at The Berries when we had all been there together: "Those were good times and I suppose we were lucky to have had them, if only to look back on. There is very little such tenderness in the world or in people these days, and I doubt very much whether we are going to be worthy of the peace when it comes."

She was, she continued, starting work on her autobiography. She planned to make the journal she had kept during her tour for ENSA the core of the book, as the experiences seemed to her the most important in her career, outweighing her theatrical successes in London and New York. What did I think of this, or that, for a title?

Simultaneously she was preparing to do a play called *Errand for Bernice* for Gilbert Miller, who had been one of her friends and admirers since she starred in his production of *Candlelight,* supported by Leslie Howard and Reginald Owen.

Errand for Bernice was a war play. It appealed strongly to Gertrude, who believed audiences should be made to feel all the emotional impact of the war. In this I disagreed with her, believing that war plays and novels come into popularity after, and not during, conflict; and that the public, in wartime, wants comedy as an escape from anxiety. However, in line with the pact we had made never to interfere with each other's work, I made no attempt to press the point. Having given my opinion as requested, it then became a point of honor for me to keep silent on the matter.

The play opened out of town during the 1944 Christmas holidays and went on a brief tour. Gertrude received her usual excellent reviews, but the consensus of opinion was that the play would not be accepted on Broadway without changes in cast and script.

"Always Right Aldrich again," she wrote when telling me her play was closing. "Actually, I am thankful for some months in which to finish my book. And then, I hope the USO will send me back to Europe to entertain American troops, as I entertained the tommies for ENSA. After all, I have a double obligation—to your countrymen as well as my own."

Her letter reached me through Lady du Maurier, at whose home in Cornwall I was a frequent guest.

At that time I was stationed at Fowey, on the Cornish coast, quartered in makeshift barracks which offered little protection from the penetrating cold. I was particularly grateful to Lady du Maurier, who offered me both a hospitable fireside and a mailing address at which I could receive letters from Gertrude in less than half the time required to pass through the regulation Navy P.O. Lady du Maurier's daughter, Daphne, authoress and wife of General Sir Frederick Browning, was at a house only a few miles distant, with their children.

When I had found Gertrude ill at the Savoy I had accepted unquestioningly her assurance that there was nothing more serious the matter with her than strain and fatigue. However, during the next few months, a picture of her kept appearing before me. Gertrude's most memorable features were her eyes—large, widely set, and emphasized by her high cheekbones. It was these eyes which I saw recurrently on waking or in fitful sleep. But now they appeared to me not brilliant, not mischievously mocking, nor tender, at which time their blueness was ineffable. I saw them clouded over with weariness, full of the sights of the battlefields.

Therefore, I was increasingly determined to exert whatever influence I could to keep Gertrude from accepting an assignment which would again overtax her strength. When she wrote me early in 1945 that she intended signing up for the USO, I replied instantly, opposing the idea. I continued my opposition until I heard that John Hoysradt, the impersonator, later known in motion pictures as John Hoyt, would be in command of the unit. I knew John through our mutual friend, Joseph Verner Reed, who had been his classmate at college and thought very highly of him.

I then gave my consent, but under the complete misapprehension (for which I can only blame the pressure of my own duties) that the USO tour would be confined to camps and hospitals in the United States. Gertrude let me continue to think so up to the very day the troupe departed. Her heart was set on returning to Europe, something which I had vetoed.

Had I been against the tour unqualifiedly, would she have abandoned it? I am not sure she would. She might still have contrived a way around my ban, using all her cleverness in getting what she wanted while making it appear to be what I wanted, too.

The first week in April, 1945, Gertrude delivered to the publisher the manuscript of *A Star Danced* (the title was her own creation and she kept it a secret from me until she airmailed me a copy of the manuscript, calling my attention to the dedication—"*For Richard*"). Ten days later she was on a plane with her USO unit, bound, not for a swing around the United States nor for Europe as she had hoped, but for the Marianas in the Pacific.

I learned later that up to the very moment of the take-off she did not know the destination of the unit, which, besides Gertrude and John Hoysradt, consisted of Nancy Barnes, accordionist, and George Tapps, the dancer.

Aside from the unexpected destination, Gertrude had another reason to be disappointed. Not being primarily an "entertainer" in the American tradition, she had proposed to the USO that they present *Private Lives.* With but four in its cast and two easily contrived sets, the production was admirably adapted for a war-front tour. Unfortunately, the directors of the USO at that time still cherished the notion that the men wanted variety shows only; moreover, *Private Lives* was deemed censorable, a judgment which seems ridiculous in view of some of the material used by individual performers when on tour.

Gertrude's letters from the Pacific were not very informative. Neither the climate, nor the exigencies of a six-weeks' island-hopping tour playing two shows a day, were conducive to literary expression. But she set down some of her impressions in a diary. Her comments on her experiences were spontaneous and characteristic.

"But this is the Army, Mrs. A," she wrote on the first day, consoling herself for the disappointment of being sent to the Pacific. "Pam, Fanny, and David saw me off. They are all very depressed and quite sure I shall return looking like Mahatma Gandhi. . . . Dearest Richard, I love you very much today up here in the sky. Please keep your feet on the ground. We are twenty-two aboard, including captain, pilot and stewardess—Navy personnel, USO, and medical technicians. Including 200 mice. Nancy Barnes has just unpacked the squeeze-box. Now we can try out our new unit on the passengers before we drop down from the clouds into Reno to refuel. . . ." ("Squeeze-box," a pet term of Gertrude's, is the English music-hall artist's slang for accordion.)

"This is April 19th and we are on our way in a huge B24 on the thirteen-hour hop to Hickam on our way to Kwajalein—fifteen A.A.C. men, the crew, and our unit. No bucket seats this time—really comfortable and spacious, which is just as well, as our Mae Wests are fairly bulky. We are now about to consume five glasses of water each in case we are forced down. . . . The briefing at Hamilton Field included lectures on first aid, on how to live on a life raft in case we have to ditch the plane, and another on tropical diseases. We were informed that none of the shots we had taken would do us any good if we were bitten by a mosquito, and that a plane seldom survives a ditching, so when the officer asked: 'Any questions?' I nearly said: 'Yes. Where can I phone and say I've changed my mind?'

"Before our take-off at 5 A.M. we got the news of the death of Ernie Pyle from Jap sniper. Everybody terribly depressed. That's two in a week. Darling, keep your fingers crossed for me, because this trip is going to be very hard to take. I promise that if I get through I shall go no more aroaming.

"We have been in the air nine hours and there's been no more motion than in a Rolls on the parkway. The sea below is Virgin Mary blue glimpsed between egg-white puffs of cloud. . . . Our co-pilot brought me *The History of the Theatre,* which he is reading (at 9,000 feet!), in which he showed me that I am mentioned once under Noel Coward and once under Rachel Crothers. It turns out he is Lieutenant George Slavin, Herman Shumlin's nephew.

"*Arrived Oahu,* 5 P.M. Pacific Time, and greeted as V.I.P. Dined with the colonel and motored around Pearl Harbor. Took off again 12:30 for Johnston Island. Arrived 4:30 A.M., met by very gay colonel in shorts, had breakfast and left immediately for Kwajalein. Referred to on Johnston as 'Four red balls,' meaning Very Important People. Wonder what we shall be called at Kwajalein.

"*Kwajalein.* Well, now, I am all confused . . . having crossed the International Date Line, it is now the day before yesterday. We were met by General Ross and taken to lunch with his staff and later—after a much-needed shower—on a jeep tour of the island with the general. This is the main base for the maintenance of all the other islands. The B29's come in on the newly built airstrip—6,000 feet long—on the way to their bombing raids. So do the Air Transport Service planes, which bring the mails and reinforcements. With 14,000 Japs surrounding the island, Kwajalein is still a danger zone. From here we take off for Saipan, and then by shuttle plane to Guam, where our shows begin.

"*Guam,* April 22. . . . Tonight we break the ice. Golly, how I wish there were some! Nancy and I are billeted in tents on the

Officers' Command Reservation of the U.S. Marines. The settling-in process is always hard at first, and the humidity and the tropical wind which blows constantly make my head ache. It's a bit heavy going, having to eat with the Big Brass—General Blake, Colonel Murray, and the Dutch Governor General, Dr. Van Mook. They couldn't be nicer, but we feel we are intruding. Actually, they say they like having us because they are not very popular with the nurses, who prefer the company of the younger officers. Privately, so do we. However, as honored guests, it's up to us to suffer the penalties of our ivory-tent existence. . . .

"We gave our first show at 6:30 to a battalion of Seabees—fifteen hundred of them, in an outside theatre. Very efficient. Our second show at 8:30 was about half an hour away to 5,000 very noisy Seabees (72d Battalion). Here the mike was very poor, the stage enormous, we had to scream, and we were feeling the heat terribly. . . ."

For ten days they were on Guam, giving two shows a night. In the afternoon they visited the hospitals to entertain men recently flown in from Okinawa, and take recordings of messages from them for rebroadcast to their families and the public in the United States. Her Guam experience brought home to Gertrude that "this is an entirely different kind of war to the one I witnessed in the ETO. The prospect of peace in Europe makes no difference here. Mussolini's death brought a few comments, but Hitler's didn't cause a palm leaf to quiver."

From Guam the unit flew to "treeless Tinian," as she called it. "No shade and boiling hot all day, but cool at night," she wrote. "I find it hard not to give in to the tropical torpor. . . . We can't bathe, as the beaches have not been cleared. Nancy and I are in the Army Nurses' Compound . . . we live by the clock: 6-7 breakfast; 11-12:30 lunch in the mess; afternoons at the hospitals or the Red Cross recreation rooms; dinner with the enlisted men at 5 P.M. and a show at 6:30. Afterward we go to the officers' club and we are back in our compound at 11."

Here, as on Saipan, where the unit never moved except under strict guard, the intense heat, humidity, insects, and the beginning of the rainy season added greatly to the difficulty of giving performances on open-air stages. "We are constantly unpacking, pressing, and packing. . . ."

Gertrude's experience in Normandy nine months before had taught her that the troops were sick of the sight of uniforms; they wanted to see entertainers in costumes that were pretty and suggestive of the theatre. She had cut down on her personal luggage to take with her three complete changes of stage costume. For each show she dressed and made up as meticulously as for an appearance on Broadway. She contrived flower-decked hairdos, wore glittering bracelets and earrings, and donned fluttery false eyelashes which were all but dissolved by humidity and perspiration as she sang and danced.

Even in uniform, she and Nancy Barnes caused something of a sensation when they drove up to one camp where three thousand United States Marines who had spent three years in the islands were waiting for the show. At sight of the jeep's freight, the leathernecks let out a yell: "My God, real women!" and stormed the jeep with its guard.

"We changed in tents . . . no covering on the ground, and rats scuttling about. Suddenly it began to rain as it can rain only out here. The crude stage was soon awash. I was dripping wet and steaming. But not a man moved from the soaking clay hillside. There they sat, huddled under their camouflage ponchos, laughing and happy. We gave them our full show. Halfway through, the generator broke down, all the lights went out, and the mike went dead. But the men turned their flashlights on us and we carried on . . ."

On the tiny island of Wallalopen, "having been assured that their public address system was the best in the Pacific, we did not take any equipment with us. We found the stage was a built-up platform on a corner of the main thoroughfare. Trucks and jeeps roared by every few seconds, planes took off at low level just behind us, and the public address system had no existence except in someone's imagination. We did the best we could for a while, then we got the band to play and I kept things going by dancing with the men. All comers. I got a terrific jitterbug workout. . . ."

The dreary monotony of the life of troops who had been stationed in the islands for months and even years appalled Gertrude, to whom activity, freedom, and change were essential to well-being. "No wonder they are bored, cynical and sometimes extremely bad-mannered. I ran into a most terrifying experience at one show—all was going well until I announced: 'And now a song about Brooklyn,' at which 3,000 voices yelled: 'No, No, *No.*' "

Thinking this was just "back chat, of which there is always a good deal," Gertrude persisted in singing the song. To her horror, all the men joined in and climaxed the chorus with hoots, Bronx cheers, and more vulgar noises.

"Well, that's all, fellers," she said and walked off, shaking with indignation and considerable fright.

The M.P.'s stationed backstage reassured her. "Don't mind, lady. It isn't your fault. You see, the C.O. comes from Brooklyn; he plays a record of that song all the time on our loud-speaker and the men are fed up with it."

Meanwhile the audience began to grow ashamed of its rudeness. There were calls for Gertrude to come back. She did so and asked what they would like her to sing. A voice yelled "Night and Day." "So without any rehearsal, and praying that I would remember the words, I plunged into a sloppy, corny version of the song . . ." The applause that followed was less for the song than for the display of good sportsmanship.

How closely Gertrude was identified in the men's minds with her role in *Lady in the Dark* was revealed when the troupe gave its show for the Forty-second Air Command on Guam:

". . . Afterwards a motorcycle guard of honor (12) drove me out to the airstrip, where, standing in the moonlight, was a brand new shiny C46 (transport and cargo plane). On the nose, in huge black and red letters, was: LADY IN THE DARK. I met the crew of six, we were photographed together and we launched my ship with beer. So now I fly between Guam and the front . . . It was a great thrill and a great honor. I shall keep praying for the safety of my ship and her crew . . ."

Everywhere she appeared the men clamored for "Jenny."

This presented a problem. The directors of the USO had censored this song from Gertrude's program. Insistent demands for it from soldiers and sailors who had seen her in *Lady in the Dark,* either in the theatre or in the streamlined version which her company had put on at servicemen's canteens and benefits all over the country, sent her to the resident USO director for advice. The calls for "Jenny" were holding up the shows.

After some hemming and hawing, she was told she might sing the song, provided she omitted the bumps.

"But the boys like the bumps. They yell for them," she argued.

They did indeed. They made no bones about declaring that "Jenny" without bumps was as flat as an egg without salt.

"We shall have to query the War Department," officialdom told Gertrude. Ultimately, the Pentagon issued the ukase: "Miss Lawrence may do the bumps, *provided she does them sideways.*"

It is extraordinary what problems and decisions can occupy the General Staff while fighting a global war.

Gertrude was loyal to her superiors, but she was too finished a performer to believe that bumps done sideways were any substitute for the real thing. After a traveling reporter had caught one of her shows and sent his paper a paragraph to the effect that Gertrude Lawrence was short-changing her soldier audiences, she put the situation straight to her audiences:

"And now I am going to sing 'Jenny.' Only I want you all to know that I have been forbidden to do the bumps."

The instant response was a chorused yell: "Why?"

"Because you are too young. And too innocent."

Jeers.

"Very well," Gertrude would accede. "I'll do a *little* bump. But if there are any chaplains present, I trust they will understand that this is Jenny; and *not* Gertrude Lawrence."

Later, when entertaining the war wounded in hospitals back in the United States, Gertrude resorted to still another ruse in order to do justice to "Jenny." On these occasions she was accompanied by Joe Moon, the talented pianist and vocal arranger who had been with her since she came to New York for *Tonight at 8:30* in 1935. She would explain gravely that she was forbidden to do the bumps for the youthful patients: "But they didn't say anything about my not doing them for Joe Moon. So I'll do them for Joe; and if you want to watch—well, can I help it?"

Summing up her experience of the first few weeks in the Pacific, Gertrude wrote:

". . . the men out here want more adult entertainment than they are getting. Above all, they want plays. You saw that by the way they welcomed Moss Hart's production of *The Man Who Came to Dinner*. I cannot understand the refusal of the USO to let us do *Private Lives*. Noel never wrote a vulgar line in his entire career." She added that Maurice Evans, then Major Evans in charge of entertainment in the Pacific Theatre, had interested Margaret Sullavan in playing *The Voice of the Turtle* on the fox-hole circuit but the chaplains had objected to the play as risqué.

In view of the realistic novels dealing with service life in the Pacific which have been published since the war, such decisions reveal an astounding ignorance and disregard of the kind of amusement sought by men crowded into small tropical island bases.

* * *

"Whoever talked about the 'crossroads of the Pacific' had something," Gertrude noted in her diary. "I keep running into all sorts of people I have known or who know Richard . . . Admiral Nimitz is here. He was at the prize fights last night but we expect him at our show tonight . . ."

On Saipan, where she "found an excellent radio station," she did a broadcast with Tyrone Power. Afterward he escorted her back to her quarters.

"May I come in?" he asked. "I really haven't had a chance to tell you how I have admired you for years. It seems strange that we should never have met until we both came out here. And I'm terribly lonely."

Guardedly Gertrude extended the invitation; her experiences with lonely men had not always been felicitous.

"I never thought I could be this lonely and homesick," Tyrone went on. "Would you like to see a snapshot of my wife?"

"Of course," Gertrude replied, "if you'd like to see a picture of my husband."

They exchanged photographs and family reminiscences. When they parted, Tyrone gave her a bracelet made out of the fuselage of a bomber, as a souvenir of their meeting.

Though the islands offered no amusement and very little opportunity or space for relaxation, the mere coming together of three or four friends in the proximity of a beach was enough to stimulate Gertrude to plan a picnic. Usually the group was photographed and sometimes the photograph found its way into a national publication. Whereupon several wives who had been pitying the loneliness of their husbands "out in the Pacific" promptly sat up and wrote in varying tones of chagrin: "I thought you were out there to fight the Japs, not to go picnicking with glamour girls like Gertrude Lawrence!"

* * *

As summer approached, the troupe visited many small atolls in the Marianas. The trips were always made in bucket-seat planes. The rainy season was beginning and storms of tornado force were not uncommon. John Hoysradt told me later he never heard Gertrude express fear or complain of the discomforts and privations they were all subjected to at times. He said: "I've seen her remove her knapsack, put it down on the floor of the plane for a pillow, spread her coat, and with a 'Goodnight, my dears,' tuck herself up for a few hours' nap. Once, while we were on Saipan, there was a terrific storm. We were undecided about trying to get to the place where our show was scheduled. But Gertrude insisted that we make the attempt. It was lucky that we did, for thousands of G.I.'s were already there waiting for us. We gave the show, with real thunder and lightning supplying the sound effects."

From the Ulithi islets the troupe flew south to the small islands of the Palau group, which had been German or Japanese possessions since the first world war. They had been redeemed at great cost of life as the Americans moved northward from Guadalcanal toward the Marianas.

On Angar, Gertrude wrote: "We are now by way of having gone slightly Noel Coward. We are staying with the colonel in his house. We have beds. And Nancy and I have a room apiece. We are slightly supercilious at having to share the shower, but we have a real lavatory again. And the food is excellent.

"When we stepped from the plane we had our first touch of South Sea Island color—we were greeted by two rows of smiling natives (women and children) who sang an island song for us *in English*. They usually speak Japanese although they are Chamorros. One stepped forward and made a perfectly memorized speech of welcome to me and the company. Then we were decked in *leis* of heavily scented flowers, and presented with gifts of hand-woven bags, belts and cigarette cases . . . After dinner with the colonel we went to a movie. Everybody stood up when we arrived and when we left and I felt as though I had stepped right into the pages of the Coward Diary . . .

"After the show on Angar the natives gave a dance recital for us in their grass skirts, floral wreaths, and bare feet. During the German and Japanese occupation of these islands they were not permitted to do these dances, so the art almost died out. When the Americans came, the custom was revived and the old people are now teaching the children the steps. It was most picturesque and I felt greatly honored to have the dances dedicated to 'Miss Lawrence and her party from the U.S.A.'

"This island is small but it was very difficult to capture. Here is Bloody Ridge, which the marines took after having to climb and clean the Japs out of 977 caves which honeycomb the mountain, and which were full of guns and other weapons. There is a monument on top of the ridge—the most dramatic sight I have seen out here . . . We played to 8,000 men on Angar, and in Petelini to another 3,500. Score is mounting. So far we have appeared before 168,700 troops . . ."

As the tour progressed, it became more and more apparent to Gertrude that her greatest contribution would be to visit the wounded in hospitals.

"John Hoysradt has sent a telegraph to Special Services on Tinian and Saipan," she wrote, "saying that we can only do one show a night. This is to enable us to visit more hospitals. Those broadcasts by the men to their folks back home are very important and we want to do as many as we can . . . The morale in the hospitals is very high in spite of the temperature and the discomfort of the heavy plaster casts . . . One boy—that's all he was—started a bad hemorrhage from a shrapnel wound in the neck which had gone right through into his mouth. We quietly went on chatting to the other men while the nurses and the doctor attended to him . . .

"On the visits to the hospitals I have appointed myself the mailman. I take the names and addresses of the wounded men's wives and mothers and girl friends, and write to them giving cheerful news. Yesterday I wrote 50 letters, and I have another 50 to do. It is quite a job as it all has to be done in longhand, and individual letters, of course. But I think those at home will be glad to get fresh news of their loved ones."

On every island she visited, Gertrude continued to spend hours in the hospitals and to write her short, cheerful letters telling the men's families small but vastly important details of her visit to them, and enclosing personal messages. It was a labor of love and one which not only taxed her strength but engaged all her sympathies. Her diary continues:

"*June 5*. We are once more in the plane, headed for an island-hopping trip of 9 hours (bucket seats all the way) back to Guam. The rain is blinding . . .

"*June 7*. Arrived here on Kwajalein at 11:30 last night, exhausted, cold and with a gnat rash which is driving me crazy. Met by General Ross, who took us to his beach house. No more Noel Coward; strictly G.I.

"*June 9*. Airborne again. This time for Honolulu. When the end came during the performance last night (4,000 men at the Richardson Theatre) it was quick, quiet, and painless—a dispatch from Washington releasing Nancy Barnes to join her husband who has been released from a P.O.W. camp in Germany, and calling the rest of us to return to headquarters on Oahu. Wonder what our orders will be there. Our total attendance now stands 200,000 men in seven weeks. Received my Pacific Theatre ribbon today from General Ross. . . ."

* * *

Returning to Honolulu in early June of 1945, the company duly reported to Major Maurice Evans. Their account of the tour bore out Maurice's own conviction that the troops were satiated with variety entertainments and were hungry for good plays. Several years later, when Maurice starred in my production of Shaw's *The Devil's Disciple,* he told me that, as an army officer, he had found himself nearly strangled by the red tape which entangled the Special Services and the USO. He welcomed Gertrude's offer to appear in a play at the camps on Oahu. The play selected was Noel Coward's *Blithe Spirit;* Maurice rounded up actors for the various roles and rehearsals commenced.

This was Gertrude's first opportunity to play Elvira, the ghost of the first wife, whose materialization disrupts the widower's second marriage and provides the high comedy of Noel Coward's "improbable farce." She had always wanted to appear in the role, which fitted her with the same glove-like smoothness as Amanda of *Private Lives.* Elvira, in point of fact, is Amanda who has died and who—Amanda-like—annoyingly refuses to stay dead. Noel had written it with Gertrude in mind; as, he has said, he wrote the star part in every one of his plays. She had missed creating the role because, when it was ready for production, she was appearing in the long run of *Lady in the Dark.*

The company was billeted at Moana Hotel, next to the celebrated Outrigger Canoe Club and on Waikiki Beach. Gertrude took a quick but comprehensive look around and announced to John Hoysradt: "I have several friends here."

"Who are they?" John asked.

"First, the Walter Dillinghams," Gertrude enumerated. John appeared properly impressed. "And," she continued with increasing pride, 'one of my very good English friends, Nadine Alexander, is married to a Polynesian nobleman, the Duke of Kahanamoku."

Well aware that Gertrude's penchant for aristocracy had led her into an understandable error, John nevertheless kept a straight face. "Oh, yes," he said solemnly. "I've heard of the Duke."

"Of course you've heard of him," Gertrude assured him. "The Duke is an internationally famous athlete."

"And you *really* know them?" asked John in an awed tone.

"I know them *very well,*" Gertrude replied haughtily as she went to the phone and told the operator, "Please connect me with the residence of the Duke of Kahanamoku."

A moment later there was a look of triumph in her eyes as she said, "This is Miss Gertrude Lawrence. May I speak to the Duchess of Kahanamoku?"

The triumph gave way to dismay and a slight frown drew her brows together. She spoke with even greater distinctness: "I wish to speak to Her Grace, the Duchess of Kahanamoku."

"What's the trouble?" John asked solicitously. "Royalty out on strike?"

The pleasantry drew no riposte from Gertrude. Bewildered, she replaced the receiver, saying: "He keeps talking about 'Mrs. Kahanamoku.' He says 'Mrs. Kahanamoku' is at her office . . . 'Mrs. Kahanamoku' will call me when she comes home."

"Royalty is so democratic, these days," John observed. Grinning, he strolled out.

"But, Gertie," Nadine explained later, "Duke isn't a title. It's a name. Like Earl. My husband was named for his father, and he was called Duke because he happened to be born the day Queen Victoria's son, the Duke of Edinburgh, arrived on a state visit to King Kamehameha. Darling, I'm terribly sorry to disappoint you, but although my husband does have royal blood I'm just plain Mrs. Kahanamoku of Oahu, just as you are Mrs. Aldrich of Cape Cod."

Gertrude's disappointment over the nonexistent title was her only one. Each morning, she hopped out of bed, put on her swim suit and joined Duke and Nadine for coffee at the Outrigger Canoe Club. Finding Gertrude a good and fearless swimmer, Duke took her surfboard riding, between rehearsals for *Blithe Spirit.* The long, narrow board, with Gertrude and Duke straddling it, soared across the Big Surf, high on the crest of powerful combers.

Gertrude paid no attention to John Hoysradt's remonstrances

that she was likely to break her neck or be drowned, or both. The exciting sport, with its constant imminence of danger, was exactly her cup of tea.

She boasted to John that Duke had told her in all seriousness: "If you ever want to quit the dry stage, Gertrude, I will train you for an Aquacade show, and you can swim while you earn."

"Darling," John came back, "you can break your pretty neck any way you choose—after we get back to the States. Until then, I have a responsibility to your husband. I promised him, God help me, to look out for you."

When these appeals had no effect he reminded her of her professional obligations to the USO. What would happen to *Blithe Spirit* if she were drowned?

"Think how much better I would play Elvira if I were really a ghost," she said. "Oh, Noel understands me. I would be the most infuriating spirit to have fluttering around. Perhaps that is why Richard made you promise to bring me back alive. I am much more manageable alive than I would be dead."

"If Dick figures he can manage you at all, when you don't want to be managed," John retorted, "he's living in a dream world."

* * *

During her play's two-week run at the various camp theatres, Gertrude continued to spend much of her leisure with Nadine Kahanamoku. The two girls had plenty of opportunity to catch up on events since King George the Fifth's Jubilee Year in London, when they had been the favorite supper and dance partners of two gay young princes of Hyderabad.

As Gertrude remarked: "If you've been born on Clapham Common you can't help having an awe of royalty." Consequently, she was profoundly impressed when an island friend of the Kahanamokus dropped in one evening and said that the native Hawaiians were tired of being kept on territorial status. There was talk, he added, of restoring the old monarchy and making Duke king.

Nadine's reply that she knew her husband would oppose any such movement, as would she, was promptly reported by Gertrude to John Hoysradt with the comment: "Nadine is more than a duchess. *She has turned down a crown.*"

A few days before they were to return to San Francisco, John was sunbathing on Waikiki, when, looking out to sea, he saw beyond the surf a strange object protruding from the water. It occurred to him that it might be the periscope of some small new type of submarine, and that it was his duty to report it promptly to the Navy guards.

The object had not escaped the watchful eyes of the United States Navy. Before John could sound the alert, a plane had been sent to investigate. It circled low and swooped, then rose and flew back to shore.

No submarine, the pilot reported; only Miss Gertrude Lawrence floating underwater, wearing a glass mask such as skin divers use, to which was attached a two-foot-long plastic tube for breathing.

"With a thing like that you can stay in the water for hours and hours," she said happily. "I was having a marvelous time until you sent the Navy after me."

"Save your gadget for the Cape," John retorted. "Play mermaid there, where there are no sharks. I've lost ten pounds on this tour—and most of it because of you." John reminded her of a week-end party at Sam Pryor's place in Connecticut, where the guests had included John and his wife, Gertrude and myself, the Wendell Willkies, and the Joseph Verner Reeds. "When I remember how we men got together and expressed our envy of Dick, all I can think is: what a pack of chumps! What Dick Aldrich rates is sympathy and, as of this moment, he has mine."

Chapter Thirteen

When Gertrude and I were married, a good many people announced flatly—and gratuitously—that it would not last. Everything, they said, was against it: our backgrounds, our values—and above all, our temperaments. The optimists gave our marriage two years; the pessimists counted its chances for survival in months.

That it would last for life, and become more richly rewarding year by year, is something nobody—not even Gertrude and I—could have foretold; success in marriage is not something you can contract for in advance.

As time went by, the oracles reacted with increasing peevishness to our stubborn refusal to fulfill their gloomy prophecies. One gossip broadcaster publicly rebuked Gertrude for permitting a mere husband to keep her out of the spotlight of Café Society. The entire brood rejoiced, like vultures wheeling over dying prey, whenever reasons of career or wartime service forced Gertrude and me momentarily to go separate ways. Someday the columnists may learn the facts of life: two adults can enjoy an enduring love, even when they are not holding hands under the table at the Stork Club.

Halsman

After her return from the European front, Gertrude proudly wore a sweater bearing the insignia of the many military units she had entertained.

Signal Corps Photo

The actress turns spectator. Gertrude watches machine-gun practice in the Pacific.

Gertrude and her USO troupe arrive at Angar, from Ulithi.

This is not to say that Gertrude and I never had our differences. In this account of our life together, I cannot pass them over. For they were a vital part of our relationship—tests that we had to meet together and for which we had to find our own solutions.

Some of our quarrels were heated, even violent. In the early years of our marriage Gertrude occasionally flew into a hysterical tantrum, at the height of which she might hurl at me whatever was nearest at hand. My own temper, though slower than hers, works up, like my father's, to fairly stormy proportions. And, like my father, I am apt to shout . . . An additional irritant was the essentially different way in which we reacted to grievances. Gertrude got all the anger out of her system in one fine pyrotechnic outburst, after which she was all smiles and forgiveness. My tendency, by contrast, is to sulk and smolder at great length over something that irks me.

We were able to overcome these conflicts of personality, and the equally serious strains imposed by external circumstances, only because we were both fundamentally determined to make our marriage work. We realized that a successful union is an achievement accomplished not all at once, in a month, or a year; but little by little, day by day. It was Samuel Johnson, I believe, who said that "a man needs to keep his friendships in constant repair." The same might be said, with more telling truth, about a marriage. Gertrude and I were each prepared to give our relationship as much attention —if not more—than we gave to our individual careers.

The first major test of our resolution came in the summer of 1945, when we had an unexpected wartime reunion in Chicago. Paradoxically enough, whereas the deprivations of war had revealed to us our deep need of each other, our coming together again brought us to the verge of separation.

I cannot explain the tensions we both felt; though I suspect they will be familiar to any couple who were forced apart for long periods by the war. I only know that, deeply in love as I was with Gertrude, and as I believe she was with me when we said goodbye in London in the autumn of 1944, by the following July, when we came together in Chicago, our relationship was painfully askew.

We met in Chicago as a result of a wartime coincidence between unexpected naval orders issued to me, and Gertrude's return from Honolulu.

In the Navy everything moves at two speeds: either with exasperating slowness, or at a pace that doesn't allow you to catch your breath between the issuance of your orders and your arrival somewhere half the world away. I had had every expectation of being kept on in the ETO for some time when, early in July, I was suddenly ordered to attend a naval conference then convening in Chicago. Before taking off from England there was no time or opportunity to get in touch with Gertrude, whom I supposed to be in Honolulu.

Not until I reached the United States and called David Holtzmann by telephone did I learn that Gertrude had arrived in San Francisco two days earlier. With that city playing host to the organizational meeting of the United Nations, Gertrude had found it impossible to get a hotel room. She had gone directly to Fanny Holtzmann, who was there as counsel to the Chinese delegation. Fanny gave her a bed in her suite at the Mark Hopkins and put her to work in place of an absent secretary. Gertrude enjoyed making herself useful to the diplomats and political advisors, among them Adlai Stevenson; she was working there when she received my wire asking her to join me in Chicago.

My message, as I later learned, caused a dramatic commotion. Until she ripped open the yellow envelope, Gertrude was under the impression that I was six thousand miles away.

The Overland Limited was due to leave from Oakland in exactly forty minutes. Gertrude made a mad dash across town and managed to get aboard the last of the Limited's five sections. She left her chances of getting a berth to luck.

Brief but affectionate wires from Mrs. A announced the Limited's progress from stop to stop. Meanwhile Fanny had communicated with Gertrude's New York publishers, telling them that their author would be in Chicago on the day her book, *A Star Danced*, was to be released. The publishers, on their own, dispatched a publicity man to Chicago to promote book and author.

Thus, when I took time off from the naval conference to hurry down to the station to meet my wife, I walked into a huddle of newsmen, photographers, radio broadcasters, lights, microphones and several hundred gaping spectators. Our reunion promised to have about as much privacy as the proverbial goldfish in a bowl.

Irritation made me self-conscious, awkward, and brusque. More than three years of being in uniform, and being treated with the respect it commands, did not fit me to deal imperturbably with a swarm of reporters who buzzed around demanding what it felt like to be the husband of Gertrude Lawrence, what I thought of my wife's book, what she had said in it about me, and—were I to write a book—what I would tell the world about her.

I was having my first taste of being "Mr. Gertrude Lawrence," and not finding it very palatable.

I was there to meet Mrs. A, not the author of a potential best-seller. To have half a dozen cameramen snapping our first embrace, while shouting at us to "Hold it!", did not lessen my annoyance. I felt myself freeze up.

Gertrude looked at me wonderingly. And smiled at the cameras.

"But, Richard darling," she protested when I called over a cab and told the driver to take her to the Ambassador East, "aren't you coming, too?"

I explained that I had already been absent from my conference longer than I should have been.

"But you're meeting your wife."

I replied that the Navy was entirely uninterested in that. As far as it—the Navy—was concerned, I was in Chicago on duty. That came first. I would join her at the Ambassador as soon as I was free to do so.

"What will the press think if we separate at once, like this?" Gertrude demanded. "They'll hint all sorts of things. That you don't love me. That there is some other man, or other woman."

I said that for all of me, the press could think and say whatever it chose. I had not asked any of them to be there.

* * *

It was close to the dinner hour when the conference broke up and I was at liberty to rejoin Gertrude. Before I reached the door of our suite I heard her singing happily. Inside, I found her unpacking the clothes which her maid had sent on from New York; she was surrounded by flowers, with more being delivered as the news spread through Chicago of her arrival.

The phone rang repeatedly. Everyone, it seemed, was eager to welcome her, to fete her. I heard her promising to lunch with one caller; to meet another for cocktails. To dine at someone's house, "Not tomorrow night. We have an engagement. What about Thursday? Wonderful! My husband and I will be delighted . . ."

"Gertrude!"

I found myself shouting at her. It seemed the only means of breaking through the glittering shell which enveloped her, to the reality of my Mrs. A.

"Don't make engagements for me," I roared. "I can't promise to go here, there, and everywhere."

"What do you mean—here, there, and everywhere?" she retorted. "I met the Hughston McBains on an Atlantic crossing. They want to meet my husband. Especially, considering all the nice things I've said to them about you."

Again I repeated what I had said at the station—that even in Chicago I was still in the Navy and subject to orders.

"But you and the captains and admirals can't be conferring all the time," Gertrude observed with clipped sarcasm. "They must let you have some time off. Suppose you devote a little of it to your wife—or are you too busy taking care of your friends in the Waves?"

"What do you mean, Waves?"

"Don't forget, darling," she replied with such cloying sweetness that I felt an impulse to slap her, "I've been around. I've seen a few Navy boys out in the Pacific."

I retorted that for my part I'd be glad of a chance to have a little time alone with my wife. If her friends and well-wishers and her publicity man would permit it. "After all," I pointed out, "this isn't the sort of thing I looked forward to when I asked you to meet me here."

"I know," she said, still with that annoying sweetness. "But, you must remember, all this is terribly good for my book."

I said I didn't care if it was. I wanted my wife. Not a successful author.

There were several copies of *A Star Danced* on the desk waiting for her to autograph. She took one, opened it, and showed me the dedication: *"For Richard."*

"This book is as much yours as it is mine," she said. "There's no need to be jealous."

"I'm not jealous," I snapped. My tone, I realized with some shame, was that of the Officer of the Day bawling out an incompetent yeoman. It did not salve my feelings to realize that Gertrude had put her finger unerringly on my weak spot. I *was* jealous.

* * *

When we went down to dinner I found that the ballyhoo had preceded us. Ernie Byfield, back at his job as host of the Ambassador East, was too fond of Gertrude not to pay her every tribute within his domain. The last time I had seen Ernie was when he came into my headquarters and begged me to get him aboard an LST crossing the Channel in order that he might score a "beat" on the invasion for the Chicago paper he represented. Because I had found a place for him on one of the eighty craft attached to my command, he had additional reason to extend himself for us, and did so by reserving the choicest table near the entrance and decorating it especially and elaborately. A banner above our heads proclaimed WELCOME TO GERTRUDE LAWRENCE. Colored lights played on us. The orchestra performed one after another of Gertrude's popular songs.

I had the feeling of being in a brightly lighted shop window, displayed to public view and public opinion. Lacking Gertrude's stage experience and stage presence, I writhed inside my uniform.

The position of our table at the entrance to the Pump Room made it almost obligatory for everyone to stop and say hello to us. There were greetings, reminiscences, references to persons I did not know, and to experiences I had not shared or even heard about. As Gertrude introduced me, I found myself cast in the role of Gertrude Lawrence's husband.

One of those who welcomed Gertrude most warmly and enthusiastically was Irving Kupcinet. His column in the Chicago *Times* was always appreciative of her, and "Kup" had long been one of her very good friends. When she played Chicago he was frequently her escort to supper parties. Through the years he and Ernie Byfield had gradually assumed the responsibility of "looking after Gertrude" while she was in Chicago—for which I was always very grateful.

Kup's companion that evening was a well-set-up and well-tailored gentleman whose gray hair added not so much the effect of age as of distinction. It was obvious to me from Gertrude's manner that she did not know him. And equally obvious that she intended to remedy this at once.

Though Kup made no move to introduce the stranger, and the man himself held back as if not wishing to intrude, Gertrude leaned forward slightly, silently but pointedly drawing him into the conversation at our table.

Kup reluctantly made the introduction Gertrude had rendered unavoidable: "Miss Lawrence, Mr. Fisher."

Mr. Fisher's manner was impeccable. There was just the right amount of appreciation in his eyes as he told Gertrude that meeting her, after admiring her for years, was one of the high spots in his life. His deference to me was, I felt, to the uniform. Kup had introduced me as Commander Aldrich without reference to my status as Miss Lawrence's husband.

"What a charming man!" Gertrude murmured appreciatively when "Charlie," as Kup had addressed him, and Kup moved on to their table.

"I wonder who he is. I'll have to get Kup alone and find out. Darling, this is fun, isn't it?" She was as joyous and radiant as a little girl at her own birthday party.

I agreed with her that it was fun and said I was sorry I couldn't stay and see more of it.

"Darling! What do you mean?"

"I mean the war is still on and I'm an officer on duty, not on leave," I said. "I told you I had to report at headquarters tonight."

I had mentioned that fact while we were dressing for dinner and the telephone was ringing incessantly. Apparently Gertrude had not grasped my meaning. She stared at me now. Her eyes, always indicative of her mood, seemed no longer blue, but steely gray.

I looked at my watch and stood up. "I have to go now," I said stiffly. "I'll be back as soon as I can."

"Which will be when?" Gertrude demanded with the hauteur that indicated she was hurt and angry.

I was angry, too. Everything had gone wrong all that day and I was feeling it. I spoke brusquely: "I don't imagine it will matter much to you when. From all indications, you won't be lonely."

Her head came up.

"I don't intend to be," she snapped.

* * *

It was an effort to keep my attention centered on the subject of that evening's conference. We sat around a table in the bare, impersonal room—a dozen or so men, thoroughly schooled in the detached courtesy which the services make a requirement of those who bear their commissions. For all anyone could tell, no one at that table had an emotion deeper than resentment of the heat wave which blanketed the city. Not a flicker of a facial muscle, not a single inadvertent gesture revealed that any of us might at that moment be suffering torments of anxiety, envy, anger, jealousy, bad temper. Or remorse.

It was, from the viewpoint of a producer, a very interesting and provocative production.

At twenty minutes past eleven I sprang out of my cab and pushed through the revolving glass doors into the lobby of the Ambassador East. A call on the house telephone brought no answer from Gertrude's suite. I realized that I had not really expected one. I asked at the desk if any message had been left for me and the clerk handed me a folded slip of paper on which was written in Gertrude's hand:

Richard,

I have gone on to Chez Paris with Kup and his friend.

Join us, if you feel like it.

Gertrude

I was turning over the paper in my hand, and its suggestion in my mind, when Ernie Byfield caught sight of me and came over.

I said: "Gertrude has apparently gone to Chez Paris with Kup."

"Joe E. Lewis is playing there," Ernie said.

Chez Paris was, I knew, Chicago's most popular night club. All sorts of people went there, if they had the price.

"What about this Fisher who is with Kup?" I asked Ernie. "Charlie Fisher. Gray haired. Very smooth."

Ernie's lips pursed in a soundless whistle. "Is Charlie along with them? With Gertrude?"

I said he was. "Who is he?" I asked.

"Did you ever hear of the Fischetti brothers?" Ernie demanded. "This is one of them—Charles. Socially known as Charles Fisher." To make things clearer, he added: "The two Fischettis are supposed to be cousins of Al Capone's. This one was Capone's lieutenant. Since Capone's exit, he's become one of the most powerful figures in the Chicago underworld."

I sat tensely in the cab all the way to Chez Paris, wondering what I was going to find and what I might be in for.

By all the signs, Gertrude had been in one of her reckless moods, inclined to flirt with danger . . . in this instance, Charlie Fisher. That she had been attracted to him I could not doubt. And she was sufficiently irked with me to want to make me thoroughly angry and very much worried about her. The wind was blowing us straight into a high old row. If not into something much more devastating. My one consolation was that Kup had gone along; I could only hope that he would stay with them.

Chez Paris was doing big business. There wasn't a vacant table, and the dance floor was crowded. I noticed a lot of uniforms. The headwaiter shook his head before I had a chance to speak.

"I'm looking for Mr. Kupcinet," I said. "He expects me to join him."

The headwaiter looked at me dubiously. Kup's name was usually a password, but the look implied that it would not help me this evening.

"Tell him Commander Aldrich is here," I said.

The waiter sent to locate Kup was gone some time. I stood at the barrier, trying to see whether Gertrude was among the dancers. At last my eyes found her.

I readily recognized the gray-haired man who held her close, guiding her with a skill and grace which, even in my mounting annoyance, I was compelled to admit was superior to anything I could show. With a partner so worthy of her, Gertrude was dancing as beautifully as she ever did on the stage. She seemed to be enjoying herself to the full. The spotlight played on her and her partner and a buzz of admiration and applause rose above the sound of the orchestra as the supper crowd recognized her.

It was inevitable, I realized, that many in the crowd should also recognize her partner.

Long legs have their advantages at times. This was one of them. Eluding the shocked protest and the restraining reach of the headwaiter, I stepped high over the rope and strode between the close-packed tables onto the dance floor. There was no grace in the summary way I cut in on Gertrude and her partner, but I was beyond caring.

Before I felt Gertrude's reaction I was aware of Charlie Fisher's aghast surprise that such a thing could happen to him. Evidently the spectators shared this feeling, for there was an audible gasp.

"Richard!"

Gertrude was struggling against my chest. In her white, strained face her eyes were like sword points. I tightened my hold on her.

"You're getting out of here," I whispered between my teeth. "Now. Before anything happens."

"I'm not," she panted. "How *dare* you behave like this!"

"Be quiet."

"But that nice man. Kup's friend . . . You're a boor. You're . . ."

"Save the names for later."

I steered her toward the entrance. I nodded curtly to the disapproving headwaiter, who lowered the rope and let me guide Gertrude past him into the lobby and up to the door. The cab I had told to wait was just outside. I shoved Gertrude unceremoniously into it and got in after her, telling the driver, "Ambassador East." My left arm pinned Gertrude against the seat while my right reached across her and gripped the handle of the door, which she was trying desperately to wrench open.

Back in our hotel suite the storm, brewing all day, broke in unrestrained fury. Taut and stiff as a stretched bowstring, Gertrude let fly at me the barbed arrows of her anger. I was rude, she asserted; sullen, resentful, domineering.

I let her have her fling. I felt I could afford to. My anger had expended itself in the brief moment it took to snatch Gertrude from Mr. Fisher's arms into mine, and in the relief of getting her and myself out of the night club without further incident.

Gertrude continued to berate me for what she termed my crudity, my rudeness "to that charming man. Kup's friend. What must he think of you?"

Finally I broke in: "That charming man, for your information, is Al Capone's cousin and successor—and the Number One gangster in Chicago."

It took a minute for her to assimilate this. She blinked. But it turned the spate of her wrath.

"Oooh!" she breathed softly. "Really, Richard? Is he?"

"He is." I repeated what Ernie had told me about the Fischetti brothers. Gertrude's look of pleased wonder grew.

"I've always wanted to meet a gangster. I've wondered what they were like, really. Outside the films." Her tone became accusing. "And now, when I do have the luck, you come along and spoil everything!"

I said nothing.

Suddenly, a totally new thought occurred to her. I could see her eyes widen as she turned slowly toward me.

"Richard, suppose he was armed? What if he had bodyguards there?"

"He probably did."

"They might have done something terrible."

"You've been seeing too many gangster movies."

"Richard! They might have shot you!"

She regarded me a moment as if unable to take in the full import of this. Then color flooded her cheeks, her eyes became an indescribably soft blue. "Darling Mr. A," she breathed. "Whatever would I do without you?"

She ran straight into my waiting arms.

* * *

I let the telephone ring several times. Finally, when its insistence permitted of no refusal, I growled into it: "Commander Aldrich."

"Charlie Fisher," said the voice at the other end.

"Yes?"

"I just phoned to say I didn't know you and the little lady were married," the voice went on. "Otherwise, I hope you realize, Commander, I wouldn't have presumed."

"That's all right," I said. Feeling that I owed the polite Mr. Fisher an apology, I added: "You understand, Mrs. Aldrich and I haven't seen very much of each other for the last couple of years. Naturally we want to be together all we can."

"Just what I'd feel if I was in your place," said Mr. Fisher gallantly. "About what happened tonight, Commander," he continued, "don't give it another thought. You and the little lady aren't to worry about anything as long as you're in Chicago. You have my word of honor for it."

"That's very kind of you," I said.

"You don't have to worry about the newspapers. We've taken care of that."

That was a welcome reassurance. Up to that time I hadn't given the matter any thought, but upon a moment's reflection it was obvious that a sensationalized account of the scene on the dance floor would not benefit Gertrude's reputation. Nor would the Navy be pleased.

"Thank you very much," I said.

"Okay, Commander. My regards to the little lady."

With that Mr. Fisher retired, graceful to the last.

Though Gertrude and I never saw him again, he became one of

our legends. When Gertrude played *Pygmalion* in Chicago two years later, among the flowers she received at her opening was an enormous white urn filled with the longest-stemmed lilies I ever saw. The card read: "To Mr. and Mrs. Aldrich, from Charles Fisher."

* * *

The naval conference went on for several days, during which Gertrude kept the appointments her publishers made for her, and *A Star Danced* shot high among the best-sellers. I had applied for and was granted a one-month leave. As soon as the conference closed, Gertrude and I returned to New York, preparatory to going up to the Cape. I had every expectation that when my leave was up I would be sent out to the Pacific Theatre.

A month would have been little enough time for us, but, as I discovered as soon as we reached New York, we were not to have even that to ourselves in peace.

It was not only that the publishers were determined to make Gertrude's book sell more copies in New York than in Chicago, and showed an ingenuity in publicizing it that allowed us almost no privacy; but the publicity was producing an overwhelming amount of mail. Gertrude's fans demanded autographs, signed photographs, and personal mementos.

Although two secretaries were hastily installed to deal with the mail, Gertrude insisted on signing each letter herself.

The rattle of the secretaries' typewriters, the ringing of the telephone, and the appearance at all hours of interviewers, photographers, and persons soliciting Gertrude's endorsement of every sort of product drove me out of the apartment early in the morning, not to return until evening.

Meanwhile my few days of freedom were slipping by. I would have insisted on Gertrude's leaving all this and going with me up to the Cape but for the recollection of her remark to me in Chicago: "There's no need to be jealous." I felt unwilling to say anything that Gertrude might interpret as a return of the emotion which had possessed me there.

So we stayed on in New York.

If I had had an office of my own to go to and business of my own to engross me I might have been more philosophical about the delay. But this was 1945. During the four years I had been in the service a great many changes had taken place on Broadway, including the temporary dissolution of my own firm. The war had not only drawn hundreds of young actors into the services but had radically altered production conditions. I found myself in an alien land, without ties or prospects. I drifted aimlessly from the Players Club to the Harvard Club, to the Union Club.

As long as the Navy had use for me, I was able to tell myself that I was serving my country. What would happen when the war ended and I, along with millions more, was demobilized and had to start out looking for something to do? Frankly, I did not know.

I had pointed out to Gertrude before we married that play producing is a precarious livelihood. I had been out of production and consequently out of possible profits since December, 1941. I was now four years older, and enough wiser to realize that getting started again in the only business I knew was going to be the most difficult step of my career.

Meanwhile, I was the uniformed husband of the successful star and author, Gertrude Lawrence.

I did not like it.

However, for the present, there was nothing I could do about it. In desperation, and to take my mind off my own problems, of which I said nothing to Gertrude, I undertook to help plough through the mass of fan mail cluttering our apartment. It might help us get off to the Cape before my entire leave was up.

Gertrude welcomed my assistance. Going through her mail, I became aware of something which disturbed me.

Gertrude had been writing letters and sending packages—and unwittingly creating sentimental attachments—among English, Canadian and American fighting men scattered all along the various fronts. Some she had met at the Stage Door Canteens, others in Normandy, in the camps in Britain, and in the South Pacific and in veterans' hospitals. When these lonely and homesick men had started writing her, she had replied with characteristically generous warmth. In more than one instance this had been misinterpreted by her correspondent as a romantic interest in him.

True, the majority of letters from overseas (they came from colonels and corporals; Gertrude's notes and parcels were sent with proud disregard of rank) were simply genuine expressions of gratitude. A G.I. in Cairo thanked Gertrude for trying to place two songs he had written; another in the Marianas forwarded to her an invention which he wanted marketed (she promptly had it sent to a patent lawyer).

But there were more personal letters that bothered me; obviously, the writers had no idea Gertrude was married. I showed one or two to Gertrude with the observation that she had gone beyond the bounds of common sense.

"But Richard!" she exclaimed. "I just sent those boys warm, friendly notes. You couldn't possibly take such letters seriously, could you?"

"*I* couldn't . . . but what about the boys? Do *they* realize that all those lavish 'darlings' in your letters mean nothing at all—that they are just part of the patter of the theatrical world?"

Gertrude appeared momentarily impressed. Then she said lightly, "Don't be so *glum* about it, darling—it's all past."

The whole thing would probably have ended there had it not been for the annoying insistence of one of her overseas admirers who suddenly turned up in New York. Answering the telephone one morning, I heard a high-pitched male voice with a distinct southern drawl ask for Miss Lawrence. The speaker identified himself as "an old friend—a close personal friend" of Gertrude's from overseas.

I explained that Miss Lawrence was not taking any calls, but that I would be glad to relay a message to her.

"Oh, she'll want to take this call, all right."

"I'm afraid that's not quite possible."

"Now, look here . . ." the voice paused impressively. "You just go on and tell her it's R—— D—— calling. She'll come quick enough," he added confidently.

I repeated with a slight edge of impatience that I could not disturb Gertrude; she was fulfilling a heavy schedule.

"You just don't understand." The tone became irritatingly patronizing. "Miss Lawrence is looking forward to my call. We have been corresponding back and forth for months."

"And *you* don't understand"—I realized I was raising my voice—"that Miss Lawrence has been corresponding with a number of young men in several Allied armies. I am sure it was all very pleasant at the time, and a help to morale, but now the war's almost over. Miss Lawrence has returned to her own life. I suggest that you do the same!" I slammed down the receiver and turned around to see Gertrude standing in the doorway. The look in her eyes left no doubt that she had heard my final remarks.

"So it's censorship now, is it?" she inquired acidly.

"Not censorship," I corrected her. "Just common sense. I am trying to protect you from possible embarrassment."

"How very, *very* chivalrous!" She glared. "Who was on the telephone—if I may pierce the veil of secrecy?"

"Oh, one of your pen pals. A rather . . ." I groped for a word that would annoy her—"dull-witted young man who said he was R—— D——"

Gertrude bristled. "He's *not* dull-witted; he's very talented and intelligent."

She caught my skeptical glance. "He writes poetry," she added defiantly. "Free verse."

"Dedicated, no doubt," I said drily, "to that modern Helen of Troy, Miss Gertrude Lawrence."

Gertrude's head went up—a familiar storm warning. "It happens that some of them *were* dedicated to me—and it also happens that I would like to see R—— again." She advanced a step toward the telephone. "He's in Army Public Relations. Their people can tell me where to reach him."

I grabbed her wrist. "You're not touching that phone!"

"How *dare* you stop me!"

Eyes blazing, she tried—unsuccessfully—to wrench herself away. For a few seconds we struggled, our fury rising. Then the doorbell started ringing insistently. The mood was broken.

I went to the door. It was one of the typists, apologetic for being a few minutes late. I left the apartment and went downtown.

I did not see Gertrude again until that evening, when I returned home. The apartment was filled with people—when they left, we had to hurry out to keep a dinner engagement. This was hardly the occasion for us to pursue our differences. But throughout the evening I could not forget the morning's unpleasantness; I felt that some decisive action had to be taken—at a time and place of my own choosing. Later, when I had a few moments to myself, I telephoned Fanny Holtzmann and asked her to let me have her apartment the following day.

"What for?"

I said I found it necessary to have a serious talk with Gertrude. Because it was a matter of importance, I preferred not to use our own apartment, where we might be overheard by secretaries or interrupted by visitors.

"Very well. My apartment is at your disposal from ten o'clock on; the housekeeper will let you in and disappear. You and Gee can then fight it out in peace and privacy."

Gertrude came along docilely enough, when I told her there was something I wanted to discuss in complete privacy. I am quite sure she had a very good idea what the subject would be.

Mrs. Jenkins, Fanny's motherly housekeeper, left us alone in the living room. Far off, I heard a door close.

"Well?" Gertrude said rather too brightly.

"I want to talk to you about the man who phoned yesterday—among other things. Not that I think *he* himself is very important."

"If you're aware of that, why bring him up?"

"Because of what he represents."

Gertrude laughed. It was a brittle laugh, and it irritated me.

"Oh, Richard, don't tell me you're being jealous again!"

"No," I said grimly. "Not jealous. Disgusted."

"Disgusted?" Her quick reaction told me the shot had found its mark.

"Yes, disgusted. You're supposed to be a grown woman, a responsible adult. You've achieved great things in your profession. Yet at times you behave as if you had no respect for your position in the world—no respect for yourself—and no respect for your husband. In fact, you behave like a juvenile delinquent!"

She turned on me, white-faced, and stony-gray-eyed with anger.

"How *dare* you presume to speak to me like that, Richard Aldrich?" she demanded.

"Because I'm your husband," I shot back. "And don't forget it."

"What if you are—do you think that gives you the right to find fault with me? Criticize what I do? Scold me? Give me orders? I'm not one of your men, Commander Aldrich. How dare you presume to tell anyone that he shall not write to me, or call me up, or come to see me in my own home?"

"Your home is my home," I reminded her, "while you and I are married, and I want you to know it."

"And I want you to know," Gertrude flared back, "that, married or not, I'll see whom I like, and when I like. And where. I don't need anyone to manage my life for me. I did it pretty successfully for some years before I ever heard of Richard Stoddard Aldrich."

We were now launched on the "high old row" of which she was to remind me several times in later years. It was worthy of the name. Gertrude blazed at me for attempting to dominate her. She accused me of surliness; of being a dog in a manger ever since I had come home. According to her, my behavior in Chicago and lately had been a revelation to her—and an unpleasant one.

If she spoke of revelations, I retorted—and I found myself shouting—what did she think her conduct had revealed to me?

She chose to take this as an accusation of unfaithfulness. How dared I make such a charge against her, she demanded?

"I didn't!" I shouted.

"You most certainly did." She followed this by pointing out that she had not once questioned me about the women I must have met in England. Well, then, why shouldn't she make friends of men she had met in the service?

"No man likes finding that his wife is an indiscriminate flirt."

"Don't call me promiscuous!" Gertrude outshouted me. With a gesture of total defiance she pulled off her hat and threw it at my face. I ducked, and the hat sailed past me, to land behind the sofa.

I said nastily: "I'm glad you know there is such a word."

Her anger had now risen beyond flood-water mark. I thought for a moment she was going to attack me with her bare hands. I caught them both and gripped them tight while she struggled to free herself.

"Northfield . . . Northfield . . . NORTHFIELD . . ." I commanded.

It was so long since either of us had used our code word that it was several seconds before its significance pierced Gertrude's rage. Then suddenly I felt her go limp. I gathered her into my arms.

In the peace after the storm we arranged to get out of New York that same afternoon, leaving our worries and differences behind us, and go up to the Cape.

We let ourselves out of the apartment without another thought of Gertrude's hat.

Years later, on Easter Sunday, Gertrude and I were walking along Fifth Avenue with her newly acquired West Highland terrier, Angus, when we met Mrs. Jenkins similarly engaged with her Trixie.

While the dogs rubbed noses we exchanged compliments.

"Why, Jenkie," Gertrude exclaimed with genuine admiration, "how smart you look! And what a sweet hat!"

"I'm not surprised you like it, Miss Lawrence," Mrs. Jenkins observed.

"You aren't?" Gertrude asked, apparently puzzled.

"Well, that's the best of a really good hat when you get one," Mrs. Jenkins said blandly, favoring me with a wink. "It never dates."

* * *

For several days our vacation at The Berries left nothing to be desired. However I could not completely put away the thought of my own future. Each day's news from the Pacific made it clear that the war in that theatre was entering its final stage. I faced the probability of returning to civilian life before long, and with no business to go back to.

One day when Gertrude and I were at the Hydes' and Dr. Fritz had taken Gertrude off to see his paintings, Dr. Harriet asked me a few straight questions about my plans.

There was no reason not to tell her the truth—that they were nonexistent—and I did.

"How does Gertrude feel about all this?" she asked.

"I haven't discussed it with her."

"Don't you think you should?"

I said I would rather not until I had thought out a method of procedure. Dr. Harriet looked grave.

"Marriage should be a full partnership, Richard," she said. "The responsibility for success rests equally on husband and wife. One partner must never shield the other from facts that affect them both. Don't pamper Gertrude," she added. "She can take it."

Then she changed the subject. Perhaps she felt she had said enough.

* * *

If I had followed Dr. Harriet's advice, would things have been any different? Perhaps. But, as Gertrude used to say, I am a stubborn Yankee. I cherish the idea that I know best. "Always Right Aldrich," to quote Gertrude.

Perhaps, too, our quarrel, like a long spell of torrid weather, could not be dissipated in one storm, however violent. It continued to hover on our horizon. I was aware of its rumblings on Sunday morning, when I answered the telephone and was told that it was the Western Union office calling; they had a telegram for my wife, and would I mind if they read it to me? The message came from a man I had never heard of. It said he had forty-eight hours' leave in New York before sailing, and he counted on Gertrude's promise to spend part of that time with him.

I had thought we were clear of such difficulties. Gertrude had assured me of it. This new one was the final straw.

I determined not to give Gertrude the message. Let her admirer cool his ardor and carry his disillusionment abroad with him. I got out my car and drove down to the village to pick up the papers. When I returned, I heard Gertrude at the upstairs telephone.

Presently, she came down, singing blithely.

"Darling, I have to go back to town this evening," she announced. "Just for two days."

"What for?" I inquired from behind my paper.

"I forgot all about an engagement I'd made for tomorrow. It's a party at the Stork Club that the publishers are giving for me."

"Is A—— going to be there too?" I asked. "He has leave. His ship is in port."

She stared at me a moment. I lowered the paper and stared back at her. The thought that was forming in my mind was: I've had enough.

Gertrude said slowly: "And do you have any *other* fascinating tidbits of confidential information?"

I said that this was hardly confidential. A—— had telegraphed, and with a lack of reserve that reminded me of her. By this time dozens of people knew that she had promised to spend part of his leave with him. "I would not be surprised to read it in the columns on Tuesday. Perhaps Jimmy Fidler will have a flash on it tonight."

The idea that she had aroused my jealousy inspired Gertrude with the irresistible impulse to torment me. I realized this, but in my mood I was powerless to circumvent her.

"Thank you, darling, for reminding me about A——," she said airily. "I'll invite him to the party. He'd love it. And he can take me. There's no use asking *you,* since you seem to resent my literary career."

She avoided meeting my gaze, but I kept it on her unflinchingly.

"I want you to get this," I said, "because it's final. If you go to New York to meet that man, no matter what your pretense is, I'm through."

"What do you mean, Richard?"

"Just that," I answered. "I won't put up with a woman who insists on acting like 'My Last Duchess.'"

"Your *what?*"

"She was the subject of one of Browning's poems. An incorrigible flirt. '*She had a heart too soon made glad, too easily impressed. . . . Oh, sir, she smiled, no doubt, whene'er I passed her: But who passed without much the same smile?*' That was too much for her husband, the Duke. And it's too much for me! I won't live with a woman who treats my name so lightly!"

Gertrude had contained herself as long as possible. She burst out: "And I will not live with a man who suspects me constantly—who does not trust me. . . . Oh, everyone said it wouldn't work. They were right. The sooner you and I go our separate ways, the better."

"If that's your final decision," I said, "there's no point in any further discussion. Go to New York. Or anywhere you wish. Or stay here, if that suits you. I'll move to the club."

She made no reply. Suddenly she turned and ran up the stairs. I heard her door slam.

Because of gas rationing, I could not leave the Cape earlier than by the evening train. I remained downstairs, prepared to go out of the house should Gertrude reappear. I felt frozen, dead. Yet my resolve was unshakable. I felt Gertrude had pushed me to the limits of patience and forbearance.

Perhaps an hour passed. Then Dr. Harriet walked in. Her mien revealed this was no casual visit.

"Where is Gertrude?" she asked.

I told her.

"Ask her to come down," Dr. Harriet said. "I want to talk to you both."

I hesitated. Dr. Harriet continued firmly. "It's high time someone talked seriously to you two. I seem to have been selected for the honor."

"How did you know anything was wrong?"

"Fanny Holtzmann telephoned. She said Gertrude had called her brother David and asked him to make a reservation for her at the Plaza. Gertrude said she was leaving you. For good. As Gertrude's lawyers, and as friends of you both, the Holtzmanns are very much distressed. I don't usually meddle in my neighbors' affairs," she concluded grimly, "even on occasions when I believe I know better than they do. But in this case, and acting at the request of Gertrude's lawyer, I feel justified.

"Please ask Gertrude to come down," she repeated. "What I have to say, I wish to say to you together."

At first Gertrude refused to reply to my request. But her affection and respect for Dr. Harriet triumphed. Quiet, tense, and resolutely disregarding me, she came down and sat with her hands folded, like an obedient, injured child.

Dr. Harriet took off her glasses and polished them with a corner of her handkerchief. I realized she was finding her assignment difficult.

"This is the second world war I've lived through," she said at last. "In every war, the casualties are not confined to the battlefields. What I have come here for is to prevent one more casualty, if I can. As a doctor, that is part of my responsibility. And as your friend and neighbor, as someone who is very fond of you both, I feel that responsibility is doubled."

Dr. Harriet pointed out that both Gertrude and I had been subjected to severe wartime strains. We had been living abnormally, under great tension, and amid confusion. We showed the effects of it. We were edgy, sensitive to slights, suspicious, quick to take affront. We were in no state to make a decision which would affect our entire lives.

She reminded us that after the first world war many homes were broken up because husband and wife could not find a common meeting ground after their long separation.

"It would be a pity for your marriage to be destroyed for no sounder reason than this," she went on. "You are two fine, intelligent people. And you love each other. I'm convinced of that. Are you so careless that you would throw away what you have built together, right in this house, because of a temporary misunderstanding?"

I started to speak, but she checked me.

"I don't want to hear the cause of this or of your other quarrels," she said firmly. "I'm not interested in proving that either one of you is right, and the other wrong. My guess is that neither of you is right, and the other wrong. You are equally at fault; though, perhaps, in different ways. That is something you must talk over together, honestly and calmly. Gertrude may need to remember that when she married, she assumed a responsibility toward you, Richard, and toward society, and she ought to live up to it. Gertrude, my dear, no woman ever achieved happiness in a career alone, at the expense of her personal life. Believe me, I know what I am saying. Don't think that Dr. Fritz and I have our careers and our happy marriage without having gone through our own struggles."

Gertrude was crying. But quietly.

"And you, Richard," Dr. Harriet addressed me, "may need to remember that when you are at home you aren't an officer on duty, who must be obeyed without question. You have been living that sort of life for years, and it isn't easy to change. But you must. And I repeat what I said the other day: don't underrate your wife. Don't be too proud to ask and accept her cooperation. You should know by now the stuff she is made of.

"I ask you just one thing. A promise. I want you to promise me that you will try for one year to get along together. I ask only a year; but I ask that you make a serious attempt, during those twelve months, to reach a basis of understanding. Not for me, but for yourselves. Because you owe it to yourselves. Will you promise me that?"

Dr. Harriet rose from her chair.

Gertrude darted a tentative look of inquiry at me, then started across the room toward our friend. Dr. Harriet stretched out her arms silently to enfold her.

"I'm willing," Gertrude said slowly. "If Richard is . . ." Her face —now cleared of resentment—was that of a bride tremulously taking her marriage vow.

Her loveliness and sincerity were irresistible. I strode over to where she and Dr. Harriet stood arm in arm.

"I'm willing," I murmured.

Dr. Harriet joined my hand to Gertrude's. I leaned over and kissed both my wife and the good friend who had brought us together.

"Now," Dr. Harriet said, "I'm going. I advise you to get out of the house for the rest of the day. Go down to the beach. Or drive up to Groton. And don't discuss your problems for at least twenty-four hours. Then you can start making a clean breast of them."

I saw the wisdom of this and accepted it. Gertrude appeared troubled.

"That brings up the cause of our quarrel this morning," she said, speaking pointedly to Dr. Harriet, not to me. "I do have an engagement in New York. My publishers' publicity man rang up this morning to remind me of it. Richard chose to think I wanted to go for another reason; one, which, it so happens, I knew nothing about. That was what set us off; he suspected me unjustly, and I was hurt and angry."

Dr. Harriet looked at me with lifted eyebrows. Embarrassment and shame overcame me. I realized that I had jumped to my own conclusions, and in the direction away from the truth.

"You will have to be patient with Richard, Gertrude," Dr. Harriet said quietly. "He is in a difficult situation—a situation many men are finding themselves in at this time. He will tell you himself. Then you will understand and be able to help him. That's the best foundation to build any marriage on."

* * *

Gertrude and I went to New York together. On the way I gave her a picture of my business affairs and what I was up against.

Our quarrel, seen in retrospect, was a turning point in our lives. Before the twelve months of trial were up, it seemed incredible that we could ever have said to each other with bitter finality: "I'm through."

Years later, when Gertrude was in Hollywood for the filming of *The Glass Menagerie*, I flew out to spend Christmas with her. One evening we drove away from the lights and the hectic holiday mood into the desert. There the air was clean and pungent; the deep blue sky above us was ablaze with stars.

Gertrude's head was on my shoulder. She had been silent, deeply moved by the natural beauty. Suddenly I heard her recite, more to herself than to me:

"All that I know
Of a certain star
Is, it can throw
(Like the angled spar)
Now a dart of red,

Now a dart of blue,
Till my friends have said
They would fain see, too,

My star that dartles the red and the blue,
Then it stops like a bird—like a flower, hangs furled;
They must solace themselves with the Saturn above it.
What matters to me if their star is a world?
Mine has opened its heart to me; therefore I love it . . ."

I had not heard Browning's poem "My Star," which he wrote to his wife, since Professor Copeland read it to us at Harvard. Schoolboy's lines, I had thought them then, even when delivered in his spellbinding voice. But now, spoken by my wife, they were all that I, had the gods made me a poet, could have found to say about her and our marriage.

I told her this, adding as a sop to the self-consciousness that nearly always overcame me when I attempted to express my deepest feelings in words, that Browning's "star," like mine, must have furnished her husband a good many moments of eye-winking bewilderment.

I brought the conversation around to the subject of our own marriage, which was then entering on its tenth year. I called on her to notice that we had successfully rebutted all those who had given us at most two years from the starting post to Reno.

"It's all been a miracle from my point of view. And you can't say it's been dull, either," Gertrude said. "Or can you?"

I replied that "dull" was the last word which would occur to me to describe our marriage. There had been too many red and blue darts for that.

"Aren't you glad?" she sighed. "I'll tell you something now that I never quite dared admit to you before. When we were first married I was awfully disappointed in you for a while because when I started a quarrel—and you know, I began nearly all of them—all the best ones," she added proudly, "you didn't quarrel back. You were like a log of green wood on the fire. Absolutely no blaze. I almost despaired of you. I said to myself: If he's going to stay like that forever, I don't think I can stand it. But you got the idea. You caught on. And you must admit, we've put on some really slap-up rows in our day. Regular rousers, some of them. Like that time when you hired a hall to deliver me a lecture on my manners and morals. Or when you quoted 'My Last Duchess' to me. Remember?"

I said I was not likely to forget it.

"The best part about all our fights has always been the making up," Gertrude went on. "You're always so sweet afterwards. And I feel so purged and relaxed. And so eager to fall in love all over again. Darling, I think it would kill me if after one of our rows you were to stamp out and slam the door, the way you always do, and never come back. I would *die* if there were no red roses the next day."

I told her that I had more than once suspected that she was not above promoting a quarrel with me for the sheer excitement it afforded her, and the chance to go into a big scene.

"But, darling, of course," she admitted. "I'm a woman. As well as an actress. And you can't tell me you don't enjoy it yourself, Mr. A."

Nor could I, at that.

Chapter Fourteen

IN THE CLOSING WEEKS OF 1945, the following release went out to the New York press:

THEATRE INCORPORATED

Richard Aldrich, Managing Director

Presents

GERTRUDE LAWRENCE RAYMOND MASSEY

in

Pygmalion

a ROMANCE by

BERNARD SHAW

This announcement represented a departure from the rule Gertrude and I had established for ourselves at the start of our marriage, never to either interfere with each other's career or to merge our professional activities.

At the time we were married, there was general expectation in theatrical circles that I would produce her plays and we would become another husband-wife, producer-star team. To our friends who asked when this was going to happen, our invariable reply was: "Never." Each of us wished to keep our relationship purely personal. Gertrude had an established, brilliantly successful career and was sought after by the greatest producers in England and America. I, for my part, had no desire to "present" my wife or be married to my star.

Apart from Gertrude's few appearances at the Cape Playhouse, we had observed our "separate-careers" rule meticulously. Now we were temporarily setting it aside for a project that we both believed in.

Theatre Incorporated was a group of young men and women intelligently and creatively interested in the theatre. They had just been organized to produce first-rate plays for limited engagements on Broadway and in a few other cities. They intended to operate on a non-profit basis on a total capital amounting to less than the cost of one Broadway musical. Profits from the successful plays were to be paid into the corporation to make possible other, and perhaps less commercial, productions.

Shortly after Dr. Harriet had figuratively banged our heads together, the Theatre Incorporated directors approached me as one who could contribute the practical experience of a Broadway producer to the project and yet would share and appreciate the enthusiasm which they felt for the theatre. Beatrice Straight, one of the directors, had already spoken to Fanny in an effort to get Gertrude to star in a play for the new organization. When Gertrude learned that I had accepted the post of managing director of the group, she immediately wanted to give it her enthusiastic support.

I reminded her that she would have to forego the large percentage of profit that she usually received, and that she would be working for me.

"It isn't really working *for* you—but *with* you. And for something we both believe in. Let's do *Pygmalion*. I've wanted to play Eliza for a long time."

I believed that a comedy like Shaw's *Pygmalion* would be a fine starting point for Theatre Incorporated; but Shaw had already turned down our request for permission to do the play. In fact, for the past decade Shaw had been refusing to let *Pygmalion* be done. Many stars and producers had approached him, but, as he wrote Fanny Holtzmann, he considered *Pygmalion* "a pot-boiler that had been done to rags."

However, Fanny, who was in London on United Nations business, undertook to re-open the matter with Shaw, and soon we received a cable that Shaw had accepted Theatre Incorporated's offer, and we began to plan our production.

Following *Pygmalion,* and before returning to my private business with the producing firm of Aldrich and Myers, I, as managing director of Theatre Incorporated, succeeded in bringing to America for the first time, in 1946, the Old Vic Theatre Company, starring Laurence Olivier and Ralph Richardson. This visit created a sensation. Later, Theatre Incorporated brought over the Habimah Players from Palestine. The following year, when I had resumed my old partnership, Dick Myers and I sponsored the first visit to this country of the Dublin Gate Theatre Company.

In all these ventures Gertrude gave me her enthusiastic support. She not only participated directly—at considerable financial sacrifice—in Theatre Incorporated's first offering, *Pygmalion,* but kept up her interest in our plans and her pride in our achievements for as long as Theatre Incorporated existed.

So did my mother.

I think Mother had been ignorant of the blaze of glory surrounding the name of George Bernard Shaw, and oblivious to his social gospel, until the topic of *Pygmalion* became part of our daily conversation. With considerable diffidence, she asked if she might read the play. It must have been one of the few plays, other than Shakespeare's, that she had ever read, and I suspect that she approached it with the feeling that she was doing something daring and unconventional. Her excuse to herself, no doubt, was that the unconventionality was condonable, since *Pygmalion,* like our cranberry bog, was a family enterprise.

Before she reached the end, Mother was a Shavian. Having whetted her appetite, she went on through "Plays Pleasant" to Ditto

Unpleasant, until she was brought up short by *Mrs. Warren's Profession.*

She closed the volume grimly and put it into a corner of the bookshelves, where she hoped Aunt Alice would not discover it. Then she sought me out and demanded my assurance that, no matter how highly Gertrude regarded the works of George Bernard Shaw, I would never countenance her appearing as Mrs. Warren.

When Gertrude visited Shaw several years later, she told him this story, which caused him to grin impishly. When Gertrude knitted mittens for him during his last years, he inquired whether her very proper mother-in-law had helped her make them, despite his authorship of *Mrs. Warren.* A few days before his last illness, he sent Gertrude an unpublished collection of playlets, entitled *Far-fetched Fables,* which he had just completed and for which he had set down stage directions in his own hand. He suggested that Gertrude read one of the sketches to her mother-in-law. It was a futuristic play dealing with deviationists in love.

* * *

Pygmalion opened in New Haven the second week of December. Its success was phenomenal. In four performances the play broke the house record for a non-musical. Gertrude's amazing variety was evident in the role of Eliza, as was her exquisite sense of balance. Her flower-seller was never grotesque; and, as a fine lady, her veneer of elegance had something touching about it.

She divided honors with Sir Cedric Hardwicke, who directed the play, and with Raymond Massey, whose Professor Higgins was so effectively annoying that it exasperated everyone who had ever suffered from meddlers.

It was this, I believe, that made the audience sigh disappointedly when, during a scene in the last act, Gertrude snatched up one after the other of the Professor's slippers and flung them at him, only to display a feminine inability to hit the mark.

"I knew Gertrude actually had the accuracy of a big-league catcher throwing to second base," Ray Massey said, recalling those days. "I pleaded with her to use her powers. The audience wanted her to hit me. Or at least to come gaspingly close to it. But it was no use. She was really afraid that my powers to dodge were inadequate. But after a week or so the tomboy in her—and that was considerable, God love her—or perhaps the role itself, overcame her caution and kindness.

"One night, when I'd given up expecting anything, a whizzing slipper caught me on the nose. Gee was as startled as I. 'Oh!' she exclaimed. 'I've hit you . . .' She dropped the other slipper in horror.

"Then she caught my gratified laughter and the delighted hilarity of the audience. She picked up the slipper and let me have it. For a season afterward I had to duck pinpoint pitching."

During the play's run in Boston, Mother joined Gertrude at the Ritz Carlton and had her first exhilarating taste of being related to a great popular star. Her horror of the theatre had been swept away by her pride and by the late release of a long-suppressed love for what was dramatic and beautiful. At eighty-five, she began for the first time to understand my lifelong interest in the theatre. She no longer frowned on it as something slightly disreputable which could never have been inherited from her side of the family. Instead, her eyes twinkled appreciatively when I said gravely, one day, that I must have acquired my interest partly from her. The ultimate seal of her approval was granted when she invited Dr. Donald Ward, Groton's Congregational minister, to be her guest at a matinee. Only a few years before, she had been at pains to keep secret from her neighbors my connection with the theatre, and my marriage to an actress.

She took an ingenuous and charming delight in lunching with Gertrude at the Ritz, where several of her Boston friends caught sight of her and were properly impressed. And in going shopping with Gertrude in the city, though her conservatism was still occasionally disturbed when Gertrude insisted on buying her a becoming dress or hat. Gertrude's wily way of circumventing Mother's protest was to tell her that the dress in question was just what the Dowager Queen Mary wore.

Gertrude could never resist costuming Mother for her role and surrounding her with suitable "character" props. She was always picking up Victorian ornaments and sending them up to Groton. Any presents Gertrude received that had an aura of age and quaintness were immediately set aside for "Mother Mary."

Passing on gifts made to her was an incurable habit of Gertrude's. "Take it, dear," she would say while giving an expensive handbag, a Hattie Carnegie blouse, or a piece of jewelry to a member of her cast or a friend visiting backstage. Since she was the constant recipient of many presents, her penchant for giving them away sometimes resulted in strange situations.

Thus, she once presented Fanny with a pair of earrings, saying, "You simply must take these. Every time I look at them, somehow they remind me of you."

"For a very good reason," Fanny remarked, as she examined the earrings. "I picked them up in Helsinki—and gave them to you years ago."

Far from being embarrassed by her short memory, Gertrude burst out laughing. "That proves something that I've always said," she added. "It's much more pleasant to give than to receive!"

Pygmalion opened in New York the day after Christmas for an engagement limited to two months. The notices were warm in their praise of the cast, the direction, and the idealism which made the production possible. They hailed "a new Gertrude Lawrence . . . she is funny, very funny; she shows heart and tenderness and grace . . . she is pitiable, she is gallant . . . and she is beautiful . . ." "She makes the role a lustrous addition to an already impressive list of memorable stage portraits . . ." Do I show favoritism if I say I agreed?

One of the tributes Gertrude prized most was this note from Uncle Jim.

January 30, 1946

Mrs. Richard Aldrich
Eliza Doolittle
Gertrude Lawrence

Dear Miss Doolittle:—

Despite my lame ears, my good eyes served me so well last Saturday that I shall surely seize my first opportunity to revisit "Pygmalion." I wish to thank you—and through you, Richard—for the

Vandamm

Eliza Doolittle, before and after her transformation by Professor Higgins —Gertrude as she appeared in Shaw's play *Pygmalion*.

Maurice Seymour

A producer-star team. For *Pygmalion* we broke our long-standing rule that our careers should be separate.

great pleasure your performance has given me. It is a satisfaction to learn that your presence in New York for the rest of the season will keep a host of people away from the theatres which offer only "Follies" and "Scandals." (You see how old-fashioned I am.)

With best wishes for your long continuance in your brilliant career.

Yours cordially,
James R. Joy

Our Christmas celebration that year came up to Gertrude's anticipations. She had begun planning for it while we were at The Berries in the late summer, and she kept on adding to the plans, to the presents for everyone, to the humorous verses she wrote and attached to the gifts, and to the decorations for the tree. This was so large it threatened to push us out of the apartment.

The boys were with us that Christmas Eve; both grown tall, and Dick shockingly like myself at his age. He was a senior at Choate, and hoped to enter the University of Virginia the next autumn.

"Our first Christmas in a world without war," Gertrude reminded me as we gathered around the lighted tree: my mother, Barbara, Pamela and her husband, Dick and David, and my first wife with her husband and son. Missing from our little group was the cheery presence of Barbara's husband, Harrison Hobart, killed in an accident; Gertrude had been a sorely needed pillar of strength to Barbara ever since.

* * *

When *Pygmalion* closed its New York run and the company went on tour, Mother stayed on with me in New York at Gertrude's suggestion. I think Gertrude felt I should have a home atmosphere after my years in the service. She left detailed orders with Helen Mahoney about serving Mother's breakfast in bed, and surrounding her with the little luxuries that Gertrude herself delighted in. These included Gertrude's Parisian bedjacket of billowy chiffon. It came as something of a jolt to see my mother, so attired, sitting up against the lace and satin pillows in bed, having breakfast from a tray—without even the excuse of a temperature or a broken leg to justify such indolence to her Puritan conscience.

One day, Mother asked Helen where Gertrude would be playing the following week. Helen didn't know, but volunteered to look it up in *Variety.*

"What's *Variety?*" Mother asked.

"It's the theatrical trade paper," Helen explained, as she showed her a copy. "We get it every week."

Mother scanned the headlines on the legitimate theatre page. "What does '*Pygmalion* Boff' mean?" she inquired.

Helen explained that it meant very big or very successful. Mother took to reading the paper herself, principally the reports on Gertrude's play. Though she was continually mystified by much of the theatre journal's vivid vocabulary, she persevered until she had a reading knowledge of that foreign language, Varietyese. Later, when she returned to Groton, she expressed the wish to continue this reading as a means of keeping up with Gertrude's and my plays. I had the paper sent to her and she took to reading her *Variety* as regularly as any theatrical veteran on Broadway.

On Sunday mornings Mother did not linger abed. Perhaps she was unwilling for Aunt Alice, who came with Uncle Jim every Sunday morning to take her to church, to catch her indulging in such frivolity.

Once, on the night the show ended its Philadelphia engagement, Gertrude arrived home long after midnight to spend Sunday there before going on to the next city. She refused to rest, but insisted, instead, on accompanying Mother, Uncle Jim, and Aunt Alice to church. After services they returned, bringing Bishop Welch for the old-fashioned Sunday dinner which Helen Mahoney had prepared for them.

It was a strange feeling to sit in surroundings which were so intimately associated with Gertrude, and find myself lapped in the Sunday atmosphere of my childhood and of family gatherings at Uncle Sam Aldrich's. My elders discussed the sermon, the choice of the hymns, and the inspirational value of the service they had attended. Bishop Welch remarked with satisfaction on the number of worshippers that morning.

"Yes," Gertrude and I heard Mother say, "as *Variety* would put it, it *was* a boff congregation."

* * *

In *Pygmalion's* coast-to-coast tour, Dennis King took over the role of Professor Higgins. Following her usual practice, Gertrude kept a day-by-day journal of her experiences, in which her co-star and the other members of the company figured frequently.

"Just had a cup of tea in the diner with Dennis King," she wrote. "He has taken up painting and is most excited to find that he really can paint. He has found that everybody needs a hobby—no matter who the person or what the hobby. He now sees colors, and shapes and shadows which he can capture on canvas. This enthusiasm is shared by several friends of mine. I am going to watch Dennis and see whether I respond . . ."

Gertrude was soon to join her friends who had taken up painting as a hobby. She started working in oils with Fanny Holtzmann. Her forte, however, turned out to be finger-painting, in which medium she produced interesting and unusual pictures. Several of her pictures were exhibited and sold for charity in New York and London, one being bought by the wife of the mayor of New York for his official residence, Gracie Mansion.

Gertrude encouraged her daughter, Pam, to renew her interest in painting, first through lessons at the Art Students' League. Later she made it possible for Pam to continue her art studies in Florence under the guidance of Bernard Berenson.

Gertrude was very proud of the abstract paintings Pam did and sent to her. Once an artist's agent, who had selected many of the paintings used by Hallmark greeting cards, came to visit Gertrude backstage. She thought Hallmark might find some of Gertrude's paintings suitable for reproduction as greeting cards. But when the subject was introduced, Gertrude abruptly dismissed her own work. She brought out a portfolio of Pam's work and tried to interest her visitor in her daughter's art.

"I think she has great talent," Gertrude said enthusiastically. "Don't you agree?"

The agent agreed wholeheartedly but felt that Pam's work was not of the genre which would interest greeting-card buyers. "But from what I've heard about your work," she told Gertrude, "I think the Hallmark people would be glad to buy it."

Gertrude shook her head. "Have you ever thought what it is to be the daughter of a woman whose name is up in lights? Pam has talent as an actress, but is always labeled as my daughter. She has writing talent—more than I will ever have—but I'm the one with the best-seller book to my credit. I love dabbling in paint, but this is one field where I will leave all the honors to my daughter."

* * *

The *Pygmalion* company traveled south. Gertrude wrote in her diary: "Just came from lunch at the home of the James Forrestals in Georgetown. Excellent food, and plenty of it. The Secretary was in California but Mrs. Forrestal had invited Admiral Sherman, Joe Alsop of the *Herald Tribune,* Alice Longworth, and John L. Sullivan, who is Under-Secretary of the Navy and who acted as host.

"It was informal and most charming and John Sullivan interested us with stories of the American mothers who at one time were writing to get their sons sent home and now are writing to get their sons into the service . . ."

Another entry records: "Lunched today at British Embassy with the Ambassador, Lord Inverchapel, M. and Mme. Bonnet from the French Embassy, the ambassador's social secretary Miss Boyle, and a charmer named Robert Murphy, just back from China . . ."

An innovation in Gertrude's tour was a week in Mexico City, playing at the Gran Teatro de Esperanza Iris. This was the first time a star of the American theatre had performed in an English play there, and Gertrude and her company were welcomed at the airport on arrival by a band of Mexican musicians, children with flowers, photographers and diplomatic honors.

"I rode to the Reforma Hotel in a car which looked like a hearse full of calla lilies," she wrote . . . "but this is a happy place, full of flowers and friendly favors . . ."

At a reception at the American Embassy she "met Señora Esperanza Iris, for whom the theatre was named, and Dolores del Rio, who looked like a living close-up of her famous self—simply beautiful. . . .

"Dined at the Ambassadeurs, a quiet restaurant, good music, excellent food including doves served like tiny quail rolled in bacon. Scalding hot coffee. Then a stroll home along the Boulevarde in calm clear moonlight such as one used to experience in Paris in the old days. I feel no fatigue—the altitude is like a tonic to me. Looked longingly at the shops but decided to resist temptation until Richard arrives on Wednesday from New York. If his new play looks like a success we shall feel more affluent . . ."

I might have known what to expect. Four days in Mexico City, I discovered upon arrival, had already given Gertrude ideas about buying silver, pottery, glass, gems, rugs, baskets, and souvenirs for everyone she knew.

The play had opened with much fanfare and an advance unprecedented for a play in a foreign language. The theatre was festooned with flags. All the ambassadors were present as well as high dignitaries of the Mexican Government.

No matter how late she went to bed in Mexico—and it usually was very late, as evening performances did not begin before 9 P.M. and there were always supper parties and dancing after the play—she was up, and getting me up, at eight o'clock in order not to miss the morning market.

She teased me about my trip to Mexico with Pam, which now seemed to have taken place untold ages ago. She insisted on my taking her on all the sight-seeing trips in and around the city. To my astonishment, I heard her speaking better than passable Spanish with a fluency I could not account for and which she would not explain.

One morning, however, I was awakened by a masculine voice in the next room speaking some of the same phrases which Gertrude had used so fluently. I opened the door quietly and found Gertrude intently listening to a Holt Army Course phonograph record, which she confessed she had studied for several hours a day before I arrived in order to astonish me.

"I thought I could sneak in a few new phrases," she said, "so I let you sleep a little late. Why did you get up and spoil it?"

One day, more as a joke than for any other reason, I bought Gertrude a ring. It was just a band of Mexican silver with some Aztec symbols which the shopkeeper told us meant good luck, love, fidelity, and happiness. Gertrude stood silent and suddenly solemn in the dark, low, little shop while I slipped the ring on her finger. I felt the silversmith's eyes on us both and I imagined that he was speculating about our relationship. I was confident he took us for lovers. Or a honeymoon couple. I am sure he did not suspect we had been married almost seven years.

Part of Gertrude's constant fascination was that she never acquired that long-married, uninterested, bored, I've-said-everything-I-know-to-you-and-you've-told-me-everything-you-have-to-say-too-many-times look and manner which brands so many wives. She had a way of making you feel, when she was with you, that she would rather be with you than with anyone else.

Though the purchase of the inexpensive silver ring had been made in jest—she had teased me to buy her something as a keepsake—I believe we both realized that it symbolized a new stage of our relationship. The twelve-months' trial we had promised Dr. Harriet had passed and we were still together. Moreover, the bond that united us had strengthened and deepened. We knew each other better. We were more tolerant of each other, more tender, less demanding.

Gertrude always kept the silver ring with her, and she wore it sometimes, as if—or did I fancy it?—it carried a message to her heart which she sometimes felt in need of.

Some months later, in Boston, she suddenly missed the ring. Frantic search of her suite at the Ritz failed to turn it up. Her dresser, Hazel, emptied out all of Gertrude's luggage, shook everything, but the ring did not come to light. Gertrude was sure she had left New York with it on her finger; she believed she had worn it at the dress rehearsal the night before. When Hazel was unable to find it in her dressing room, Gertrude telephoned the play's publicity man, Harry Forward, and begged him to announce she had lost a ring and was offering a substantial reward.

Harry demurred, saying not unreasonably that the story would sound like a hackneyed publicity stunt—"Star Loses Jewelry."

Only because Gertrude insisted and seemed so upset, did he consent to report the loss to the Boston police. Because of the legend that Gertrude's jewels were priceless, no one even considered the possibility that the ring had little intrinsic value.

Gertrude went to the theatre with Harry Forward and the detective who was detailed to the "case," to see if they could turn up any clues. As the detective questioned the employees around the theatre, Gertrude roamed backstage restlessly.

In the wings stood a bed which she had used in a rehearsal the night before. The sight of it seemed to give her an idea. She tore off the pillows and covers, shook them energetically—and the silver ring dropped to the floor.

She pounced on it with a joyful cry. Harry and the detective ran over to where Gertrude stood clutching the ring.

"Is *that* what we've been looking for?" the detective asked disgustedly. "That piece of tin?"

Gertrude looked at the detective with an expression compounded of equal parts of indignation and pride. "My husband gave it to me," she said.

* * *

The customary arrangements made for Gertrude when she went on tour included a suite with two bedrooms at the leading hotel; one for herself, the other for her maid. It meant a great deal to her comfort and convenience to have someone within call at all hours. When she found it impossible to fall asleep there was someone to talk to until the tension subsided and she felt drowsy; someone to read aloud to her until she dropped off.

Gertrude even disliked eating alone; rather than do this she would go without food. Among her maid's responsibilities was seeing that Gertrude ate proper meals at proper times. To accomplish this, Hazel was always unobtrusively on hand to have lunch or dinner with Gertrude whenever Gertrude wanted her; to go out with her for a walk, to shop, or to do any of the innumerable small errands which a star on tour requires to have done for her. In nearly all Gertrude's plans for the future, Hazel was included. "Hazel is seven people in one to me," she would say. Her reliance on Hazel's calm, imperturbably good-humored competence increased during the years.

On her *Pygmalion* tour, Gertrude arrived at her hotel in Washington, D.C., to find her suite filled with flowers; telegrams and telephone calls pouring in; and no Hazel to deal with them or to unpack the luggage. Twenty minutes passed. Then Gertrude answered a call and heard a plaintive voice say: "It's me, Miss L. Hazel."

"Why aren't you here?"

"They won't admit me."

"Why not?"

"Because I'm colored."

Gertrude's reaction to this was to make an outraged protest to the hotel manager. When this resulted in no more than an apologetic reference to "rules" which allowed no exceptions, she stalked out of the hotel and, arm in arm with Hazel, toured the city looking for a hotel that would admit them both. After several rebuffs, Gertrude hit upon an ingenious solution. She told the next hotel manager that her friend was in the diplomatic service of a foreign power, and they were immediately ushered to a suite of rooms.

As Hazel wrote me:

Dear Mr. Aldrich:

Thanks for letter. I took care of pkg at post office. Miss L—feeling fine. We don't have no more trouble about hotel because Miss L make the reason for me being her guest she is diplomated service. Miss L says to hotel I am her friend. She promoted me into diplomat. We had good time and laughed a lot. We have to eat in drug store account of strike and everybody come over to our booth and Miss L says Hello. Please tell them to send the grey suit to Pittsburgh. Miss L says, Hazel, you write Mr. Aldrich about now you are diplomat. Love,

Hazel

During her engagement with Theatre Incorporated, Gertrude's salary, as I have already suggested, was considerably less than what she had long been accustomed to. She found it hard to remember this and limit her expenditures accordingly. Hazel was instructed to do what she could to discourage Gertrude in her shopping orgies. Nevertheless, David Holtzmann was compelled to remonstrate with Gertrude from time to time.

After a scolding by David, Gertrude would economize on food for herself and Hazel. At times when she wanted money—often to give to some member of the company or an employe of the theatre who was in straits—she held a sale backstage of some of her personal belongings. Clothes, shoes, and handbags would be offered at ridiculously low prices—a twenty-five-dollar blouse for two dollars, a crocodile leather bag for five dollars. In the course of a tour, her Molyneux and Hattie Carnegie wardrobe might disappear and she would be reduced to a simple dark suit which she had bought "off the peg" in a Junior Miss Department. And in which she looked so well that half the force of one's protest was lost.

When the regime of economy interfered with the satisfaction of Hazel's healthy appetite, I would receive a letter such as the following:

Mark Hopkins Hotel
San Francisco, California

Dear Mr. Aldrich:

Hope you well. Hope you will tell Mr. Holtzmann not to scold Miss L about bills. My poor stomach can't take it. She goes to Gump's and buy up all the antiques and robes and pyjamas and when the bill come and the office scold she says Hazel we must have only one meal every day.

Now Mr. Aldrich the Lord made me a three meal a day girl. My job calls for 3 meals a day and no hot dogs meals like Miss L wants us to save money on. Yesterday I went out and bought some hot dogs for myself. She came in and smelled them and said they are good, and so I go hungry. I tell her I get wrinkles in my stomach, and wrinkles in stomach show on face. She says all right Hazel you order what you like but only soup for me. Now, Mr. A, I am no sea gull. I cannot eat when Miss L go hungry, so I go hungry with her.

Mr. Smith, hotel manager, came up to see why all sea gulls was on our terrace. There was hundreds from all over Golden Gate.

Mr. Smith should have looked at bill then he see Miss L every day is throwing parties to sea gulls. She says Hazel you tell room service send up double orders crack crab, shrimps, lobster which Miss L says sea gulls like and she feed them on terrace.

Mr. Smith he is mad. He said Miss L should not do that because hotel spends lots of money to keep birds away and now they all coming for Miss L free lunch.

Where Miss L get the strength to give a show I don't know. I ask Mr. Potter take her out after the show and see she eats good. I send back lots of antiques to Gumps and Magnin's so tell Mr. Holtzmann please not scold Miss L. Sunday Miss L and I are going out on picnic and Mr. Potter give me some money and say buy some ham and chicken. Business is good. Miss L in good health but misses you.

Much love,
Hazel

At all times Hazel was Keeper of the Book. This was the handsomely bound green leather guest book which always had a prominent place in Gertrude's dressing room. The book was the first thing to be unpacked and the last to be packed in the theatre trunks. The collected volumes, covering Gertrude's long stardom, contain the autographs and admiring and affectionate sentiments of nearly every celebrated person in England, Canada, and the United States during that period.

One unceasing source of amusement to Gertrude was the fact that Hazel had once taken a course in embalming and had worked for a fashionable Hollywood mortician; one of those whose funerary extravagances had inspired Evelyn Waugh with the idea of *The Loved One*. This was a constant joke between the two. When Ithaca College in upstate New York conferred an honorary degree of Doctor of Fine Arts on Gertrude, among the letters and wires of congratulation which she received on her doctorate was this telegram:

YOU KILL 'EM DOC AND I'LL BURY 'EM
LOVE HAZEL

* * *

It was during the summers after the war that Gertrude became closely associated with the Cape Playhouse. In fact, but for her efforts, I might have lost the theatre completely during the war.

Back in 1944, when I was in Southampton, caught up in the feverish preparation for D-Day, I received a cable warning me that the Playhouse trustees could no longer hold the theatre for me and were about to lease it to someone else.

Nothing was further from my mind at that moment than a summer theatre.

My answer was brief: "Please don't bother me. And tell Gertrude to have nothing to do with it."

Gertrude, however, was unwilling to see the Playhouse I had built up fall into other hands while I was in service overseas. Threatening to pawn her jewels if need be, she arranged with her lawyers to allow her to put up the necessary money to save her husband's business until his return from the war.

The Playhouse was reopened July 1, 1946, with a week's run of *Pygmalion*. Gertrude's play was followed by Gregory Peck in *The Playboy of the Western World*. The engagement was in the nature of a homecoming for Greg, who had served his apprenticeship and played bit parts at Dennis for several seasons before the war.

It was traditional for Gertrude and me to give a party at The Berries in honor of each visiting star during the ten-week season. After a while, despite all our efforts and Gertrude's ingenuity, these developed a wearying sameness.

"Let's do something altogether different for Gregory," Gertrude proposed when we were making plans.

"What do you suggest?" I asked.

"A clambake," she said instantly. "On the beach after the play. We'll have a big fire of driftwood and whatever they have to eat at clambakes, and we'll sit around the fire and sing and tell stories."

It was, of course, just another version of the picnic which Gertrude adored in any form. We tried it out and it proved extremely popular, especially with those stars who were having their first experience of the Cape.

Another of Gertrude's pet diversions was a hay ride. She would arrange for large trucks piled with fragrant, dry salt hay to carry the guests along moonlit country roads and to bring them back for a hot country-style supper.

One day, when I was still feeling the cramps in my long legs after one of these ten-mile hay rides, I observed: "You're a frustrated Girl Scout."

"I'm not a frustrated anything," she retorted. "You should know that by this time, darling. I decided a long time ago to do the things I want to, when I want to do them. You have to take your tarts as they are passed. Otherwise, you'll miss them. And I don't want to miss anything."

In addition to entertaining the visiting stars, Gertrude entered into much of the fun of the young people connected with the Playhouse at Dennis, and later with the summer theatre we opened at Falmouth.

She became the leader of the Dungaree Set, and an active promoter of the square dancing which followed nearly every performance. Dick and David, who were now old enough to hold summer jobs at the Playhouse, became Gertrude's regular escorts to the dances.

Once, when she did not come home until long after midnight, I scolded Dick for keeping her up.

"I don't keep her up," he objected. "It's she who keeps me up."

"No matter," I insisted. "It's your duty to look after her. Hereafter, I want you to bring her home by twelve o'clock. Otherwise I'll put a stop to the dances."

My son regarded me pityingly. "Look, Dad," he said, "you and Gertrude have been married eight years. Don't you know by this time you can't stop her from doing anything she wants to do?"

In getting to know the young apprentices, Gertrude was always on the alert for talent. It was she who first detected "star quality" in June Walker's son, John Kerr, who put in several summers doing various jobs at the Playhouse, from ushering to playing bit parts.

In one of Gertrude's appearances at the Playhouse her choice for an important supporting role was John Kerr.

"She was exceedingly stimulating to work with, as I imagine everyone knows," he wrote after his own success on Broadway in

Tea and Sympathy. "But what I remember better than anything about her were the numerous occasions when she would talk with us apprentices and try to disillusion us slightly of our romantic preconceptions of what the theatre was.

"That she was realistic without being discouraging was a good indication of her interest and concern with those who were young in the theatre, and we were all extremely fond of her . . ."

"To be successful in the theatre," Gertrude frequently said, "you have to *love* it. Its ups and downs. Its constant changes. As for me, I'm an adventurer at heart. A seeker. I'm always curious about what may lie just around the corner."

To the younger actresses who would gather around her when she went down to the Playhouse to watch a rehearsal, she said: "Everything depends on your attitude toward your work. If you are stage-struck and want to study dramatics because you think it makes you glamorous, then you aren't good enough to succeed. Success in the theatre requires more than that. If you have the money to study at a dramatic school, that's all to the good. But I still believe the way I started out is the best. I say it's the best way because when you're hungry you learn more quickly. If you go into the theatre because that's the way you choose to make a living, you will develop what talent you may possess in order to get ahead and to earn more. I have had every kind of role—in the chorus, as understudy, bit parts; I learned something valuable from every one of them."

One of the young actresses during the season of 1948 was Mary MacArthur, the lovely daughter of Helen Hayes and Charles MacArthur. In casting *Susan and God* for Broadway, John Golden had originally thought of Mary for the part of Gertrude's plain, neglected daughter. Her parents had been willing enough, but Mary was too pretty and had too much charm for the part. Since then, it had been her ambition to be associated with the Playhouse, which had already acquired the reputation of being a "cradle of stars."

Once Mary joined us, Gertrude, as a friend as well as warm admirer of Helen's, naturally took a keen interest in the progress of Helen's daughter. When Mary was cast in Noel Coward's play *The*

Marquise, starring Lillian Gish, Gertrude began dropping in at rehearsals.

Unfortunately her presence made Mary self-conscious and constrained.

Gertrude decided the young girl needed the reassurance that only her mother could give. At the time, Helen was appearing in New York in *Happy Birthday*. Gertrude picked up the phone and told Helen: "I think you and Charlie ought to come up to The Berries for the weekend."

We arranged to have Mary spend as much time as possible with her parents at our home, where she could regard Gertrude simply as a family friend. A special dress rehearsal was held on Sunday for the MacArthurs. Helen and Gertrude gave Mary not only pointers on acting, but a measure of confidence in her own ability. The following night, Gertrude was able to telephone Helen in New York that her daughter had given a fine performance and done her proud.

The next summer it was arranged for Helen and Mary to play together at Dennis in *Good Housekeeping,* a play selected by Helen because there was a good role in it for Mary. When, in the subsequent week Helen moved on to repeat the show at Falmouth while Gertrude opened at Dennis in *September Tide,* two of the greatest stars of the English-speaking stage were playing on Cape Cod simultaneously.

In that summer Gertrude struck up a friendship with another MacArthur, Mary's ten-year-old brother, Jamie. The boy had been chosen to play in *The Corn Is Green,* with Eva Le Gallienne. Like a shadow, Jamie followed Gertrude wherever she went. He had no use for the young apprentices, who loftily termed him a "pest," but he regarded Gertrude as a "regular guy." The two became inseparable companions; by the time Jamie left the Cape, Gertrude had acquired another devoted male admirer.

Mary MacArthur's death shocked thousands of people who knew and loved Helen Hayes and Charlie MacArthur. Gertrude, then in Hollywood, was grief-stricken. She wanted to go to Helen at once but this was impossible. Helen Hayes's simply worded reply to Gertrude's letter of sympathy was put away among Gertrude's treasures. It reads:

October 31, 1949

Dear Gertrude:

We love you and we love your letter.

Thank you, dear.

Your boy Jamie is fine. We thank God that he is a normal, healthy boy and therefore resilient.

We are improving all the time. Don't be worried about us. We are protected by the happiest of memories.

Good luck to Amanda! You will be wonderful.

Love,

Helen

From the summer we moved into The Berries, Gertrude thought of herself as a permanent resident of the Cape—one who "belonged"—even though she spent no more time there than others who were content to be part of the summer colony.

In large measure Dr. Harriet and my mother were responsible for this. They both preached long, often, and forcefully the importance of putting down your roots into the soil. These arguments found a quick response in Gertrude. Though she had been a gypsy all her life, she had always yearned for a home to which she belonged as much as it belonged to her. And to her, as to many English men and women, home meant infinitely more than a house on land which she owned; it meant a place in the community, relationships with the people living nearby. It meant lasting ties and responsibilities; the very things so many men and women in her profession were forced to do without.

She was constantly thinking of the welfare of the community. One summer she was invited to give a talk at the Dennis Union Church on a topic of her own choosing. The mere announcement that she would appear brought an unprecedented response, not only from devoted members of the congregation, but from people who had not seen the inside of a church for years. I hesitate to hazard a guess as to what this latter group thought they would hear from Gertrude. Perhaps they hoped for a cut-rate performance of *Susan and God,* or that Gertrude would reveal the intimate secrets of a star or discuss her soul in a sort of Salvation Army testimonial. Whatever they expected, it is quite certain that they were surprised, if not utterly disappointed, when, after she was introduced and the enthusiastic applause had subsided, Gertrude announced to the audience: "My subject for this talk is the use of hydroponics in the infertile sandy soil of Cape Cod."

Unlike most of the women of the summer colony, Gertrude never did her marketing by telephone. Every morning she drove the station wagon into the village, and, basket on arm, went shopping along the one street. Thus she, sooner than I, knew everyone who had a business there—as well as most of the children and all of the dogs.

Dennis has three grocery stores. First there is Goodspeed's, which is also the post office and which enjoys the distinction of a community club. Goodspeed's, like Shattuck's in Groton, has been provisioner to the locality for several generations. In the course of time it has stocked up with various things which Cape dwellers have required, and the residue of these are still on the store shelves, in the storeroom, or down-cellar. If the Playhouse suddenly needed a lamp wick, harpoon, a pint of sulphur and molasses, a yard of Turkey red flannel, a button-hook or a kit of salt mackerel we would go confidently to Goodspeed's, knowing that if Mr. Goodspeed could not produce the object from his store, he could say where it was waiting.

Davidson's, like Goodspeed's in business for many generations, was the Tiffany of Dennis grocers, catering especially to those who consider the tempting line of delicacies sold by S. S. Pierce and Company a prime necessity of life. During our first season on the Cape I tried to impart to Gertrude some of the reverence which Bostonians feel for whatever bears the Pierce label. I pointed out that to us, S. S. Pierce and Company are Crosse and Blackwell, Huntley and Palmer, Fortnum and Mason, Harrod's and the Army-Navy Stores rolled into one. Davidson's opened later and closed earlier than the other stores.

The third grocery is owned by Louis Terpos. Louis is a Greek, a recent arrival, and originally was without knowledge of Cape traditions.

Our trade had always been equally divided between Goodspeed's and Davidson's. When Louis took over the third store the change did not affect our household until Gertrude said one day at lunch: "Louis Terpos is trying so much to get ahead."

"Well," I said, "the hard fact is that Dennis doesn't need a third grocery. Goodspeed's and Davidson's give us all we want."

"I know," Gertrude said pensively, "but I think he could make a place for himself."

I could see that her instinctive sympathy for the underdog had been aroused.

Later I learned from Louis how that sympathy was translated into action. He said that Gertrude came into his store one morning and looked around the shelves. She asked how business was.

"Not so good," Louis told her.

"Hmmm!" Gertrude rejoined. "Why don't you do something different from the others?"

Louis asked what she meant. A grocery was a grocery; or wasn't it?

"It can be whatever people want," Gertrude expounded. She pointed out that in the theatre no one ever succeeded by imitating someone else. "Running a successful grocery store must be quite similar," she said. "Take you, for instance. Instead of trying to compete with Mr. Goodspeed and Mr. Davidson in their lines, why don't you offer the public something entirely different?"

"Like what?" Louis demanded.

"A sandwich counter, for one thing," Gertrude answered. "Think of all the young people at my husband's summer theatre. If you had a sandwich counter and a soda fountain they would be dropping in here at all hours for snacks."

Following her suggestion, Louis installed the equipment for making sandwiches and served sundaes and sodas. Immediately his business began to look up.

Gertrude took a proprietary interest in the new venture. She liked to drop in whenever she was in the village, slide onto one of the stools at Louis' counter and have a hamburger and a mug of hot tea, while she and Louis exchanged views on problems in the Near East, the Marshall Plan, and their common acquaintance, Mr. Spyros Skouras. Louis was proud to be a member of one of the Aid to Greece Committees headed by Mr. Skouras, while Gertrude reveled in the compliment reportedly paid to her by Mr. Skouras, who is said to have commented that even if he saw Gertrude Lawrence cleaning out a stable, "to me she would still be glamorous."

Gertrude dropped in at Louis' grocery one day when the Playhouse was opening for the summer, and Dennis and the surrounding countryside were full of new arrivals. Louis was wrestling with a mountain of unpacked cases of goods, while a line of customers in the adjacent soda shop waited to be served. Gertrude took one look at the situation, pulled a white apron off a hook, tied it on, and stepped briskly behind the counter.

"Well, we're ready," she announced. "What will it be?"

"Cherry coke," a dazed voice replied.

"She went ahead," Louis said, "jerking sodas just like she'd done it all her life. Chocolate malts, frosted coffee, pineapple mint frappes—they were all one to her. And neat! There wasn't a splash on the counter. 'This is a lot easier than drawing beer,' she said. 'I was a barmaid once, for a week—when the show I was with was stranded because the manager ran off with the leading lady and the funds. I asked the proprietor of the inn for a job to pay for my room and board until something turned up. The landlord told me when I left that I could have a job in his bar any time.' "

Chapter Fifteen

BREAKFAST WITH GERTRUDE was apt to be more exhilarating than restful. Being one of those who wake full of zest and exploding with ideas, she usually arrived at the breakfast table having set half a dozen activities in motion and prepared to tackle problems of world importance.

Among these momentous problems was my manner of attacking my soft-boiled egg; early in our married life Gertrude had dedicated herself to bringing about a change in this field.

"Why don't you do it properly, darling?" she inquired.

I am no more touchy than most men about wifely criticism of my manners, but Gertrude's tone carried the unmistakable ring of the reformer.

"What do you mean—properly?" I demanded resentfully.

"As I do. As everyone in England does it."

I have listened to and read countless suggestions on the subject of improving Anglo-American relations. I have not much hope of a real accord until a moratorium is declared on criticism of each other's ways with knives and forks, boiled eggs, corn on the cob and tea and coffee making. If we would agree not to become testy with each other over these basic but irrelevant differences, possibly we would find ourselves getting together cosily on the more important matters. I pointed this out to Gertrude. She agreed with me; yet whenever she saw me tap on my egg, break it in half and dump its contents into the larger half of the eggcup, her nose would wrinkle with disgust. "Ugh!" she would exclaim (the monosyllable dripped with contempt). "How *can* you, Richard?"

I told her that I could because I had been brought up to deal with a soft-boiled egg in this way. It was the way of my parents—the way of all Joys and Aldriches since the first hen laid the first egg on the soil of Massachusetts. My reply left her unconverted—and undaunted.

Similarly, I always shuddered when I saw her take up a knife in one hand, hold the defenseless egg steady in the small end of the eggcup with the other hand, and with one nonchalant stroke cut off the end. I fully expected to see the contents of the shell spattered on the wall of the breakfast room. That this never happened, and that the top of the egg was always neatly severed, leaving the yolk exposed but intact, I put down as one more proof of Gertrude's extraordinary talents.

It also disturbed her that I let my breakfast egg lie for five minutes or so to cool off before breaking it.

"But, darling, cold egg is so *nasty*," she said.

"Not as nasty as burned fingers."

"Your fingers wouldn't be burned if you would eat your egg properly."

We were right back where we came in. I delivered the ultimatum: "Either no comments, or no eggs."

"Mr. Aldrich needs eggs for his breakfast," Helen Mahoney protested. "You can't send a man out to do a day's work on an empty stomach."

The imputation that she was starving her husband fired Gertrude's imagination. Off and on, for several days, she fiddled with some pieces of wire, saying nothing of her purpose until one morning—at breakfast—she handed me a gadget which she said was an egg gripper of her own invention.

"Try it," she directed. "See if it holds the hot egg so you can open and eat it before the inside congeals."

The thing really worked amazingly well. Gertrude made some minor improvements. Then, quite on her own, she asked David Holtzmann to take her and her invention to a firm of patent attorneys. She laid the model and a set of working drawings before Mr. Charles Keel, who gave his opinion that she had produced something practical for which there was a market. The application for patent was filed at the United States Patent Office, Ser. No. 710,-838, and Mr. Keel undertook to have the Gertrude Lawrence Egg Gripper manufactured and put on sale. Unfortunately, he became ill shortly afterward and died; meanwhile Gertrude's attention was fully taken up with a new play, and the egg gripper was laid aside to await a more propitious moment.

In any case, it had served a domestic purpose. Gertrude thereafter tolerated my American egg-eating habits without further protest, turning from the sight of me stirring my soft egg with a spoon, to bury herself in the letters which usually arrived while we were at breakfast.

The first thing Gertrude always did was run through her stack of mail swiftly, looking for a letter from Pam. After this, her expectation was for letters from England. She maintained a steady correspondence with a number of women friends there, including Evie Williams, Lou Hollis, and Boxie, who had been her dresser. They were, in a sense, her family. She depended on their love and loyalty, and she responded to it by becoming 100 per cent British whenever she wrote to them, assuming the role of a homesick expatriate who longed to exchange comfortable life in America for the rigors of war-battered London.

The arrival of a letter from her friend Polly in particular never failed to turn Gertrude's thoughts nostalgically toward the world she had left behind when she sailed for America in 1937. She could not believe pre-war Mayfair did not still exist; that it was not waiting for her return; stacked up like the sets and props of a play, to be brought out, dusted, and put in place for the lights to go on and for her to make her entrance.

She had seen England in battle dress, but she was confident that the khaki would be taken off and the white ties and tails brought out of the wardrobes when the war ended. This had happened in

1918. London after the first world war had been feverishly gay, sparkling with all the bright young people who made the pages of Aldous Huxley and Evelyn Waugh, and the comedies of Noel Coward. In that galaxy Gertrude had blazed among the brightest. It did not occur to her that history might not repeat itself.

The relationship between Gertrude and Polly was the sort which frequently exists between sisters, and which rests more on friction and an instinctive rivalry than on mutual affection. It dated from the days when Gertrude was in the chorus of one of the West End revues. Polly, then married to a wealthy business man, was stage-struck to the extent of taking part in a show for some war charity, at which society and the theatre came together. Polly was reputed to have been in the chorus herself a few seasons before; but this phase of her existence was now well out of sight and remembrance.

The acquaintance developed into a friendship. No doubt Gertrude was ingenuously flattered to be received by Polly in her Mayfair house. She looked on it and on Polly's financial security and position with envy. In her eyes Polly was a girl who had done well for herself. Polly, for her part, very possibly enjoyed patronizing the promising young actress who, at that time, was beginning to attract favorable notice and develop a following.

Through the years, and always with an undercurrent of unexpressed rivalry, the friendship had gone on with a seesaw motion. When Gertrude went up, becoming the toast of London's smartest set, a friend of the young royal princes, a personality whose activities, clothes, jewels, romances, pranks, and repartee figured almost daily in the gossip columns, Polly's married security appeared somewhat stuffy in comparison. When Gertrude's inability to handle her own financial affairs sent her end of the seesaw down—even to bankruptcy and eviction—Polly's status rose proportionately.

As Gertrude struggled and worked her way out of debt and into much wider fame in her profession, she sometimes spoke wistfully of the ease of Polly's life. Not, she always added quickly, that she would give up the theatre, even for a wealthy or a titled husband.

If she could have all three—wealth, title and career—her cup of happiness would be full.

Envy of Polly had lessened almost to the vanishing point during Gertrude's successful and happy seasons in America just before we met. There may have been a forgivable note of triumph in her letter announcing our marriage and our plans to Polly, who had divorced her first husband. When Polly came back with the announcement of her own forthcoming marriage to a handsome young man of unimpeachable position in English society, Gertrude reeled for a moment. By all the standards of Clapham Common, in which Gertrude was reared, Polly was about to move several squares ahead of her, who had only a Yankee theatrical producer to match against the most awe-inspiring uniform in the British Army. It was ironical that just when Gertrude and I were dropped from the New York Social Register, the gates of *Burke's Landed Gentry* should be thrown wide for Polly to enter on her groom's arm.

Nevertheless, I don't think Gertrude entertained regrets when she thought of or heard from Polly during the next few years. I have every reason to believe that her life as Mrs. A satisfied her. Everyone who had known her for some time observed that she matured in those years; that some of her former recklessness abated as she found herself.

Even her extravagance, long the hallmark of Gertrude's irresponsible years, was virtually disappearing.

One day she and Fanny were walking up Park Avenue when they passed a show window in which an extraordinarily beautiful —and costly—car was displayed. Gertrude stopped to admire it. Fanny remarked that with Gertrude's affairs in such a flourishing state, there was no reason why she should not buy the car if she liked it so much.

"No," said Gertrude, "that belongs to Gertrude Lawrence *circa* B.A."

"B.A.?"

"Before Aldrich!"

With Gertrude's gradual emotional growth, her charm as a

woman and her talents as an actress deepened perceptibly. A sense of this underlay a remark she had made, in explaining her desire to play Eliza Doolittle in *Pygmalion;* she said she had "outgrown the old tricks."

That she might also have outgrown a former phase of her character, and the friendships and loves associated with it, was something which neither she nor I then knew.

Soon after Gertrude arrived in London to start her ENSA tour, she had dined with Polly. In Southampton, later, she told me she felt a sense of guilt when she contrasted our bountiful existence at The Berries with the way of life the war had forced upon her friends. On her return to America, she immediately inaugurated an active parcel service not only to her old retainers, fans, and theatre associates, but to her rich and titled friends as well. She envied them their opportunity to make sacrifices in rebuilding her beloved England.

In May of 1948, with no suitable play in immediate prospect, Gertrude was restless and worried. She was never happier than when she was working, and always miserable and fearful when "resting" between plays. I suggested that she go over to London and Paris for a few weeks to see what the theatres there offered, and to renew her friendships after the long break occasioned by the war.

Though her stay was very brief, when I met her at the airport on her return I saw at once that the trip had done her good. She was radiant, bubbling with news, and frankly delighted to be home again. We flew immediately to Ithaca to attend the commencement exercises at Ithaca College, where the president of the college conferred on Gertrude an honorary degree of Doctor of Fine Arts. She was justly proud of this honor. Her irrepressible sense of humor never let her let me forget that in the academic world her doctorate gave her precedence over my Harvard A. B. She also cited her new degree in defending some of her baffling idiosyncrasies of language.

"As Doctor Lawrence," she argued, "why shouldn't I invent a word now and then to fill a need? Like 'ethicasy.' "

"I don't know about the ethicasy of this," she would write in all seriousness. And then be indignant when I questioned the "ethicasy" of the word.

She gave me in a series of vivid flashes a picture of life in England after nearly three years of the Labor Government; not in statistics, but in facts in the lives of women like Evie Williams, "whose rent and rates are exactly double what they were. And coal between ninety-five shillings and five pounds per ton and so poor, Evie says if that is what we're exporting, I bet we don't get many orders."

"How does Polly make out?" I asked.

"Oh, Polly manages to bear up," Gertrude replied. Her tone made me sure that Polly had pulled another fast one, leaving Gertrude (or so she felt) a few paces to the rear. Polly and her second husband, Gertrude explained, had separated. Polly was living in the country, not too far from an attractive and possibly not unwilling viscount. Polly had driven Gertrude over to the viscount's moated manor house to have lunch.

"And to collect eggs and vegetables and fruit and cream and butter. And all these on a magnificent silver tray that took her eye. She annexed this so neatly I could not resist gathering up an armful of other silver things about the house and dumping them in Polly's lap and asking why she left them behind."

She laughed, but I had the feeling that the viscount rankled. Not that Gertrude wanted him. Only, why should Polly edge up on the peerage in this manner?

Shortly after we went up to the Cape that summer, an ecstatic letter arrived from Polly announcing that the viscount was now entirely willing. Her divorce was in process. Before many months she would don the coveted coronet.

"Fancy Polly pulling off a trick like that," Gertrude exclaimed indignantly. "Polly a *viscountess!* And he's rich, too." She glanced quickly across the breakfast table and caught my look, which was more amused than impressed. The long-sustained rivalry between the two friends had always entertained me.

But the comedy of it was lost on Gertrude. Her temper went up.

"It's all very well for you to smile, Richard, but it isn't funny. When I think of Polly, a peeress, and me just sitting here. . . ."

My amusement threatened to explode into a burst of laughter, but with an effort I controlled myself. This was an opportunity for a tongue-in-cheek ribbing of Gertrude that I could not resist.

I banged my fist fiercely down on the table. "Say that again," I shouted.

"Say what?"

"That you're just sitting here . . ."

"Well, I am. And what is it getting me? And meanwhile Polly is . . ."

I pushed back my chair with a loud scraping sound and stood up. "That's enough from you," I interrupted. "So long as you feel so sorry for yourself I'll give you a present."

She stared up at me in surprise. The mention of a present never failed to have an effect on her.

"What sort of present?" she demanded.

"What you seem to want," I answered. "Your freedom. Go back to London and beat your friend Polly at her own game, if that is what appeals to you! I'll be in Reno if there's anything more you have to say."

"Richard!" Gertrude was on her feet, too. Polly's letter fluttered to the floor, forgotten. "Do you know what you are saying?" Her voice deepened. It had the tragic, throaty sound that never failed to make audiences quiver. "You're not going to Reno. Or anywhere else, without me. Are you out of your mind?"

I grinned and relaxed. "No," I told her, "but I sometimes think you are. If you don't outgrow this schoolgirl envy of your friend Polly, one of these days it will choke you."

She flashed me an impudent smile. "Darling, you don't know how it relieves my mind to discover we can still get mad enough to fight. Even over anything as silly as Polly's coronet. For months and months you haven't shouted at me once. You just bury your head in a newspaper or a script and let me seethe alone."

I asked if by this she meant that she was satisfied to remain plain Mrs. Aldrich.

"If I ever come across someone like you with a fortune and a good title, I might consider letting you run off to Reno," she retorted. "Until that happens, please remember that you belong to me, Mr. A."

* * *

But though she could laugh at her former envy of Polly and assess this properly as a hangover from her early days of struggle and insecurity, she was, I realized, genuinely homesick for England and more than a little anxious about her continued prestige in the London theatre world.

It was more than ten years since she had played there. In that time new stars had been born. It was inevitable that she should wonder whether her brilliance remained unchallenged. Greatly as she respected the position she had attained in the American theatre, her appraisal of herself was based on her rating "at home." Her greatest pride was in belonging intimately to both countries, loving and serving each. She was always eagerly alert to anything that would increase my appreciation and liking for England and the English—hence, I believe, her frequent reading aloud to me of the letters she received from "home." Including many from former suitors, who might have been surprised to learn that some of their tender messages and the longing they expressed to see her . . . *"and if only I had a pocket full of dollars I would whip over straight away and stand every night outside the stage door with a large posy of red roses waiting for you to come out . . ."* were shared with me across the breakfast table.

Gertrude's delight in these proofs that she was not forgotten, and that she continued to evoke romance, was unaffected. It did not interfere with her appreciation of the humor of what the Earl of Dudley wrote her about Gertie Millar, the musical comedy star who was his stepmother. As Countess of Dudley, Gertie Millar had reigned over the segment of London society in which the peerage and the theatre mingle. The earl had gone down to see his paralyzed stepmother a few days before she died, when she was barely conscious. "Darling," he said to her, "such millions of people send you love and good wishes." The old Gertie Millar gleam came into the dying woman's eye. "Oh, really," she said. "Any men?"

Gertrude's nostalgia for England was increased when, in the spring of 1948, she did a coast-to-coast tour in Noel Coward's *Tonight At 8:30*. She undertook the tour eagerly because she had never before gone on the road with these deft little plays, which were among her favorite theatre pieces. Noel directed the two bills of three short plays each which, as in the original production, were presented on alternate evenings.

The casts were almost entirely British in these sharply etched vignettes of British life. The characters were as far apart as the down-at-heels variety artists of *Red Peppers* with their rough-and-ready "squeeze-box" music, the elegant and slightly decadent Gayforths in their Mayfair house, and the slatternly Doris Gow of *Fumed Oak*.

Gertrude took an intense pleasure in playing all the roles which, of course, Noel had written for her. She prided herself on her ability to change from an enchanting, glamorous, and highly sophisticated heroine to the whining, drab and repulsive Mrs. Gow. When the reviewers applauded her versatility, and audiences marveled at the metamorphosis, she would exclaim: "There, that shows I am an actress."

The tour was successful, especially on the West Coast, where Gertrude had a large and devoted following. "George Cukor gave a lovely party for Noel and me," she wrote from Los Angeles. "Of course everyone was there—Dietrich, Crawford, Irene Dunne, Otto, Cobina, the Colmans. Bea Lillie, too. Irene Dunne is giving us a supper on Thursday night. The Brian Ahernes called and sent you their love, and I am dining with them next Sunday. Otherwise I am lying low, as everything is miles away from Los Angeles, and it is too late after *Peppers* to drive fifty miles to a party."

But I knew by her letters that she was frequently lonely and literally homesick. Life on tour was no longer attractive to her. She wrote and spoke wistfully of The Berries. Did I think Ed, the gardener, was feeding the wild birds as she had left instructions he should?

"I don't think I ever want to make another long tour," she said during one of our long-distance calls.

Whenever I could arrange to do so, I flew out to wherever she was and spent a few days with her. Once it was to San Francisco, where *Tonight at 8:30* was having a successful run. Gertrude wrote me a few days after my return to New York:

". . . I have been in bed since you left, only getting up in time for the show. Today I had 24 hours special dose of penicillin, and a most imposing oxygen tent has been installed in my bedroom to break up the congestion in my chest. Two shows tomorrow. Then I shall stay in bed over the week-end to fully recover. Business is tremendous and I will NOT stay out. . . . Bless you for the pink valentine. I hope you got my telegram. I love you, my darling. Please believe that always . . ."

She was not the only member of the company to be laid low by the prevailing virus. Her leading man succumbed to it. At the last moment Noel had to step into the roles, to the surprise of the audience, who recognized and welcomed the "understudy" enthusiastically.

More and more her thoughts turned to England and to the idea of playing in London again.

Soon after we went to the Cape the following summer, I received the manuscript of Daphne du Maurier's new play *September Tide*. She wrote expressing her hope that Gertrude and I might find it suitable for production on Broadway.

Gertrude and I read the script together. It was the story of a self-centered young artist who marries a very young girl because he feels he can trust her to clean his paintbrushes and not bother him. Dragged to Cornwall on a duty visit to his mother-in-law, he falls in love with the older woman. She is swept away, too, but recovers her footing and sends the young couple off to America to a fresh start.

We were agreed that the play would not be successful in America.

"But the part of the mother—Stella—is a role I could do something with," Gertrude said thoughtfully. "I could play it. And I could make a success of it in London."

How much her desire to go home was influenced by the situation in which she and I then found ourselves, I did not, and still do not know. We were facing for the first time a problem which has taken a severe toll of marriages in the theatre, and which sooner or later almost invariably confronts every producer married to a star.

Let me put it this way: how does a wife who is a great actress, and thus not immune to the subtle, if petty, rivalries of the theatre, feel when her producer husband stars an actress who has been her rival not only in the theatre, but in love?

Richard Myers and I were then arranging the production of *Goodbye My Fancy,* a play by a new author. We had engaged Madeleine Carroll for the star role, with Conrad Nagel. Earlier, Gertrude had read the script on her return from her tour and had expressed interest in playing it. I did not think it was right for her, nor did I wish to appear to exploit her by having her introduce the play to the highly critical New York first-nighters. I said so. I reminded her of our fixed intention at the time we married to keep our careers apart.

We had made a partial exception in the case of *Pygmalion,* but that arrangement had come about in the post-war emergency. The fact that we had been fortunate once did not mean we should cancel our rule. I reiterated my firm view that business and love could rarely be combined successfully; and then only with individuals whose temperaments were less liable to explosions than hers and mine.

Gertrude did not contest the point. She had read the scripts of *Goodbye My Fancy* and *September Tide* at about the same time. She much preferred playing the enchanting, susceptible Stella of Daphne's play, in clothes designed by Molyneux, to the congresswoman heroine of *Goodbye My Fancy.*

Nevertheless, I realized fully that she disliked the prospect of her husband's presenting Madeleine Carroll as his star.

In her autobiography, Gertrude wrote with disarming frankness that Madeleine Carroll's marriage to Philip Astley caused her considerable heartache. This had taken place in 1931. For years before, Captain Astley of the Guards, known as "the handsomest man in London," a charmer and a close friend of the Duke of Windsor (then Prince of Wales), had been Gertrude's constant companion.

The romantic attachment between Gertrude and Philip became

part of the rapidly growing Gertrude Lawrence myth. The two figured spectacularly and memorably in the gay life of Mayfair and the English colony on the Riviera during the latter years of George the Fifth's reign. It is striking that not a single book of fiction or fact which treats in any way of the English social scene during that period is without at least a passing reference to Gertrude; not merely as a star of the theatre, but as an influence in and a symbol of England's life. She became in those years part of her country's romantic legend.

At that time, her career took her to New York to star in a number of successes culminating in *Private Lives,* in which I first saw her. Gertrude left the play in June, 1931. She sailed immediately for England, as she did every summer, to spend her holiday with Pamela, then a schoolgirl at Roedean.

Her first evening in London, she had dinner with Philip Astley. Only then did she learn what, in her excitement at coming home, she had failed to read in the papers—that his engagement to Madeleine Carroll had been announced two days before.

All this was many years past when Gertrude and I met. Philip Astley's marriage to Madeleine Carroll was dissolved by divorce a year before Gertrude and I married. In that year Gertrude had had full opportunity to choose between a new love and an old one. She had chosen me, and I had no reason to think that Philip Astley meant more to her than an old friend means to anyone. I was always rather amused when Gertrude's acquaintances would make wistful reference to the charming Philip Astley, as if they regretted the passing of a romantic tie from which they had derived vicarious pleasure.

Only one aspect of Philip Astley's current presence in London concerned me at all. This was the realization that, should some paragraph of trans-Atlantic gossip link my name with that of Madeleine Carroll, Gertrude would have a most convenient foil handy for retaliation, in the person of the handsome ex-Guardsman.

Gertrude made no comment about Madeleine's appearing under my producing banner. Nevertheless, the situation, if only unconsciously, must have increased her eagerness to return to London and to score a brilliant new success there. This is something which I believe most women—and every actress—will understand.

* * *

Gertrude was to sail early in October to start rehearsals for *September Tide*. Hugh ("Binkie") Beaumont was to produce the play and the London opening was set for mid-December, after a five-week tryout in the provinces. I had promised Gertrude to go over for the opening, if at all possible, and to spend Christmas with her.

A few days before Gertrude sailed, she and I drove up to Groton to visit Mother. The countryside was at its loveliest—the maples scarlet and gold, the oaks russet, and the fountain elms a dusty copper color against the cloudless blue sky.

Mother loved that season of the year. Until well in her eighties she had always taken long walks each fall to enjoy the trees and would write us descriptive letters, enclosing in each a pressed maple leaf. Now, close to ninety, she walked only to the village post office and to church. She was like an autumn leaf—frail in appearance but still holding on to its tree with summer strength.

She sat in the living-room window enjoying the view across green pastures and colored woodlands to the line of the New Hampshire hills. "You will see nothing more beautiful than that in England," she told Gertrude with pride.

I had expected her to express some disapproval of Gertrude's going so far, and for an indefinite length of time; Mother believed, as she often said, in husbands and wives staying together, and staying put.

"It will do Gertrude good," she said. "I am sure it does not mean that she loves you less, Richard, or is less fond of the home you have made together because England still is 'home' to her. It was always 'coming home' to me when I would leave Boston and my husband and children for a few days and come to Groton, where I felt I belonged."

The analogy did not seem very close, but I understood it.

"While you are abroad, Gertrude," my mother continued, "it might interest you to look up some of Richard's ancestors. For

Look Magazine

Breakfast with Gertrude—but here a play, not an egg, is the subject under consideration.

Gertrude and Noel Coward—in the spring of 1948 she toured in his *Tonight at 8:30*.

Gertrude has her picture taken at The Berries. A few moments earlier the bush was flowerless, but when the photographer demanded blossoms she nimbly taped on some marigolds.

American Home

She was on chatting terms with everyone in Dennis.

She could never resist an ice cream cone.

though our families have been in New England three hundred years, our roots are in England. We came from Aylesbury in Buckinghamshire, and our forefathers still lie buried there."

Gertrude dutifully promised Mother to look up our ancestors. On the drive home, however, I told her, "Really, Gertrude, you needn't have humored Mother. You'll be busy enough in London, without scouring the countryside looking for ancient graveyards."

"Of course I shall do it," she replied indignantly. "I want to. Especially now that Mother made me the custodian of the letter."

"What letter?" I asked.

"You know, darling. *The Letter.* The one accompanying the last will and testament of your great-grandfather Joy, who is inside the white iron fence in Groton cemetery. Look!"

She opened her handbag and showed me the creased, stained, and yellowed sheets, covered with my great-grandfather James Joy's writing. The letter was one of my mother's most prized possessions; hers because she was the eldest of the three Joys. And she had given it to Gertrude! But why?

As if she read the question in my mind, Gertrude said, touching the pages with a reverent forefinger, "She told me she knew I would value it and take care of it. I am to pass it on to young Richard when the time comes. Meanwhile, as Mrs. Richard Stoddard Aldrich, wife of the Head of the Family, I am Guardian of *the Letter.*"

Her voice was light, but without mockery. I thought: if Mother in any way suspected that there might be considerable hazards in our approaching separation, she has used the most powerful means at her command to give Gertrude the feeling that she belongs to me, and to no one else.

The Letter, which was kept in her strong box with our marriage certificate, all my letters, Pamela's, and other papers and mementos which Gertrude treasured, bears this notation: "In 1857, James Joy of Groton, Mass., in his 80th year wrote the following letter to his wife, Sarah Pickering, to be read after his death, which was then near."

James Joy wrote:

My dear beloved Wife,

We are both old and feeble, and I find old age is fast bearing us down to our final rest. I am well aware that I shall not be here much longer. We have lived together many long years and seen many happy days together.

We were both young when we were united together in Durham, and spent many happy days there surrounded with good friends and neighbors and a young family of pretty Sprightly children.

Many days & years have passed away since our family have been separated; we have been called to mourn the loss of several of our dear Beloved Children, taken away from us by that all wise God that rules all the works of his hands for his own glory and agreeable to his own plans from the beginning.

But, my Dear Wife, we have great reason to be thankful for those dear Children that have been spared to us in our old age. They are all Respectable, and in good Circumstances, and we have reason to hope they will live for a Comfort to us while we live, and a Comfort to each other—so long as they are permitted to live.

Now, my dear Wife, I must bid you a *long, long* farewell and I do believe and hope that we shall all finally meet in that happy world where peace forever Reigns.

I am at peace with all men, and I trust and hope with my God and Saviour.

I once more bid you farewell, and before you receive this I shall probably be far advanced on my journey to that final home from whence no traveller ever returns.

With sincere affection I remain your loving husband as long as life Shall last.

James Joy

* * *

Gertrude sailed on the *Mauretania.* A note on the ship's writing paper, dated October thirteenth, announced:

Dearest,

We have arrived. Just saw the glorious white cliffs of the Isle of Wight. Wonderful morning—sunny, calm and all-embracing. Seems really to be saying "Welcome Home."

Shall write later—

All my heart,
Mrs. A

Later, from London, came more details of the trip and her initial experiences of austerity Britain:

> I am at the Savoy, as you see, but as yet my trunks are still outside the hotel because Binkie had ordered me a single bedroom, which, for some strange reason, is air-conditioned. It's beastly cold, not a sausage of heat in the whole place, and no way of turning the thing off.
>
> London is packed—every hotel crammed to the gunwales as there is a Conference of Foreign Ministers going on. The Savoy is full of them with their secretaries, under-secretaries, shoeshine boys and concubines. By golly, they certainly manage to cost their countries a lot. And they take up every inch of space. Jean Nichol is away for three weeks with MUMPS. The manager is away until Monday but I have been promised a suite as soon as possible. Meanwhile here I lie, surrounded with floral offerings of all shapes and sizes—even the bathroom is filled—but I can't unpack anything but the two suits I had on the boat.
>
> I brought over a huge parcel for Polly which I got through without duty and which she jolly well called for directly. She didn't even send me a bunch of roses; just motored back to the country and left word I was to let her know when I would like to go down.
>
> I can see that money is going to be a problem. Remember, David only gave me 15 quid in cash. After I did my ship's tipping there was nought left except enough for tea and tips on the train to Waterloo and the porters each end. I was passed through Customs without a key being used but a lot of palms were offered in greeting and welcome, all of which had to be filled with a little more than my own. So—when the customs asked for £3.17.6 duty on the three bottles of whisky in my shoe-bag which they opened—it not being locked—bang went another $20.00 traveller's cheque in addition to the two others I had to cash aboard ship for my huge radio bill, etc. Sixty dollars in all out of my measly 200 bucks. Breakfast here is 4/ for tea with a roll and no butter.
>
> Dearest heart, I miss you so. Please rest. Don't catch cold. *And don't get interested in somebody else.* It's *me* you belong to for always, remember. Even little adventures aren't worth getting bothered by.

Think of our home in Dennis—think of our love, and remember my wedding ring.

It binds me to you,
Mrs. A . . .

". . . Rehearsals are going fine," she reported a few days later:

. . . Of course the problem was where to put the set up, as all the theatres have plays in them. Finally it was decided that although the "Queen's" was completely gutted out in 1941 and has not yet been rebuilt, the stage and all the back part are fairly safe. So I returned to the theater where I held sway in the good old days in Clemence Dane's play *Moonlight is Silver.*

The whole place is a shambles—peeling plaster, staircases torn up, no light, old ropes dangling like forgotten scaffolds, a torn and tattered asbestos curtain separating us from the ruins of the auditorium where now rats two and a half feet long hold sway.

We were a strange little group huddled in blankets trying to recreate a warm Cornish day out of such surroundings. However the rain stayed away, although it was very foggy, and we took the set down again and up will go the second act on Monday if the weather permits.

They have been hoping to have the theatre rebuilt by now, but Permits get bogged down and even when and if it is ever finished it will take at least 9 months to dry it out before it can be opened to the public. Actors, meantime, being crazy, go in there in all weathers, amid the rats, and think nothing of it. Or, if we do, we consider ourselves lucky to have a place to rehearse in and a play to rehearse.

Strangely enough, there was no play running at the Queen's when it was hit, but all the scenery for *Rebecca* was stored there ready for the opening. Quite a coincidence that we should be in there now with another du Maurier play . . .

The cast is splendid, and our director, Irene Henschel, is a fine director, patient, kind and cheerful. She is the wife of Ivor Brown, the drama critic on *The Observer,* which should be to the good. Edward Molyneux has done lovely clothes—smart, simple and in character with *Stella,* who, I must say, is emerging with great dignity, serenity and character . . .

It is getting awfully cold and I need my fur coat. As yet I have no maid. Evie comes each day at one, but she has to leave to get a train at seven to be back to get her husband's dinner. However, she will go with me when we go on the road, to keep me company and eat with me. Helen Hayes sent me lovely flowers. I have not seen her for the reason that we rehearse from 10 A.M. to 6 P.M. and the theatres open at 1. I'm tired at night after walking most of the way home. One spends a fortune in cabs.

I have not attempted a social life but I made my first bow to the British public on Thursday at the Carleton for the premiere of *The Guinea Pig* for the Actors' Orphanage. I got a tremendous ovation, and cried a lot, but made a pretty good speech. We took £3000 odd at the premiere and I got it up to £5000 at supper.

I had written her from Detroit, where *Goodbye My Fancy* was playing. Curiously, I voiced little optimism, mentioning only what was still wrong with the play. She replied:

You do sound depressed, darling, and I must say there seems to be good reason, but maybe it will all be a great surprise and a success after all.

Never mind, pet, we shall be together soon. I have the bit in my teeth and shall do my best to romp home a winner. After that—Dennis, and *you.* Don't worry, there is no one else.

Can you say the same?

September Tide opened its pre-London tour with a week's run in Oxford. "Terrific social event," Gertrude reported. "All very top drawer, with printed invitations: *To Meet Miss Gertrude Lawrence.* . . . From here we go from the sublime to the ridiculous—good old Blackpool, Leeds, Liverpool and Manchester."

"A peasoup fog and a fuel cut," she reported from Leeds. "Pray the Lord we don't have a bad winter. But with it all, dear, it's worth it. Even the food poisoning I had in London from tainted meat. I'm now sticking to tripe. And eggs . . . A matinee today, and we ring up at 6:30 so there are only about 25 minutes between shows. But we are sold out solid for the entire week and we shall do just over £3000. Top price, 8/9. Some big theatre! But I'm glad I came."

Meantime, *Goodbye My Fancy* opened in New York and was highly acclaimed by the critics. Pleased as my partner, Dick Myers, and I were to have a hit, I was a little anxious about how Gertrude would take it. Her letter was indicative:

Dear Mr. Producer

Congratulations again and again. Your star owed me a good turn and I am *thrilled* that we can enjoy it *together!*

Binkie called me last night and said that *we* could fill the Albert Hall with first nighters for December 15th. And that *we* already have an advance library deal with Keith Prowse for 12 weeks . . .

In spite of a continual blanket of fog here [Leeds] and buses all stopped and taxis not running, *we* are breaking house records and shall take over £3,000, which is all you can take in the provinces. Binkie is *jubilant.*

Her approaching opening in London had Gertrude in a fever of excitement. But even in the full swing of her triumphal return to her homeland, and with an ocean between us, she did not duck her domestic responsibilities.

"Darling Germy," began Gertrude's next letter:

I am worried about your cold. Be a good boy. Use your sunlamp. Have Dr. Rubin (he says you are difficult when I am away), and get here as soon as you can.

I loved your letter about the little house and Ed.

Daphne, Tommy [General Browning] and Mo [Lady du Maurier] are thrilled that you are coming. Don't bog it up, ducks.

Such a night will never happen again in my lifetime and you MUST be there. It would be an empty night for me if you were not there . . .

Am very excited.

Much love,

Mrs. A . . .

I arrived four days before the opening of *September Tide* at the Aldwych. The joyous expectancy surrounding Gertrude on her first appearance in London since before the war, already was running high. Wherever she went—in the restaurant and lounge of the Savoy, in the streets, shopping in Bond Street, where she took me to choose ties to take home to Dick and David and other gifts for Barbara and Mother, she was recognized and greeted with a genuine affection. I had never seen anything like it.

What impressed me quite as much as the warmth and the extraordinary popularity of her reception, coming as it did from people of all ages, classes and types, was Gertrude's own humility in the face of it. She had none of the bored and arrogant assurance frequently found in motion-picture stars of global fame. She was like a queen who had returned to her people from a long exile. There were tears in her eyes much of the time; but they were happy tears. They turned her eyes the misty-blue of the forget-me-nots she had planted and tended at The Berries.

"This is my husband," she said again and again, presenting me to total strangers whose slightly critical, though friendly, scrutiny left me somewhat embarrassed.

"Who do you think you are?" I teased her. "Victoria Regina? With me as Prince Consort?"

"Darling, you don't mind, do you?"

"Not at all. Not as long as I don't have to wear side whiskers."

"Victoria's Prince Consort was a foreigner," Gertrude said thoughtfully, as though this fact gave her an idea to work on. "But for her sake he turned into a proper Englishman."

"Don't get notions in your head," I advised her. "Much as I like your countrymen, *and you,* I still think it extraordinary that in the three hundred years in which *my* country has changed from a wilderness to the greatest country on earth, the British have not improved their cooking or their house-heating systems."

"You wouldn't feel the cold so much, darling, if only you would learn to drink—"

"Scalding hot tea," I finished for her. "After eight and a half years of marriage, haven't you given up hope of converting me? Though, if anything could change my habits, it's what passes for milk over here. It's as blue as the blood of a viscount."

"Of course, if you have no soul above your stomach," Gertrude said loftily . . .

We expected Fanny Holtzmann to arrive the following day, which was the day before Gertrude's opening. Fanny's plane was delayed, and it was early afternoon when we drove to Heathrow to meet her. Fanny descended the steps from the plane with her usual imperturbability. Gertrude's eyes lighted on the parcels Fanny carried.

"Did you bring them, Fan?" Gertrude asked eagerly, as soon as Fanny cleared customs.

"Of course I brought them."

"That's our Wonder Girl!"

She quickly relieved Fanny of the parcels as we got into the car.

"I was awakened by a telephone call early yesterday morning," Fanny informed me. "It was Gertrude Lawrence Aldrich entrusting me with a most important international mission. Would I bring a bottle or two of homogenized milk to London? Oh, yes, and a quart of chocolate ice cream. 'Richard loves it,' she made sure to explain."

"You can have some *real* milk for breakfast tomorrow, darling," Gertrude said, giving me the container to carry. "So you'll start the day right for my opening. No. I'll carry the ice cream."

She continued to hold the package in her lap on the drive to Claridge's, where Fanny was stopping. The ice cream had been in the plane's refrigerator, but it was no longer frozen solid. We arrived at Claridge's after dusk. There the attendants, in their evening livery of scarlet, ushered us across the threshold and offered to relieve us of our plebeian packages. Gertrude motioned them away.

"No, no," she said. "We'll carry these ourselves." Gertrude swept across the crimson carpet that has received the footprints of most of the earth's royalty, serenely unaware of the dribble of melted chocolate ice cream that marked her trail.

* * *

The opening of *September Tide* will go down in London's theatre history as the first gala First Night since the beginning of the war. It was completely in the pre-war tradition. The men had taken their white ties and tails out of storage and the ladies, freed some six months before from eight years of clothing rationing, blossomed forth in dazzling new creations. There were the queues of devoted fans waiting patiently for hours—many stood in line all night—in the chill and murk of London's December weather. There were the lights blazing on the angle of the theatre's front, making a beacon of the name *GERTRUDE LAWRENCE* to illumine the curve of Aldwych, which had been dark and silent when I had known it during the war. There were the knots of shivering but staunch onlookers, the flower-sellers and hawkers that are always drawn like moths by the glitter of the lights and the promise of a view of the fashionable world.

I had known First Nights in New York, exciting, nerve-wracking occasions, but with none of the romantic, storybook quality that attended this one. I began to realize that Gertrude had missed something in all her successes in America. It was for this, I thought, more than any other one thing, that she had longed to "go home."

I went with her, well ahead of time, to the theatre, where I met Evie Williams and "Boxie," who was Gertrude's dresser as she had been years before. I realized how retentive Gertrude was of people who had helped her at various times in her career. They were the ones she wanted close to her on an important occasion like this. They knew her tastes, understood her moods, and served her with love; more for love than for the good salaries she always paid.

Two dressing rooms had been set aside for her, and they were needed. Both were filled with flowers. Evie brought a box in which a single large mauve orchid lay on crisp ferns, and showed it to Gertrude without comment. Gertrude lifted the flower and held it against her cheek. Her eyes were moist.

"They haven't forgotten," she said softly.

The single orchid, she told me, was the emblem of the group of her fans headed by Lou Hollis. For many years they had sent her an orchid whenever she opened in a new play, although the purchase of such a costly flower entailed a good many small sacrifices on the givers' part. Through the years Gertrude had become sentimental and a trifle superstitious about the orchid; its arrival now after the lapse of all these years, proof that she was remembered, loved, still a part of the old life, was like a blessing. It gave her strength and assurance.

"Kiss me, Richard," she said. "For luck. I'll see you after the play."

The royal box had been dusted and regilded for the occasion. Lady du Maurier sat there with Daphne's husband, General Sir Frederick Browning, an officer of the Royal Household, on her left. I was on her right. I was conscious that many eyes were turned on me, and that there was considerable interest in and speculation about Gertrude's American husband.

The play fulfilled my expectations of it and I found my opinion confirmed by the critics, who drew a sharp line between its merits and Gertrude's performance. To quote W. A. Darlington's report to the New York *Times:* "When Miss Lawrence takes the stage we find . . . that . . . inevitably (and, I imagine, since she is a serious and conscientious actress, without special intention) she transcendentalizes the part . . . Everybody agreed that the occasion was a triumph for Miss Lawrence. For Miss du Maurier hardly a good word was said. All the same, there she is, with what looks like another smash hit on her hands . . ."

When she first read the play Gertrude had said the part was one she could do something with. I have reason to believe that there were moments during the rehearsals when the director was troubled by what she considered Gertrude's liberties with the role. How well taken those liberties were, and what they did to give the play success, was evident from the reaction of press and public.

Backstage, after the final curtain, joy reigned. The crowd waiting with me outside Gertrude's dressing room was eager, enthusiastic, and confident that *September Tide* would run for many months. It had swept Gertrude onto their shore and they had no intention of letting her drift away again, if they could prevent it.

A distinguished-looking man who was wedged close to my shoulder said as much to me. My reply was noncommittal. I was in the difficult position of husband versus wife's career. The similarity between me and a character in one of the soap operas Gertrude regularly listened to, made up in irony what it lacked in comfort.

"There's no one like her," the Englishman said with a fervent sincerity that I could not help liking.

"No one," I agreed.

"It's high time she came home. America is all right. But her place is here. We need her."

My reply that I needed her, too, was cut off by the sudden opening of the dressing-room door, revealing Gertrude smiling, her eyes searching the throng of cheering, applauding men and women. They found me.

"Richard," she called. And instantly: "And Philip! So you two know each other."

I took a long look at the man beside me. "So you're Philip Astley!" I said. At the same moment he was saying, "So you're Richard!"

That night, and several times during the next three weeks in London, I had opportunity to increase my spontaneous liking for Colonel Astley. Gertrude was pleased, I saw, that we got on well together. "Philip has done so many kind things for me," she told me. "He kept an eye on Pam in school, when I would be in America for months. And he'd run down every so often to see Mummy and Granny."

The day before my return to New York, early in January, 1949, Gertrude, Fanny Holtzmann, Bill Conway, who was Binkie Beaumont's manager, and I were lunching at the Savoy Grill, when an incident occurred that gave me a deeper insight into Gertrude than anything she had ever said to me about her life before we met.

We were a very sprightly group, and Gertrude was the sprightliest. The restaurant was crowded and a great many of those lunching there that afternoon recognized Gertrude and greeted her. The success of her play was current news. It had brought to the war-wearied and financially and politically worried Londoners not only a reminder of other, happier days, but some measure of hope of a return of the kind of world they had known—the world in which Gertrude's star had risen.

I was aware of an elderly woman, obviously well born, with a haughty face etched with lines of discontent, lunching alone at a nearby table. She seemed to be paying more attention to us than to her meal. Presently she rose, and was making her way to the lounge when abruptly she turned back. She stopped at our table and bowed to Gertrude.

Gertrude's vivacity was instantly frozen. Her body stiffened. She appeared to grow in height; her blue eyes turned to steely gray. She gave no sign of recognition.

"You don't remember me, Miss Lawrence," the woman said.

Gertrude's voice, in reply, shocked me. I had never known her to speak like that to anyone. Low, vibrant with bitterness, her voice cut like a whip-lash. "Oh, yes, indeed, madam," she said. "I remember you only too well."

The woman's face flushed slightly. Her lips moved as though she would have said something. Then, as she changed her mind, they settled into their former petulant droop. She shrugged slightly and moved on.

"Lady ——"; Bill Conway mentioned a name well known in England and on the Continent.

"But why the Sarah Bernhardt pose," I asked, "and that line straight out of a Pinero third act?"

"That was no line," Gertrude assured me swiftly and bitterly. Her eyes followed the old woman as she went out. "I have good reason to remember her, though we met only once. I knew her son. He wanted to marry me. One day she wrote a note asking me to call at her house in Mayfair. Naively, I went, believing she meant to receive me as a friend. Instead, as I entered her drawing room, she took out her checkbook. 'Miss Lawrence,' she said, 'how much money do you want not to marry my son.'"

Fanny was silent. I had the feeling that I was in the presence of something old, ugly, and cruel.

Under the table, my hand grasped Gertrude's. It was cold and trembling. But suddenly her voice was light again.

"Darling," she said, "promise me that as soon as you get home you will send flowers to Mother with this message. Tell her, as much as I love England, I love being your Mrs. A more . . . and her daughter-in-law."

Chapter Sixteen

WITH THE ASSURANCE that her play would run in London until spring, Gertrude set about finding a furnished apartment there. She never liked living in hotels, no matter how luxurious. "FLAT-HUNTING AND STILL ADORINGLY YOURS," was the cabled message that greeted me on my return to New York.

The flat she finally settled on was a small one in Fountain House, Park Street, W1. She described it briefly:

> . . . No work room, spare room or dining room. It looks out on a courtyard and faces the backs of other apartments, so it's really attractive only at night, just when I'm not there except to sleep. But it is *cheap*. And I am determined to save money . . . And while we are on the subject of money, let me tell you I have a woman who comes in each day except Saturday and Sunday at £2.0.0 a week plus 5s. for her fares from Wimbledon. My rations for the week come to 1 shilling, 3 pence, 3 farthings and consist of:

1 rasher of bacon	4 pence	
1 oz. lard	1 "	½
1 oz. cheese	2 "	

¼ lb. margarine	2	"	3f
¼ lb. butter	3	"	
½ lb. sugar	2	"	½

But don't get worried. It's amazing how one learns to eke things out with a few stores from outside and meals with friends. I never dine alone after the play. I am becoming a real spiv over my meals . . .

Actually, of course, she was playing the role of a surtaxed, severely rationed British housewife, and deriving sufficient satisfaction from it to make up for the actual discomfort and privations. Not that these were allowed to go far. Generous food parcels went to her regularly each week, as well as other luxuries for herself and to give away.

"Thanks for the pkgs of socks and men's clothes. I can give them to my fashionable hostesses to give to their boy friends or their husbands," she wrote.

Evie Williams acted as secretary to "Lady Jane," as she called Gertrude; she also took upon herself the task of writing me a series of newsy letters addressed to Lord Richard, a title which both I and Debrett utterly disclaim.

Gertrude's letters were full of the number of invitations and requests for her services on committees that poured in on her. "I would never have believed it possible to do so many things for so many people," she wrote, "but these are the days when to say 'No' to anything or to anybody's invitation would bring the accusation of cutting one's old friends."

The invitation which she valued most highly came from Shaw. A telephone call from Blanche Patch, Shaw's faithful secretary through thirty years, on a dismal Saturday morning in February, asked if Gertrude could come out to tea that afternoon. Gertrude drove down to Ayot St. Lawrence feeling alternately excited and fearful.

The dark green wrought-iron gates bearing the name of the place—Shaw's Corner—stood open, leading into a short driveway. Miss Patch came out of the house to meet her and took her into a sitting room, where a fire burned and tea was laid.

Shaw was asleep, but they "took a peep, just in case," Gertrude wrote me.

The peep through the carefully opened door of the study revealed a capacious wing-backed chair, "and snuggled down in its depths a gnome such as Walt Disney might have created—wicked and wise. Two pink cheeks glowed in the firelight out of a mass of white hair and flowing beard. One would not have been surprised to have seen a pointed scarlet cap aslant his brow and long, pointed green shoes with bells on them instead of the country brogues he was wearing."

While Shaw finished his nap, the two women renewed their acquaintance, begun during Gertrude's short stay in England the year before. At that time, Shaw was closing his apartment in Whitehall Place and was disposing of many of its furnishings by auction. Sitting beside Blanche Patch at Sotheby's, Gertrude had bought some of the books for our library, including a presentation copy of H. G. Wells's *Short History of the World* inscribed: "G.B.S. to improve and steady his mind," and a facsimile set of the four folios of Shakespeare's plays for which she paid £163.

After a quarter of an hour it was deemed time for a second peep. Miss Patch said softly: "She's here."

"At once he was awake," Gertrude wrote. "I went forward and kissed him on the cheek. It seemed a perfectly natural thing to do, and he was a bit surprised although his eyes sparkled as we went into the sitting room. He sat in his chair and began to talk. That was at half-past three, and at half-past five we were still at it.

"We talked about taxation, actors—old school and new. He does not approve of the modern form of underplaying. He thinks it has gone too far and that present-day actors lack gusto and power. This he believes is due to so many of them doing film acting, which restricts their emotions as well as their movements.

"We got to pantomime and he said the first one he remembered was *Aladdin,* in which Ada Reeve played Aladdin and sang *Up in a Balloon, Boys.* I remembered the song from Granny singing it to me. Shaw and I sang it together, loud and clear, with gestures:

"Come, little girl, for a sail with me,
Up in my bonny balloon,
Come, little girl, for a sail with me,
Round and round the moon.
No one to see us behind the clouds:
Oh, what a place to spoon.
Up in the sky—ever so high,
Sailing in my balloon."

Miss Patch's comment on the performance is worth repeating: "Few can have been audience to so astonishing a duet."

After this musical interlude, Shaw spoke of a one-act play he had written for marionettes, which was to be the feature of his birthday celebration at the Malvern Festival on July 26. Gertrude seized this opportunity to tell Shaw about the Cape Playhouse, which, she explained, was run along the lines of Malvern and Stratford. He was immediately interested and asked a number of pertinent questions. He then told her that he had written a new, modern play which was to be done at Malvern, starting on his birthday.

"Who is to act in it?" Gertrude said.

"You," was Shaw's reply. "Can you play the saxophone?"

"I could learn," Gertrude answered.

The subject was dropped there, but on Monday night, when Gertrude arrived at the Aldwych Theatre, there was a bulky envelope addressed to her by Shaw containing a copy of *Buoyant Billions,* inscribed on the cover: "To Gertrude Lawrence, for her consideration—in case—G. Bernard Shaw."

Gertrude was not able to clear the time to appear in *Buoyant Billions,* so she asked for Shaw's permission, which he granted, to send the play to me with a view to my producing it at the Cape Playhouse at some future date, when she would be free.

Another negotiation which Gertrude managed on my behalf was to get Shaw's consent to my producing *Caesar and Cleopatra* in New York the following winter with Sir Cedric Hardwicke and Lilli Palmer. One Sunday, Gertrude drove Lilli down to Ayot St. Lawrence to meet Shaw. Our friend Radie Harris was included in the party on condition that she did not reveal to their host the fact that she was a newspaperwoman.

As it turned out, this agreement to hide Radie's profession was a fortunate one.

Shaw greeted Lilli with the demand: "What did you mean by saying that on the wireless last night?"

Lilli, appearing as a guest on the B.B.C. Saturday night program "In Town Tonight," had remarked that she was looking forward to her visit to Shaw the next day. As a result, five newspaper correspondents had applied at Shaw's house for permission to be present at the meeting. It may have been this that put him in a cantankerous mood. At any rate, he refused to sign the contract which Gertrude proffered for the production, putting her off with a vague, "Yes, that's all right," which, of course, was *not* all right from a business standpoint.

Then he scrutinized Lilli Palmer and asked suddenly: "Are you a Jewess?"

She bristled and countered with, "What has that got to do with it?"

"Everything," Shaw answered. "Are you?"

"Yes," she said.

"Good!" He beamed at her. "Then you may play Cleopatra." He added that he believed a Jewess would play the role best.

His mood mellowed by Gertrude's imperturbable good humor, he walked with the visitors to their car. Radie had her camera, but Gertrude had exacted a promise from her not to use it, and in any case there had been no opportunity to photograph Shaw. At the last moment, Gertrude threw her own precaution to the winds. While Shaw was pointing out something to Lilli, Gertrude seized the camera from Radie and snapped a view of his back, quite unknown to him. "If he had caught me," she told Radie, "he might have been angry, but not so furious as he would have been at my smuggling in a reporter with a camera. The photograph, if it turns out at all, is just for us."

Shortly afterward, plans were being made for Gertrude to broadcast her Success Story for the B.B.C. She wrote Shaw herself, asking permission to include a scene from *Pygmalion* in her program. His reply, on a postal card and in his handwriting, read:

18/6/49

Miss Gertrude Lawrence is hereby licensed to include Act III of *Pygmalion* or anything of mine she likes in the broadcast of her Success Story, in consideration of her knitting a pair of mittens for my personal use next winter.

G. Bernard Shaw

Gertrude submitted samples of wool for him to choose the color, and went to work with her needles. She finished the mittens and forwarded them to Shaw a few months later.

* * *

Meanwhile her play continued to be a popular success. She wrote me:

"They fight with umbrellas to get into the matinees as though we had announced nylons going free. Binkie sends me flowers for breaking records . . . H. R. H. the Duke of Edinburgh was in front the other night and came back afterward. We are hoping Their Majesties will come. Queen Mary has returned from Sandringham and she usually comes to the plays first, and then the reigning monarchs . . ."

She was now, I saw, all Englishwoman and intensely royalist. I detected a slightly patronizing note in a letter written early in March telling me:

Last Wednesday night I dined after the play at St. James' Palace with Sir Piers Leigh. He is Comptroller of the King's Household. He came to the play first with a large party (his third visit) and I joined them at the Palace by 10:15. He has a perfectly charming house in the corner of the Palace facing Marlborough House, so he is near Queen Mary also. He lived there with the Prince of Wales in earlier days.

We dined, about fifteen of us, in a charming cosy Adam room, and all left the table together, the ladies rushing to powder their noses and put on their long gloves.

Then all assembled in a circle in the drawing room, where a lovely fire glowed and the flowers shone in the reflections on the polished floor, from which the carpet had been raised to permit the guests to dance. Why the circle facing the door? Word had come that THEY were on the way.

In a short time the door was quietly opened; in came "Tommy" Browning followed by the Edinburghs.

Piers had told me he had a surprise for me, and this was it.

It was a charming evening. We danced—I with [Prince] Philip, singing old songs with Carroll Gibbons playing the piano. It was not until 3 A.M. that the Edinburghs finally went home. It was the first time Elizabeth had stayed out so late since the baby was born.

When leaving, as I curtseyed very low, she told me that she is most anxious to see the play and is coming soon. So we are all waiting again at the Aldwych.

They are wonderful together, and most obviously very much in love. This time I dare you to laugh at me . . .

This challenge was issued to me because of a running argument we had about the authenticity of publicly displayed affection. Gertrude would never fail to come home with stardust in her eyes after seeing a couple who were—by my New England standards—much too obviously in love. I had a chronic skepticism of what seemed to me suspicious overplaying; and Gertrude was invoking the evidence of the royal couple—whose mutual affection was beyond any question—as the crusher to prove I was wrong.

The ten months which Gertrude spent in England were one of those disturbing periods of psychological readjustment during which she examined and appraised, however unconsciously, all the various personal relationships in her life, including her relationship with me.

I think I have said enough about her character and mine to make it clear that the tempo of her life was the exact antithesis of my own. The law of my nature is to progress steadily, as one mounts a stair—a single step at a time—having one foot resting solidly on the past while the other feels its way into the present. But not Gertrude. Her movement through life resembled the flight of a bird which soars, wings its way into the distance, then comes to light on a branch from which it looks about and examines the terrain. Our marriage, Gertrude's long stay in America, her gradual identification with American life—especially our family life at The Berries and the intensely American community activities centering around the Playhouse—represented a long flight away from the old familiar surroundings.

Perhaps she was a little startled by the extent of her flight, and suffered a degree of panic fear that she would never find her way back again.

This, I am sure, was one of the compelling motives behind her desire to go to England, and her determined effort to recapture not only the world she had known there, but the self she had been in that world.

Gertrude was one of those persons in whom certain childlike qualities persist. They contributed as much to her charm as an individual as to her talents as an actress. Yet her evanescent moods, her instinctive as well as deliberate play-acting, her touching dependence on affection and admiration, even her little ingenuous vanities existed side by side with a magnificent simplicity and directness. All her ingenuous traits, which could be annoying as well as endearing, would be swept away by her courage, her clear perception of truth, and the divine compassion which could flood her heart and lift her to the heights of nobility.

I am sure that she was frequently bewildered by the rapidity and mutability of her own impulses. Possessed, as she was, of an intuitive rather than an analytical intelligence, I doubt that she really understood herself clearly, any more than did most of those who thought they knew her intimately. An exception in this regard was Daphne du Maurier.

During those months in England, Gertrude and Daphne formed a warm friendship, which continued unbroken after Gertrude's return to America. Daphne later returned the visit by being Gertrude's guest in New York. Daphne's subsequent best-selling novel *Mary Anne* was originally planned as a possible starring vehicle for Gertrude.

It was chiefly from comments made later by Daphne that I was able to reconstruct the full picture of Gertrude's inner conflict during her stay in London. Daphne spoke of Gertrude's moodiness, her variability, her sense of vague self-dissatisfaction. To other English friends, Gertrude talked wistfully of wanting to remain in England, "where I belong."

However, long before this, I had made my own analysis of the forces working on Gertrude. Above all, I reasoned, she was experiencing a deep and disturbing longing to escape the necessity of being an adult. Our life together in America challenged her to put away the childish things—the frivolities, the free-and-easy ways which had occupied her before we married and which she associated with England. It was the only life she had known there, away from the hard work of the theatre. It glittered in retrospect, and the glitter temporarily put out of her mind the fact that she had been deeply dissatisfied with that existence at the time that she turned from it to become Mrs. A.

For I am convinced that one, and perhaps the dominant, reason why Gertrude had been willing to marry me and embark on a life so different from her former life in London, and on the Riviera, was that the latter had begun to pall on her. She longed for something else; for a reality which would give her opportunities to express a part of her nature—the richest and best part—which was then frustrated and undeveloped.

In our building of The Berries, in the healthy, happy outdoor life we lived on the Cape, occupied with the Playhouse and its people, above all in her relationships with my mother and my sons, Gertrude had found the outlet she craved and needed.

But with fulfillment came increasing responsibilities. There came an obligation to be fully adult. This she was not quite sure she wanted to be. At any rate, not yet. So she had evaded it by flight and by immersing herself in a world which did not expect her to be more than gay, charming, and amusing.

I realized that our marriage was running in shallow water among reefs which I had not charted. I could not ignore the fact that strong influences—strong because they were of longer duration than our marriage and because they spoke a familiar and seductive language—surrounded Gertrude. They separated us more effectively than the Atlantic.

Just how seductive her return to the English stage and London society was proving, I did not completely realize until David Holtzmann came back from a trip to England, where he had gone principally to take care of some business matters for Gertrude.

As he got up from his desk to greet me when I went to his office the next day, I noticed that he had lost weight.

"David," I remarked, "the austerity diet has streamlined you."

"Austerity my eye," he snorted. "I dined magnificently in London."

"Then how ——?" I indicated his trim waistline.

"Exercise, Dick. Disgustingly vigorous exercise. And, I might add, on your behalf."

I was understandably curious to hear more.

David went on: "I have explored every empty, draughty mansion in Mayfair. I have trudged with Gertrude up and down rickety stairs from Belgravia to Berkeley Square, inspecting studies for you and top-floor bedrooms for the boys. I haven't been through such a workout since my days at college!"

"What on earth would I do with a study in Berkeley Square?"

"A very good question," David replied. "And one that usually struck me with particular force toward the end of the day, as I staggered up the fourth flight of stairs."

"And the answer?"

"Gertrude has visions of you becoming an international producer—a theatrical Colossus with one foot in Piccadilly Circus and the other on Broadway."

This was a notion about which Gertrude had given me no advance knowledge. I could see, however, that her house-hunting was a daydream in action—an evasion of the reality of being married to an American.

"And did she say anything about coming back home?" I asked David.

"No," he answered, and then added quickly, "but she often said she wished you were *there*."

In the meantime, Gertrude wrote to me, "We are playing to

capacity since Easter." Surely I would not advise her to drop out of her play while it was making money?

She emphasized the Cinderella aspect of her life by telling me how busy she was with causes and benefits under royal patronage. "This committee, 'Dogs for the Blind,' is very important because the Queen will be present," she explained. "My job is to procure the glamour gals for selling programs."

Now and then a note of wistfulness crept between the lines: she was sending Ed, our gardener, some seeds. She did hope we had rain. Young Fritz Hyde had been to see her. "He says his father cannot go anywhere without his wheelchair and they are worried how they are going to get him into the Playhouse. They do so want to keep their same seats. I've been wondering if it would be possible to build a small ramp at the side entrance so that they could wheel him into the theatre. Do think up a solution . . ."

"London is jammed," she reported. "I am going out with Larry, Vivien, the Garson Kanins and Danny Kaye to supper and dance at the Café de Paris . . ."

But her next letter was written, she said, while she was seated on the fire-escape of her flat, getting a bit of sun and with her back against the garbage can. "Polly has her coronet and is now on 'er 'oneymoon, but I just love you. I get very tired and lonely at times. Can't you come over for a week?"

The obvious course was for me to go to England and try to persuade her to leave the play and return to America and me as soon as the terms of her original contract were concluded. But I did not wish to do this. First, because I always steadfastly refrained from interfering in Gertrude's career and from urging a course of action on her. Second, because I felt that for me to cross the Atlantic and plead with her to return home would be to defeat myself and our future. Gertrude must *want* to return. The initial impulse must be hers. Otherwise nothing would have been accomplished by her stay abroad.

And so I replied it was impossible. It was as much as I could do to get a second playhouse at Falmouth in operation, starting my season with Tallulah Bankhead. I added that it might be a good idea to rent The Berries for the summer, particularly since she seemed to have made no plans to come home before autumn.

Her reply came by return post:

Dearest,

Please do not let or lend our little house to ANYONE. It's ours and I shall be back sooner or later and want to go straight there. And in any case I want to know that *you* are in it.

I adore you, *please.*

Mrs. A . . .

I felt that the sky was growing brighter.

Still, my refusal to fly over "for a week" to make a personal appearance as Consort nettled her. Her letters became less frequent, and in each she was "terribly busy" . . . "The Prime Minister was begging me to go to Australia when he was here last week." She thought of flying over to Paris for the week-end . . . She had motored out into the country with Radie, who had turned up to interview celebrities in town for the season, and England was "an enchanted Isle, earth had nothing to show more fair . . ."

Much later, I learned the facts of that drive with Radie into Bucks. Gertrude and Radie had lunched together at Caprice. Radie spoke of the columnist's constant worry—how and where to get good copy. "Come along with me this afternoon," Gertrude said. "I'll give you something you can write about." Gertrude refused to say anything about where they were going, other than, "It's a surprise."

They rode through the suburbs in the direction of Hertfordshire. Passing through the village of Aylesbury in Buckinghamshire, the car stopped in front of the parish church. Gertrude sprang out. Radie followed, wondering. She wondered still more when Gertrude opened the gate into the cemetery and began examining the tombstones.

"I'm looking for some of Richard's ancestors," she explained.

"You don't mean *this* is the surprise?" Radie asked.

Gertrude ignored Radie's obvious disappointment and said, "Yes, isn't it wonderful to think that, after all these centuries —"

"And how do you figure," Radie interrupted, "that I can score a beat with a batch of three-hundred-year-old gravestones?"

"Radie, darling," Gertrude replied, "You're from Boston. You ought to know that an Aldrich, no matter how defunct, is still news!"

* * *

The Fourth of July was the most important day in Gertrude's calendar. By being married on her own birthday, she had cheated her sentimental nature out of having two separate occasions to celebrate. But, by the same token, she had created a day loaded with a double charge of emotional significance.

Under such circumstances, it was always difficult for me to find a present to match the calibre of the day. This year, it seemed impossible to me, for any physical gift would have subjected Gertrude to the bother and expense of customs. I therefore sent her a check, suggesting that she choose her own present.

She made no reference to this when she replied, but in a note to David Holtzmann, which he showed me, she told him of the gift, adding the terse comment spread across the page:

"HOW ROMANTIC!!!"

After viewing the incisive flash of those three indignant exclamation points, David did not have to urge me to make one of those extravagant gestures, ridiculous to me, which so delighted Gertrude. I arranged to have a birthday anniversary cake baked in New York—in itself a simple enough task. Then, after complicated negotiations, the cake was placed in the hands of an American Airlines steward who was to guard it as if it were the Kohinoor diamond, and deliver it to Joe Rile of their London office, who in turn was to present it in person to Gertrude on her birthday.

I tried to reach her by telephone several times on the Fourth, but with no success. It was 1 A.M. on the fifth in Dennis, and 6 A.M in London, when I finally heard her voice in response. After our greeting, I asked her how she had spent the day.

It had been gay, full of fun, she told me. In the afternoon there was the July Fourth garden party at the American Embassy. Lew and Peggy Douglas were friends of Gertrude's and I knew that they liked having her at their parties. Then, after her play, there had been a dinner party at Larue's. Afterwards the guests had gone on to dance at the 400 Club. She had come home at dawn.

There was no mention of the cake. After a short pause, I ventured a hesitant question: "Anything else happen today?"

"Yes, something very nice happened," she replied. "It's about Philip."

I wondered what was coming next. I had tried not to let my mind dwell on Philip Astley.

"Well," Gertrude said, "he's married. I just heard it today and I've been celebrating."

I may have seemed unresponsive because she went on, "Such a nice girl! She'll be a good wife for him!"

"And you've been celebrating with them?" I asked.

"No, not with them—but for them. But more than anything else —for me. I'm happy because when I heard the news I didn't feel a thing. Only pleasure at the thought of them being happy together— like we are. We *are* happy, aren't we?"

"When we *are* together."

"Sometimes you act as if you don't want me back. I was alone— very much alone today, despite all the people."

"I never wanted you to go away. Or stay away," I said.

"I don't suppose you could come over and fetch me?" she asked.

"No," I said. "I think you'd better come back under your own steam."

"That's not a very cordial invitation. And it's very late. Let's say goodnight."

After a few more words, we hung up. I lay awake for a time, staring disconsolately around the empty room; then dropped off into a troubled sleep. . . .

I was awakened by the overseas telephone operator: Gertrude was calling me from London. In a voice tremulous with excitement, she announced that the birthday-anniversary cake had just arrived, a day late and somewhat the worse for wear.

"Darling, it was the nicest thing you've ever done for me," she said. "When I opened up the box and read your sweet note, I knew I had been away too long. And I knew that I didn't belong here any more. I thought I did. But I don't. I don't think that I belong completely to America—but I belong to you—wherever you are."

"But are you coming back?"

"I'll have to see. I must talk it over with Binkie."

Though, at the time, I thought this was just procrastination, it was only a few hours later that I received this cable:

SPIT ON THE BRASS. CLEAR THE DECKS. GET THAT WOMAN OUT OF THE HOUSE. LEAVING SHOW IN ONE MONTH AND COMING HOME.

MRS. A

* * *

The special present she brought me for my birthday, August seventeenth—which, she said, would be *our* birthday this year—was a handsomely carved ship model. It was a full-rigged brigantine, made by the stage doorman at the Aldwych Theatre. Gertrude had seen him whittling the ship and had arranged to acquire it for me.

She told me that as a result of her genealogical research, she had been able to trace the early origins of the Aldriches, Joys, and Hartwells. To prove it she proudly produced meticulously painted copies of their coats of arms.

"There isn't a viscount to show among them," I said. "Your friend Polly wouldn't give them a second glance."

"Poor Polly," Gertrude sighed. "Imagine wasting a whole lifetime chasing a will-o'-the-wisp. I can't understand it."

"You understood it well enough to help her get her viscount. Come to think of it, he's part yours!"

"Mine?"

"Of course. Aren't you the one who kept her supplied with rubber girdles and beauty aids all through the war? It was like Lend Lease; you gave her the tools and she finished the job. You ought, at least, to rejoice in her victory."

"I would if I really thought it was a victory. It isn't. Peeresses' robes are no guarantee of happiness."

"Aren't you the least bit envious?"

"Of course not. I'd rather have my untitled Aldrich than any item catalogued in *Burke's Peerage!*"

Chapter Seventeen

I HAD HOPED to have Gertrude with me at the Cape and in New York that autumn and winter of 1949. She had no play in immediate prospect, though she was interested in several then being written.

However, at that point, Hollywood and *The Glass Menagerie* entered our lives. Shortly before Gertrude returned from her long engagement in England, feelers had been put out from the film capital to inquire whether she would accept the role of the mother in a motion picture of the Tennessee Williams play. Laurette Taylor had created the part on Broadway. Gertrude saw her when the play opened. A paragraph in her diary expressed her admiration for "this great and distinguished actress."

By a strange coincidence the name of the mother was Amanda. It would be difficult to conceive of a role further removed from the beautiful, *soignée,* sophisticated Amanda of *Private Lives* than this faded, slatternly Amanda, living in penury and still clinging to her Deep South accent and her unrealistic memories of a romantic past. To many it was a mystery that Hollywood possessed the imagination to offer Gertrude the part.

As a matter of fact, she talked herself into it. Her interpretation of Doris Gow, the mother in Noel Coward's *Fumed Oak*—one of the short plays comprising *Tonight at 8:30*—had been widely acclaimed by critics. Influential members of the motion-picture hierarchy marveled at her willingness to dispense with the "glamour" generally associated with her. She had replied that she was an actress, first and foremost.

Her own words were a boomerang. Warner Brothers now asked her to star with Jane Wyman and Kirk Douglas in *The Glass Menagerie.*

Gertrude asked for my opinion. I was opposed to her accepting the offer, and I made no bones about it. I called to her attention that she had just come back from ten months in England. She had not been seen on Broadway since the record-breaking run of *Pygmalion* nearly three years before. I suggested that she take time to select a play to appear in, that season. I pointed out that there were a number of talented, older actresses, capable of playing Amanda, who might be thankful to get the role. Why should she, and the studio make-up department, struggle unduly to turn her into something she was not?

"I know, darling," she said to all my arguments. "Always Right Aldrich! But just the same, I feel it is a challenge and I'd like to have a go at it."

Once more she was acting on her uncontrollable impulse to respond to a dare.

"All right," I told her. "Go ahead, if that's what you really want to do. However, I insist on two things. First, they must write into the script several flash-backs to show Amanda as she was in her heyday, young and beautiful, and as *you* really are. Perhaps *you* don't mind if you appear before the movie-goers of the globe made up with a wrinkled neck and sagging cheeks and a middle-aged spread, but *I* do."

"Richard!" Gertrude was out of her chair and across the room, studying herself in a mirror. "What do you mean—middle-aged spread? I don't bulge anywhere."

I grinned at her. "Exactly," I said. "Then why let anyone think you do? Art or no art—that's why I insist on the flash-backs. It's a long time since you made a picture; not since *Rembrandt* with Charles Laughton in 1935. The audiences all over the world who will see *The Glass Menagerie* will be made up largely of people who never saw you. Let them have their first view of Gertrude Lawrence as she is."

Gertrude admitted the wisdom of this. "What is your other condition, darling?" she asked.

"That you take a small house in Beverly Hills. Have Hazel to look after you. I'll fly out to spend Christmas with you and as much more time as we both can manage. With luck, the picture should be finished by the first of the year and I can bring you home with me."

The idea pleased her. Characteristically, she began at once planning for us to drive home from California, stopping at motels and seeing what she called "the real America," as she had long wanted to do.

* * *

Beverly Hills
Tuesday, 4:30
October fourth, 1949

Dear One,

Here I am, another 3000 miles away again. It was a splendid flight but a desperately sad parting. Dearest, I suddenly felt so awful about us. But it won't be for long this time. Please take care of yourself, be good and come here soon.

Your very own
Bunkie

Her welcome at the airport, I learned later, had been strictly according to Hollywood tradition. The director, Irving Rapper, accompanied by studio executives, producers, publicity men, newsmen and cameramen, was on hand to receive her. For a moment, she was nonplussed. The fanfare exceeded anything of the sort she had ever known.

"Flowers—and such concoctions—have arrived and keep arriving," Gertrude wrote. "They tell me that after the announcement

A present from London. "I get very tired and lonely at times," she wrote. "Can't you come over for a week?"

London, 1948–49—she played the role of Stella in *September Tide* with "great dignity, serenity, and character" and renewed old ties with her English friends.

Angus McBean

Gertrude's snapshot of G. B. S. had to be taken when his back was turned. "If he had caught me, he might have been angry," she said.

As Amanda Wingate in *The Glass Menagerie.* insisted on the insertion of this scene, so that the motion picture public would know Gertrude as she really was.

Acquiring a Southern drawl for her role in *The Glass Menagerie.* Unfortunately, Hazel's accent was too British.

Warner Bros.

that I am here and the pictures taken at the plane reach the press, there will be many more offerings. This is a mad, crazy world. But, oh, darling, I'd hate to be on the ash-can out here. . . ."

Accustomed as she was to the formal social life of London, Gertrude was nevertheless staggered by the elaborate elegance of Hollywood soirées. "It's the Savoy and Mayfair again—only much more so," she commented in a letter.

Hollywood parties, Gertrude discovered, rarely lasted until midnight; work at the studios began too early.

She reported: ". . . Today has been another long gruelling test—costumes, hairdos, dialect and dialog, all alone but with the cameras grinding and everybody staring. To my horror I looked up and saw a well-known newspaper columnist on the set. Of course I couldn't order him off. That would have proved fatal. However Irving Rapper assured me that the columnist had been very impressed by what he saw me doing and that we need not fear his typewriter—yet. All this is so different from the theatre. . . ."

It was indeed. In the world to which Gertrude was accustomed, no critic or newspaperman would be admitted to the first reading or to the working rehearsals of a play. As she commented:

> Believe me, it's tough to go through what I have put up with today without any rehearsal or even a general reading of the script. And to play three scenes with three different people *with not one of them there* is like some horrible dream.
>
> Tomorrow I have off, thank Heaven. Thursday I go back to the studio to finish the costume and hairdo tests and to see the results of what I did today, which I think will be quite dreadful.
>
> I saw Joan Crawford today. She dresses next to me. She said she did all this for *five weeks* before she started shooting the picture she is now on. I suppose it gets better when each individual actor has tested alone as we all have to do, and when we begin rehearsing the scenes together . . .

"It's difficult to dress Amanda like an out-of-date belle," Gertrude commented, "without making her look either like Whistler's Mother or Nurse Cavell after a night on the town." Several days later she wrote:

I must admit these people—actors, directors and technicians—are the most thorough people I ever met.

Up to now I have tested thirty different costumes and about two dozen hairdos. They have made an entire padded foundation for me which adds about fifteen pounds to my weight and makes me stick out in places where I don't. Bette Davis wore such in *Now Voyager.* I must say it helps the character for the contrast between the present and the flash-backs. Without the pads I look too young for the present-day scenes.

They have cut all Jane Wyman's hair off so she can wear a blond stringy wig, and they have dyed her eyebrows to match. We are a pretty pair . . . .

Merle Reeve, the hair-stylist assigned to Gertrude, who was constantly at her side during the three months of work in the studio, has said that she never saw an actress work so hard and so unselfishly to help bring about a characterization. "I don't look old enough, Merle," Gertrude would say. "Put more gray on my hair, and dampen that lock to make it look stringy. Make my face look harder and give me more wrinkles . . ."

"It was no joke to make our Miss Gee look frumpy," Merle told me. "Milo Anderson, the designer, Eddie, the make-up man, and I had a job which was just the reverse of what we usually are required to do, which is to glamorize the star. *De*glamorizing Miss Gee was some assignment. Changing her walk was part of it. One of the interviewers said that she walked 'like a young deer.' Irving Rapper had an awful time teaching her to walk heavily and clumsily."

"Like a young deer" was an exact description. From the first time I saw her in *Private Lives,* I had been fascinated by the precision and grace of her movements. To watch her walk across the room or stride across the lawn at the Berries, or run from our beach house fifty feet across the sand to plunge into the bay, was like seeing a virtuoso playing a great instrument to produce a passage of exquisite clarity and beauty. If there was ever a woman with whom a man could fall in love for her walk alone, that woman was Gertrude.

Gertrude's figure and her walk were not the only things that had to be changed to fit her for the role of Amanda. There was her voice—that clear, clipped enunciation of each syllable which made her a joy to every director who had worked with her.

Gertrude's voice could do a great many things to an audience; it could stir tears and laughter. But it could not suggest, even over a sound track, the jasmine, magnolias, and romance which motion-picture audiences associate with a belle of the Deep South.

She was told summarily that she must have a voice coach.

"I don't need one," Gertrude replied confidently. "I already have Hazel." Gertrude knew that Hazel had been born in the South. She would have Hazel go over the lines with her, and would come to the shooting of the picture drawl-perfect.

"When Hazel gets through with me," she assured Irving Rapper, "I'll be Miss Issippi from New Orleans."

He took a look at Hazel, nodded, and said, "Very well."

Having spent all of her adult life in stars' dressing rooms, Hazel was delighted to find herself promoted to what amounted to a director's chair. While Gertrude relaxed on the cot in her dressing room at the studio, Hazel took the script and read aloud Amanda's lines. The idea was that Gertrude would repeat them after her, memorizing the words and the pronunciation at once.

Unfortunately for the success of this plan, Hazel proved to be a born "ham." Carried away by the melodrama of the role, she forgot completely about waiting for Gertrude to repeat the lines after her. Worse than that was her accent. Either through over-exposure to the plays of Noel Coward, or to Gertrude and her English friends, Hazel read Amanda's lines with inflections more appropriate to Birmingham, England, than Birmingham, Alabama.

Gertrude gave up and switched to the coach who had prepared Vivien Leigh for her role as Scarlett O'Hara.

* * *

She and Hazel had settled contentedly in a charming bungalow in Beverly Hills.

"It all works out beautifully," Gertrude wrote me. "As I have a dresser provided by the studio, there was nothing for Hazel to do at Burbank, so she has taken over the house and cleans and cooks for me. Now we are only awaiting your arrival. . . ."

Her Sundays were spent in the garden, or shell-hunting on the Pacific beaches near Santa Monica. She had first become interested in the design and sculpture of seashells in Waikiki, when Nadine and Duke Kahanamoku took her on a shell-discovery tour. She needed relaxation from the arduous toil of perfecting herself in her role.

"We continue to progress into the picture," she wrote . . . "It's a dreary business trying to record a mood over and over again for the camera. You must be photographed for the close-up, for the middle shot, and for the long shot, and every time you must look and act the same. . . .

"There is much more comedy mixed with the pathos of the story than I remember on the stage. For a picture with only four actors, it is amazingly alive. The rushes are 'sensational,' according to those concerned, and the Big Boys seem very happy.

"Irving Rapper is all right. He is known to be demanding. However, he is a great director and does get results, even though his actors get ulcers. Now all is fine and everybody understands everybody. Jane and I pull his leg and josh him along. I am now more house-broken in this business. . . ."

Gertrude was beginning to relax a little, as I later learned from Merle Reeve. During one interminable wait for a lighting change, Irving Rapper was startled to hear an exuberant chorus of "Jenny" ringing out from the crew platform high above the set. His precious star was perched recklessly a few feet from the ceiling, entertaining an enthralled group of electricians. Some, who had served in the Pacific, joined her in a rowdy parody or two before Rapper could persuade Gertrude to come down—a precarious descent by the same ladder that she had climbed up.

However, despite such occasional releases, Gertrude was essentially not attuned to the Hollywood social climate.

"They all behave as though the sword of Damocles were hanging over their heads," she told me. "I have never been in such an atmosphere of fear. The top ones—the producers, directors, writers—even many of the stars—are all afraid of what the 'bosses' will do.

The studio heads fear the New York office. The Big Boys in New York are scared of the bankers. Everyone is jumpy and nervous and unsure. How actors go on working out here under these conditions for years is more than I can understand. This isn't the *Theatre*. Their name for it is right—the Industry."

This fish-out-of-water feeling was accentuated for Gertrude by the depressing atmosphere of the set on which she worked every day.

The setting for *The Glass Menagerie* is a dreary tenement flat in the slums of St. Louis. The windows overlook a narrow, grimy alley and a network of fire escapes. The furnishings are cheap, ugly, and shabby. As a final touch of realism, the technicians arranged to have steam coming out of the sewer manholes in the street, and a sour smell of cooking pervaded the set.

At no time in her life had Gertrude spent hours in such sordid surroundings. Now she lived ten to twelve hours a day surrounded by hopeless and unredeemed ugliness.

Even more undermining in its effect on her morale was the part that she played: the poverty-riddled mother of a lame, lonely daughter and a rebellious son. Gertrude always threw herself into a role unsparingly, with such emotional completeness that she invariably lost part of her own identity while playing it. Now some of the frustration and failure inherent in Tennessee Williams' tragic story was impregnating her normally blithe nature.

All this was to have a direct bearing on our personal lives together.

I have described Gertrude's flight to England and her prolonged stay there as, in part, an attempt to escape from the necessity of growing up. If her return to me represented an acceptance of this necessity—as I think it did—the fulfillment took some time. After all, psychological and emotional growth, like physical growth, does not take place overnight. Nor does it proceed symmetrically. There is always a period when, figuratively speaking, one's legs and arms are too long, one's shoulders and chest too narrow, and when one's voice wanders uncertainly up and down its register.

During the three to four months she spent in California that winter of 1949–1950, Gertrude was in such a state. I could tell from her letters and our telephone talks that she was making a persistent effort to meet her working problems at the studio wisely and impersonally:

Dear One,

I didn't mean to blub over you today on the telephone.

Please don't worry. I shall snap back and learn to take care of myself as time goes by. And at the rate we are moving at the studio I shall have several months in which to toughen up . . .

A greater threat to her peace of mind was the Hollywood pattern of syndicated gossip. Gertrude was never a gossip-gatherer. She enjoyed the drama of a good story, particularly a true one about persons she knew; but the malicious tittle-tattle, the innuendoes, the allegations of infidelity and worse, the printed cruelty which destroys a reputation in a phrase and which sacrifices generosity to cleverness, had always offended her.

Until the present, she had always been able to keep aloof from such things. She had never needed the people who deal in this form of tender. In the theatre her position enabled her to be a law unto herself.

But Hollywood, as she pointed out, was unlike the theatre. From the moment of her arrival, it had been impressed on her that she would have to woo the columnists, since her fate in pictures rested largely with them. Inevitably, she could not help being receptive to what she heard on all sides.

Both of us would have found those months a great deal easier to live through if some of the gossip current in Hollywood had not concerned me. For the first time in her life as Mrs. A, people came to Gertrude and, under the guise of friendship, repeated to her bits of alleged "news" about me. It was just the reverse of what had happened early in our marriage when the radio commentators and gossip writers had suggested that our marriage was floundering because Gertrude had been seen several times with this or that man, when we were separated by her tour or by the war.

A play producer deals in stars as a publisher deals in authors, and a shoe manufacturer in hides. The shoe manufacturer is fortunate in that not even the most imaginative gossip-monger can work up an incriminating story about his attention to the commodity on which his business is built. For the first time in my life, regret for having made play producing my livelihood mingled with annoyance when Gertrude wrote that one of Hollywood's busiest "little birds" had taken time to tell her:

> . . . how divine you are! And how —— —— fell for you and how *she* kept you both from visiting public places together. She said you never failed to arrive without bringing iced champagne!!!
>
> I said you were always most *romantic* and thoughtful. . . .

The italics, and the exclamation points which punctuated these paragraphs, spoke for the writer's mood.

No man likes feeling that he must account to his wife for small amenities he pays other women whom he meets socially or in connection with his business. My dislike for wagging tongues and for those who make a paid profession of purveying gossip mounted, while I put in a call from New York to Beverly Hills to inform Gertrude that my acquaintance with Miss —— had been limited to meeting her through Mike and Fleur Cowles and then having a drink with her at "21" to discuss the possibility of her starring in a play.

We both laughed about it. But both of us, I think, felt uneasily that this sort of thing would happen again, and many times, as the producing firm of Aldrich and Myers became busier and busier.

Now Gertrude was facing new problems of adjustment.

"Everyone out here tells me how wonderful *you* are, and how lucky *I* am . . ." she wrote.

I thought I detected a wistfulness between the lines. After all, it was a new experience for Gertrude Lawrence to be congratulated on the possession of her husband. She was accustomed to hearing all the luck ascribed to me.

This mood of self-doubt was apparent to anyone who had known Gertrude over a long period; as it was to Edmund Goulding, whom she saw several times during a visit to Palm Springs, when some scenes were being filmed without her. British like herself, Goulding too had had an extensive experience of the theatre before becoming a top-flight director of motion pictures. He understood the artist's sensitivity to a role.

"Don't let this part get you down, chum," he advised.

She confessed that it had. "It's odd that while my professional ego is puffed up because I know I'm doing a good job, my personal ego feels like a punctured tire. It's getting so that when I look in the mirror I don't see *me*. I see that dreary has-been, Amanda. She's even begun to color my thinking . . . about myself, and . . ."

"And Richard?" Goulding asked.

Gertrude nodded.

As Goulding described it to me later: They were stretched in long canvas chairs beside the Racquet Club Pool after a swim. Goulding looked at her as a casting director might consider an applicant for a part.

"I don't see anything that reminds me of that old bag in *The Glass Menagerie,*" he said. "Since Richard has never seen you made up for the part, there's no reason to believe he thinks of you except as you are—beautiful, desirable, entertaining, and valuable. Many women possess two of these qualities. Very few have three. Having all four makes you quite a packet. Yankees are shrewd traders. When they get hold of a good thing they hold on to it."

"Still, I wish people wouldn't hint things," Gertrude said.

He knew what she was referring to—a paragraph and a photograph in a gossip column which reported me at the Stork Club with Hedy Lamarr. The item had been flashed about Hollywood. Half a dozen people had repeated it to Gertrude and had watched for her reaction. This was revealed to me when she sent me a note mentioning what long hours she was working every day, with the postscript: "How nice to know you are not too busy to go out with Hedy Lamarr."

"People will always hint," Goulding told Gertrude. "It's a tribute to you that it becomes news when the man you are married to takes another woman out to dinner. Without the element which *you* inject into the situation, what is there about a producer being seen with a star at a place like the Colony or the Stork? They're safer there than in church. Stop worrying, chum. When Richard

Aldrich is noticeably not seen at any of those places, then it will be time for you to start worrying."

Edmund Goulding's common sense put at least a momentary check to Gertrude's brooding suspicion. She rang me up and asked me to send her an enlarged photograph of myself in uniform—"with all the scrambled eggs"—that she could put in her dressing room at the studio.

"Perhaps you would ask Hedy Lamarr for her photograph and let me have it to put beside yours," she suggested. "That would fix the twitterers out here."

I said that I would make the request.

Hedy came through handsomely. A colored photograph which she inscribed: "To Richard Aldrich . . . Brunettes prefer gentlemen. Hedy Lamarr," was forwarded to Gertrude, who proudly displayed it. She took a mischievous count of the comments that were *not* made when certain people caught sight of it.

* * *

I knew Gertrude's tension had been eased somewhat by her visit to Palm Springs. But I felt that it was important for us to be together as soon as possible, if only briefly; there could be no better antidote to the rumors that had upset her. So I made an all-out effort to clear my desk, and was able to get aboard a Los Angeles-bound plane a full week before Christmas.

The timing of my trip was fortunate; Gertrude's picture was drawing to a close, and there were whole days when she was not needed on the set.

That week together did a great deal for both of us. From the moment of my arrival, we found ourselves laughing—as we nearly always did—at the same things: the Santa Clauses and reindeer in neon lights, and the angels who derived more from Walt Disney than from Fra Angelico, floating over the tops of palmettos. My own experience of Hollywood was limited, and I was delighted to have Gertrude as a tourist guide.

"Everything is pushed ahead of schedule out here," she said as we drove from the airport to her bungalow. "And that goes for

Christmas, too. They start putting up the decorations weeks and weeks ahead of time. By the time Christmas comes, it will be a bore even to the children."

To anyone who loved Christmas as much as Gertrude did, and who cherished all the religious and family associations connected with its observance, the comic aspects of the Hollywood Christmas were mingled with a sense of considerable shock.

Hollywood Boulevard was renamed Santa Claus Lane, decorated with lights, silver bells, red stars, and wreaths of chemically frosted evergreens. Every evening Santa Claus rode down it in his toy-laden sleigh mounted on a decorated float, and his parade was reviewed by specially invited motion-picture stars who divided camera honors with the saint.

In Beverly Hills, many houses boasted both an indoor and an outdoor Christmas tree. Some of the latter were sprayed with red, blue, purple, and silver paint.

At one house where we were invited for cocktails, log fires blazed in several rooms while the air-conditioning worked at full blast to keep the temperature endurable.

In the midst of this synthetic Yuletide Gertrude, as usual, found the shining exception: columnist Frank Scully's home high above the Hollywood hills. Here at Bedside Manor, overflowing with babies, dogs, and stacks of photos that recalled Frank's early days as the *Variety* roving correspondent in Europe, we enjoyed a real Christmas Eve. It was here, too, that Gertrude and I constituted the entire adult audience at a special reading by Charles Laughton given for the numerous Scully children. They—and we—listened raptly as he read passages from the Bible, Shakespeare, and Dickens. It was only when their eager faces left no doubt of their response that Laughton decided to launch his since-celebrated tour and TV program.

* * *

I returned to New York immediately after the New Year, having arranged to join Gertrude in Florida as soon as the studio released her. This was in the middle of January. She took a plane to Tampa, where I met her at the airport.

She came down the steps of the plane, carrying one of those canvas bassinets the airplane companies furnish to transport infants. It held something completely swaddled in a pale blue afghan.

"What is *that?*" I demanded before I kissed her.

She laid a finger to her lips. "Sssh! darling."

Gertrude glanced around warily. Seeing that no one was watching, she gently pulled down a corner of the blanket—exposing a plant with glossy leaves. She explained that this was a small orange tree on which she had grafted other citrus fruits—all California varieties. It had occurred to her that it would be interesting to experiment, adding Florida specimens to the collection, to see what such a union would bring forth.

"But why the blanket?" I asked. "There's no frost here."

"It's not the climate I'm afraid of," she replied. "Don't you remember the time I arrived at LaGuardia Airport with some English plants for the garden? I was detained a long time. It even got out that Gertrude Lawrence was suspected of smuggling."

I pointed out that there was no customs inspection for travel *within* the United States.

"But this is Florida," she rebuked me. "And I'm coming from California. How do you know what regulations they have? I'm taking no chances."

Passing a bored policeman in the doorway, she gazed fondly down at the bundle in the basket and then up at me. "Darling," she said sweetly. "Everyone says he's the image of you . . ."

* * *

We drove to Naples, where we were to stay with the Julius Fleischmanns. Our entertainment, by Gertrude's wish, was simple and unexacting. There were hours when she sunbathed on the sand in a sheltered spot. She took me fishing and shell-hunting. We confined our fishing to the pier—I having shown myself no sailor. As an officer in the Naval Reserve, my acute susceptibility to seasickness brought jeers until Gertrude defended me with the reminder: "Lord Nelson was seasick, too." Out of consideration for me she gave up going out on the Gulf while I was there, though this was a sport she greatly enjoyed.

It was a perfect holiday, made the more so by our sending for Dick to join us for his short vacation after the mid-year examinations at the University of Virginia, where he was a student.

Leaving Gertrude to bask longer in the sunshine she loved, I returned to New York, where the problems of a busy season demanded my attention.

I had made two long trips—one to California and one to Florida—both for the express purpose of spending some little time with Gertrude. I remained, as always, in constant communication with her. It therefore did not occur to me that my return from Florida without her would be taken in some quarters as an indication that Gertrude and I were not getting on.

Although our marriage was on as even a keel as ever, we had spent no time together in New York for two years. Now that no necessity of career held Gertrude away, whenever I was seen around town with this or that star with whom I had business dealings, eyebrows were raised. There were pointed questions or very careful avoidance of references to her. All this betokened that rumors were flying, and flying fast.

As I see it now, perhaps I should have been more sensitive to the atmosphere around me. I remember in particular one incident when, feeling lonely, I rang Gertrude and asked when she thought she would come north.

"Do you really need me, Richard?" she asked.

I said I missed her and wanted her back home.

"I'm beginning to feel much more rested," she said. "If you can do without me a little while longer, maybe I ought to stay on."

I thought of the miserable February to which Gertrude would be returning. I knew that I had really very little free time to devote to her, since we were about to open Shaw's *The Devil's Disciple*. Instead of coaxing her, as perhaps she wished to be coaxed, I encouraged her to stay in the sun.

There are times when consideration for one you love can be interpreted as indifference. It is clear that, logically, my consideration for Gertrude had put me in the position of saying that I could "do without" her—a highly unflattering situation for her.

As far as I knew, Gertrude had heard none of the tittle-tattle about us. Therefore I was totally unprepared for the letter which reached me on Valentine's Day, and which read:

Naples, Florida

Dearest,

I guess you will have your old lady back pretty soon after all, and I shall be very happy to go around the town with you, so there! But I do wish "little birds" wouldn't write hints to me that have horrid interpretations about you.

Please tell me if you aren't happy with me—or if you are bothered by trying to be in more than one pair of arms! I couldn't blame you—darling—it would be my fault—I want you to be happy, but my work has always made a mess of my personal life, so I could face it again I guess & go on my way.

Don't for God's sake stay with me because of habit, or because of the fear of hurting me. Be in love, be free, but *please* be truthful for both our sakes.

Your own
"Mrs. A"

Chapter Eighteen

WHEN MY EYE came to the end of that letter, my hand went out toward the telephone. I put in a call to Gertrude at Naples. In a voice which I tried to keep quiet and steady, I said I was taking the plane south that afternoon. She could expect me that evening.

"But, Richard, what about your play? Haven't you a lot to do?"

"There's nothing in my life so important as our being together," I said. "If you doubt that, even for an instant, I must come down at once and make it clear."

The connection was excellent. I heard her quick intake of breath. "Richard, you're not saying that just to make me feel happy?"

"Of course not. I want to be happy myself. But I can't be, unless you are. So I'll be on the evening plane."

"No, darling," she said quickly. "I'll fly to you. It's my place to do it. And it's what I want. You never wanted to be a star's husband. And right now, what *I* want more than anything else in the world is to be Mrs. Richard Stoddard Aldrich. *Your* Mrs. A . . ."

* * *

Although *The Glass Menagerie* was not to be released until the following autumn, glowing reports of Gertrude's performance in it were current in Hollywood before she left the West Coast.

While she was still in Florida, Joseph Mankiewicz had approached her agents to secure her for the lead in his forthcoming picture *All About Eve.* On her return to New York she discussed the proposal with Fanny and David Holtzmann. I refused point blank to take part in the discussion. The script, which I read at Gertrude's earnest request, gave promise of becoming one of the best pictures of the year; the starring role would give an actress plenty of opportunity to qualify for an Oscar. Not least of the inducements of *All About Eve* was the salary which the studio was prepared to pay to get Gertrude.

"I'm turning it down," she informed me.

"Are you sure that's wise?"

"I'm sure it's very foolish—financially speaking. And it won't help my career. But I told you—I want to be Mrs. A. *Now* will you believe me?"

I hastened to assure her that I did. In the face of Gertrude's behavior since her return from Florida, only a fool could have believed otherwise. She had plunged into the role of Mrs. A with an intensity that left me breathless. No man I knew was so lovingly looked after in all matters of comfort, health, and companionship. It was even better than during our honeymoon winter on Long Island, when she had tried to turn me into a country squire—or during my first early months in the Navy, when she was grooming me for a hero's glorious death.

She was standing beside my bed, folding the silk bedspread, which she had removed.

"You must nap, darling," she said briskly, "if you are going with me to Maurice Evans' party tonight after the play. When will you learn that sitting around yawning over the paper when you come home from the office does you no good? Two hours' sleep before you dress for dinner will carry you through a long evening as fresh as a daisy."

I took off my coat. Before I could drape it over the back of a chair, Gertrude had taken it from me and was hanging it neatly on the proper hanger.

I watched her cross the room, slim and alluring as ever—yet crisply efficient.

"I wouldn't dare let Dick Myers or Don Oenslager or any of my other friends know how well I'm taken care of," I said. "Their wives would gang up on you . . . But I'm onto your game. You're just working to make me realize how much I'll miss you when you go into your next play."

She turned quickly. "Who said anything about a play?"

"No one. But I've noticed quite a flurry of calls to and from the Holtzmann office the past few days. You've been closeted with them for several hours every day. Something is *up*, Mrs. A."

I was in bed and Gertrude was bending over me, pulling and smoothing the covers about my shoulders. She could never resist an opportunity to play nurse.

"Always Right Aldrich," she said lightly. "Something *is* up. Something big and very wonderful. I can't tell you yet. It's still too uncertain. But Fanny is working on it and we'll know soon, and then I can tell you everything."

"Including when I am going to lose my Mrs. A?"

She leaned over and kissed me quickly. "You'll never lose her for long again, darling. I'm resolved on that. Even if everything turns out as I hope it will, there can't be a play till next year. For the first time you and I will have *a whole year* to ourselves without my career getting in our way."

The "something big and very wonderful" was the plan for *The King and I.* Gertrude's interest in the story of Mrs. Anna Leonowens, the English governess at the Court of Siam, began when she and my mother went to see the film *Anna and the King of Siam,* in which Irene Dunne and Rex Harrison starred. They were both extremely impressed by it. Mother had been fascinated by the adventure of the Englishwoman in Bangkok ever since, as a young girl, she first encountered it in the pages of Mrs. Leonowens' original story, *The English Governess at the Siamese Court.*

As the film unfolded, Gertrude found herself sharing Mother's enthusiasm. She was deeply intrigued by the unusual personal story of the governess and the king, the picturesque background, and the clash in attitudes between East and West—frequently comic, yet with overtones of sadness. It occurred to her then, watching the motion picture, that herein lay rich possibilities for a beautiful musical play.

While Gertrude was in Hollywood, a copy of the book by Margaret Landon from which the motion picture was made, came into her hands. Reading the story, she was still more impressed by its values, and her interest in playing the role of Mrs. Anna was revived. When she refused the offer to star in *All About Eve* she asked Fanny to look into the possibility of securing for her the right to have a musical made from *Anna and the King of Siam.* Gertrude was eager to do a musical; she had not appeared in one since *Lady in the Dark* closed six years before, in 1943.

While awaiting word concerning production rights, Gertrude and Fanny had made tentative plans for the play. They had selected a composer, an exceedingly well-known one who had provided the score for one of Gertrude's big London hits. Anton Dolin was to supervise the choreography, bringing over Frederick Ashton of the Sadler's Wells Ballet from London for the dances.

When word arrived that Gertrude could obtain the production rights to *Anna and the King of Siam,* provided she would star in the play, she triumphantly laid the whole plan before me, stressing the preparations already made for the songs and dances.

"So you see," she concluded, "we have just about everything but a producer. And my choice of a producer is . . . you."

Though Gertrude and I had been married nearly eleven years, I was still unprepared for her amazing magic in pulling rabbits out of a silk hat.

"We can't lose, darling," Gertrude went on. "Everyone today is interested in the Far East. Very soon people will be flying to Siam and India as nonchalantly as they fly now to France and Italy. The setting of the story is perfect. And the theme—the conflict and the possible sympathy between East and West—is right out of today's headlines. Best of all for me, the real Mrs. Anna was an Englishwoman. I tell you, we can't lose."

It was a great temptation to say I would produce the play, either with Dick Myers or alone—perhaps the greatest temptation that has come to me in my career in the theatre. The story was sound, beautiful, and moving. With Gertrude in it, it had all the elements of a great hit. It was a potential bonanza to anyone who presented it.

Yet I knew I must not be the producer. Our relationship as husband and wife had survived many vicissitudes; it had confounded the skeptics by growing stronger through the years. Others might consider it quixotic of me, or just plain stupid, to make a considerable financial sacrifice in order to maintain the separateness of my life and Gertrude's in the theatre; but I felt the principle had served me well for eleven years, and I chose to abide by it.

Gertrude was frankly disappointed. My decision meant her original plans might have to be drastically revised. Yet she recognized the essential soundness of my argument. "If you *have* to say no, darling, I couldn't ask it to be for a better reason."

We discussed the merits of several Broadway producers. When we came to Rodgers and Hammerstein, Gertrude said she was favorably disposed, for two reasons: "First, they have Morrie Jacobs as general manager. He was my manager in *Lady in the Dark* and we were happy and successful. Then, R and H keep their shows on Broadway for years. I would like that. I want to stay put in a play, in New York; so while I'm working I can go on living here at home with you, and be Mrs. A."

On this reasoning, early in 1950 Gertrude took the rights she had acquired to Rodgers and Hammerstein, who contracted to write, compose and produce the musical which became *The King and I*. To permit preparation, the production was not scheduled until the following year—1951. Meanwhile Gertrude gave her undivided attention to getting the most out of her well-earned year off.

* * *

The supper party at Maurice Evans' Tenth Street house had pleasant consequences for the Aldrich household. After coffee, Maurice brought in his West Highland terrier, Bridget, and her litter. The fat white puppies, balancing unevenly on their short legs, stumbled and tumbled about, apparently delighted to have an appreciative audience. Only one of them rejected the troupe and its act. He trotted purposefully across the floor to Gertrude and, after sniffing her approvingly, lay down as close as possible to her foot and rested his chin on it.

Since Mackie's death, Gertrude had refused to have another dog. "Another dog means another heartbreak," she would say. And though her eyes always followed wistfully any rough-coated little white terrier she passed in the street, she never expressed a wish to own one. In fact she often remarked that there were no West Highlanders bred in the United States equal to those of Mackie's aristocratic strain.

But now, I recognized, she was wavering. The small white-haired ball curled against her instep was shattering her aloofness. He had chosen her out of all the guests and had deserted his dam and his brothers and sisters for her. It was a compliment she was unable to resist.

His name, already registered, was Angus of Casterbridge, and he gave promise of being a champion.

I took Maurice aside and asked if he would sell me the puppy; I wanted it as a birthday present for Gertrude. He said he would. I said nothing about it to Gertrude that night because I had to be sure she wanted the dog; that the infatuation was not a passing one. She spoke of Angus so wistfully the next day that I told her of my tentative offer to Maurice. "He is my birthday present to you if you want him."

Her eager response left no doubt I had better clinch the deal. By Gertrude's birth date, July Fourth, when we would be at The Berries, Angus would be old enough to move in with us. Gertrude began marking the calendar. It was a long time to July by her count and, as we were going to the Cape early in June, why, she demanded, put off the acquisition of Angus so long?

"Couldn't I have an advance birthday present, darling?"

Angus went up to The Berries with us and immediately approved of what he found there. Gertrude reported to Maurice Evans:

Just a note to give you news of Angus. He is a character. Full of fun, affection and *such good manners.*

He never leaves my side . . . eats well, sleeps right through the night—paper on waking—"big affairs" immediately outside with the maid. Then orange juice and cereal.

We walk for miles, we sleep, we hide *everything.* He is such a grand house dog. We do *not* chase the birds, and we don't mind being deticked at the end of each day.

In fact, we are a great success. Thank you, Mister Evans.

I brush him often and he is in good health and excellent spirits . . .

Richard is wild about Angus, but Angus only really loves me.

All the best to you,

Gertrude

Undoubtedly, Angus was the most successful present I ever gave Gertrude. I never had her talent for thinking of and finding the uniquely appropriate gift. At Christmas and at the boys' birthdays, her ingenious suggestions usually left me speechless until I could summon my forces and protest that such lavish generosity would spoil them. Gertrude would counter that I was being a puritanical parent, a carbon copy of my own father, who had believed that more harm was done to the young by leniency than by sternness.

Gertrude believed that people—especially young people and very old ones—should have whatever would make them happy. One of our typical wrangles on this point involved Dick and the car.

When Gertrude was playing *Pygmalion* in Baltimore, she wired young Richard at college in Charlottesville, Virginia, inviting him and as many of his friends as he wished, to be her guests at the play on Friday and to spend the week-end with her at the hotel. Dick declined regretfully, explaining that, although the distance was not excessive, the connections were so poor as to make the trip impractical.

Gertrude's reaction to this was to suggest to me that Dick should have a car of his own. I replied that I did not approve of a college freshman having a car; nor, I was sure, would the dean. She pooh-poohed this as an example of New England stinginess. Of course college boys needed cars and should have them. Furthermore, she pointed out triumphantly, I would not have to buy a new car for Dick; there was that extra car standing idle in the garage at the Cape.

The altercation over Dick and the car went on for months until I finally gave in. But even my eventual retreat on this point did not wholly satisfy Gertrude. The delay caused by my natural caution in giving had destroyed the opportunity to make the large, magnificent gesture which she so dearly loved.

The same sort of argument had arisen when we were in Beverly Hills at Christmas and we discussed what we should give the boys. Gertrude suggested that, since they were in New York, we should make them a present of several charge accounts: at supper clubs, at a florist, and at Carey's, where they could hire chauffeur-driven cars.

At first, I put my foot down hard. But I recognized some merit in the idea if it were limited, so I agreed to a compromise; we would pay the bill for one gala evening for each boy.

When Dick joined us in Florida we told him of his present. At the same time I wrote to David, who was a sophomore at Harvard.

Dick heartily approved the idea. When he came to town for spring vacation, he dropped into my office. I asked him whether he was set for his big evening.

"I get to New York so infrequently that all the girls I know are probably dated up—it's going to be rough getting the right girl on such short notice."

"What sort of girl is the 'right girl'?" I asked.

"Oh, somebody attractive and lots of fun. Somebody like Gertrude."

"There's only one like Gertrude," I replied. "How would you like to take her out?"

Dick looked at me incredulously. "Really, Dad?"

"As a matter of fact, I have to go to Washington for a couple of days and Gertrude will be alone. You're welcome to ask her for Friday evening—if you care to."

"Would I!" he exclaimed delightfully. His face clouded over. "Would you give me a few tips, Dad?"

"Like what?"

"Well," he began hesitantly, "I'm okay on most things that Gertrude would like—but how do you order champagne?"

I told him what little I know on the subject.

He asked one other favor: I was not to let Gertrude know he had come to me for advice. I agreed readily.

Actually, she did not tell me of her "date" for Friday.

When I returned from Washington on Saturday afternoon, I found that Dick had just arrived to have tea with Gertrude.

"Where were you last night?" I asked her sharply. "I tried to telephone you."

"Out," she said with an air of great mystery. "With a tall, handsome young man." She looked meaningfully at Dick, who kept a straight face.

"Hm," I grumbled. "I tried you three times and there was no answer. Who was it? Some long-winded millionaire?"

Gertrude looked offended.

"It was someone very nice," she said.

"I can imagine!" I remarked testily. Dick was still controlling his smile but with difficulty.

Gertrude gave up trying to tease me. "If you must know, Richard Aldrich," Gertrude replied haughtily, "Richard took me out. And I had a lovely time. Champagne and everything."

I mumbled a reluctant apology to Gertrude. "But, Dick," I said sternly, "the next time you take out *my* wife without my permission, I'll horsewhip you."

* * *

The very thought of a picnic—of packing sandwiches into a basket to eat out in some cold damp spot among the caterpillars and ants—was enough to make Gertrude glow with excitement.

During her few weeks at Dennis in 1949, I had heard her divulging this enthusiasm to Dorothy Wheelock, the drama editor of *Harper's Bazaar,* who was vacationing on the Cape.

"That would make a wonderful story for us," Dorothy said. "We could run it in the July issue next year. And we could illustrate it with photographs of you picnicking, modeled after the famous paintings of Renoir and Manet. How would you like that?"

Gertrude was delighted by the notion; and I, as I found out later, must have agreed to take part.

Nothing more was said on the matter until the following April. It was a raw morning and unseasonably cold. A damp, blustery wind chilled the streets of New York. As I was about to leave for the office, Gertrude said blithely:

"Remember to come home at noon, darling. We're going on the picnic."

"Picnic?" I protested. "On a day like this? What picnic?"

Gertrude reminded me of the project and said it had been entered several times on our social calendar and postponed.

"But why today?" I asked. "We can't possibly picnic in weather like this!"

"Because this is our last chance to make the deadline for the July issue," Gertrude said firmly. "I've made all the arrangements with Dorothy Wheelock."

Gertrude had invited Pam to join the party, bringing paints and sketch book for artistic atmosphere. Bea Lillie had agreed to be photographed at an easel. Bea was bringing along Robert Fleming, then appearing in *The Cocktail Party*.

"That adds up to five cases of pneumonia," I commented. "Tell Dorothy to postpone the *al fresco* to next August."

Gertrude insisted that further postponement was impossible. Bea was not always available. There would be the usual rainy days of April. And besides, there was the deadline and we could not let Dorothy Wheelock down.

Writing about it now, it seems incredible that I should have yielded to Gertrude's persuasion and taken part in anything so fantastic as that out-of-season picnic. But I did. Before me, as I write, is the photograph to prove it. It is a most skilfully taken picture. The photographer has managed to create an illusion of early spring. The five persons basking in the filtered sunlight of the little glade seem peaceful and content. You would say that none of us had a self-conscious thought, that nothing from the outside world intruded on our artistic solitude. Whereas the truth is . . .

I came home at noon to find Gertrude and Helen Mahoney packing the picnic kit with sandwiches and delicacies they had made.

"Where are we going?"

Gertrude was vague about this. "Westchester, Connecticut, Jones Beach—wherever the photographer suggests."

"That's out," I declared. "I refuse to leave Manhattan Island. Why drive fifty miles to catch our deaths? We can do it just as easily ten blocks away in Central Park!"

On the arrival of Karen Radkai, the photographer who was assigned to the story, I explained my position forcefully. Miss Radkai, dressed in slacks and carrying an inconspicuous camera so as to look like another picnicker, was amenable. She agreed to my suggestion about Central Park. "But I can't use the lower end of the park," she said. "It's too familiar and the skyline is unavoidable. However, there's a hilly, wooded section up near Harlem that will photograph like the forest primeval."

We set out, chilled even in our warm coats, in a safari of two cars, to search for a location. We found one in a wooded area off a park drive near the Harlem boat lake. There, under the direction of Dorothy and Miss Radkai, we began to re-create Edouard Manet.

From *Harper's Bazaar* came a basket of photographic delicacies, including impressive bottles of Scotch and champagne. An easel was set up for Bea Lillie. Gertrude, like the others, took off her coat; then, despite my dire predictions of a cold, she stepped out of her covering skirt to pose in white shorts. Marveling at the patience and fortitude of the others, all of whom were actors, I still kept on my pullover to cut some of the chill. A canvas deck chair was produced for me, and I tried to appear relaxed in it, although, unlike my picnic partners, I fretted at every moment's delay. If this was an example of what performers had to go through at rehearsal—and I knew that essentially it was—I was fortunate to be a producer and not an actor.

At this point I discovered we were attracting an audience. The younger set from Harlem had found us. They were creeping through the bushes. They were clinging to every available branch that gave them a vantage point, literally hanging from the trees. In vain did Dorothy plead with them to stay out of view of the camera. The longer we postponed the picture, the greater was the crowd which gathered around to "watch the funny people having a picnic."

We were finally posed satisfactorily, when a police patrol car hove into view.

"Hey, what's going on here?" the driver shouted from his seat in the car.

"It's just a picnic, officer," Dorothy replied.

"Picnic, is it?" the policeman snorted. "On a day like this?"

He motioned to his partner, and the two of them got out of the car. They strode over to our summer-clad party.

"But it *is* a picnic, officer," Gertrude said in her most blandishing tone. "Not a real one, of course. We're taking pictures of it for *Harper's Bazaar.*" She introduced Karen Radkai, who showed a Park Department permit.

The policemen were momentarily appeased—until they saw the wine and spirits.

"Don't you know that's against the law?" One of them yanked out a summons book from his back pocket.

Again Gertrude drew upon her charm. "But we're not *drinking* anything, officer. That's just for the photographs. The moment we finish, we want you to donate all those bottles—on our behalf—to the Patrolmen's Benevolent Association. For your next party."

The guardians of the law looked at each other, hesitating. Gertrude smiled her most winning smile. "And you *will* help us keep the kids out of the picture, won't you?"

As for us, we ate lunch in a small, not overly elegant, but very warm restaurant.

* * *

All in all, in that spring of 1950, Gertrude was finding life as Mrs. A full of a great number of things.

Foremost of these was the musical tent-theatre—a new form of summer theatrical entertainment which had developed recently out of the theatre-in-the-round idea. Staged in the center ring of a large circus tent, the musical tent-theatre presents popular musical comedies and old operettas to an audience seated around the arena. There was a great deal of interest in the idea that spring, and I had been toying with the notion of opening such a theatre at Hyannis on Cape Cod.

However, being very busy, I had done nothing positive about getting it started. I was also held back by the suspicion that I might merely be competing with my own summer operations on the Cape at Dennis and Falmouth. Some of my associates agreed with me; others were equally insistent that this kind of production would draw an entirely different audience. As yet, I had not actually seen a music circus performance myself.

I kept putting the matter off until one morning an advertisement appeared in *Variety,* announcing the sale in Florida of a tent and one thousand chairs from the Miami Musical Tent, which was about to close its season. If I wanted to take advantage of the offer, I could no longer postpone a decision. I could not, however, spare the time to fly down to Miami to take in the performance and inspect the property.

"It's a big decision," I told Gertrude. "I'd better not think of opening until next year."

Gertrude pondered a moment. "Couldn't I help, Richard?"

I told her that of course I trusted her judgment, especially in matters of showmanship. "But it would mean a frantic trip to Miami, which I'm sure you don't want to make."

"You can be wrong sometimes, darling," she replied.

We made reservations which would enable Gertrude to arrive in Miami in time to see the closing performance. Before I put her on the plane, I emphasized to Gertrude that the purchase of the tent and seating was the biggest single investment involved in setting up such a venture. I would buy or not, depending on her report of the show.

Gertrude came out of the performance enthusiastic. "The whole atmosphere," she told me, "is different from the playhouses. It's colorful and gay. The audience comes in a carnival spirit, wanting to have fun. They're not in a critical mood. They'll accept fresh young talent at the tent, where they would demand stars in the playhouse."

On Gertrude's say-so, I bought the tent and launched this new enterprise.

But that was only the beginning of her participation. Together we selected a site in Hyannis, on the Cape, on which to raise our big top. The next problem was to set up the dressing rooms, box office, and other facilities which would be required before we could open our season.

Knowing how busy I was in town, Gertrude proposed that she go up to the Cape and help round up the necessary building materials. I agreed to this, provided one of the young men from my office went along with her to drive the station wagon and assist her generally, and (though I left this unsaid to her) to control any sudden urge she might feel to buy lavishly and without regard to price.

Gertrude reported to me daily by telephone. The tent had arrived from Miami. It was in good condition, but since it had faded slightly in the hot Florida sun, it looked very drab. "However, darling, it will look very well if we paint it white with peppermint pink stripes," she said.

"No painting," I adjured her.

"But it's so ugly like this. Why can't it look gay, like the circus scene in *Lady in the Dark?*"

I reminded her that a painted tent could not be fireproofed. And a tent fire could be a catastrophe. Faced with this reality, Gertrude suppressed her artistic urge—at least temporarily.

Estimates for the construction of the dressing rooms and other buildings on the lot ran high. Gertrude suggested that we try to find some old buildings and move them to our lot. She scoured the countryside until she acquired the needed structures, which were set up around the tent according to her working plan.

I flew up to Hyannis to inspect the arrangements, and remained to marvel at my wife's efficiency. I found that during her visit to Miami she had observed carefully the physical layout necessary to stage musicals in the round with an orchestra, chorus, and dancers. This was very different from what was required in the playhouses.

Following her usual fashion, she had made careful lists of what was needed, including several innovations of her own for increasing the comfort and convenience of the cast.

The praise I gave her acted like a stimulant. A few days after I returned to New York I received a call from the worried young man I had sent to act as manager. He said that Mrs. Aldrich had called in a nurseryman and was giving him the order to landscape the grounds around the main tent.

"She wants to have roses climbing up on the trellises to hide the tent because you won't let her paint it red and white," he complained. "And she wants lawns, not sand. And some flowering trees and shubbery. It will run into thousands."

I headed back for the Cape. There I explained to Gertrude as tactfully as I could that landscaping, no matter how attractive or smart, would destroy the circus atmosphere, which evidently was one of the features that attracted the audience. "It has to be rough and ready. Cheerful but not too frou-frou."

Thwarted again in her plans for beautifying the circus, Gertrude retreated reluctantly.

"Richard, I can't paint the tent. I can't landscape the grounds. Now, what sensible male objection can you find to my decorating the women's rest rooms?"

"None whatsoever," I assured her.

"At last I've found my place," she exclaimed puckishly. "Our tent theatre is going to have the gayest, most colorful, and most chic powder rooms on the whole Cape!"

* * *

One morning in that spring of Gertrude's "sabbatical" year, I had a phone call from Arthur Brooks Harlow, one-time Harvard football hero and secretary of the class of 1925. Our class, he informed me, would be celebrating its twenty-fifth anniversary with a grand reunion in June.

I'm afraid I answered with a vague "Uh-huh," or words to that effect.

Cheerily disregarding my evident lack of fervor, Brooks said the reunion was to be launched at a series of cocktail parties in New York, where the necessary committees would be formed, and would Gertrude and I give the first one?

I was so emphatic in my refusal that, as I put down the phone, Gertrude looked up from her mail and demanded: "Darling, what was *that* about?"

I explained, adding that reunions were not "my cup of tea." Such classmates as I had kept up with since college days I thought of as friends—not as Harvard alumni. I had an inborn shrinking from the synthetic geniality and forced back-slapping of large banquets and business luncheons.

"I think you're making a mistake, Richard," Gertrude said with a gravity that surprised me. "These groups of men are very constructive. I've seen them when I've been on tour, in practically all your big cities. And I've been at a couple of their lunches. They don't just *talk*—they get things done."

I said the Harvard class reunion wasn't quite the same thing as the Kiwanis and Rotary Club groups to which she referred. Those were civic and business organizations; a reunion was purely sentimental.

"Well?" she demanded. "Don't you have any feeling at all for Harvard?"

I admitted the name evoked pleasant memories, but these were highly personal. "They couldn't be refreshed by sitting down to filet mignon with men I would hardly recognize."

Gertrude shook her head. "I don't know, Richard. If *I* had ever been lucky enough to go to a fine old school, I'd be devoted to it. I'd help, if called upon."

I threw her a sour sidelong glance. "I believe you *want* me to give that cocktail party."

"I do. And go to the reunion, too. For years I've been hearing about all the fun American girls have at college." Gertrude was on her feet now, excited, as she always was at the prospect of catching up on something she felt she had missed.

Of course we gave the cocktail party. Gertrude was at her most enchanting—although distinctly in the role of a housewife. As Mrs. Aldrich she was appointed a member of the ladies' entertainment committee, which was headed by Gardner Cowles' wife, Fleur, and which had Mrs. Stanley Marcus as vice-chairman. Another member of the committee was John Lodge's wife, Francesca.

Gertrude and Francesca had known each other since the *Charlot's Revue* days, when Gertrude was appearing in New York and Francesca—then Francesca Braggiotti—opened the first school of modern dancing in Boston. This was in the same year John Lodge and I were graduated from Harvard. Later, as Navy wives, Gertrude and Francesca had become warm friends.

The chief job of the wives' entertainment committee was to work up a comedy sketch with music, to be presented after the traditional ladies' dinner at the Hotel Somerset, and then repeated when the men, after their class banquet, joined the ladies in the Somerset Ballroom for the gala dance which ended the three-day celebration.

In the weeks before we left for the Cape at the end of May, Gertrude worked with the committee when not occupied with preparing for the Hyannis musical tent. She refused to discuss the comedy sketch except to say that Parke Cummings had written it for the ladies and Ruby Newman, whose orchestra was to play for the ball, had arranged the music. Other than that, I could learn nothing; Gertrude had gleefully discarded her professional standing and was reveling in her new status as a member of an amateur theatrical group. By the time we went up to Cambridge, she was as full of wifely excitement, as bubbly with mysterious hints as to the devastating contents of the sketch, as the most theatrically uninitiated of suburban matrons.

Watching Gertrude during our three days in the Harvard Yard, I wondered more than once what some of her super-sophisticated international friends would make of this transition from the glamorous actress to the self-effacing wife. Throughout our stay at Harvard, Gertrude was nothing more than the personable wife of a member of the class. She was so retiring that I am sure the majority of those attending the reunion had no idea who she was in her own right; that is, until the last night, when the girls presented their skit in the ballroom as prelude to the ball.

The printed program carried on its cover a photograph of Mrs.

Richard Stoddard Aldrich, star of *Charlot's Revue,* 1925. The six performers in *There's Nothing Like a Guy* were billed as:

Miss Girl Meets Boyden	1925
Miss Fishing Lodge	1925
Miss Marcus Twins	1925
Miss G.L.Q. Aldrich	1925
Miss Hot Cowles	1925
Miss Nixon Dixon	1925

What the lyrics lacked in sophistication was more than balanced, for that audience, by the personal allusions to the husbands of the performers. This sort of buffoonery appealed strongly to Gertrude. When she danced up to the mike, she sang so directly to me I felt my ears redden:

"Now Pinza may sing better than the
husband that I picked,
And frankly, as a playwright, Noel Coward's
got him licked.
Fonda's profile is better, and Fred Astaire's
more spry,
But I wouldn't swap—for my Harvard Guy.
The theatre life is often pandemonium
But I wouldn't lose that man of mine for
fifty million mountains of plutonium . . ."

"Darling, isn't it fun!" she cried when I claimed her for the first dance. Judging by the light in her eyes and the lightness of her step, she might have been a teenager at her first prom.

Halfway through the ball, Gertrude made it a point to go up to Ruby Newman, the orchestra leader, to thank him and his musicians. Ruby begged her to sing a few numbers. Gertrude looked at me inquiringly. I nodded; she stepped to the mike and, as the orchestra swung into "Jenny," Gertrude began to sing.

At the first sound of her voice—tremulous, haunting, inimitable—heads began to turn. Soon a circle of eager spectators had formed around soloist and orchestra.

Not an actress in the world could have resisted the demand in their faces. Before my eyes, Mrs. A changed to Eliza Elliot, the fabulous career girl of *Lady in the Dark*. Gertrude gave them "Jenny" as she had given it to that startled first night audience in Boston years before, with a mischievous audacity and the finest bumps ever produced at Harvard since its founding in 1636.

After that she couldn't beg off. For one solid hour the crowd called for her most popular recent songs, for old numbers she had done years ago, and for numbers whose lyrics she did not know.

Brooks Harlow, whose spectacular touchdown runs nearly three decades before had placed him in the ranks of Harvard's athletic immortals, stood beside me, aglow with admiration.

"Dick," he said, "she's great. She deserves the best. . . . The class must do something to show its appreciation. How d'you think she'd like it if we gave her the Harvard cheer?"

Before I could reply, Brooks rushed forward to stand beside Gertrude as she finished her song, and raised his right hand for silence.

"Ladies and gentlemen," he began, "Mrs. Aldrich has given us a thrill here tonight that we'll all remember a long, long time. I propose we try to do the same for her—by giving her a real, straight-from-the-heart Harvard cheer!"

There was a roar of applause. Then Brooks led the crowd in that ancient rallying cry, so rich in its association with last-minute football rallies, stirring crew-race finishes, and similar climactic moments in Harvard's athletic history: "H-A-R-V-A-R-D! H-A-R-V-A-R-D! H-A-R-V-A-R-D! HAR—VARD!"

As the long drawn-out, quivering cheer rang up to the rafters, staid business men cast off the accumulated dignity of years and shouted their affection; a feeling of exultation and good fellowship ran through the entire crowd. It was a thrilling and unforgettable moment. Never, in the memory of anyone present, had that tribute been paid to someone in the theatre; and certainly never to a woman.

I kept my eyes on Gertrude, alone and indescribably humble. I saw her sway momentarily at the microphone. Her lips trembled, and she put out a hand to steady herself.

I realized she was on the point of collapse. The intensive activ-

Karen Radkai

Picnic in Central Park—after Renoir. At the left: Beatrice Lillie and Robert Fleming. At the right: Pamela, Gertrude, and myself.

Fay Foto Service

Harvard reunion, June, 1950—David, Gertrude, Dick, Jr., and myself.

Hyannis, June, 1950—time out for a drink of water with some friends during the raising of the Melody Tent.

ity, topped off by her hour of solo singing and now the excitement of the crowd's ovation, had been too much for her.

I bolted toward Gertrude, and was soon at her side. I put my arm firmly around her. With my free hand, I made a quick, frantic signal to Ruby Newman to start playing something—something, I hoped he would understand, that would break the feverish mood and restore a quieter atmosphere.

Ruby did not disappoint me. His baton came down and the orchestra swung into a spirited rendition of the waltz "Two Hearts in Three-Quarter Time."

I led Gertrude away from the microphone and onto the dance floor.

At this point something peculiar happened. Perhaps the exhilaration of Gertrude's success was responsible; or maybe it was the urgent desire to provide her with a physical release from her tension. At any rate, I suddenly whirled her around sweepingly and in a moment the two of us were spinning across the floor.

"Mind your step," she whispered. "We're alone."

I looked around.

We were. Alone on the floor, whirling to the music like an exhibition dance team, watched by nearly a thousand spectators.

And I did not mind. Although I have never been considered more than a passable dancer, I felt myself gliding along easily, smoothly, borne without effort on an everflowing tide of rhythm.

Was it a miracle or an illusion? To this day, I do not know. But miracle or illusion, it was created by Gertrude on that strange and wonderful night.

Our exhibition dance was brought back vividly to me, as it was to others who were present at our reunion ball, by the "Shall We Dance" number which was the high spot of the second act of *The King and I.* When the King seizes Mrs. Anna in his arms and waltzes her away and about the stage, it is as though that incident at the reunion ball were transferred to another country and another era. I had not seen the rehearsals; therefore when I came up on a Saturday from Washington to see the tryout of the play in New Haven, the "Shall We Dance" number was a startling surprise.

"What did it remind you of?" Gertrude asked when I went backstage after the performance. I told her.

"Of course, darling. I never once do it without closing my eyes and reliving our dance at the reunion."

* * *

Gertrude's Harvard triumph was crowned the following winter when the Hasty Pudding Club chose her as "The Woman of the Year." As vice-president of the club, my son David had invited Gertrude to the annual show, always an event of the late fall. At David's request, Gertrude gave the producers and actors valuable help at the final rehearsals. In recognition of this, the club president, after the final curtain call, stepped to the front of the stage and informed the audience of Gertrude's contribution. He asked her to join the cast on the stage and take the bow. Later, Gertrude told me this request caused her first and only experience of stage fright. She was reluctant to turn the audience's attention away from the director and cast who had worked so hard; she therefore merely rose in her seat in the audience and acknowledged her thanks.

After the performance, Gertrude stayed on at the request of the boys for an informal party and to show them how to add a professional touch to the rendition of the numbers. She worked with them until far into the night, when David and I finally had to tear her away from the theatre.

* * *

That summer at The Berries was dedicated largely to bringing up Angus—a proceeding complicated by Gertrude's wanton disregard of the feeding rules which she had insisted the veterinary should draw up. Thus she inculcated in Angus an appetite for caviar and for hollandaise sauce which gave us a good deal to reckon with later in town.

The hollandaise sauce was plentiful that summer. Gertrude had prevailed upon Barbara Winslow Davies, one of our neighbors and an inspired cook, to take her on as a pupil. Soon several friends joined her in an informal class.

The first lesson was the making of three essential sauces—mayonnaise, béchamel, and hollandaise. According to her teacher, "Gertrude was capable in every way from the start, when she arrived for the first lesson at 8:45 A.M., dressed in a girl's white shirt and blue pedal pushers, and with her hair tied back in a pony-tail. Her hands were confident when she used the kitchen hardware. Every operation was neatly done according to directions. When handling the chopped onions and parsley, or bruised fresh tarragon leaves (her favorite among the pot herbs), she would repeat little homely admonitions she had heard from her grandmother long ago: "Keep it tidy, girl," "Make yourself useful, Gertrude, every day!"

From the sauces, Gertrude advanced to miracles in aspic, lobster mousse, and a chicken cooked in wine sauce to which, in her honor, Barbara gave the title *Coq-au-vin Gertrude* when she wrote the cook book which Gertrude persuaded her to do.

Eventually the pupils in the cooking class held a graduation party. Gertrude received a diploma, of which she was inordinately proud.

"Richard!" she declared enthusiastically, "hereafter we shan't ever have to go to one of those expensive restaurants for epicurean food. I can cook anything on their menus. Come, let me show off! I'll fix you something right now. Tell me, darling, what would you like?"

I furrowed my brow as if pondering the culinary delicacies of all Western civilization. At length I replied, "A glass of cold milk!"

"Richard!" Gertrude exclaimed.

* * *

This was the summer of Gertrude's greatest triumph as a homemaker. The final accolade came when *The American Home* magazine requested permission to do an illustrated feature story on her household at The Berries. Gertrude was delighted.

However, it was early autumn before all the details could be arranged and a cameraman from the magazine arrived. His pictures were to be shot entirely in color. This arrangement presented no problem as far as the interior of the house was concerned. The exteriors, however, were another matter. The barberry bush in the garden, essential to the composition of his front-view photograph, presented no color contrast to the green of the lawn. Disappointed, the cameraman said, "We'd better skip this one."

"Not quite yet!" Gertrude exclaimed.

Quickly, she darted around to the back of the house where there was a bed of marigold. She scooped up an armful of the blossoms, called for some Scotch tape and, before the bewildered cameraman knew what was happening, the hardy barberry perennial was sporting bright golden-orange flowers.

"With apologies to Mother Nature," Gertrude beamed. "Snap away!"

* * *

Only one thing clouded the happiness of that summer. This was my mother's failing health. When we drove down to Groton to see her, we found her a little weaker, a little nearer the end. She was in her ninetieth year. Age, not illness, was lowering her hold on life, which until that year had been exceptionally strong.

Uncle Jim and Aunt Alice were with Mother much of the time. The three Joys held staunchly to each other. Mother, well aware of the approaching shadow, spoke several times with dissatisfaction of the Aldrich custom which would result in her being buried in Upton and not in her beloved and beautiful Groton.

"I will be alone with Father in Upton, away from my family," she sighed to Gertrude on our last visit. My sister Joy, who had died during the war while I was overseas, and Barbara's little Peter were both buried in Groton.

Gertrude tried to comfort Mother. "But, darling—Richard and I and young Richard and David—we will all be there with you one day."

My mother always seemed better and brighter when Gertrude was with her. She was keenly interested in the forthcoming musical version of *Anna and the King of Siam.* As is often the case with old persons, she remembered easily and vividly experiences and stories heard during her younger years, and she brought forth for Gertrude innumerable things the missionaries she had known had told her about Siam in the days of Mrs. Anna's king, and about Anna Leonowens herself. Because of these reminiscences, Gertrude said she always had the feeling that she herself had known the real Mrs. Anna. One of my mother's last gifts to Gertrude was a first-edition copy of Anna Leonowens' book *The English Governess at the Siamese Court,* which had stood on her bookshelf for over sixty years.

As autumn came, we all knew that Mother would not see the winter.

Just before Mother died, I was sitting with her looking through some old snapshot albums. She treasured these as a record of her children's early years, and of our summers at Sunny Shadow and our trips abroad. It was a long time since I had seen many of the photographs. I discovered that a good number of them had been mutilated; they had been cut into, apparently with manicure scissors, and figures and faces removed. In reply to my query, Mother explained that it was her custom to go through the books from time to time and censor them. Anyone appearing in the album who seemed to her to have behaved wrongly, or to have disappointed her hopes, was snipped out. Barbara's first husband had been dealt with in this fashion, leaving a hole in several groups in which he had been a member. A boy I had played with, and who later figured in Mayor Curley's political machine in Boston, had been excised from a picnic gathering, leaving a leg behind.

But the most extraordinary renovation had been given to a photograph of my father, taken in Egypt when he stopped there on the way to the Holy Land with several leading members of the Northfield Movement. The picture was a posed one made by a professional photographer. It showed several tourists mounted on camels, with the pyramids and Sphinx carefully displayed in the background. All but one of the camels were supervised by Arab dragomans. This last camel, mounted by a plump lady in black basque flowing skirt and a neat black bonnet, was held by Father. With a dark woolen suit, his imposing gold watch and chain, and his stout umbrella, Father looked more than a match for any camel.

The photograph had been familiar to me since earliest childhood. There was a family joke about Father carrying his umbrella into the Sahara Desert. Lest there be any doubt about his identity, Father had inscribed his picture in white ink—"E. I. A., 1904."

But Mother's scissors had wrought a strange change in the familiar scene. The camel remained. So did Father, still assertive and competent. But the lady in the basque skirt had vanished. Over her, Mother had pasted a head of Gertrude cut from a picture. Beside the Sphinx, Gertrude smiled demurely at Father and his fellow-pilgrims to the Holy Land.

At my exclamation of surprise, Mother placed her hand on mine. "He would have liked it, Richard," she said. "I have regretted many times that your father never knew Gertrude."

With her scissors and paste, Mother had done what she could to make up to Father for this loss. No daughter-in-law could have been given a higher accolade.

Chapter Nineteen

As THE YEAR 1950 drew to a close, Gertrude wrote to her English friend, Evie Williams:

It is ages since I wrote, but now that there is nothing to do, I am busier than ever.

I am co-chairman with Mrs. Vincent Astor of a gigantic ball which we are giving to raise funds for the American National Theatre and Academy on New Year's Eve. I am on the fund-raising Committee for the Memorial Center for Cancer and Allied Diseases. I am making recordings for the Voice of America, which we hope reaches into the Communist-occupied countries. There are personal appearances in connection with *The Glass Menagerie,* and soon there will be costume sessions for *The King and I.*

I went to Boston for United Nations Day and at a press conference I was told that the picture is Academy Award material. But who knows? It is in its sixth week at Radio City and still going strong.

Things are not too gay these days. Richard's boy, young Dick, has been called for the Army, but as he is in his senior year at University of Virginia he is allowed to graduate and will go in June. The Korea mess looks *horrible.* Big Richard, I believe, is due for special duty in Naval Intelligence. This is all hush-hush. Even I am not being told what his actual job is to be, or where he will be sent. They have been investigating and questioning and interviewing him for months, in secret. He leaves for Washington early in January about the same time rehearsals start for my play, so I shall be a Victorian grass widow. Not a pleasant thing to look forward to.

Pam and Doctor Bill have cracked up. She is living out in the suburbs and doing odd jobs in TV and radio. Well, they both seem happier now they have parted and I suppose one should admire their courage in facing facts.

Having been absent from West 54th Street three years running, and not knowing where any of us may be next year, we are going to have Pam, Richard's two boys, their mother Helen, her husband and their young son and Richard's sister Barbara all for dinner on Christmas Eve.

I do hope you are well and have a decent Christmas and that this new meat rationing won't make things too impossible.

I don't know what my status would be as a British subject if the U.S.A. and we ceased to be allies. Guess I should be deported or interned.

As Gertrude's letter indicates, the new year 1951 was to come in under a shadow.

The news from the Pacific troubled her exceedingly, as did the possibility of young Dick's being sent to Korea, should the war last much longer. When the time came for me to leave, she did something I never knew her to do before—she broke down completely.

"I don't see how I can live through it all again," she said as the tears welled up in her eyes. "I could be brave when you went the last time. But it's different now. It breaks my heart to think that nothing was really accomplished by all the agony and death. Peace is no nearer. Are we going on forever wasting lives and happiness?"

I could neither reassure nor comfort her. She sat there dutifully stitching name tapes to my shirts, underwear and socks, as she had done back in 1942, proudly refusing to turn the dreary job over to anyone else. When I tried to inject a note of humor by saying that she was sewing so thoroughly no Korean washerwomen would ever rub the labels off, she was not diverted.

"Not Korea, darling. I can't bear it if they send you to Korea. We were lucky before. God has been so good to us. I'm choked up with thankfulness all the time. But will we be lucky always? It makes me afraid, and I've never been afraid before."

Apparently she sought spiritual counsel, because soon afterward I found on her dressing table a little printed card which stressed the value of living one day at a time: "One secret of a sweet and happy Christian life is learning to live by the day . . . Anyone can carry his burden, however hard, for one day. This is all life ever means to us—just one little day . . . God gives us nights to shut down upon our little days. We cannot see beyond. Short horizons make life easier and give us one of the blessed secrets of brave, true, holy living . . ."

Gertrude carried this card in her purse, wherever she went. That she did not merely keep it near her, like an amulet, but assimilated its philosophy, was shown more and more in the months that followed. All of us who knew her best realized that she had acquired a peace of mind which lifted her above worrying, above daily annoyances, even above physical pain.

She had always been courageous, especially about refusing to allow illness or pain to interfere with her work in the theatre. In the summer of 1950, when she was appearing in *Traveler's Joy* at my Falmouth Playhouse, she suffered a fall while wading on some rocks one afternoon. That night, just before her entrance cue, she fainted. Dennis King, who was appearing with her, had to announce that Miss Lawrence had had a "slight indisposition"; he asked the audience to wait for more definite news. Suddenly, Gertrude's voice was heard clearly, protesting: "I'm all right." She came on and went through the play, despite excruciating pain in her back. The next day, when her back was X-rayed, it was discovered she had suffered a fracture. The injury troubled her at times for a long period.

Though her physical courage never deserted her, Gertrude was constantly groping for spiritual reassurance.

Very early in our life together she spoke of a talk she had had with a friend who was a staunch Christian Scientist. "I don't know whether to try it or not," she said reflectively. "I have always wanted something to hang onto. Something to make me know that all this does include Heaven, too. You see, I don't know how to pray alone."

She said sometimes, wistfully, that she wished she had a religion. My reply was that she seemed to be confusing religion with church membership. And that whatever she chose to do about the latter, she had the former in a very live and flourishing state, very much according to the pattern of the early apostles.

"But what is religion, Richard?" she asked.

I referred her to the definition Professor Whitehead gave us at Harvard: A man's religion is what he does with his own solitariness.

Gertrude, more than anyone I ever knew, dedicated her solitariness to love. All her work for and her generous gifts to others were illumined by love. She wanted to help people, severally and en masse, because she loved people—all people. It hurt her when she had to work with someone for whom she could not find some love. Those she had once found lovable she kept loyally in her heart and in her life.

Service was an article of her creed. She wrote the Reverend Robert C. Dodds, pastor of the Dennis Union Church, explaining why she could not do something which she had discussed with him: "It is really frightening to have to write such words as 'there will not be time.' We are given so much time in which to serve each other in His Name, yet we squander it so thoughtlessly. Please help me in this."

She looked constantly for help, for direction, for an explanation of the mysteries that confront us. She had a number of correspondents among the clergy, including all denominations. Father Francis Slattery was one. After attending a memorial service for King George VI at the Church of the Transfiguration, she wrote the rector, the Reverend Randolph Ray, to say she would like to be a member of his parish.

Several times she attended services with me at the Fifth Avenue Presbyterian Church, of which I had long been a member. But

Gertrude did not have in her the making of a churchgoer such as my parents were. She liked to drop into a church—any church—from time to time, as a traveler might rest gratefully for a few moments in the shade of some tree by the road—any tree.

Sometimes when she and I took a walk on Sunday afternoon and passed a church where a vesper service was going on, she would say: "Darling, let's go in." We did this once when on our way to a cocktail party. Arriving at the party, Gertrude apologized for our being late, explaining we had stopped to chat with Bruce Barton and his daughter Betsy after vespers at the Central Presbyterian Church.

Our hostess's jaw dropped. "Vespers," she repeated as if she had not heard. "Don't tell me you and Richard go to *church* Sunday afternoon?"

"You'd be surprised who goes to church!" Gertrude retorted.

* * *

Gertrude was greatly interested in Memorial Hospital and its work to relieve cancer. This interest began soon after the war, when one morning I read aloud at breakfast a letter from Mrs. Ralph Hines, chairman of the Woman's Committee of the New York Cancer Society. I had known her many years before when she was Mrs. Betty Pirie of Chicago. Her sister Ellen was married to Adlai Stevenson. Betty wrote that her committee would award prizes for work done in a recent fund-raising campaign, at a reception to be given in her home. Could I, as a producer, produce an actress who would give the awards?

"I'm free that afternoon," Gertrude said. "Would I do?"

I put the question in a telegram to Betty. The reply came back: "JUST!"

As Betty recounts the story: she told her husband the morning of the reception, "Gertrude Lawrence is coming this afternoon to make the awards. You will get home in time to be here for it, won't you?"

Ralph Hines looked suddenly embarrassed. "I'm afraid I can't," he murmured.

Betty suddenly remembered that when she was Mrs. Pirie and living in Chicago, Ralph Hines, one of Chicago's most eligible bachelors, had been spoken of as one of Gertrude's ardent admirers. She smiled mischievously.

"I want to meet her," she said to Ralph, "because I've known her husband, Dick Aldrich, for many years. Suppose we ask them both to dine with us after the prize-giving."

Ralph agreed to this. Following this evening together, Gertrude and Betty became fast friends. Through Betty, Gertrude became a member of the Board of the New York Cancer Society. To the surprise of some of the other members, she was a very active one, attending every meeting which was not held on a matinee day. If she were absent she would ask to have the minutes sent her. In 1952 she accepted the co-chairmanship of the American Cancer Society Membership Drive.

As with every cause, the ever-present problem was how to raise funds. When the Ritz Carlton was to be torn down, Gertrude suggested at a board meeting that they ask the right to auction the discarded fittings of the famous hotel.

"But who would buy them?" someone asked.

"Everyone," Gertrude said promptly. "Think of the numbers of people who have taken teaspoons and ashtrays and towels as souvenirs. They would all come and buy something, if only to legitimatize what they already have."

* * *

When rehearsals were called for *The King and I*, Gertrude necessarily stopped all her other activities. Her letters to me (I was in Washington on duty) were brief. They spoke of the length of the play and the amount of work there was in it for her. She was very happy that Yul Brynner had been engaged to play the King of Siam. She had wanted him for the role since the day she arrived early to rehearse a broadcast and had inadvertently opened a studio door and heard a commanding masculine voice say, "Come here."

The command was not addressed to her, but to an actor in a play in rehearsal. Gertrude, however, had chosen to obey it. She recognized Brynner—she had see him in *Lute Song*—and remained to watch him work. She informed me that evening how wonderful she thought he would be as the King.

"I'm sure he can do it," she assured me. "He has the appearance, the forcefulness, and the ability that the part requires."

"But can he sing?" I asked.

"No, but that's not important. He doesn't have to sing. They can give him a song and he can talk it."

She was very pleased that Sandy Kennedy was engaged to play the role of Mrs. Anna's son Louis. Gertrude had known Sandy's family for years. Originally Philadelphians, they had welcomed her to their homes whenever she played there.

After moving to New York, Mrs. Kennedy had sent Sandy to dramatic school. When the school put on a play at the Cosmopolitan Club, eight-year-old Sandy's performance resulted in several offers of professional roles. But his mother turned down all offers until the casting director of *The King and I* offered him the role of Mrs. Anna's son, adding, "He is to play with Gertrude Lawrence."

"Oh, that's different," Mrs. Kennedy said.

When Sandy came to his first rehearsal he was shy and plainly in awe of Gertrude. She recognized this and immediately set about putting him at ease. "Hello, Louis, I'm your Mummie," she said cheerily. From then on, she helped Sandy identify himself with the role he played. She put on his make-up until he learned how to do it himself. After that, he would present himself at her dressing room, before every performance, for what they laughingly called "inspection."

While she was, as she used to tell him, his "backstage Mummie," between shows she gave Sandy the sort of companionship that made him feel that he and she were contemporaries. It had been the same years before with my sons. Few adults have this ability; but Gertrude had it.

After seventeen months in the play Sandy grew out of the part. He was disappointed at leaving the play, but he accepted the ruling philosophically, as part of the cost of growing up. He told his mother he wanted to give Gertrude something to remember him by.

"What would you like to give her?" Mrs. Kennedy inquired.

"I'd like to give her a diamond necklace," Sandy answered. "But I suppose that costs a lot of money."

Mrs. Kennedy said a necklace would be rather expensive. Besides, she added, it would be better to give Gertrude something Sandy was sure she would like.

"I know," said Sandy suddenly. "A house."

"A house?"

"Yes, don't you know how she is always telling the King he promised her a house? In the play the King says he'll give it to her, but he never does!"

Sandy went to work and produced a two-story Victorian doll house. For its furnishings he combed the Third Avenue antique shops for miniatures of Victorian furniture. Sandy was exacting. "We must have a tea-kettle," he said. "She is always drinking tea." He remembered that once, when he had lunched with his mother and Gertrude, Gertrude had ordered *vin rosé*. "We must find a little bottle of *vin rosé,*" he insisted. He did. He also found many other valuable miniatures for the bedroom and sitting room of the promised brick house.

On the night Sandy was to leave the play, the house for Gertrude was completed. When she reached the St. James Theatre she found it in her dressing room. A card tied to it read: "With love from Louis."

Hazel was there when Gertrude discovered the house. She said she had never seen Gertrude more deeply moved by any gift or token of appreciation and love. Gertrude cried when she thanked Sandy, telling him:

"You've given me something I wanted all my life. When I was a little girl I always wanted a house I could play with. I never had one."

Gertrude kept Sandy's house in her dressing room. It became one of her treasured souvenirs.

The seventeen little Puerto Ricans who played the royal children became fanatically attached to Gertrude, whom they called "Missis Anna." They came to her with their childish troubles, as when one little girl lost her shoes and was afraid of parental discipline when she went home. Gertrude sent Hazel out with the child to buy new ones.

The children added immeasurably to the charm of the play, but they also appeared to constitute an almost insurmountable drawback to a London production. Gertrude wrote one of her English friends in the spring of Coronation Year:

"As for being home for the Coronation, that is very debatable. Naturally I want to be there but I am sure the play will not be over by then, as we are selling tickets into the New Year already.

"I had set my heart on playing at Drury Lane but there is great doubt whether we can do *The King and I* in London at all, due to the Child Labor Laws. We have seventeen children in the play and they must be *children*. Not midgets. Ours here range from seven to eleven years and they are divine. Real children, not academy kids. So it presents a grave problem, as we cannot do the play without them. . . ."

The large number of children in *The King and I* created some problems here, too. During rehearsals there was an epidemic of colds among the children, which spread to the adults in the cast. Gertrude went on at the New Haven opening with a raging fever of 103 degrees.

After the New Haven opening, the play moved to Boston. There it was subjected to cuts and alterations, but everyone felt the first act was still too slow. It needed something. But what?

"Give me a number with the children," Gertrude suggested.

This suggestion resulted in the number "Getting to Know You." John van Druten, the famous playwright who directed the play, wrote in an article published in the New York *Times:*

"Her biggest number, 'Getting to Know You,' was added in the last week in Boston. She arrived in New York with no time to become certain of her performance. Everything had been indicated, nothing had been set.

"On the opening night she came on the stage with a new and dazzling quality, as though an extra power had been added to the brilliance of her own stage light. She was radiant and wonderful.

I asked her afterward whether she had been aware that this would happen to her. She said that she had sensed, at the morning's session for last-minute notes and comments, that we were none of us quite certain of what she would give. That was enough of a challenge to her. She had said to herself: 'I'll surprise them.' And she did. The opening night audience cheered her in 'Getting to Know You.' "

Just as I was struck by the similarity between her number "Shall We Dance?" and our dance together at the Harvard reunion, I experienced an eerie feeling of familiarity at the New York opening in Gertrude's scene with the children, when she showed them the map and sang "Getting to Know You." It puzzled me for a moment. Then I remembered a photograph we had of Gertrude with the British orphans in the Bronx. She had gone up there to talk to them about the United States and "Home"—a lesson in geography and international good-will. What she did in her "Getting to Know You" number was precisely what she had done in all seriousness with the little refugees, ten years before. No wonder it went across the footlights straight to the hearts of the audience.

To Gertrude, the affection given her by the cast was the richest reward for the hard work of the role. Knowing that this warm feeling of camaraderie was so strong among all the members of the cast, I grew indignant at the recurrent gossip-column rumors that a feud existed between Gertrude and Yul. Gertrude, however, was more tolerant. "Such talk is inevitable, darling," she said. "But it doesn't really matter. The important thing is that Yul is wonderful to work with, just as I knew he would be. Each performance we do is better than the one before."

Gertrude was right. Their scenes together improved steadily, as they became an acting team. When, after playing for nearly a year without missing a performance, she was stricken with pleurisy, Yul kept her heartened with the kind of amusing messages she always loved and responded to. One wire read:

MY TIMING SICK WITH HIVES CUES SICK WITH ARTHRITIS AND ATMOSPHERE HERE WHOOPING COUGH I MISS YOU BELOVED ANNA YOUR VERY OWN KING

To which Gertrude replied:

DEAREST MAJESTY I AM SORRY TO BE AWAY FROM DUTY BUT CANNOT UTTER A SOUND SO AM QUITE USELESS AND FEEL RIDICULOUS BUT HOPE TO RETURN IN FULL VOICE DEVOTEDLY MRS. ANNA SIR

The costumes for her roles were enchanting and beautiful. However, it was especially difficult for her to accustom herself—she who moved naturally "like a young deer"—to the weight of the skirts which were held out by heavy steel hoops.

Gertrude attacked this problem with customary thoroughness. Before the play opened on the road, she borrowed a hoop from the Brooks Costume Company and wore it around the apartment until she could move with the grace she wanted to achieve on the stage.

Still the hoops were to cause her trouble. At a matinee of *The King and I* in Boston, when she made her entrance for the scene with the King's wives before they welcome the British ambassador, the heavy steel hoop holding out the very wide skirt of her pink satin gown became caught in something, pitching her forward. There was a horrified gasp as the audience saw her totter, saw her gloved hands reach out and find nothing to cling to, saw her fall, her body hidden by the billowing skirts of the royal wives. Fortunately, she was not badly hurt.

One Saturday, as I was going upstairs to her dressing room to see her between shows, Hazel called me aside.

"Mr. Aldrich, someone gotta do something about those steel hoops," she said. "She'll never complain, but I'm burnt up. Her knees and legs are just black and blue with bruises. Every time Miss L curtsies to the King, the hoops hit her—and she curtsies more than fifty times in each performance. I've counted."

I knew that Gertrude would adhere to the tradition of being a good trouper, and say nothing about the steel hoops, since she thought they were an essential part of the performance. Therefore, without her knowledge, I requested the Holtzmann office to ask the management to have lightweight metal or bamboo hoops substituted.

While Gertrude's costumes were all in accord with a glorified Victorian tradition, those of the rest of the cast were made of beautiful silk imported from Thailand (Siam). They were the finest products of the Thai Silk Company in Bangkok, which, despite its name, was the creation of a man named Jim Thompson. Thompson was an American who had found himself in Bangkok when the war ended. Falling in love with the place and the life it offered, he decided to turn his architectural training and his instinct for color into rebuilding the almost defunct Siamese silk industry.

When his silks were selected by Irene Sharaff, costumer for *The King and I,* Jim met Gertrude in New York and a friendship was established which bridged half the world. Thereafter, whenever Jim flew to New York on business, he went directly to call on Gertrude. She introduced him to friends such as Fleur Cowles, who were planning trips to the Orient; to other friends she gave letters to Jim. Joshua Logan and Ward Morehouse were among the theatre people who dropped down out of the skies above Bangkok so equipped.

Gertrude's interest in Thailand extended to its people and especially to the royal family. The currently reigning Chakri dynasty is descended from the King represented in the play. It amused her that His Majesty, King Plumiphon Aduldet, drives a Jaguar, instead of proceeding by royal elephant.

Thai statesmen and business men soon realized that Gertrude was, in her way, a very effective ambassadress without portfolio and they began to treat her with appropriate respect. Her dressing room became a mecca for Siamese dignitaries visiting New York. From these visitors she received gifts of Siamese products, books on Siamese history, and much information about native customs, until she became, in effect, the adopted daughter of this land which she had never seen.

* * *

Those who had followed Gertrude's career, like John van Druten, were impressed by what they considered a change revealed in her playing of Mrs. Anna. The gaiety was there, but veiled. As John said, "her comedy in the part was gentler, Victorian, almost evasive, and her touch on the sweeter and more personal notes was stronger and surer than New York had seen before." The radiance was there—the star quality, "indefinable but intensely vivid, that comes from something other than the human or technical talents of the actress, giving her an iridescence, a power to move not only the audience but the very boards of the stage as she steps on them. Whether Gertie was giving a good performance or a bad one, that quality was never absent. The radiance was always there."

Those who knew Gertrude's instinctive tendency to identify herself with whatever role she played spoke often of what "Mrs. Anna was doing to her." I viewed it somewhat differently. What I saw was not a Victorian English governess exerting a transforming influence on Gertrude Lawrence, but, for the first time in the theatre, the emergence of Mrs. A.

It took Gertrude a long time to find herself; to discover and express that part of her personality which was the core of her individuality. She had played so many roles through the years, starting in childhood, that she had had scant opportunity, time, and strength to develop what was essentially and truly herself. Much of the time she was not sure what she herself was, and she tried to be a great many selves. Noel's phrase comes to mind: "Seven women under one hat."

Her inner indecision and instability was what fascinated many people as much as it disturbed them. They realized that much of the time she was play-acting to herself, as much as to the world. They wondered, as one of her friends said, "would she ever alight?"

During the year she had been out of the theatre—the year she spoke of dedicating to Mrs. A—Gertrude had made an important discovery. She came to realize—not without some sense of shock—that the woman she was with me, in our moments of greatest clarity and tenderness, was her innermost self. Mrs. A, which many of her old intimates suggested was "just another role that Gee was trying out" for as long as it amused her, was actually the basic truth of her.

Returning to the stage, Gertrude brought a new set of values, a maturity and self-confidence that greatly enriched her talent. She was a greater actress because she was greater as a woman.

* * *

With Gertrude's play a success at the St. James Theatre, and the probability that it would continue to run at least for three years, the problem of her getting to and from the theatre at night and in all weather arose. We had not kept a car in New York for years.

"I'll have Roosevelt on a regular basis," Gertrude said.

Roosevelt Zanders, citizen of Harlem, owner of a Cadillac limousine for hire, driver of celebrities, was a friend of Hazel's who from time to time acted as Gertrude's chauffeur. Roosevelt had a proprietary attitude toward Gertrude which was assurance that he would take good care of her.

On one of my week-ends off from my duty in Washington I had a talk with Roosevelt and outlined to him his responsibilities while he was working for us. At no time and on no excuse was he to permit Gertrude to take a stranger into the car.

Gertrude had a persistent readiness to give a lift to total strangers. Whenever she emerged from a stage door on a cold or stormy night she would ask the waiting crowd of fans cheerily: "Anybody going my way?" Then she would slide into the front seat of her car beside the driver, and offer the rest of it to any person or persons unknown who accepted her cordial invitation.

Later, when I asked Gertrude in the course of one of our daily telephone conversations how the arrangement was working out, she replied: "Wonderfully. Angus has taken to Roosevelt and is so happy to go driving with him."

I said that the point of our having Roosevelt was that he would be of use to *her*, not a companion for Angus.

"I know, darling," she said, "but with Angus going into the dog show it's terribly important his psychology should not be upset. If he's not happy, he might not win. Roosevelt keeps him happy."

Angus, who had taken his first blue ribbon at an autumn show, was rapidly developing the temperament of an opera star. His vanity was fostered by the brushing, clipping, and rubdowns given him at the handler's in Syosset, Long Island. When Angus was "on" at the Westminster Kennel Club Show, Gertrude lavishly bought tickets at $7.50 apiece, and distributed them far and wide among people she knew at the theatre. She was determined Angus should have a good house. I accused her of being a theatre mother, fussing and bridling over her infant prodigy.

As at the Cape the summer before, Gertrude had a careful diet for Angus drawn up by Mr. Brumley, the trainer—and then violated it regularly by feeding him the caviar and asparagus that she and the terrier both loved. When I noted this contradiction, she protested: "But Angus adores caviar. You don't want him to be frustrated, do you?"

I retorted that some frustration might do Angus good. "It might cause him to stop making what you call 'mistakes' in my room."

"It's his reaction to your being so stern with him," Gertrude insisted.

When I came to New York for week-ends, I would pick up Gertrude at the theatre and take her home. As we entered the house, she would connive for me to go straight to the kitchen to raid the icebox, while she took a quick survey of the bedroom and removed any incriminating evidence. "My Anguish," I would hear her say. And know that Angus had made another mistake.

* * *

Angus rose rapidly to stardom.

Early one Monday morning, as I was packing to leave for the airport, the telephone rang. It was a news photographer who wanted to know when he could come over to take some pictures. I relayed the query to Gertrude, who said, "Tell him to come right over." After I had hung up, Gertrude added, "Of course, they will want a few shots of us together, darling."

Twenty minutes later, as I was downstairs in the hall, bag in hand and glancing anxiously at my watch, the photographer arrived. Gertrude was obviously relieved.

"I am so glad you made it in time," she told the photographer with her most charming smile. "Commander Aldrich has to leave for Washington in a few minutes."

The cameraman looked at me suspiciously, obviously puzzled.

"Where's the dog?" he demanded. "The dog who won the prizes? That's what my editor wants."

I glared at Gertrude. But as she stood up on tip-toe, her face tilted to kiss me goodbye, she whispered mischievously, "I'm sorry, dearest; that's what happens when there are two stars in the family."

Angus' beauty treatments figured heavily on Gertrude's engagement pad. On the afternoons when these were scheduled, she never took the car to the theatre; she walked or took a cab. Once I was in from Washington on special leave on a matinee day, and said I would like to use the car that afternoon to attend to some business. "I'm terribly sorry," Gertrude replied. "It's Angus' day to be clipped."

"Does he have to be driven there? Why can't he walk? Exercise would be good for him."

"Angus doesn't like to walk on the streets," she said. "He likes to drive with Roosevelt and look out the windows and see the people in the streets."

I more than suspected Roosevelt of encouraging Angus' devotion to and dependence on him. But there was nothing I could do —except take a taxi.

As the warm weather came on, I became concerned about its effect on Gertrude. She was committed to remain in *The King and I* throughout the summer. It would be the first time she had played during the hot weather for many years, and I dreaded it for her; she always wilted in New York summers.

As an alternative to the confinement of our midtown apartment, I suggested that we take a house on Long Island or along the Connecticut shore from which she could motor back and forth to the theatre.

"I won't take a house more than one mile from the theatre," Gertrude declared. "Then I won't be dependent on transportation because, if necessary, I can walk to work."

When Gertrude told our friend Betty Hines that she was looking for a house with a garden in town, Betty said, "Don't look any further; I want you to have my house for the summer."

Ralph Hines had died a year earlier, and Betty planned to spend the summer in Europe. Before leaving, she not only had her house on East Sixty-first Street put in order for Gertrude's enjoyment; she also had it air-conditioned. This was the sort of thing Gertrude would do for a friend but, as she told me, it was the first time in her experience that a friend had been so graciously generous to her. She moved in joyfully, taking with her only her most cherished personal belongings. Her maid Dorothy and Dorothy's husband, Hood, were re-engaged on a full-time basis to live in the house. Hood became Gertrude's chauffeur and Angus' chaperone. I felt easier in mind about Gertrude when, early in the summer of 1951, I was ordered to special duty in Europe.

To Daphne du Maurier, whom she had invited to stay with her when Daphne came to America for the publication of *My Cousin Rachel,* Gertrude wrote:

> Darling Dum,
>
> The new house is blissful. I have a garden, birds, trees, a butler and a cook who cooks like a Ritz Carlton chef.
>
> I hardly know this is New York. And it is even cooler on this side of town than Fifty-fourth Street.
>
> Let me know when you are actually arriving so that I can send the car for you. Am very excited about your coming. . . .

The prospect of a house guest—her first—sent Gertrude into a happy whirl of preparations. She had the window boxes planted with long hanging ivy and brilliant red geraniums. Tubs of hydrangeas were placed on either side of the front door. This was left wide open much of the time when she was at home—in strict disobedience of my orders and to the startled surprise of many passers-by. Her excuse was that she thought it was pleasant for people in the hot street to look through the hall into the green back garden.

As the summer wore on, Gertrude Lawrence's house, with its bright flowers, became a neighborhood landmark. She loved and felt at home in the locality. Many of the residents of the block got to know Gertrude and were soon on chatting terms with her. These included Major George Fielding Eliot, about whose backyard herb garden Gertrude was intensely curious, and Allen Dulles, subsequently head of the Central Intelligence Agency.

Despite the heat and my being away from her, I think Gertrude was very happy that summer. She liked entertaining friends who passed through New York, and having "the girls" to lunch, or to tea in the garden. The girls were usually Englishwomen like herself, connected with the theatre, who had known each other since the start of their theatrical careers. They included Norah Howard, Constance Carpenter, her understudy in *The King and I* and other plays, and Christine Brooks, who had been her vocal coach since *Lady in the Dark.*

Gertrude had disliked the idea of leaving The Berries vacant that summer. She liked knowing that the house was being enjoyed and lived in even during her absence. But she never wanted strangers in it. When I was recalled to the service and had to arrange for someone to supervise management of the playhouses and the musical tent on the Cape, it was Gertrude who suggested that my former wife, Helen Corballis, and her husband Teddy might be interested. Teddy could manage the summer enterprises for me, and the Corballises could have our house for the summer. Gertrude pointed out that this would be a continuance of the family tradition at The Berries, and that David and Dick might spend their summer holiday there.

The fact that this was a somewhat unconventional arrangement did not prevent any of us from realizing its advantages to all concerned.

One of Gertrude's letters to my former wife reads:

237 East 61st Street
New York 22, New York
27 June 1951

Dearest Helen,

Bless you for your letter. I am so glad you are happy at The Berries, and after the rain the gardens should be looking wonderfully green.

Keep Ed spraying the roses everywhere because last year we had a lot of aphids, and they eat them up; also de-bud the roses and cut them for the house—this will make them bloom more. Keep all beach towels, bathing suits, etc., in the Beach House—this saves bringing them back and forth, and they dry quickly down there and are brought up and laundered at the end of the season. All Star Cottage laundry including blankets can be stored with Mrs. Fagan at the theatre, as the girls and boys bring their own, although if it is cool they sometimes need an extra blanket which they can borrow and sign for and return to her. Don't bother about the face cloths—they are very cheap and always get mislaid. The bed pads I like to let them have at the cottage because the mattresses are not too good.

The carpets at the house are a bit spotted I know, but they are due for a cleaning this year, so don't worry. Relax. You can imagine now how "restful" my summers have been up there with all the overseeing and entertaining to do.

None of the bedroom doors in our house are ever locked, and, anyway, the same key fits all of them, so don't worry about that either.

I am a real summer grass widow, living in this most beautiful house alone, but it is cool and quiet, and I love it. Richard spent his last week-end here before going overseas and he loves it too. So now I am looking for a house for us instead of No. 17 West 54th Street. I have birds, trees, a garden, an elevator and a butler, my dear. And it's bliss! Richard is well, he writes, but gives no news, of course. What a crazy world this is these days.

Give my love to Teddy and the boys and *do* enjoy the house.

Ever fondly,

Gertrude

The information that Dick had enlisted in the Air Force immediately after his graduation in June, 1951, reached me in Paris in a cablegram from Gertrude. She had seen him off to Sampson Air Force Base. He took with him a photograph of her as Mrs. Anna in the pale pink satin gown she wore in the "Shall We Dance" number. There was no reference to their relationship on the photograph, which Gertrude signed: "To dear Private Aldrich, with love—Gertrude Lawrence."

Below the autograph she added her own special mark for those dearest to her—the heart pierced by an arrow.

This photograph went with my son through his training period. He took it with him when he left for Korea the following summer. Gertrude was his "pin-up girl," admired by all the other fellows. None of them knew that she was his stepmother.

During the summer of 1951 the heat in New York was worse than it had been in many years. Backstage at the St. James Theatre the temperature in the stuffy dressing rooms stood in the high nineties. For Gertrude, condemned to wear hoops, heavy satin costumes over many petticoats, a luxuriant wig and bonnets, the prolonged heat wave was torture. Friends who came backstage to see her after a performance marveled how she stood it.

One of the friends who came was the chairman of the board of an electric appliance company, on whose radio program Gertrude had made a guest appearance when her autobiography was published. The friendly relations established then had continued through the years. Mopping his brow, her perspiring visitor said to Gertrude, "You mean too much to your public for us to let you melt away. We will air-condition this dressing room for you."

He was as good as his word, but unfortunately the location of the dressing room presented a difficult engineering problem. Gertrude asked them to put the air conditioner instead into the room where the chorus dressed.

The girls' delight and gratitude was shown at the next performance, when the King's wives presented themselves in their new Victorian crinolines for the King's approval before the reception of the British ambassador. Standing at one side of the stage, Yul Brynner inspected the row of wives drawn up opposite him with Gertrude standing behind him. Suddenly, at his bark of command, the wives prostrated themselves. Up went all the crinolines, disclosing to Gertrude's startled view the underpants. On each was a single letter in lipstick. The letters spelled the message: WE LOVE YOU.

Later the ever-resourceful company manager, Morrie Jacobs, managed to install a cooling device in Gertrude's dressing room.

The appliance company asked Gertrude to select something from their catalogue for herself. She went through it and settled on a deep freeze. She wrote me in Paris that she looked forward to placing one in our kitchen at The Berries; she and Helen Mahoney would freeze our own garden fruits and vegetables.

Then she read in the paper that people in Washington were dropping in the streets from heat prostration. She canceled her request for a deep freeze, and asked instead for an air conditioner to be installed in the flat I kept in Washington.

When I flew back in August, dreading the clammy weather I would have to face, I entered my apartment to find the temperature a refreshing sixty-five degrees and one of Gertrude's notes:

DARLING, PLEASE EXCUSE THE COOL RECEPTION.

Chapter Twenty

July 20, 1951

Dear Heart,

Here I am all alone up in my balconied bedroom. All the servants are out. Angus and I are quite happy until it's time for me to drive through the sticky streets to Siam, where I get all hot and sticky again. The weather is 'orrid and torrid, and the smell of burning flesh on our crowded matinee days is really quite *something*. I miss the Cape and the sea . . . Business continues at a never-changing top figure and one just struggles through, giving the best performance one is capable of, and longing for Saturday night and the peace of Sunday. . . .

Your red hot and sticky Momma
Mrs. A . . .

In another letter, Gertrude wrote:

In spite of the heat, or perhaps because of it, the house grows more divine every day. When you return to America, we *cannot* go back to the mousetrap on Fifty-fourth Street. I am looking for houses, and I shall keep on looking. . . . I hope to have a lovely home for you when you come back to me. . . . I do miss you so. I have sent the cold pills. Directions are on the labels. You take one white and one brown together. As to your umbrella . . . I realize, darling, how attached you are to it, but I can't send it to you as almost everyone we know has already gone to Europe for the summer. I really believe it would be cheaper and more advisable for you to make the effort to overcome your New England thrift and go to the Galeries Lafayette and buy yourself a new one . . .

I wonder if you got my cable, dearest. It is frustrating not to have an address which will find you direct. Even in the war I had that. . . . Yesterday was *awful.* When I got to "Young Lovers" my voice almost gave out. Our meetings and partings are always so casual, yet when you go from me I miss you terribly. I realize how lucky I am to have you in my life but I often wonder also whether you feel the same about me. Now that we are apart again you may be thinking about whether you get much enjoyment out of being married to me. If you had a wife who did not have a career she could be with you. Should you decide against me, please let me know. I want you to be happy above all things. You deserve someone who appreciates you more obviously than I do. I love you deeply but am self-conscious and usually spent by work and I know you need more actual loving than I give.

But if you go off me I'll spit in your eye!

Do take care, Angel. Write whenever you can.

Ever thine,

Mrs. A

After eleven years of marriage, I knew Gertrude well enough to realize that a sense of inadequacy in her personal relations was always a symptom of fatigue. But since I could not offer to come to her, as I had when she wrote in a similar vein from Florida, I cabled her from Paris:

DARLING HOLD SALIVARY SALVO KEEPING SAME WIFE GETTING NEW UMBRELLA

During this period of strain for Gertrude, when I was unable to be with her myself, it was a source of great comfort to me to know that she was growing closer to my younger son, David. Now that his brother Dick was in service, David escorted Gertrude whenever he was in town; he had grown to be a young man of a creative turn of mind, who shared Gertrude's interest in the theatre, particularly in writing and direction.

David had been a tower of strength to her during the difficult tryout weeks of *The King and I* in Boston the previous March. He attended every rehearsal and performance, taking Gertrude to and from the theatre, and frequently phoning me in Washington afterward to report that she was all right. On opening night, he flattered Gertrude by bringing the whole company of the Hasty Pudding Show backstage to congratulate their "Woman of the Year."

I was eager for Gertrude to be happy with our housing arrangements. So I wrote to her at length, and more soberly, encouraging her to find a house to move into when Betty Hines returned. I was quite content with our "mousetrap" on Fifty-fourth Street, which was our first home, but any house she would grace, I told her, would be home to me.

In October Gertrude telephoned me to report triumphantly that she had obtained a lease on the Dulles home at Number 239, next door. She said she had also obtained permission from Clover Dulles to redecorate according to her taste.

I received this news with grave misgivings. Gertrude had a liberal way of interpreting "redecorating." I hastily sat down and wrote a note to the Holtzmanns, asking them to be sure to arrange privately for the insertion of a clause forbidding the tenant to make any structural changes; thus I was reasonably sure that Clover and Allen Dulles would not return to find unfamiliar wings and balconies sprouting from their home.

So Gertrude had to limit her fun to painting the walls in light colors, hanging floral drapes at the windows over white curtains, and scattering her personal possessions about the house.

Gertrude's passion for redecorating rooms was to lead to an amusing incident that fall, when I had returned from Europe and was stationed in Washington again.

She decided she ought to redo the bathroom on our bedroom floor in the Dulles house. She recalled that someone in the theatre had mentioned to her a few weeks before that an ambitious but indigent young actor named Paul Phillips was looking for odd jobs of painting.

Gertrude sent out an SOS for young Mr. Phillips. When it developed that all he knew how to do was paint walls and woodwork, whereas she wanted the bathroom walls papered, Gertrude offered to show him how.

They stocked up on paper, brushes, roller, and paste at a store around the corner; then she set up a card table and spread the roll of paper on it, applying the paste while Paul climbed a stepladder to put the strips in place.

They were half finished when Gertrude looked at her watch. "I'd almost forgotten my date at the Court of Siam. We'll finish tomorrow." She dashed off to the theatre, leaving Paul behind.

As he was putting the brushes away, Paul had what seemed to him a bright thought. As he expressed it later, "Miss Lawrence had a theatre to go to, but *I* didn't. Why shouldn't I stay and surprise her by finishing up the job? After all, she'd been very kind to me."

So he went back to work. It was a hot night. The confined and crowded quarters made it hotter. Paul yanked off his shirt and tossed it over a chair. . . .

At the end of that day, I caught a late plane from Washington back to New York for an unexpected early morning appointment, and went directly from the airport to pick up Gertrude at the theatre.

When we arrived home, I went upstairs to put away some papers. Passing the bathroom, I was startled to hear faint scraping sounds. Then, a low humming—unmistakably male!

I advanced cautiously toward the half-open bathroom door. The humming stopped.

As I watched, baffled, the door swung open. A young man stepped out into the hallway—clad only in a pair of shorts.

"Oh!" he spluttered. "I didn't know—I mean—*pardon me!*"

He ran back into the bathroom.

"Gertrude!" I roared.

She came flying up the stairs. "What's the trouble, Richard?"

"A man"—I pointed to the bathroom—"in there!"

Gertrude's quick mind rapidly fitted the pieces together, even before Paul emerged, now more conventionally clothed, to offer the still-wet wallpaper as confirmation of his story.

It was a glorious opportunity for me to rib Gertrude by playing the indignant husband—but my acting talent wasn't equal to the occasion. I burst out laughing—to Paul's enormous relief. It appeared that, apart from his personal embarrassment, he was scheduled for an audition for a job at my theatre!

* * *

The house pleased Gertrude enormously, especially the impressive library overflowing with books on international affairs, and the old dining-room table downstairs.

Whenever we had guests for luncheon or dinner, Gertrude would impress them by narrating the table's history. It had originally belonged to John W. Foster, Allen Dulles' grandfather, who was Secretary of State in the Harrison administration, and then to Allen Dulles' uncle, Robert Lansing, who served similarly under Woodrow Wilson. For over half a century, world-famous figures—statesmen, royalty, diplomats—had gathered around it at state dinners.

Gertrude treated the table with reverence. To protect its surface, she had made a long green felt cover, reaching almost to the floor. When she scolded Angus for scratching the legs of the table, she said: "Angus, do be careful; this table has a longer pedigree than you have."

At the time of the Harvard reunion my duties as a class marshal had obliged me to wear striped trousers and a cutaway. I had noticed Gertrude eyeing me speculatively as I stood next to the guest of honor, Dean Acheson, then Secretary of State. "You know, you would make a most attractive diplomat," she observed. Now, no doubt under the influence of the atmosphere of the Dulles house, she returned to this theme. She made the solemn suggestion that I should cut down my interests in the theatre to my enterprises on Cape Cod, and devote the rest of my time and energy to the diplomatic service. She cited the British idea that men who have established themselves in their professions should take up public duties when they reach a certain age.

As an extension of this notion, she took to enthusiastic conversations in French with Dick Myers' attractive French wife, Suzanne.

In the shadow of the Sphinx my father holds a camel with Gertrude on its back—courtesy of my mother, who combined two photographs to make this one.

Vandamm

The English governess dances with the ruler of Siam—Gertrude and Yul Brynner in *The King and I*. In this, her last play, she scored one of her greatest triumphs.

A sweet sentiment on a cake: "Happy birthday to our dear, dear Mrs. Anna from her loving pupils—July 4, 1951."

Talbot

After an evening with the Myers, she announced she was going to start intensive French lessons. When I protested that she already had too many activities on her hands, she countered, "But, darling, let's be logical. When you become an ambassador, I'll *have* to know French!"

Her schedule at that time was indeed staggering. Apart from her daily (and sometimes twice daily) stint in the theatre, she was an active member of the Women's Advisory Committee of the New York Cancer Committee, and had just made three cancer campaign motion pictures in the children's ward of Memorial Hospital. She had succeeded Gilbert Miller as chairman of the Mary MacArthur Memorial Appeal of the National Foundation for Infantile Paralysis. And, with Alfred de Liagre, she selected plays for the "Five Enchanted Evenings" sponsored by the Hospitalized Veterans Music Service.

This, plus a few odds and ends such as housekeeping and singing lessons, did not complete the inventory of Gertrude's activities. Early in September she calmly announced that she had accepted an appointment to the Faculty of Columbia University, in the School of Dramatic Arts, of which Dr. Milton Smith was Director. Her particular post was to conduct Class 107 in the Study of Roles and Scenes. The class met on Thursday afternoons in the Brander Matthews Theatre on Morningside Heights.

I voiced my disapproval of this undertaking in no uncertain terms. I said it was a waste of her time and talent to teach a class, most of whose members would never make the grade professionally. "Why should you exert yourself to train a group of high school dramatics teachers?"

Gertrude refused to consider my objections.

"I shall be teaching an advanced, not an elementary course," she pointed out proudly. "Dr. Smith and I have screened all the students. They've had preliminary work in voice, speech, and pantomime. Many of them are already working professionally in radio and television. But, more than that, if I can find one person of real talent, and encourage and train him, I'll feel that I've done something worthwhile."

With this I could have no quarrel.

As the weeks went by, I began to see that, rather than taxing Gertrude's strength, the work at Columbia stimulated and revived her. She looked forward to Thursdays. Frequently she would ask people with whom she wanted to talk seriously to come to lunch with her on that day, and then drive them up to the campus. She was reaching out to a great many people of widely varied interests, frankly eager to learn from them.

She also drew an ingenuous pleasure from being on the faculty. She loved talking about "dropping in at Dr. Smith's office to discuss class problems."

Like other professors who want to improve their standing in the academic world, Gertrude was working on a book. A leading publishing house had sent her a contract for its publication. It was to be on the principles of acting, and she had collected a large volume of hand-written notes for it.

Gertrude had always kept in touch with André Charlot, who, with his family, had settled in Hollywood. One of the first things she did after joining Columbia was to turn to him for advice.

"Dearest Guv," she wrote Charlot soon after her class opened:

> You may have heard or even read that I am now a member of the Faculty of Columbia University and am in charge of Class 107 of the Dramatic School.
>
> From Clapham Common to Columbia, eh? Well, anyhow, that is the story, and I have a class of 50 young hopeful students of the DRAMA—and I am learning many things from them which I did not ever realize were necessary, and which I had not time to learn during adversity, but which *they* are taught during university.
>
> Well, they are, in many instances, muddled, befuddled, and bogged down and cluttered up with "theories" and the "technique" of acting. While I cannot argue against this most worthy approach, I am trying to impart simplicity and honesty in place of a lot of it. The students have been selecting their own material for their class auditions and directing themselves up to now. And of course their vehicles have all been most ambitious. They choose scenes from Shakespeare, Shaw, O'Neill, Tennessee Williams, etc., with which even experienced actors have great difficulty even under fine directors.

My thoughts have gone constantly to the wonderful training school of André Charlot's Revues, and how tremendously important an experience they were for me. I long to give my students the benefit of working on some of your splendid dramatic and comedy sketches.

There is no public demonstration in these classes and my faculty fee is used as a scholarship at the end of each year. Would you help me by lending me a few of your sketches? I do not want songs or recitations—just dramatic or comedy sketches. I will have them typed out here and return the originals to you.

My students range in age from 18 to 23. Most of them are in radio, television, or have done some summer stock. Some are just "green" and may be eliminated. But the sketches will teach them how to create character and develop a story through to its climax in a short time.

I do hope you will feel like helping me in this worthwhile endeavor; and if you could accompany the sketches with a few well-chosen words of wisdom, I would read them to my class. Professor Milton Smith is head of the entire Brander Matthews Theatre at Columbia and would write you a most grateful letter of thanks.

My fondest love to you, Flip, Joan, *et al.* When are you coming east to the Court of Siam?

Devotedly,
Gertrude

Charlot sent her the material she sought, and with it some valuable advice to young actors, which Gertrude gave to her students.

Gertrude also consulted her old friend John Golden. To him she wrote: ". . . the students seem to want to latch onto Shakespeare, Shaw, and Christopher Fry. While there is nothing wrong with the writings of these illustrious gentlemen, I do feel that the students are trying to run before they have even gotten their eyes open."

As when she had helped out at the Cape, in her teaching Gertrude always stressed the practical, believing that she owed a double duty—to her students and to her profession—to make the young actors realize that acting was hard, serious work; not arty self-expression. As she foresaw, several of the "hopefuls" did not have the necessary talent to sustain their hopes. These she would take aside and suggest that they give up the dream of going into the theatre. "Get yourself a job," she told them. "Make the theatre your pleasure, not a place to work. If this seems hard now, believe me, it is a lot less hard than a long, futile struggle ending in disappointment."

A few weeks before Christmas, the university trustees and faculty gave a Sunday night reception "to welcome Miss Gertrude Lawrence as Professor." Seldom had Gertrude been more flattered about anything. She made her list of special guests with extreme care. As was always her way, she was particular that those who loved her most should be invited. She also let the women among them know that she expected them to do her proud that evening.

She herself went to Hattie Carnegie and ordered a new evening dress. Radie Harris, who had planned to leave for Hollywood, yielded to Gertrude's request and put off her departure in order to attend the reception. Obedient to a not-too-veiled hint from Gertrude, she too went out and bought a gown for the occasion.

Before the reception, there was to be a performance, supervised by Gertrude, of *A Comedy of Errors* by the drama students. No first night of her own had ever been attended with such breathless expectancy on her part.

She had Hazel come to the house to dress her. At Hazel's knock on my door, and her message: "Miss L says, come and see how she looks," I followed her into Gertrude's room. Gertrude turned from the mirror and came a few steps toward me.

"Well, Richard, will I do?"

Poised there, in her long, shimmering gold gown, she was as radiant, as beautiful, and as suggestive of imperishable romance as she had been on that Sunday morning on which our decisive trip to Northfield began. Eleven years had passed since then, but she was still the most desirable and exciting woman in the world.

I told her so. More lights seemed to shine in her eyes.

"Then you're pleased with me, darling?"

With Hazel busying herself about the room I found it difficult to say how very pleased I was. I took refuge in pleasantry. "No one," I told her, "would ever take you for a school teacher."

It was as if the words had pulled a switch. All her lights went out. Gertrude stood there looking at me in sudden consternation.

"Oh, then I can't go like this," she exclaimed. "I'm wearing the wrong costume. Tonight I'm not Gertrude Lawrence, the actress; I'm Dr. Lawrence of the Columbia faculty, and I must look it. I'll have to change."

Nothing I or a thoroughly irate Hazel could say would move her from that decision. The glittering golden gown had to come off. She might seem to be overdressed, showing off.

"Nonsense," I argued. "Everyone expects you to look your best. They'll be disappointed if you don't dress like a star."

"No, Richard," she persisted. "I'm surprised that you don't see it my way." Disregarding Hazel's mutterings, she took a quick survey of the dresses hanging in her closet and selected a woolen one with blue and gray checks, and a matching jacket. "I'll wear that," she said.

"What got into you, Mr. Aldrich, to go and say what you did to Miss L?" Hazel demanded sullenly. "You'd ought to know by now that everything she does is playing a part and she's always got to be dressed right for it—if it's school teaching or horseback riding. The trouble with men is they don't know when to keep their mouths shut."

I withdrew in as good order as possible.

When Gertrude joined me in the lower hall, she looked demure and disturbingly efficient. On the drive up to Morningside Heights, the efficiency and impersonality came more and more to the fore. It was not a great star, nor my wife, whom I was escorting. It was Professor Lawrence of Class 107.

Hazel's back, clearly visible in the front seat beside the chauffeur, indicated what she was thinking.

Hazel's chagrin was as nothing compared to that which appeared on Radie Harris' face when Gertrude came down the aisle to join her "family" in the reserved seats in the front.

"And I went to Bergdorf and splurged on a brand new gown to do you proud," Radie scolded.

"But, dear, you're dressed to perfection for what you are," Gertrude responded with a sweet condescension which must have maddened Radie. "You are a guest. But I work here!"

"How about the professors' wives?" Radie shot back. "They've all come in formal dress."

"Because they are guests, too," Gertrude replied imperturbably. "They aren't members of the faculty. I *am*."

As usual, Gertrude's dramatic instinct did not let her down. She was the cynosure of all eyes—the only woman at the reception who was underdressed.

* * *

Gertrude by this time was carrying a schedule that, piled onto her eight performances every week in the theatre, seemed to me definitely dangerous. Anna was by far the most exacting role on Broadway. The physical effort involved in playing it was tremendous. Dr. Horace D. Worrell, the podiatrist who had taken care of Gertrude's feet ever since she had played in *Charlot's Revue* on Broadway, got her to wear a pedometer during a performance. It registered four miles.

Far worse than this physical exertion, however, was the nervous strain of the role. Gertrude's capacity for playing it night after night and still carrying on with her numerous outside activities, was a source of amazement—and concern—to a great many others besides myself. Shortly after Christmas, Helen Hayes wrote to her:

> Darling Gertrude,
>
> I have been wanting for some time to write this note of thanks for your work on the Mary MacArthur Memorial Fund. I'm told by the Foundation for Infantile Paralysis that you accepted Chairmanship of Mary's Fund and have arranged a "do" for the Oliviers for the Fund. I stand in awe of you. How can you play that taxing role *and* make all those costume changes *and* lecture at Columbia *and* pull out of pleurisy *and* take on outside obligations—it's all beyond me.
>
> I hope that you're giving yourself a little coddling and that you're getting better every minute.

I still think with a glow in my heart of the beauty and freshness of you the night I saw you.

Love,

Helen

The pleurisy to which Helen referred, which sent Gertrude to the hospital just before the 1951 holidays, had been the latest in a series of developments that made me feel Gertrude was doing too much.

Gertrude had run a high fever in the spring, during the early weeks of the play in Boston. Then, she had been taxed badly by the sweltering New York summer—doubly so because of her heavy costumes. When I returned from Paris in the fall of 1951, I had found her tired. I begged her to cut down on her commitments. This she refused to do, but she finally agreed to go to a hospital for a thorough check-up. She spent a week undergoing tests of all sorts, returning to the hospital each morning and remaining there until theatre time, then coming home after the play directly to bed.

The doctors agreed in finding nothing wrong with her; in fact, they reported, she had the physique of a woman in her twenties. She was somewhat tired, but that could be ascribed to working through an excessively hot summer without a vacation.

"Don't do too much," they suggested.

But there was nothing specifically that they banned—and that was all the excuse Gertrude needed for carrying on exactly as before. Beginning with the first rehearsals of *The King and I* in January of 1951, and continuing through a year of arduous appearances, Gertrude did not miss playing a single performance, although epidemics and assorted fevers were constantly laying low other members of the cast, and she had repeatedly been ill herself. Until Gertrude was struck by the attack of pleurisy, her understudy was never called upon.

* * *

One afternoon in late fall Gertrude insisted on taking me and Angus for a walk. We had turned toward the East River. Going through a side street in a neighborhood of shabby tenements, we had been stopped while movers carried a piano from a house into a waiting van. At a ground floor window, a woman and a little girl watched the proceedings. Sadly, we both thought.

"I know just how they feel," Gertrude said. "It used to happen to us. Poor Dad would have a little luck and the first thing he and Mummie would do to celebrate would be to get a piano on the hire-purchase plan. Dad loved some music when he drank his beer. And the idea was that a piano in the home was not only elegant but would be good for me, as I was going on the stage. But no piano ever stayed with us long. Dad couldn't keep up the payments. The company would come and get it. Those two at the window might be Mummie and me. It's funny, I don't believe I've ever owned a piano all my own. I've rented them, or there's been one in a rented house, but I've never had one that was really mine."

Though I said nothing, I realized with relief that this was one Christmas when I would not have to rack my brain about what to give Gertrude.

I arranged to have the piano delivered at 8:00 P.M. on Christmas Eve, when Gertrude would normally be making up at the theatre; that way, it would be a surprise for her when she came home around midnight.

My surprise went awry. The piano arrived on schedule, but Gertrude had been sent to the hospital with pleurisy the day before.

On Christmas Day, she was of course still in a hospital bed. Scores of gifts came to her there. Conspicuously absent, however, was anything from me, except for assorted inexpensive presents accompanied by appropriately humorous verse.

Finally Gertrude inquired, "Richard, haven't you a real Christmas present for me this year?"

"Of course."

"Well, where is it?"

"There's a package near the tree for you."

Her face brightened. "Oh, do be an angel and bring it! The doctor says I'll be here a week. And it's so silly to open a Christmas present on New Year's Day!"

I promised I'd bring it—but only if I could manage one day to get to the hospital directly from home. Otherwise I might mislay it, I warned.

Gertrude let it go at that. But the Christmas present stayed very much on her mind. The moment she returned home, she asked for it.

"It's still up in the living room near the tree," I told her. "You can open it on the way to bed."

She darted an odd, disbelieving look at me, and moved swiftly up to the stairs. Opening the living room door, she discovered the new Steinway Grand, wrapped in cellophane and decorated with Christmas trimmings and a huge red bow.

"My very first own piano!" she exclaimed. She tore off the cellophane and sat down to play until I literally carried her off to bed.

The piano opened a new world to Gertrude. Until this time her interest in music had been confined to popular songs. Now she expressed a desire to study "real music." She discovered that Frederick Dvonch, orchestra conductor for her play and a talented composer in his own right, was a graduate of the Juilliard School of Music with a rich background in the things she wanted to know. Freddie became her frequent guest at lunch, where he would talk to her about music history, theory, and similar matters, and would afterward give her lessons at the piano. Gertrude became so keen about keeping up with her practicing that she asked Morrie Jacobs, the company manager, to put a small rehearsal piano in her dressing room at the theatre. Morrie, as usual, obliged.

As a surprise for me, growing out of her newly awakened interest in the classics, Gertrude learned to sing a Bach hymn which had been a favorite of my mother's.

In February, Gertrude had a touch of bronchitis. To Evie, in England, she wrote: "Been away another whole week with day and night nurses, antiphlogistin, cough medicine, penicillin—everything the doctor can think of. Could you please send me some Owbridge's Lung Tonic? Also please find out if they still sell Sanderson's Specific in Manchester. It can only be bought there but it is a Miracle Medicine and my father and I never used anything else for colds and sore throat . . . I pray to get to England soon. . . ."

I was increasingly disturbed by her tendency to colds and by the recurrent fatigue of which she complained. When I was discharged from the Navy early in 1952, I determined to do something about making her take a rest. Setting aside my established rule never to interfere in Gertrude's work, I urged her to leave the play to go south. I pointed out that she had created the Mrs. Anna role and had made it her own. She had been awarded the "Tony" for her performance. (The "Tony," named for Antoinette Perry and given by the American Theatre Wing, is the theatre's most cherished prize.)

She refused to listen to my plea. She admitted she was tired, but she had never in her life dropped out of a play before the termination of a contract. It was a matter of pride.

But I learned it was more than mere pride and obstinacy. The earlier obstacles to a London production of *The King and I,* caused by British rules against the employment of children, no longer appeared insurmountable. Gertrude had set her heart on doing the play at the Drury Lane during the Coronation season.

"I promised myself that," she told me; and from that I could not budge her.

Nor could Noel Coward.

He passed through New York late in the winter. I talked to him privately, asking him to prevail on Gertrude to take a rest. She used to say that she always took his advice, and that he understood her better than anyone else did.

Noel took her to Sardi's for lunch and did what he could to help me. But her answer to him was the same she had given me. She wanted to play Mrs. Anna at Drury Lane.

"The doctors say there's nothing the matter with me," she told Noel, "except that I've been playing the role a year without a rest. The only times I've had off were the brief periods of illness. If I could have one week off, just to lie in the sun and rest, I would get over this fatigue and then, after my six weeks' holiday this summer, I could carry on to the end of my contract in June, 1953. Then I could go home in the play, if it goes to London. Or if it doesn't, maybe you will have a play for me."

I asked the Holtzmanns to discuss with Rodgers and Hammerstein the possibility of closing the show Holy Week, when, by Actors Equity rules, a play can shut down without paying salaries. David Holtzmann did so on Gertrude's behalf. They denied his request, saying that unfortunately it would be too expensive for them to close the show.

Gertrude took the disappointment philosophically. "I'll just stick it out," she said, "and dream of flopping down on the nearest beach the moment the curtain falls on June twenty-eighth. I would like to go where people wear nothing, after carrying those enormous hoop-skirts for so long."

A letter to David Holtzmann speaks for itself:

May 1st, 1952

Dear David,

I am most concerned about myself, my health and my career.

In taking stock lately of the amount of money which I have spent on doctors since the last week of rehearsal for *The King and I* when I had virus, it is really alarming that any human being could have treated its constitution so brutally.

I do not know whether you have ever seen a bullfight, but I have. The horses are blindfolded and are padded on the sides but the bull is smart and manages to displace the padding with his horns. The padding also gets dislodged by the action of the rider so that the bull then can gore into the horse's belly. This I have seen. The horse is then taken from the arena, stuffed up with sawdust or straw, sewn together and sent back into the arena.

This is exactly how I have been treating myself *of my own accord.* And this is where conscientiousness becomes crass stupidity if not *criminal.*

My early illness should have made us postpone the opening of the play, but we carried on. Consequently when we ran quickly into the hot summer it was an additional strain on me. When winter came I was already too worn out to withstand attack and as a result I spent eleven days in hospital. Even then I did not go away to recuperate but went back to work, with the result that I next came down with bronchitis.

Because of being absent I did not insist on an Easter break, which would have helped me. Now the doctors say that two needles twice a week (Wednesday and Saturday) are only patchwork or the equivalent to what is done to the horse at the bull-fight, who is sewn up and sent back into the ring.

Under these conditions, plus an arduous and demanding role, plus the singing, dancing, and the great weight of the costumes, I find that after a year and three months I am physically and mentally worn out. . . .

This is torture to me because I love the play, and my work for the public is very sacred to me, and I feel disappointment for both sides.

So hurry along, June 28th, and let's hope the rest and sunshine will be a better natural healer than my poor harassed medicos.

I would like you to send a copy of this to Dick and Oscar if you think they could get Celeste [Holm] in a few weeks earlier. Say June first. Think it over or wait for Fanny and the doctors to decide.

Love,
Gertrude

David did not wait but immediately traced Fanny until he found her at an airport in Rome, about to board a plane for England. Fanny changed her plans on the spot and switched planes for New York. There she tried to arrange for Gertrude's vacation to commence earlier but was informed this could not be done; Gertrude would have to wait for the date specified in the contract.

* * *

I had been looking forward to Gertrude's six weeks' holiday as much as she had. In the course of our two busy careers, many things were, of necessity, left unsaid, many things left undone. The world outside us always encroached on our lives with demands on our time, with needful separations, with inescapable tasks.

But in these six weeks, I resolved that nothing would interfere with our privacy. Arranging my affairs accordingly, I dedicated myself to making Gertrude's vacation the complete and placid relaxation I knew she needed.

So we spent our days on the beach and in the garden doing nothing—a luxury which most couples take for granted, but which in the past we had had little opportunity to enjoy. Relieved of all tension and strain, Gertrude blossomed. She appreciated my sharing her pleasures—even the sand in the picnic sandwiches—and my toleration of the interminable soap operas which went with them.

Gertrude went off her soap-opera diet temporarily to tune in on the excitement of the political conventions. She followed the fortunes of Adlai Stevenson in particular with such close attention that I commented on it.

"But naturally!" she replied. "I was once his secretary."

"You were WHAT?"

"It was in San Francisco, at the United Nations meeting. Don't you remember when I stayed with Fanny at the Mark Hopkins for a few days? Adlai needed somebody to take notes and make phone calls. I was drafted."

Such friends as we entertained were old and comfortable ones—Bea Lillie, Jules Glaenzer. None of the children was with us. Dick was at Scott Air Force Base. David, at Gertrude's suggestion and partially as a graduation present from her, had gone on a trip to Europe. Pamela was bicycling around France on a sketching tour.

"What's the matter with us?" Gertrude asked one afternoon as we sat by ourselves in the garden. I was half-dozing while she was listening to the little radio which continued to supply her with an incessant flow of drama. "We've been together weeks. Do you realize, in all that time, we haven't quarreled about *anything*? Are we getting adjusted, or just middle-aged?"

"Whatever it is," I replied, "I find it comfortable, don't you?"

Gertrude snapped off her radio and reached across to the chair in which I was lounging. "It's like peace on earth," she said. "I used to see couples in restaurants sitting opposite each other and never saying a word and I'd pray, 'Dear God, please don't ever let me be like that!' But they had something that I never had—peace. And it isn't at all dull. It's rather exciting in a strange and deeply satisfying way."

"More than that. It's earthshaking and revolutionary," I teased. "Do you realize, Mrs. A, that you are now content to leave things as they are? You no longer stuff the Sunday newspapers in the wastebasket the moment I drop them on the floor. It's almost a year since you rearranged my closet and bureau drawers out of all recognition. And you haven't given anything of mine away since you sent my accordion to the Musicians' Emergency Fund for Disabled Veterans."

"That old squeeze-box!" Gertrude scoffed. "You talk as if it were a Stradivarius."

"It was better than a Stradivarius to me," I retorted. "And, for the hundreth time, don't refer to it as a squeeze-box!"

The accordion was a cherished relic of my first year with the Jitney Players, a group of undergraduate minstrels from Yale and Harvard who wandered the summer-resort circuit in the early twenties. Alongside the others, all of whom played instruments or sang, I had been ingloriously mute. Then a good friend had introduced me to the accordion. The same kind soul inked numbers on the sheet music and corresponding numbers on the keys. Substituting perseverance for talent, I learned to press the right keys at approximately the right time. It was an accomplishment of which I was inordinately proud—so much so that I resented Gertrude's use of the British variety artist's word "squeeze-box" as detracting from the dignity of "my" instrument.

"Darling, if that's all you hold against me, after twelve years," she said, "I think we should be good for the full term of the contract!"

* * *

Dick telephoned us unexpectedly that he had a brief leave. He had been ordered to Korea—and wanted to come up to Dennis for a few days before saying goodbye.

We made no plans for extra entertainment for him, and I believe this was what he wanted. He seemed content to laze on the beach with Gertrude and me. Between swims we napped and talked. Nothing serious, nothing important. Nothing, I was aware, that touched on his immediate future. Gertrude made sure of that, leading the conversation deliberately towards recollections of other summers at The Berries, when Mother was with us. And those earlier summers before The Berries was built, when the boys came to the Cape: the baseball games with the English boys and the Hyde grandchildren; Harrison Hobart and Barbara; Bunny Lee and the obstreperous Bounder.

One day Gertrude spoke of Northfield and how Mother had expressed a longing to visit it again as a spot that belonged in a special way to our family. The boys had never been there.

"I'd like to see the place," Dick said, "sometime."

"Why not tomorrow?" Gertrude proposed with sudden eagerness. "The three of us."

I objected on the grounds that Gertrude needed rest and it was a long drive. "We'll go there when Dick comes back from Korea," I said. It was obvious to me that Dick was curious about Northfield, but only mildly so. After all, it held no memories for him.

"No," Gertrude insisted, to my surprise. "He should go there *now*." She added, almost wistfully, "It would be wonderful for the three of us to go together."

Dick turned to her quietly. "If you'd like me to go now, Gertrude, I'll go."

We planned to leave the following morning, after I had attended to a few things in the office. But that evening, when I drove back from the Melody Tent, Gertrude greeted me by stretching out a swollen arm.

"Poison ivy, darling. I broke out this afternoon." She had already seen the doctor and received an injection.

"How could you possibly get poisoned?" I asked. Every foot of our property had been sprayed earlier. "That means no trip to Northfield."

"Nonsense," Gertrude countered briskly. "This won't stop me from traveling. Dick has only two more days. He should not leave without going to Northfield."

Gertrude had suggested that we should drive by way of Upton, where she intended to visit the cemetery. She had fallen in love with the tranquil little town with its white houses, its settled look so unspoiled by modernization and "improvement." "I can't see why Mother objected to Upton," she had commented at the time of Mother's funeral. "There's not a more peaceful spot in the world."

The next morning was hot and sultry, with the promise of a thunderstorm. Gertrude was up early, cutting flowers for Mother's grave. Shortly before the hour for our departure, she went upstairs and was arranging piles of linen in a closet when Helen Mahoney, in an adjoining room, heard her call, "I feel faint." Helen went to investigate and found Gertrude slumped against the wall. She helped Gertrude lie down and then called me.

"It's just the humidity," Gertrude insisted. "I was bending over and there was no air in the closet. I'm all right."

The doctor whom we summoned thought the attack was a reaction to the poison ivy injections; he ordered her to spend the day quietly. The drive to Upton was off.

"But only for me," Gertrude protested. "You two must go."

I objected, and Dick was about to add his refusal to mine, but Gertrude insisted. I compromised by saying that we would make the trip in a day and be home late that night.

She came out to see us off. Just before I pressed the starter she called, "Wait! Just a moment." Taking her flower shears, she cut a handsome dark red rose, and laid it on the basket on top of the other flowers.

"For your father—for Edward Irving," she said, "with my love."

* * *

I telephoned Gertrude from Northfield. "Please stay overnight," she urged. "Let Dick see everything and meet some of the people; I'm all right."

I realized Gertrude was trying to give Dick and me two whole days together without the intrusion of other personalities. It was like her to think of this. And like her to realize the importance to us both of a quiet meeting away from home.

Freed of old associations and the earlier irritations of the father-son relationship for the first time since he was born, my son and I

The actress as teacher—Gertrude instructing her class in drama at Columbia University.

Edwin Gray, Falmouth

In the background, the Falmouth Playhouse; in the foreground, Gertrude and her new West Highland terrier.

Percy F. Williams

At the Cape Cod cooking school, Gertrude extended her talents. "Keep it tidy, girl," she told herself as she mastered the secrets of preparing chicken in wine sauce and lobster mousse.

Richard C. Kelsey

Gertrude leads the apprentices in a painting bee, as a token of our appreciation of Irene Fagan's twenty years as wardrobe mistress at the Cape Playhouse. Irene (in white) holds the leash of "Mrs. Anna," the dachshund Gertrude gave her.

Richard C. Kelse

Gertrude gazed at her handiwork (see preceding page) with satisfaction. "I can't wait to see Irene's house again. The white will look so wonderful against the bright green leaves next spring," she said. This was our last photograph together.

were meeting as men. Whatever diffidence and awkwardness had shackled us through the years was suddenly gone. I found I could talk to Dick of things close to my heart. One of those things was my father.

There in Northfield, where so much of my father's life was spent, it seemed important that my son should come to know his grandfather, and through that knowledge gain a stability, a sense of continuity with the past so sorely lacking in most of us today. In Northfield, I found myself able to summon up the spirit and recreate the portrait of my father. He was a man of firm and uncompromising belief in God, and his whole life was an affirmation of that belief. Here was a man—not an ascetic, nor a dreamer, but a man of business—who was not ashamed to avow his faith in Divine Providence boldly and without self-consciousness and, above all, with practical results.

I tried to transmit to Dick a feeling of kinship in this quality with his grandfather. For on such a pragmatic faith much of America was built; all of our moral strength in the past derived from it. Our future, so I feel and so I would have my sons feel, lies in our continued adherence to that faith.

On our return home Gertrude asked no questions, but I think she sensed that the trip had been a spiritual pilgrimage for Dick and me. He left the following day, and she followed him in thought across the Pacific, reliving her own wartime experience on Guam, Saipan, and the Marianas.

When her holiday was nearing its end, she brought up the subject of Northfield again.

"I've been thinking," Gertrude said, "that the family should have its roots reset in Northfield. With so many enterprises, you're busier on the Cape than in New York. And here, just as in New York, it is all theatre. How wonderful it would be if we had a little place at Northfield that we could run away to now and then and refresh ourselves, renew our contact with things of the spirit. If we could perhaps buy the chalet. . . ."

At Gertrude's suggestion, I began to inquire whether the owners of the chalet would be willing to part with it. Gertrude's interest in having it as a retreat was not a passing whim; she asked me several times whether I had heard from the owners.

The doctor had continued to give her injections against poison ivy. "I want to be immune for next year," she said. She was planning what she would do to the garden and the house in twelve months' time, when her contract for *The King and I* would terminate. "I'll come up to the Cape and perhaps open in the play in London in the autumn. But I'll want my rest first, and there are so many things I'd like to do around the place."

Typical of the sort of thing Gertrude liked to "do around the place" was the elaborate house painting she organized late that summer—not for our own house but for Irene Fagan's. Irene had been wardrobe mistress at the Playhouse for over twenty years. We were all very fond of her, but she was Gertrude's particular friend, having toured as wardrobe mistress when Gertrude starred in *Pygmalion*.

Irene had worked and saved to buy her cottage and keep it in repair. But its repainting had been necessarily postponed. Its color, a strange yellow with a garish blue trim—so alien to the Cape Cod scene—had always offended Gertrude's eye.

"If Irene's house were only white, like the others, the landscape would be perfect, like Upton," Gertrude said. Her eyes took on that faraway look which always meant she was plotting something. "Darling, why don't we have a painting bee?"

"A what?"

"You know, like a husking bee or a quilting bee. Your mother told me about them. Let's get the apprentices together next Monday and we'll all paint Irene's house. We'll make a party of it and have lots of fun as they did in oldtime New England."

Before I could weigh the pros and cons of the idea, Gertrude was off in a whirlwind of activity, conferring with Paul Phillips and spreading her enthusiasm for the idea to all the apprentices. She ordered the paint, and arranged for picnic lunches for the two days she estimated the job would take. As soon as she was sure that her plan would be accomplished, she asked Irene's permission, which was gratefully given.

Monday, however, arrived wet and windy—no day for painting. Tuesday was not better. Gertrude began to worry; she had to be back in New York on Friday, and was determined to see the job through. Fortunately, Wednesday dawned bright and dry. After she had gathered her forces together at Irene's house, the work began. There was a radiance on Gertrude's face as she set about the task with her many helpers. Thursday again, they all worked, with Gertrude staying till the job was completed.

During the painting bee, I was drafted into the army of painters along with the others. When I had painted as high as I could reach, I was excused from climbing a ladder, and was made the official dog-sitter, charged with the responsibility of keeping Irene's excited little Dachshund pup, Mrs. Anna, out of the paint pots.

Gertrude had given Mrs. Anna to Irene the summer before. She had heard of the death of a dog Irene had owned for many years, and sent up this new puppy along with a note:

> My dearest Irene:
>
> Here is my gift to you with all my love. She is housebroken, sweet-tempered and very gentle.
>
> Her pedigree is long but her name is short. She is called *Hilda,* but I would like you to call her *Mrs. Anna,* which is my name in this play, and also stands for "Mrs. A" (Aldrich).
>
> I hope you will keep her with you always.
>
> Love
>
> "Mrs. A"

Friday morning, Gertrude packed and wrote a long list of work for Ed, the gardener, to do in the fall. The list ended with the stern reminder:

KEEP FOOD
FOR
BIRDS ALWAYS
IN FEEDERS

That afternoon, as I drove her to the airport, we passed Irene Fagan's cottage, looking trim and sparkling white in the bright sunlight. Gertrude gazed at her handiwork with satisfaction.

"I can't wait," she said.

"For what?"

"To see Irene's house again. The white will look so wonderful against the bright green leaves next spring."

Chapter Twenty-One

OUR PEACEFUL INTERLUDE together on the Cape had lasted exactly six weeks. On Monday, August 11, Gertrude resumed her role in *The King and I*. I remained at the Cape.

Driving up to the theatre that evening, she was pleased to see a long line of ticket-buyers queued up at the box office, in obvious response to the announcement of her return.

Even more cheering was the affectionate welcome that greeted her backstage. Shepherded by a beaming Hazel, the entire company—dancers, principals, children—all flocked to Gertrude's dressing room to say hello to Mrs. Anna. Before the curtain went up, every member of the cast had stopped by to say a warm word.

Among the flowers and telegrams that filled the dressing room, Gertrude was happy to find a box of roses from Lee Shubert. Lee, owner of the St. James Theatre, had been her steadfast friend and admirer for many years. During the previous Spring, when the electric sign blazoning her name broke down and was allowed to go unrepaired for several days, she had telegraphed him:

DEAR MR. LEE: COULD YOU PLEASE DO SOMETHING ABOUT THE ELECTRIC SIGN AT THE ST. JAMES THEATRE? I HAVE BEEN LADY

IN THE DARK FOR THE KING AND I FOR OVER A WEEK WHICH IS QUITE AN ACHIEVEMENT STOP IT ONLY NEEDS INSTRUCTIONS FROM YOU TO LIGHT ME UP AGAIN MUCH LOVE

GERTRUDE LAWRENCE

The request was immediately granted and her name, in blazing lights as star of *The King and I,* illuminated Forty-fourth Street again.

Gertrude returned to the play fresh and relaxed from her weeks in the sun. The night before, she had phoned me at the Cape to report she had spent a quiet week-end practicing her music and finishing up two paintings for a forthcoming exhibition of art work by theatrical celebrities.

"I feel wonderfully fit," she said. "I'll be better than ever tomorrow night."

Those who saw Gertrude's performance during the next three days agreed that she was as good as her word. Advance sales shot upward, although the last two weeks of August are far from the best box-office period in the year.

Early Thursday morning, she rang Fanny Holtzmann: "Could you go shopping with me today, Fan?"

"Shopping?" Fanny had disquieting memories of Gertrude's onetime buying sprees. "What for?" she asked wearily.

"Don't worry. We won't go near Hattie Carnegie's. It's for Richard. He has a birthday Sunday."

"What are you getting him?"

"I was thinking of a squeeze-box."

* * *

Gertrude was to meet Fanny at three o'clock. Shortly after two, Dorothy was in the pantry when she heard a crash overhead, followed by a muffled cry.

Dorothy ran up to the library. There she found Gertrude doubled up against the writing desk in obvious distress. At her feet were a shattered vase and a bunch of white flowers. She had been arranging them when she was suddenly stricken.

Dorothy helped Gertrude to the sofa. Dorothy could see that all the color was out of her face; every step was a terrible effort for her. She had the butler call the doctor and Fanny, while she looked after Gertrude.

By the time the doctor arrived soon after, the pain had virtually disappeared—or so Gertrude said. The doctor hazarded an opinion—as had the physician at Dennis—that the attack could have been caused by the injections against ivy poisoning; there was no immediate evidence pointing to anything more serious.

"But don't go on tonight," he counseled Gertrude, "just to be on the safe side."

"Of course I'll go on," said Gertrude. "It was just a tummy ache. I've played through tummy aches before." She turned to Fanny: "Please don't tell Richard. It's not worth bothering him about."

At six o'clock that evening, Gertrude went to the theatre as usual. There she said nothing about the afternoon's incident; but Hazel, lacing her into her opening-scene costume, commented on the way Gertrude winced when the stays were tightened.

"Please, Hazel, don't say anything to Miss Fanny about it. She'll only tell Mr. Aldrich, and I don't want him upset. It's his busy time at the Cape."

Speaking to me on the phone at midnight, Gertrude did not even mention her illness. She was chiefly concerned with plans for my birthday. "I don't want you to feel neglected, darling," she said. "Next year we'll celebrate together—no matter what."

Friday evening, Gertrude went gallantly through her performance, despite the additional handicap of a late-summer heat wave. Hazel expressed growing concern as her star struggled into costumes which a few days earlier she had gotten into with ease.

Again Gertrude pleaded and bargained. "Don't tell anybody, Hazel. I'll have the long week-end to rest, once we get past tomorrow. Just let me get through tomorrow."

In spite of a valiant effort, Gertrude never did "get through tomorrow."

* * *

At one o'clock Saturday, as Gertrude was making up for the matinee, John Van Druten, director of *The King and I,* dropped in at her dressing room. She told him of her illness and of her determination to beat it. She asked about his troubles casting his own new play. Then she laughed and said, "Remember, I shall be free next June. And I'm no trouble." He kissed her and left.

After the final curtain at the matinee, as Gertrude was crossing backstage on her way to the dressing room, she fainted. Hazel was quickly at her side. When Gertrude regained consciousness, she said quietly, "I can't go on tonight, Hazel. Call Miss Fanny."

* * *

Almost three weeks later—at four o'clock in the morning—I was awakened from a deep sleep by the ringing of the telephone. I had been flying back and forth from Dennis; it took a moment to orient myself to the fact that I was in my New York home.

I picked up the phone. It was the New York Hospital calling, to tell me that Gertrude, who had been a patient there for over two weeks, had passed into a state of shock.

As I dressed, I was overwhelmed by a peculiar sense of unreality. The call was so unexpected, so at variance with what I had been led to believe was Gertrude's condition, that for a moment I wondered whether I was actually awake or was merely acting out an overvivid nightmare. . . .

After a few days at home following that Saturday matinee, Gertrude had gone reluctantly to the hospital for diagnosis. She underwent a series of tests, after which the doctors agreed she was suffering from hepatitis—a liver ailment which is painful, but rarely fatal. They assured me that they found nothing whatever which would warrant alarm, but advised that she remain in the hospital for treatment.

With medication and diet, Gertrude seemed to improve. Certainly her spirits never faltered in my presence. I remembered particularly that on the afternoon we received the report of the tests, Gertrude was immensely cheered and in a gay mood.

She sat up in bed, beguiling in an azure bed jacket, her hair falling around her shoulders. She could talk of nothing but my side-tracked birthday present.

"I didn't get it in time for the big day," she said regretfully, "but as soon as I return home, you are going to become the proud owner of the world's nobbiest squeeze-box."

"An accordion? But why?"

"To replace the old one you were so fond of, the one that I gave away. I'll mark every note on the new one myself, just the way they were on the original!"

"But what on earth would I do with an accordion now?"

Her eyes danced impishly. "I thought we might work up a variety act together. The Aldriches—Troubadours of Song! You play. I sing! We both dance. Look—"

She swept aside the bed covers and swung her legs to the floor. "We could start with the step I used in *Red Peppers*. Watch this . . ."

Stopping the rehearsal then and there, I lifted Gertrude off her feet and deposited her firmly back in bed. "You stay put, Mrs. A!" I ordered.

Squirming and giggling as I held her down, Gertrude looked like anything but a critically ill hospital patient.

* * *

. . . In a few minutes, I was dressed and out of the house. It was a hot, sultry night, quiet with the peculiar stillness of a big city in slumber. The street was deserted. As I walked in search of a taxi, I found myself praying, praying fervently, that it was all a fantastic mistake.

Just a few days before, Gertrude had been so full of eager plans. Each time I saw her, she asked whether there had been any word from the owner of the chalet at Northfield. Although I was still not certain that the chalet could be purchased, Gertrude was already decorating it in her mind. "It will be a retreat for us," she had said, "a haven where we can seek peace. This country should have more places like Northfield for busy, tense people."

Her recuperation was something Gertrude looked forward to as a new and exciting adventure. We would fly down to Florida, she decided, and take a cottage at Naples. Later, when I returned to New York, Daphne du Maurier would come over from London and finish the play she was writing for Gertrude.

"Isn't it wonderful how I timed my illness," Gertrude exclaimed to Fanny and me. "It's the off-season—I can convalesce at reduced rates." She turned to Fanny. "You must admit, Fan—after all these years, I've finally learned to economize!"

* * *

The taxi whisked through the empty streets, and in a few minutes I was at the hospital. They told me I could not see Gertrude. She was unconscious.

I paced the corridor outside her room. If only I could be with her for a moment, take her hand in mine . . . perhaps somehow the sense of my presence would break through the mist into which she was fast sinking. More than anything else, I wanted her to feel, however dimly, that I was there with her. I wanted to offer her strength, strength that would pull her back from the abyss. If only I could give back to her now, in the hour of her need, some of the warmth and light which Gertrude had given to me.

* * *

"Go back to the Cape, darling," Gertrude had urged on one of my visits. "I hate to think of you hanging around this hot town over the week-end. Besides, you ought to be there when Bea opens at Dennis on Monday.

"You must give Bea a party," she added.

"Not now," I protested. "I'm hardly in a party mood."

"Oh, do keep Bea happy while she's at the Cape. See that she's taken care of and made to feel at home."

This kind of consideration for her friends evoked an answering devotion on their part. I was sitting in her hospital room one day when we heard a commotion outside the door, which was slightly ajar.

"Why *can't* I see her?" a deep voice demanded.

Gertrude's face lit up. "It's Mister John, darling—John Golden!"

I stepped to the door.

"You tell her from me, Dick," John boomed, "that if it will help her to get well, I'll give her a coronet of diamonds to wear at the Coronation. Yes, and I'll pave Forty-fourth Street with red roses for her to walk over. She *must* get well and come back soon. We can't do without her."

* * *

"We can't do without her." John Golden's words echoed in my mind as I kept my vigil outside Gertrude's room.

Less than twenty-four hours ago, I had been feeding her in that room where she now lay motionless. As she ate, her eyes had sought mine like a child's asking approval. Never was her look more tender; never did she appear more beautiful to me.

When she finished lunch, I reached for the old volume of Browning, a gift from Mother, that was among Gertrude's most cherished possessions.

She shook her head. "Not Browning," she said. "Read me Dick's letter again, Richard."

I unfolded the airmail that had arrived the day before from Dick in Korea. Gertrude dropped her head back on the pillow and closed her eyes.

When I came to the concluding lines, in which Dick related that he had tacked Gertrude's picture over his cot as "Queen of the Pin-up Girls," she looked up at me and smiled.

To her ears, I realized, this was the loveliest poetry of all.

* * *

Through the window of the corridor, I could see the east grow gray, then pink. . . . The door to Gertrude's room opened softly, and a nurse came out. Three doctors hurried past me into the room. They were with Gertrude a long time. Intermittently, serious-faced nurses and internes hastened in or out.

I paced the darkened corridors, waiting, wondering. . . .

A nurse came down the hall, carrying a flask.

"How is she?" I asked.

"We're hopeful," was the tight-lipped reply.

I watched the nurse disappear into the room. "Hopeful. . . ." And yet. . . .

A note penned on the morning Gertrude had been stricken ill—the last letter she ever wrote—had a strange overtone of premonition. It was written to a fan who had admired *A Star Danced.*

August 14, 1952

Dear Miss Perry:

Ever so many thanks for your charming letter. I am so delighted that you enjoyed the book.

However, a sequel will have to wait quite a while, until I am either made a D.B.E. or retire gracefully into a peaceful country life or am found asleep never to awaken.

There has to be a final conclusion to the sequel, and I would prefer someone else to write it.

The previous afternoon, Gertrude had called Fanny to her bedside.

"I don't think I'm going to get out of this place, Fan," she whispered. "Don't tell Richard, but I have a feeling. There are things I want you to do for me."

She directed Fanny to write to her young friend Sandy Kennedy, telling him not to worry about her illness. And to send notes to everyone who had sent her flowers or "get-well" messages. "The cards are in the right-hand drawer. About the play—see that Connie Carpenter steps in. She has waited so long for her chance. See that she gets the role. And see that Yul gets star billing. He has earned it."

* * *

Sixteen stories below us, the city began to awaken. From the river below came the strident wail of tugboat whistles. I looked at my watch; it was nearly 7:45.

The door to Gertrude's room opened, and the doctors stepped out. One of them started toward me. Before he was near enough to speak, I knew what he had come to say. Quietly and without regaining consciousness, Gertrude had slipped away from me.

* * *

"There is no death, and no cause to mourn when your spirit lives on in those you love," Gertrude had told me once.

In the next few days, it would have been a solace to believe unquestioningly in this simple credo, but it was not in me to do so. One overpowering thought went round and round in my mind: Gertrude was gone.

A shocked world heard the news of her death. The swirl of activity which followed—the coming and going of telegraph boys with messages of sympathy, the well-meaning calls from friends, the insistent questions of newspapers—had no reality for me. Numbed, I moved back to our Fifty-fourth Street apartment, where I was joined by Pamela, who had flown over from England.

We remained alone until shortly before the scheduled start of the funeral. Services were held in the Fifth Avenue Presbyterian Church at Fifty-fifth Street, where I had been a member for twenty-five years and where Gertrude and I had frequently worshipped together.

As Pam and I emerged from my apartment house a half block away, we were surprised to see the street choked with people. The crowd was so dense that we had the greatest difficulty making our way to the church.

People of every sort were there: brokers, housewives, bobby-soxers, construction workers, salesgirls, and models from the Madison Avenue shops nearby. A musician carrying a violin case stood out in the street, staring with melancholy eyes at the Union Jack fluttering below the arched entrance to the church.

As we threaded our way through the crowd, fragments of wistful reminiscence came to our ears: "Remember Gertrude Lawrence in *Private Lives?*" . . . "I'll never forget her" . . .

Moving through the solemn throng, unrecognized and unknown

to them, we nonetheless felt the same warm sense of kinship with them that they clearly felt toward Gertrude.

As we entered the side door of the church, our path was momentarily blocked by two women.

"So young to die," said one. "Did you see her in *Pygmalion?*"

"I saw her in *everything!*"

More than ever I was aware of Gertrude's extraordinary human appeal—that divine spark of vitality, warmth, zest for life—that brought a glow to all who stood in her presence. It was more than a theatrical gift; it was the essence of her whole being. And at the moment it was a tangible force in the heart of busy Manhattan, bringing a hush to the roaring traffic and forging a link among thousands of complete strangers.

Inside the church, during the hour that followed, the luminaries of Broadway and Hollywood paid their respects to a great lady of the theatre. Outside, the nameless thousands stood in whispering reverence, mourning a beloved friend.

* * *

That day the Columbia University flag at the foot of the library steps flew at half-mast, while groups of students gathered silently outside the Brander Matthews Theatre, where Gertrude had conducted her classes.

At 8:30 in the evening—curtain time along Broadway—the lights of every theatre and movie house blinked out. For two minutes the most dazzling thoroughfare in "show business" stood dark and silent in honor of the cockney girl who had conquered America.

Three thousand miles away, in London's West End, the glittering marquees on Shaftsbury Avenue, Charing Cross Road, and in St. Martin's Lane—where Gertrude and I had first met—likewise flashed off, in tribute to a vanished star.

And on the other side of the world, in the battle-swept hills of Korea, a unit of British fighting men gathered in a dusty hollow to say their own kind of farewell. Peter Carlisle, an ENSA entertainer and old friend of Gertrude who was there, described the scene in a letter to me:

The dust was thick on the temporary parade square and the light wind blew it in little patterns. The Union Jack flapping in the breeze spattered color against the steely sky. The khaki of the men drawn up in a hollow square faded in with the sun-colored hills in the background.

A Padre, his white collar standing out against the khaki, spoke: "The news has flashed across the world, men, Miss Gertrude Lawrence has passed away. Many of you have come to the C.O. to ask him to hold a memorial service for her. Many of us knew her when she appeared, smiling and gay, in the last show. We thought it was *our* show, but it was hers, too. Her spirit was great and when she appeared in some corner of a hangar, or a NAAFI hut, she brought brilliance, color, and glamour to our drab world. No *grande dame* of the stage she, but a real performer, a bringer of laughter, a singer of songs. And she could jig as well as Paddy's pig. Boys, I have a feeling that the moon and sun will have to squeeze over a bit to make room for a star like our Gertie. And now I want to read you the Twenty-third Psalm."

In his rich Lancashire voice he read the old cry of faith in God's providence: "The Lord is my shepherd, I shall not want . . ."

After he finished he turned, saluted and moved off. For a moment there was silence. Then somewhere in the rear ranks a voice, high and light, started to sing: "Someone to watch over me." A young officer was about to move towards the singer but the colonel stopped him and joined in the singing. Soon the entire company was singing.

When the last note had died into the distance the company bugler sounded The Last Post. The flag dipped and slowly sank to half-mast. A deeper silence spread over the square. Not a dead silence, for it was one that was filled with a feeling of tenderness towards someone who had always given tenderness. And in the far distance the flat slap of mortar fire, the roar of the larger guns echoed. No, it was not a dead silence, but it was a moment's pause for someone who had gone. Again the same voice started to sing. This time, "Limehouse Blues."

The bitter-sweet music wavered and played over that odd-looking Korean landscape. When it had died down the colonel rubbed at his eyes with the back of his hand and dismissed the company with a nod.

One little cockney, stumping his way up the hill to the field kitchen, turned and looked back. The parade square was empty. The flag was flying high again. Standing there on the hill, he snapped a salute and said aloud: "Goodbye, Gertie. You was the sweetest goddamned Limey I ever saw!"

* * *

The next day, our small party—the handful of people who were closest to Gertrude—trudged up the path of the little hillside cemetery in Upton, Massachusetts. It was a perfect New England day—bright, crisp and cool. The September leaves of the maples were tinged with gold; sunshine sparkled on the lake below.

Halfway up the slope we stopped at the grass-covered knoll that, since Revolutionary days, has been set apart for the Aldriches. Around us lay Aldrich wives of earlier generations: Zilpah, Patience, Abigail, Hannah, Sarah.

There, near them and next to my mother, we laid to rest Gertrude, my "Mrs. A"—the English girl who, by her love and eager understanding, had made herself a part of America, part of my family, and a part of me.

Dearest ——
Please tell me if you aren't
happy with me - or if you
are bothered by trying to be
in more than one pair of arms!
Be in love, be free, but please
be truthful for both our sakes
'Your own' "Mrs A."

Dearest
Want the
to go here

Darling!
Look what I just found
in the Garden!!
In case you don't know,
they are forget-me-nots!!!
Mrs A."

Darling Hot

Please don
to room u
when you g
B

All my love, my Love - be a good boy,
& get some Colour in your cheeks!!!
Mrs A.

Dearest - please do not
let or lend our little house
to anyone — it's ours, &
I shall be back, sooner or later.

Dearest Da
We are le
vengeance
We have
days, b
The 28th
want to